FROST: CENTENNIAL ESSAYS III

FROST
CENTENNIAL ESSAYS III

EDITED BY

JAC THARPE

UNIVERSITY PRESS OF MISSISSIPPI
JACKSON
1978

Copyright © 1978 by the
University Press of Mississippi
Manufactured in the United States of America
Printed by Heritage Printers, Inc., Charlotte, North Carolina

THIS VOLUME IS AUTHORIZED
AND SPONSORED BY
THE UNIVERSITY OF SOUTHERN MISSISSIPPI

Library of Congress Cataloging in Publication Data

Main entry under title:

Frost: centennial essays III.

   Bibliography: p.
   Includes index.
   1. Frost, Robert, 1874–1963—Addresses, essays,
lectures. 2. Poets, American—20th century—Biography
—Addresses, essays, lectures. I. Tharpe, Jac.
PS3511.R94Z6545   811'.5'2   72–3548
ISBN 0-87805-047-7

To Charles W. Moorman
Vice President for Academic Affairs
University of Southern Mississippi
for consistent encouragement

Contents

List of Illustrations

Acknowledgments

Grateful acknowledgment is made to The Estate of Robert Frost, Alfred C. Edwards, Executor, for permission to print here for the first time unpublished material. Copyright (c) 1978 by The Estate of Robert Frost; to Holt, Rinehart and Winston to quote from *The Poetry of Robert Frost* edited by Edward Connery Lathem. Copyright 1916, 1923, 1928, 1930, 1934, 1939, 1947, 1949, (c) 1967, 1969 by Holt, Rinehart and Winston. Copyright 1934, 1936, 1942, 1944, 1945, 1947, 1951, 1953, (c) 1956, 1958, 1960, 1961, 1962 by Robert Frost. Copyright (c) 1964, 1967, 1970, 1973, 1975, 1977 by Lesley Frost Ballantine. Reprinted by permission of Holt, Rinehart and Winston, Publishers; to Macmillan Publishing Company, Inc. to quote "The Snare" from *Collected Poems* of James Stephens. Copyright 1915 by Macmillan Publishing Company, Inc., renewed 1943 by James Stephens; and to Mrs. Lawrance Thompson for permission to quote from Lawrance Thompson's correspondence.

Preface

Thus volume is the third of those associated with the Frost centenary of 1974. While neither the second nor the third volume in the series was a part of the original plan, they have derived from the original impulse and therefore retain in the title *Centennial Essays*.

Contributors to this volume have made a special effort to deal with a subject that has become increasingly difficult. Dorothy Tyler speaks at least implicitly for several of us when she says early in her essay that it seems wise for those who knew Frost to get their recollections on record. The editor appreciates their contributions as well as those from the literary critics whose essays are included herein.

President Aubrey K. Lucas of the University of Southern Mississippi, Charles W. Moorman, Vice President for Academic Affairs, and Wallace Kay, Dean of the Honors College, have consistently supported this project. And J. Barney McKee, Director of the University Press of Mississippi, has been congenial from the beginning years ago.

Documentation is generally internal and abbreviated. The bibliography is intended only to supplement the abbreviations, which are listed there. Two bibliographies were prepared in association with the centennial of 1974: Frank Lentricchia and Melissa Christensen Lentricchia. *Robert Frost: A Bibliography, 1913–1974*. Metuchen: The Scarecrow Press, 1976. Peter van Egmond. *The Critical Reception of Robert Frost*. Boston: G. K. Hall & Co., 1974.

All quotations of Frost's poetry are from *The Poetry of Robert Frost*, ed. Edward Connery Lathem (New York: Holt, Rinehart and Winston, 1969). All references are in the text with only page numbers given. The three volumes of the Lawrance Thompson (and Roy Winnick) biography are internally documented by roman numeral and page number, the roman numeral arbitrarily assigned by the editor. Frost's erratic spelling is reproduced without comment; and wherever consistency and other pressures allow, scholarly clutter is eliminated from the text.

Notes on the Essays

THE original idea for this volume was to discuss The "Real" Frost, and plans were made before publication of the third volume of Lawrance Thompson's biography, finished by Roy Winnick. Most of the public grievances over the biography had been recorded—and archived where they would be harmless.

In the first two volumes of this series of essays, we had no problem with controversies. One intent of the third volume was to be controversial if anyone felt the spleen in a gentlemanly sort of way. We might have learned something from a clash of sabers—at least about fair play.

But then volume three of the biography appeared, and things went awry. The essays in this collection have been somewhat influenced by publication of Professor Winnick's volume and especially by the reviews. But I have not influenced them, despite my preferences, though I admit to getting a special pleasure from Thomas Littlefield's anecdote, which arrived shortly after I read volume three and the reviews. Two essays not published here were not excessive in their praise. The first of these was withdrawn, and the second I could not use for lack of space. The book therefore is written by friends of Robert Frost or at least by those who respect him. So we have no controversial volume after all.

I have followed the original plan in having two sections—the first mainly biographical and written by those who knew Frost, the second mainly literary criticism. The first section is far longer than the second, and the distinction between them is unclear. Biographical material is approximately in chronological order.

Dorothy Tyler has short essays in the other volumes of this series. Herein, though, she writes at length on a period and a subject generally neglected—Frost's early years in Michigan. The essay has far more than autobiographical significance because it shows Frost in action, as a man and a teacher, influencing a variety of persons.

Among them is Miss Tyler herself. A motif of this collection is the significance Frost had and continues to have on both the likeliest and the unlikliest of the many whose lives he somehow touched.

Charles H. Foster, another of those acquaintances, had a unique association with both Robert and Elinor Frost. The narrative is self-contained, and Professor Foster's own notes obviate further editorial comment.

Luella Nash LeVee records brief interviews with some who knew Frost and also tells her own experience with him. John Jacob Niles and a young girl with a special sorrow are two of those who remember Frost. Mrs. LeVee herself is one of the articulate among many we'll possibly never hear from who in some way felt the influence of Robert Frost.

Victor Reichert took the latest episode about Frost rather personally. He tells me in a letter that his severe remarks do not refer to either Thompson or Winnick. (Thompson and the rabbi were friends.) But Dr. Reichert has a very special feeling about those who consider Frost either a bad or an unreligious man.

Reginald Cook wondered if he was merely rehashing by including his account of Frost's story about Ezra Pound. But we've all kept these leitmotifs—repetition, some may claim—in part because the variations themselves tell something about Frost. No good talker tells a story the same way twice. Professor Cook writes biography, but he devises a special organization for his material—and implicitly questions oversimplifications of an extremely complex man.

I agreed with Peter Stanlis that the few opening pages of his essay ought to deal with autobiography if the biography of Frost was to be in perspective. My regret and the author's is that we had no room for the account of all the other years when Professor Stanlis saw Frost at Bread Loaf. We might have cut a few very familiar incidents, but we didn't even condense them. Those who knew Frost like to tell their own versions of incidents well known to some of us by now, and I feel they have their rights.

Professor Stanlis was the third Elinor Frost Scholar. (The first, Charles Foster, is mentioned above.) And he spent a great deal of time with Frost, not always listening, but hearing enough to consider Frost the century's most remarkable conversationalist. Thus, the long reminiscence really deals with Frost's major topics: poetry, colleges and and education, politics and science—and the question whether Frost was anti-intellectual. The last few pages of the essay comprise an unimpassioned but earnest assessment of Frost's character.

Arthur Bleau's anecdote will be surprising for some and possibly of interest to everyone. Lesley Frost's brief accompanying note is self-explanatory.

Dorothy Judd Hall is primarily concerned with Frost's religion and not with biography. But her personal relationship, especially to Lesley Frost, helps explain how she too became a student of Frost. When I asked for details, Mrs. Hall sent the brief account that precedes her essay.

The short essay by Lesley Frost is a version of her introduction to *Contours of Faith*, a finished manuscript by Dorothy Hall, to which Mrs. Ballantine's essay refers. The brief comment is important not only for what it says about Frost's religion but also for Frost's daughter's willingness to speak out.

"An Old Testament Christian" uses Frost's description of himself to hint of both the paradox he considered himself to be and the paradox of justice and mercy that seems to be at the center of his complex beliefs. Mrs. Hall does not dismiss Christ from Frost's thinking but claims Frost specially defined Christ as an archetype who vivified the awesome paradox of justice and mercy. Yet Frost does not accept a puritanic Old Testament Christianity but appears to insist on an active pursuit of "salvation." Bergson's concept of creative evolution is perfectly at hand as a way of synthesizing ancient and modern approaches to religion and science.

A note following the notes to Mrs. Hall's essay gives all available details about the provenance of the Frost notebook to which Mrs. Hall refers and which she uses in her longer study, *Contours of Faith*.

Richard Foster, an unrelated former colleague of Charles Foster, has done the kind of literary study I hoped to use as complement to the biographical essays in this volume. While most of those writing here talk about the Frost they knew, Professor Foster studies the poetry, where he finds two images that he attempts to clarify.

Lewis Miller wrote for the first volume of this series, and he writes for the third on a subject that remains absorbing for me—the depth of William James's influence on Frost, a question the more significant because it involves Frost's religion and his world view.

Warren French looks into "The Death of the Hired Man" for an elusive Frost. In making such a study, Professor French goes far beyond a look at the poet or a persona to suggest we have miles to go if we are to find either man or poet.

FROST: CENTENNIAL ESSAYS III

A Ripton Afternoon

T. H. LITTLEFIELD

T HAT July afternoon had the heaviness that comes even to Vermont in haying season. My three-year-old son and I had driven up to Ripton, on Mr. Frost's invitation. Jamie wandered about under Kathleen Morrison's loosely beneficent care, while I sat with Frost in his cabin, listening as his talk wove in and out of anecdote, speculation, sacred and profane fancy, opinion, and conviction. He said poems—his own, Robinson's, Vachel Lindsay's, Edward Thomas's, Wordsworth's, Pope's, Shakespeare's, Horace's, and Yeats's—as they occurred to illustrate his talk or my questions. His Latin was excellent schoolboy Latin, much the same as I had been expected to learn two generations after Frost was taught. His English is well known.

I wanted to take notes, but I was playing a role. Frost thought of me (I thought) as a young poet, and poets (*I* thought) are too self-possessed to take notes. Nor did my pride let me play the mug's game of Rosencrantz and Guildenstern, those reporters who believe that nobody would dare to wear glass slippers who does not have clay feet. I was not looking to expose anybody, least of all somebody I recognized as the wise master of my tribe. In short, I was aware that Frost was beset by biographers, and I was determined not to be one of them.

Frost's description of the making of a poem—like the melting of ice on a hot stove—had a good deal to do with my having become secretly dubious as to my vocation as a poet. Once or twice I had felt its being like that. Mostly, for me, it was more like picking burrs out of Harris tweed. I wondered whether "The Figure a Poem Makes" described the way it always was for Frost, or sometimes, and whether he thought there was ever anything to metaphors linking the writing of poetry to the art of sculpture in marble.

He assured me that his poems always wrote themselves at first. Revising was something else. He said he'd talked about it with other poets. He told about one such conversation with Vachel Lindsay

3

when they were sitting together in a railroad station at two o'clock in the morning, waiting for a connection to take them on to wherever they were appearing together. Kenyon? I have a vivid image of those two, as Frost's ironic view of it went—prickly men standing one another off in the waiting room at Columbus or Cincinnati or Indianapolis. But I don't remember what either of them is supposed to have said.

He went on to tell about the last time he had visited Yeats, and how they had talked together about the way they worked, Yeats maintaining that composition was always a slow, arduous process, Frost questioning whether Yeats didn't remember it that way because he thought it ought to be that way. Frost's view was that the scholars had imposed their thinking as to how poems ought to be written, based on their own finicking practice. It had got so a skylark wouldn't admit to making up his song without perching on top of the Oxford English Dictionary (shorter). Yeats maintained steadfastly that whatever other men might do, he for one worked as painstakingly as a medieval law clerk.

Frost said he told him, "I'll bet you a—" (my memory has, shamefully, suppressed both nature and value of the stake) "that I can name a poem you wrote straight off."

"Go ahead," said Yeats.

" 'The Wild Swans at Coole,' " Frost told him.

"Ah," Yeats answered, "I sweated quill points and feathers over that one."

After laughing awhile, leaving me to wonder whether he had owned to defeat and paid off the wager, Frost beetled at me and said, "But we're all damned liars, you know."

He talked on a little more, citing as I recall the Apostle Paul's remark to the Corinthians that while everything was lawful to him, not everything was expedient. I remembered Gogarty's account of a visit *he* paid Yeats, presumably at about the same time, that led him to conclude the old poet had turned crotchety, invidious, and snotty. Frost was, that July afternoon in his cabin, about a decade older than Yeats had been, and I thought about that, wondering whether there was a touch of the invidious in Frost's tone towards Yeats. On another occasion, Frost had spoken quizzically about

Yeats's psychic experiments. And, from Frost's point of view, the "quill points and feathers" story was a story "on" Yeats. He had caught Yeats brazening his way out of a contradiction.

It all comes down to how you take the "we're all damned liars" part, I have decided now. I couldn't be sure at the time, from the way he said it, and probably it wouldn't have done me any good to ask, even if it had seemed in keeping for me to do so—if I'd thought to. Was he just underlining the point of the story, to make it clear that we don't have to believe Yeats really won the bet? Or was he, inexorable ironist that he was, turning it about one more twist, to say that it wouldn't do to take what Frost said of his own practice too literally, either?

In "Build Soil," a poem written about the time of Yeats's death, Frost has his poet-persona, Tityrus, tell Meliboeus the potato man, "Don't let the things I say against myself/ Betray you into taking sides against me,/ Or it might get you into trouble with me" (p. 320). What he doesn't say is that the risk, for Meliboeus, does not reside only in the ire of a living poet; the twin (or more) stools of Tityrus's irony stay after him.

Whether or not Plato meant to be literal when *he* said the poets are all damned liars, the irony to be found in the statement touches every poetic act from God's first "I am" to the last "Let there be" of the latest maker. When poets are most saying sooth it is "as if" (see Frost's preface to Robinson's *King Jasper*) they were all damned liars. What Frost and Yeats were quarreling about, if quarreling they were, was what god to worship as much as how "The Wild Swans at Coole" was made, and how long it took. Vulcan or Amor? Do you, like Joyce, forge your poems in the smithy of your soul, or, as Dante explained Stil Novism to Buonagiunta (Purgatory, 24), does Love stand behind you and, as he speaks, you write? Sweating quills and feathers and the melting of ice on a hot stove both sound right to me. "Come, but this isn't choosing . . ." (see the end of *New Hampshire*, p. 171).

They say nowadays that Robert Frost was a difficult man. Well, I've never known a man who wasn't, leastways a poet. But was he more difficult than most?

It is not a question I can answer from my limited acquaintance with Frost. In the course of a decade I met him four times: twice in Ripton, once at his house in Cambridge, and once at Ray Nash's in Hanover. We exchanged Christmas cards. As my experience of elder acquaintances goes, he was as kind, sympathetic, understanding, and comfortable as any. Which is just enough to lead me to suspect the judgment of his official biographer and others that he was especially difficult. And to look for some other explanation.

The explanation that comes to hand, as I remember that July afternoon at Ripton, is that Frost's personal reputation has been suffering the depredation that partial, literal readings have often worked upon the reputations of poems and other fictions. I believe that a literal-minded commentator would extract no more from "We're all damned liars" than the inferences, first, that Frost was maligning Yeats's probity; second, that Frost was admitting to his own lack of probity. Such a commentator would even be capable of receiving both those inferences without noticing that they modify one another, and conclude that Frost was both an invidious slanderer and a liar. As near as I am able to observe, that is the stuff of which (Frost's) biography is made.

As the sun waned on our talk in the Ripton cabin, three-year-old Jamie came looking for Daddy. The old man who was talking with Daddy asked Jamie how he had spent the afternoon. Jamie said he had been for a ride on a black mare. So the old man went outdoors with Jamie and gave him a ride on *his* back. And I went down to our car to get my movie camera so I could get a shot of that. It was pretty dusky, and the footage turned out so dark that you can't guess much more about the scene than it's of a sweet little boy on the shoulders of a sweet old man.

Robert Frost in Michigan

DOROTHY TYLER

S "*To* VERMONT AND MICHIGAN"
o runs the somewhat wry dedication of the poems collected in
New Hampshire (1923), published in Frost's second year as Fellow
in Letters at the University of Michigan. There would be many
years to follow those first two of association with the University
and the State—in truth, more than forty years, beginning in the
academic year of 1921–1922 and ending only in the last year of
Frost's life, in 1962, when he made no less than three visits, two to
Ann Arbor and the last, in November 1962, to Detroit.

All that begins to seem far away and long ago, certainly to the
younger generation—as if, as Lawrance Thompson suggested, those
who knew Frost appear remote and strange, as in Browning's question:

> Ah, did you once see Shelley plain,
> And did he stop and speak to you
> And did you speak to him again?
> How strange it seems, and new!

But yes, it was all thus with Frost, and before the memories are
gone forever, and those who remember with them, it is prudent to
set them down, as they relate to Frost's life and poetry and friendships in what may be called his second home in Michigan.

Frost's Earlier Connections with Michigan

By the time Frost came to Michigan as Fellow in Letters for the
academic year 1921–1922, his knowledge of the University was
substantial, newcomer as he might be to the campus. For in the summers of 1915 and 1916 Professor Morris Palmer Tilley and his family
had vacationed in Franconia, and there had known Frost and his
family. Virginia born and bred, Tilley had been a member of the
Michigan faculty from 1903 and became Professor of English in
1918.[1]

In that early year of 1915 Tilley had taken pictures of the Frost family "and where we live," as Frost mentioned in his earliest letter to Tilley.[2] One of the pictures, showing Frost and his son Carol, is published in Elizabeth Shepley Sergeant's *Trial by Existence*, a biography notable for its warmth and understanding.[3] As pictures often do, it reveals the personality of both father and son in a way that almost reveals the future of both.

In the same letter Frost thanks Tilley "for trying to make the professors out there like me. It was a good deal if you interested them even a little." The days were not yet when Frost carried on his ambivalent campaign of belittling the importance of university education while seeking honorary doctorates. Alas, then as later both Frost and the family were having "all sorts of sickness," and Frost wrote to Tilley: "The truth is I don't just see how I am going to get into shape for all the lecturing I have ahead." A chronology of the illness, mental and physical, that bedeviled the poet and his family through the years would go far toward providing an understanding of the poet's life and the Emersonian concept of compensation that applied to it.

Tilley did not waver in his affection and admiration for Frost, then or later.

Frost urged Tilley to report on the progress of his sister, Jeanie Florence Frost, who entered the University of Michigan as a Special Student in February 1916, in her fortieth year. After many trials and tribulations she managed to acquire the A. B. degree in August 1918. Her name and the year are registered in the Alumni Catalog, but nothing more. Evidently Frost had urged her to take a degree before attempting more teaching, but why Ann Arbor was chosen is not clear. Perhaps it was the "Tilley connection," which also accounted for so much in the later years of Frost's own association with the University.

Tilley reported to Frost that Jeanie had made an impression of "extreme eccentricity" in Ann Arbor,[4] and later events proved the impression to be well founded. Her letters to Wilbur E. Rowell, the family lawyer, always pleading for more funds from their Grandfather Frost's estate, are indeed pitiful.[5] The fact that she was studying German at the University, at the time of World War I, when there was turmoil and agitation among faculty members, no doubt contributed to her travail.

Though Tilley knew all these circumstances, and Frost's letters about them were in the Tilley files but have never been released, they were not generally known at the time of Frost's sojourns in Ann Arbor. Those students who knew Frost then, but knew nothing of this particular sorrow, will recall with sadness that Jeanie had been committed to the State Hospital in Augusta, Maine, in 1920, and died there in 1929. With the belated sympathy for Robert and Elinor Frost must go thoughts of compassion for Jeanie herself, who died at the age of fifty-three, after many troubles, and who shared her brother's traumatic childhood without sharing the qualities that compensated for it. Only those who know Ann Arbor can picture her wandering from lodging to lodging, and finding friendly help at times from Professor Max Winkler (1866–1930), who lived in one of the stately homes, and was head of the German Department for many years.

One of the earliest commentaries on Frost as man and poet was contributed by Professor Tilley to *The Inlander* of November 1917 —then a faculty publication.[6] Based on letters and notes of 1915 and 1916, from Franconia, in the White Mountains, when the Tilley family were summering there, it has perhaps the earliest statement of Robert Frost's theory of poetry as based on the sound of the human voice. "He felt that he wanted to get the qualities of intimate conversation into his poetry.... He is going to talk in St. Johnsbury soon on 'Sound in Poetry,' about which he has interesting theories. He thinks that the creative power of the voice is all important in poetry."

Anyone who has heard Frost reiterate and enlarge upon this theory of poetry in later years, and has heard his voice "saying" his poems, will agree that his ideas of poetry perfectly suit his own work—little as they may explain many great poems in the language. Not once but several times he would hotly dispute the theory of quantity in poetry expressed by Robert Bridges, the English poet who succeeded him as Fellow in Creative Arts at Michigan in 1923–

1924.[7] Frost expressed his contrary opinion thus: "An *O* can be as short as someone stepping on your toe or as long as a groan that lasts all night."

Several years were to elapse before Frost came to Ann Arbor for his first fellowship in the fall of 1921–1922. Though some would say it was "all Tilley's doing," and he would certainly be Frost's friend throughout his Ann Arbor association—and Frost would often be a guest at the family home on Ferdon Road,[8] it was a complicated arrangement at the time, requiring much planning and high-level agreements.

The new and spirited President of the University, Marion LeRoy Burton, whose term began in 1920 and ended with his death in 1925, was responsible for securing at the University the cultural idea of a Poet in Residence. The Regents had assented to the idea at their meeting in December 1920, and thus Michigan became the first large university to sponsor such a custom and usage.[9] It thus became heralded by Sinclair Lewis, in his 1930 address on "The American Fear of Literature," on receiving the Nobel Prize in Literature, as one of four American colleges and universities "which have shown an authentic interest in contemporary creative literature." Robert Frost was among those cited as worthy of praise.[10]

It was the smaller Miami University of Oxford, Ohio, and its President Hughes who had initiated the idea of a Poet in Residence and built a studio on campus for Percy MacKaye in 1920. Frost heard about it in December of that year at the apartment in Greenwich Village maintained by the hospitable Harriet, widow of William Vaughn Moody, as a meeting place for poets. Was there an idea for him there? Yes, for Burton of Michigan had heard about it at a meeting addressed by Hughes of Miami of Ohio.

Burton, now memorialized by a carillon tower that signals the hours in Ann Arbor and sometimes sends forth a carillon concert, was not a man to temporize or delay. He had the Regents' permission, but what was he to do about the necessary honorarium for a poet like Frost? It could not come from University funds, which were far from munificent at that time.[11]

The problem was solved when the Hon. Chase Salmon Osborn, former Governor of Michigan and a member of the Board of Regents, offered the sum of five thousand dollars to bring Frost to Ann Arbor as Fellow in Creative Arts for the year 1921–1922.[12] Called during his lifetime "Michigan's foremost citizen," and certainly one of its most flamboyant and widely known, always spoken of as "Governor," long after his term was over, Chase Osborn was the perfect donor of that first fellowship. No doubt Frost had letters from Osborn when Osborn became a celebrated resident of Possum Poke in Possum Lane in Poulan, Georgia, in a part of the country that became famous in the autumn of 1976.

The First Year in Ann Arbor, 1921–1922

So it came about that Frost was welcomed to Ann Arbor in the autumn of 1921 as the University's first Fellow in Creative Arts. President Burton had left to Joseph Bursley, Dean of Students, the selection of a residence for the Frost family, and the choice fell on the large house at 1523 Washtenaw Avenue—the street named for the county in which Ann Arbor is located. It had been the home, and now belonged to the widow, of Professor Martin D'Ooge, head of the Classics Department, famous for both wit and knowledge. It was rented with its furniture in place, a large house far back from the street, known both then and today for its handsome buildings and residences—the D'Ooge house having a surprising resemblance to the Frost house at 10 Sunset Avenue in Amherst. It is no more, for years ago it was razed to make way for a church building.

The Frosts, at least the part of the family free to come, were welcomed there by Professors Tilley and Roy W. Cowden—whose home at 1016 Olivia Avenue, not far away, was the regular meeting place for the *Whimsies* group of editors and writers, later called *The Inlander*. No doubt Dean Bursley was also among the welcomers, for he was to become a staunch friend, and in later years the Bursley family home often had Robert and Elinor Frost as guests. It is probable that Mrs. Frost was not there at first, but that Lesley took her place as hostess for her father, as she was often to do; for then, as later, Mrs. Frost's time was divided between her family members still in Vermont and her obligations in Ann Arbor.

Though the house was considered too large to be run without the assistance of a maid, the Frosts had decided not to seek such help.

Perhaps the consequences were soon apparent to Mrs. D'Ooge—a truly formidable woman from all accounts—and she evidently made her disapproval known, for Frost wrote an appalling letter to Untermeyer about the confrontation. Read in Ann Arbor many years later, when Untermeyer (p. 149) published his Frost letters—no doubt he had forgotten its contents—it caused consternation among those who had known the circumstances. A gentle missive it was not, but then as later Frost used Untermeyer as a sounding board for his offhand opinions, asking later that the letters not be published until he was "good and dead," as the saying goes.

Frost Given a Royal Reception

That first creative arts fellowship on a large scale played a large part in "The Recognition of Robert Frost," as a later book would call it. The press, of both Detroit and Ann Arbor, where *The Michigan Daily*, then widely read and respected, had an excellent welcoming interview, gave Frost all the attention he desired, and perhaps more. There were receptions both by the University, well attended, and in faculty homes. If Frost sometimes complained of the proximity of big fraternity houses to his Washtenaw Avenue home, as he did to Roy Cowden, he nevertheless liked "the boys," and welcomed them when they appeared at his door.

An element of comedy attaches, at this distance in time, to the *Washtenaw Post* reporter's view of Frost's comments on a crisis in the squirrel population of Ann Arbor. At that time (27 October 1921) a mysterious disease was proving fatal to battalions of the city's red squirrels. Noting the merry scampering of that species among the oaks at present, it becomes evident that the poet was right in viewing that onetime trouble in the animal kingdom as only a natural way of coping with their overpopulation. The reporter, however, was not pleased, and noted that "The University of Michigan is welcome to Mr. Frost and his theory of God's ways."

So, too, despite tragedies to come, there is comedy in some of Frost's family troubles at that time, notably in Carol Frost's proposal to pay twenty-five dollars for a champion rooster to improve his poultry. When his father harshly put down the idea, son Carol disappeared from Ann Arbor and made his way back to the Stone

Cottage in South Shaftsbury. His presence there was traced through frantic telephone calls to Marjorie, still in high school in North Bennington. He was to make the rooster part of the flock, defying his father, as he often did. Comical as the incident seems in retrospect, it was not so at the time.

One of the earlier of many Frost portraits, drawn by James House, Jr.—who was to follow a career as artist—was "Drawn from Life" soon after Frost's arrival in Ann Arbor, while he was being interviewed by Edwin R. Meiss at the house on Washtenaw Avenue. Both portrait and interview were published in *The Michigan Chimes* (November 1921). A persistent impression that the *Chimes* article was written by Donald Coney, later Librarian of the University of California, Berkeley, is corrected by a copy of the Meiss article from the Reference Department, University of Michigan Library.

If Frost was to say many years later that he "took the wrong way" with his son Carol, and also in that first year at Michigan took Lesley out of her University classes and transferred her to the care of Mrs. Moody in Chicago—his encouragement of nonadaptability to the world was only the fostering of his own qualities—whatever merits he assigned to practicality. As he was to say in "New Hampshire":

> I refuse to adapt myself a mite
> To any change from hot to cold, from wet
> To dry, from poor to rich, or back again (p. 166).

"And it is so," said Sidney Cox, in his perceptive book, *Robert Frost: Original "Ordinary Man."*[13]

How new and strange the idea of a creative fellowship, or poet in residence, was at that time is suggested by an editorial in *The Bookman*:

> Robert Frost has received an appointment to an "Idle Fellowship" at the University of Michigan. The "Idle Fellowship" idea is a new and notable one. Its incumbent does the university the honor of residing in the same town, but has literally no duties; if he should write a masterpiece or two while thus connected with the university, so much the better, but this is not required of him. In a time when poets are notoriously less amply rewarded by the public than are politicians and film comedians, this is not only a graceful but a useful way of

showing appreciation. The idea is being considered by more than one university, and it is understood that several of our American poets have been approached by various middle western universities with tentative offers of the same kind. The only difficulty seems to be that when it comes to idling, most of them would prefer to do it at home.[14]

The "idling" in this account was a bit overdone, but Floyd Dell, who contributed the news, had no knowledge of Frost's active life or frequent appearances about town—in themselves noteworthy, as some students were to remember.

New as the idea was, it is curious to find Ezra Pound writing from London, in November 1916, to Felix E. Schelling of the University of Pennsylvania, "on the subject of fellowships for creation as a substitute for, or an addition to, fellowships for research." It was not a new idea with him. To be sure, it was evidently meant to assist young men "whose work will stay imperfect through lack of culture," but it was to be in poetry.[15] When the creative fellowships came to fruition, of course, they were for men who had reached eminence in their fields and could inspire and lead others still on the lower rungs of the ladder. So it was with Frost.

A delightful note in the same issue of *The Bookman* with the serious announcement of Frost's new appointment at Michigan is worth preserving. Here it is, from the lead item in "The Gossip Shop."

> Sandburg and Robinson are two of our four poetic heroes. [No doubt it is the Editor, John Farrar, writing.] Which reminds us, that when we visited Ben Miller, that charming appreciator of poetry, not long ago in Washington, we were at first astonished to hear the excellent southern cook (who made me several varieties of biscuits for a breakfast that should have been served to the muses on Olympus) call "Rob't Frost, O Rob't Frost!" This was unusual. This was amazing. Where was Robert Frost? A grey cat bounded into the kitchen. "Thea you ah!" said the triumphant maidservant. "Now I'm goin' tuh find Mistah John Keats." So Mr. Miller combines his pets and his hobby. We have just bought two love birds (green and yellow). We are thinking of calling them—oh well! never mind.

The Whimsies Group and the Poetry Series of 1921–1922

An extraordinary richness of influence pervades that first year of Frost's presence in Ann Arbor, as many who knew him at that time have affirmed. It may be that Frost's later fame had its part in the remembrance of that year, but there is ample evidence that he was recognized as man and poet even then. Nor is there any doubt that the recognition given to Frost by the large and prestigious University of Michigan added luster to his fame in the world at large.

Though Frost was given to wandering, "acquainted with the night," outwalking "the furthest city light" (p. 255), often to find a friendly talker and above all a friendly listener, his closest acquaintance with the students at that time came through meetings with the *Whimsies* group at the home of the Cowdens.

Whimsies was the student literary magazine, established in 1920–1921, only a year before Frost arrived, the first issue mimeographed. It had five editors, all women students, in that first year, and it was to Dr. George Burton Grim, who died on April 7, 1922—"in his tenth year of service to our University"—that the issue of May 1922 was dedicated. By then the editors, all known to Frost, were: Lyndon Babcock, Stella Brunt, Lawrence Conrad, Yuki Osawa, and Frances Swain. Dr. Grim, the editorial noted, had been one of the warmest and most active friends of the publication, "proud when he learned that three of his own students were behind it," and who had "found our publisher for us, when we were almost in despair of ever getting into print."

The publisher Dr. Grim found for *Whimsies* was George Wahr of Ann Arbor, proudly called "Publisher and Bookseller to the University of Michigan," whose hospitable and browse-at-your-will bookstore on State Street was known to generations of students. It was known as well to Robert Frost, who autographed his books there,[16] and was often on hand for the sake of hobnobbing with the interesting folk there. In that issue and later George Wahr was thanked for his sponsorship.

Certainly by that second year, the group was meeting at the Cowdens' home, as it was to do for years thereafter. And the editors observed in the issue of May 1922: "The 'Whimsies Evenings' at the Cowdens' have brought together around Robert Frost a group of students interested in writing. This group originated the idea of the current series of lectures on modern poetry, and helped to carry

The announcements of Wahr's Bookstores, like this one from *The Inlander* of January 1926, appeared in both *Whimsies* and its successor, which George Wahr (1861–1945) subsidized for some years. Note "autographed copies if desired."

through that important movement of the present literary renaissance."

All true, no doubt, though solemnly stated. But who that remembers those evenings, then or later, will ever forget the scene? The long livingroom at the Cowdens' house—entered between two red Oriental maples—was perfectly suited to the occasion. Some twenty or twenty-five persons were present, seated far from or near the central dais, or so it seemed, at the near end of the room, near the big fireplace. On that dais, so one pictures it, if memory serves, was a large wicker chair, almost a throne. It was meant for Frost, king of kings on those occasions, but he chose instead a straight chair in a corner, from which an occasional comment would issue. The throne was more commonly occupied by Lawrence Conrad, who chaired the meetings with ease and authority. A strong editor of *Whimsies*, he later taught classes in composition at the University, and was author of the novel titled *Temper*, intended to be first in a series. He was a favorite of Frost's, who was to inquire about him in April 1962, at the University luncheon in his honor. It was Conrad who typed the manuscript of *New Hampshire*, published in 1923, while Frost was in Ann Arbor. The book was to win the Pulitzer Prize, for the first of four times for Frost.

Later, in 1930, Conrad was to publish in *The Landmark*[17] his appreciation of Frost the man and the poet, whom he had then known for nearly a decade. It had taken Frost, he said, some twenty years to give the humble grindstone "the publicity he thought it deserved. And in the end he had to run away to England and send work back across the water, in order to get really respectful attention for his message. We know him now, and have taken him to our hearts— stone wall, wood pile, pasture spring, birch trees, and all."

At the close of his essay, Conrad provides a portrait of Frost as he was in 1930: "A greying man, now fifty-five years of age, with a sparkle in his eye, and clean-chiseled lips in a perpetual whistle formation, he moves about the halls at Amherst College or tramps the farming country near South Shaftsbury, Vermont, never looking for poetry, but always sure that life holds the stuff of it, wherever he may go." (Frost, as we learned later, was fifty-six that year, but no matter.)

The Poetry Series 1921–1922

To list the names of those who came to Ann Arbor in that year of Frost's first service as Poet in Residence rings many a bell. Among the five were some of the best known and loved modern poets. Padraic Colum, gentle poet who wrote of the old woman of the roads, and was soon to return to Ireland, though he would return to America, as Mary Cooley recorded.[18] Carl Sandburg, with his "mandolute," as one friend called it, poet of the fog coming in on little cat feet, Lincoln biographer, and able to survive whatever Frost might say of him. Louis Untermeyer, poet and anthologist, great friend of Frost through many years, and the inspiration of some of Frost's best and most telling letters. Amy Lowell, great lady of Brookline, Massachusetts, poet and Keats biographer, one of the earliest to recognize the quality of Frost's poetry. And last, Vachel Lindsay, American troubadour, whose gestures and booming voice, when his poem about John Brown or *The Congo* called for it, were well remembered by his hearers. He also drew pictures for members of the *Whimsies* group, responsible for bringing the poets to Ann Arbor, though Frost often added an encouraging word and entertained the visitors.

Witter Bynner also came that year, and met with the *Whimsies*, and was entertained at the Frost home and heard the poem "The Witch of Coös," soon to be published in *Poetry*, though he did not lecture.

The series was well reported in *The Michigan Daily* by Lois Elizabeth Whitcomb,[19] often with illustrations. The success of the enterprise, the large attendance and long memories, even the Poet in Residence idea itself, were all part of the rebirth of literature then taking place, especially in the part of the country that Sandburg and Lindsay hailed from. Of these two a good friend who was a student at the time writes: "What year was it that the University brought a whole succession of poets to Hill Auditorium? I went to hear Carl Sandburg, with his mandolute, Vachel Lindsay who strode up and down pumping his arms to the rhythm of 'Fat black bucks . . .' and some others I've forgotten."[20]

One of the others, Padraic Colum, was well remembered. As the press reports indicate, most of the poets were received by Frost in his Washtenaw Avenue home, often in the absence of Elinor Frost. So it was with Colum in the spring of 1922, when the reporter found him—"a slight, eager figure, silhouetted against the window in Mr. Frost's living room. . . . We were scarcely seated when Mr. Frost excused himself. 'To make tea,' he explained. 'Padraic doesn't think I can, but just wait. Will you have plain tea or—?' 'Yes, let's have none of the calla lily stuff,' Mr. Colum cut in. . . . It was then that the tea tray appeared and we gathered about a little round table. Mr. Colum would pour his own cream from the small silver pitcher. . . . He sipped the beverage discriminatingly, and looked up. 'You're a grand tea-maker, Robert,' he approved."

As Frost's voice was his great treasure, so it was with Colum's, itself no doubt appealing to the other poet's sensitive ear—with "its depth and its singing quality . . . the delightful feathery edge of brogue, so fresh and pleasing to the American listener."[21]

Carl Sandburg was one poet no one forgot, whatever Frost's reservations of that time and later might be. Halsey Davidson, a *Whimsies* editor who would follow a career with a leading advertising firm, writes of the trouble he experienced in meeting Sandburg at the station, and of Frost's trouble in persuading him to leave his hair grooming and come to the dinner table. Davidson writes: "I recall a time when we were to meet Carl Sandburg at a train and take him to Frost's house for dinner preceding a recital Sandburg gave at Hill Auditorium. Sandburg certainly was not on the train but we did run on to him wandering up Washtenaw later, guitar over back and fur cap pushed back from his forward falling white locks. I never did find out how he reached Ann Arbor. Mrs. Frost was away and Frost put on a steak for the two after showing Sandburg to his room. Sandburg didn't show and didn't show, even after Frost had announced several times that the steak was done. Finally he went up to see what was the matter—and found Sandburg solemnly brushing his hair. 'I always do this for a half hour before any lecture,' he explained. The dinner was late—and so was the lecture. But both were good."[22]

The respective locks of Frost and Sandburg were a favorite subject of dissension both then and later. Others might laugh, Frost did not. A story current at the time had Frost approached on a train by a young man bearing a Sandburg book and asking for an autograph. Whose name did he inscribe in the book? Frost never divulged.

As for Amy Lowell and the show she put on when she lectured in Hill Auditorium on May 4, 1922,[23] with the fuse blown by her reading lamp, the ensuing darkness while she and Frost exchanged witty jokes, to the laughing delight of the audience, the tipping over of the water pitcher and tripping over the light cord by Frost— though he would not admit it in his letter to Untermeyer—it was a story that would make the rounds for years in Ann Arbor, always told with appreciation. She, like the other poets, would meet with the writers of the *Whimsies* group, with her companion, Ada Dwyer Russell, the former actress, seated quietly by. At least one of the students present, Ruth Lechlitner,[24] would find her comments helpful. They would stay in a hotel in Detroit, where Amy had addressed a group at the famous Detroit Public Library, and later go on to Chicago, where *Poetry* was published and Amy had friends.

A book of fair size could be written about the friendship, and sometimes enmity, of Amy Lowell of *Sevenels* and Robert Frost, and even the several accounts in print would make a book of sorts. But one of the most poignant passages is related by S. Foster Damon in Amy's own words concerning the book *North of Boston*, first read in London: "In the summer of 1914, I was in London, and on one occasion, when I had strolled into the Poetry Bookshop, I found lying on a counter a slim little green cloth volume bearing the allur- ing title *North of Boston*. It is a good title even when one discounts any particular bias toward it, but for an expatriated New Englander its appeal was nostalgic and completely irresistible. I bought the book then and there, and all that evening, in the impersonal bleak- ness of a hotel room, I read this most personal book, until I was sat- urated with the atmosphere of the New Hampshire hills; and when I went to the window and looked out at the moon, it was not Picca- dilly that I saw before my windows, but Monadnock and Dublin Lake shining with moonlight. . . . I immediately took off my hat to the unknown poet, and I have been taking it off ever since in a posi- tively wearying repetition."[25]

For all the contentions between them, including Amy's observa- tions about the decline of New England with the westward movement and Frost's denials—"What's wrong with it?" he asked in return, and she said rightly, "Read your own poems and find out"—they had much in common in their heritage (II, 233). Had not her review of *North of Boston* in *The New Republic* in February 1915 launched his career at home and greeted him in New York?

By the time of her lecture in Ann Arbor, Amy Lowell was already in poor health, though she carried through with her obligations as she always did. In the fall of that year, 1922, her anonymous *Fable for Critics* would appear—in emulation of her famous forebear, James Russell Lowell—though the secret of its authorship was soon guessed. One of her best portraits was of Frost "with his blueberry pastures and hills. . . ."

> He's a foggy benignity wandering in space
> With a stray wisp of moonlight just touching his face

—a good description of the countenance of Frost at that time.

As for their quarrel about the nature of New England and its people, both had their reasons, but Amy, though she had a summer home, *Broomley Lacey*, in Dublin, New Hampshire, admitted in the end that she was a "cosmopolitan," while Frost had a better understanding of rural New England.

A Banner Year—1921–1922

On anyone's scale of values, that year of 1921–1922 must have been a banner year. It was Frost's first as Fellow in Creative Arts, and though I was not there I had friends who were. Two daughters of faculty members, Sue Grundy Bonner and Mary E. Cooley, were then in Ann Arbor High School, and so knew of Frost's presence there—and would know him better later. Both became my staunch and continuing friends when all three were University students, and all three were students in Frost's only Seminar, in 1925–1926, though I was in one section, they in another.

Frost was known in the homes of both Charles Horton Cooley, sociologist, and Campbell Bonner, Professor of Greek, and so became known to their daughters from his first year there. I was still in Lansing, but heard Frost say his poems in that first year in the old Lansing Woman's Clubhouse on Washington Avenue—a warm and gracious place, now gone to seed. I still recall the excitement of that experience and the memorable appearance of the poet in that hour. I had no expectation then of knowing him personally later in Ann Arbor or in the following years.

Was it of that appearance Frost spoke to Professor Brumm of the Journalism Department, a genial spirit and an able teacher, when he said he "heard someone roaring on the platform and realized that it was he"? Then and later he often discounted the impression he had made on his listeners.

A personal note concerning the end of that first year in Ann Arbor is provided by Mary Cooley's diary for "Friday, June 16, 1922 (my High School Commencement Day)":

> While we were eating lunch the telephone rang and when I answered a voice which I did not recognize asked for Father. It was Mr. Frost! He came over shortly after lunch, and I sat in the study where I could hear his every word. . . . He spoke of many things. He said that editors knew nothing of poetry and that if we knew how little they saw in our works, we would not have the heart to send our little mind-children out into the cold world to be judged by cold, unseeing eyes and minds that do not understand. He said that criticism did not mean anything to him. He said that he did not print his poems for people to read, but that he only printed about three a year when he needed money, and then he would get so disgusted that he would not do it again for another year. He said that "The Death of the Hired Man" was refused by The Atlantic Monthly. He said that most of the people who went to hear the poets went because they thought it the correct thing to do and not because of any real desire. He said that he hoped it would be different next year. And—best of all—he said that he was coming back! Then I went in, and dear diary, he wrote a poem in the front of each of my two books of his. I was so thrilled! While he was thinking of one, he asked me to call up his wife and tell her that he would be home soon. As he sat there writing, he looked just like his picture in New Voices. I could hardly breathe, I was so happy."[26]

In *Life and the Student*, Cooley seems to be thinking of Frost's opinions of that time: "I take the ———, thought to be the best of the literary monthlies. It is admirable; and yet at times I peculiarly detest it for a sort of pose which I seem to feel in it, and for a certain proprietary attitude towards the authors. The latter seem too docile, too conscientiously urbane. . . . I miss what I have heard called you-be-damnedness. I would give volumes of this publication for a thin book by Robert Frost."[27]

Gifted Students at Michigan during the Frost "Regime"

It is difficult, if not foolhardy, to attempt a sorting out of students who were both gifted in the arts and who came under Frost's influence during his years at Michigan. But some can unquestionably be named in this category, even if—as Frost himself often insisted—they would have made it on their own without his presence among them. It was the spirit of the time and, to some degree, the place.

Putting aside any sins of omission in my listing, here are a few: *Warren Bower*, later of the faculty of New York University, who wrote in appreciation of Frost as "more than teacher," . . . "a poet, one of the American greats, standing with Emerson and Whitman, a writer who will be more and more read for his exploration of many of the dark paradoxes of life as the years lengthen from his death." Professor of English and assistant dean of the Division of General Education, Bower is listed as "a student and friend of the poet."[28]

Coming from a small Michigan college, as he wrote me, Bower found stimulation and excitement in coming to the University and finding there a poet of the stature of Robert Frost. In fairness to the "small Michigan college" it should be said that some years later it became famous for its literary gatherings under the leadership of Ford Madox Ford.

Forman Brown. As old copies of *Whimsies* for the years 1921–1922 and 1922–1923 prove, Forman Brown, remembered as one of the able and charming poets at Michigan during Frost's two years as poet in residence, contributed several poems to the magazine. He was also a member of the group privileged to attend with other students when authors were to be present at Frost's or the Cowdens' home. Frost, he writes, "was always glad to talk with even the most shy and tongue-tied, and my richest memories are of evenings when we few would receive a telephone call to come either to his house or to the Cowdens' to meet some poet friend who had dropped in, or was passing through Ann Arbor. In this way I remember evenings spent with Carl Sandburg, Vachel Lindsay, Amy Lowell, Alfred Kreymborg, Louis Untermeyer, and Padraic Colum. . . . The bolder of us would read our verses, and criticize the others. The rest of us sat and listened."[29]

That Brown was in those days "very serious about writing poetry" is proved in several ways. From South Shaftsbury Frost wrote him in early 1926 or early 1927 a letter about poems he had sent to *The Dearborn Independent,* for which Frost's daughters were then serving for a time as poetry editors. With his two Frost letters Brown found as well "a half dozen from Marianne Moore, who accepted two or three of them for *The Dial*—and paid me!"

Those poems in *The Dial* I have not seen, but Forman Brown's sonnet about "a certain writer of popular songs" who appropriated the lovely melody of "Un bel di" from the opera *Madama Butterfly* has remained with me through all the intervening years. I quote the sestet:

> Ah Cho Cho San! Still vainly hoping gaze
> Upon your eastern sea for his return!
> Still let your soul in glorious defeat,
> Twice violated, soar above the blaze
> Of tense, still balconies! Still let it learn
> To rise above defacement and deceit![30]

Forman Brown was among those who kept in touch with Frost after he left Ann Arbor. He writes: "My interests soon turned more and more to music and the theater, but I did keep in touch with Robert Frost, as my connection with The Yale Puppeteers took me to New England every summer, so I visited him in Vermont and in New Hampshire. Here, near Franconia, I found him living in a small house, remote from everything, up a wood road. When I told him I wanted to buy a place in the White Mountains, he accompanied me on long walks to inspect a good many deserted farms, and finally helped me select the one I eventually purchased on the edge of Franconia village, where I subsequently spent many happy summers. He was always much interested in the puppets, and whenever we had a performance near enough, we could count on his being in the audience.

"In later years as I became increasingly involved in things theatrical, I lost touch with him, and eventually, as his fame increased, I was loath to involve him in correspondence—although I am sure he would have answered my letters generously.

"Coming to the West Coast in 1941 I helped found The Turnabout Theatre here in Hollywood, and for fifteen years wrote all the material. I also became special lyricist for the Los Angeles and San Francisco Civic Light Opera Associations. Perhaps my failure to keep in touch was due in part to a guilty feeling that I had not lived up to his expectations for me as a poet."[31]

It should have been enough, that notable achievement of Forman Brown's, to win his mentor's approval. However, it was usually poetry alone that enlisted Frost's interest, as those who knew him were aware. Knowing his special love for the poetry of Edward Thomas, his disregard for anything he had produced in the way of prose, I was astonished to come upon an excellent biography of Richard Jefferies by Thomas, published before Frost had known Thomas in England.[32]

Stella Brunt. One of the originators of *Whimsies*, and active both as editor and contributor during Frost's first two years at Michigan, Stella Brunt later became successively secretary, adopted daughter —she was then known as "Stellanova"—companion and then wife of Chase Salmon Osborn, onetime Governor and University Regent, with whom she co-authored several books.[33] There was a special relationship, since Osborn funded the first fellowship bringing Frost to Ann Arbor.

Delbert Clark. One of *The Michigan Daily*'s excellent writers at the time when Frost was Poet in Residence, it is possible that Delbert Clark[34] was more than merely cognizant of the poet's presence. A staff writer for *The New York Times* at the time of his early death, he wrote a memorial article in explanation of the character and opinions of his fellow student and writer, G. D. Eaton, a campus radical and dissident far in advance of his time, whose hero was H. L. Mencken, and who wrote a novel, *Backfurrow*, now hard to find. Frost was well aware of Eaton, as his letters to Louis Untermeyer from Ann Arbor indicate. In one[35] he remarks that "Anything you can do to praise Miss Whitcomb will please G. D. Eaton (concerning whom consult The Smart Set for March) and anything that pleases Eaton will give you standing with what Farrar says is the best college newspaper literary supplement in the United States—namely that of The Michigan Daily." All of which, and more, proves how astonishingly Frost found his way into the University life of the time.

Lawrence H. Conrad. No one who attended *Whimsies* meetings at the Cowdens while Frost was Poet in Residence is likely to forget Lawrence Conrad, who often presided over the event. Though Frost evidently lost touch with him during Conrad's long career as a teacher, he inquired about Conrad during the luncheon held at Inglis House in April 1962, and his friendship with Conrad may have been the closest and most durable of any of his associations with Michigan students. It was Conrad who typed the copy for Frost's *New Hampshire,*[36] which was to be dedicated "*To* Vermont and Michigan,"—no doubt the first typed copy his publisher received. Editor of *Whimsies* (one of the group), contributor of both poems and prose, and writer of some of its strongest editorials, Conrad published a novel, *Temper*, and a book *The Author's Mind*, while Frost was with the University, and in 1937 a book titled *Teaching Creative Writing*, while he was in Montclair, New Jersey.

Conrad wrote a letter to President Burton[37] after Frost's second year as Poet in Residence, greatly praising his contributions and influence, and suggesting that his position be made permanent. In view of Frost's prolonged absences and many illnesses in that year of 1922–1923, some students and faculty there at the time will find the encomiums overstated, apart from the fact that, as Thompson writes, "Robert Frost did not want to be adopted by Michigan—did not want to continue there for the rest of his life" (II, 227). Still, he would be back for another year, in 1925–1926.

Anyone who doubts Frost's love for Michigan and the friends he made there should consider the many times he returned and his many letters to those he had met there. Writing to Forman Brown from South Shaftsbury on October 18, 1927—after Brown had bought a summer home in the Franconia region—Frost said: "We'll be neighbors now. I had a good letter from Lawrence. Some of us met out there in your state to stay friends."

The "Lawrence" was Lawrence Conrad, fellow student of Forman Brown.

Valentine Davies. Of a New York City family, and living in Malibu Beach, California, with his family at the time of his early death (c. 1960), Valentine Davies was a writer especially gifted in the theater and motion pictures. When the Christmas season returns with all its festivities, his ever-fragrant *Miracle on 34th Street* returns with it. It was on television on Christmas Day, 1976, delightful as always. Davies was in Ann Arbor during Frost's stays and was the son-in-law of Professor Louis A. Strauss of the Department of English, who is remembered (among more scholarly endeavors) as one involved in the farcical events connected with Amy Lowell's appearance in the poetry series of 1921–1922.

It was Strauss who later invited Frost to serve as one of the judges in the Hopwood contest and who received a warm-hearted letter of regret from the poet, who had been gadding about as usual, and returned too late to serve.[38]

Max Ewing. Of the many gifted students during Frost's reign— and he was always one to say that they would make it on their own, as *he* had—was a handsome youth from Pioneer, Ohio, who soon traveled to New York City. There he was a friend of Carl Van Vechten, who writes of him in *Going Somewhere*. I recall Ewing vividly as an unapproachable young man walking on the campus with backward tilted head and superb profile and a look of intense suffering. At that time he had already published his *Sonnets from the Paranomasian*, copies of which are in the possession of some of his fellow students, though I have yet to see one. The title always reminded me of Elizabeth Barrett Browning's book, though I doubt whether there is any similarity in content. Ewing took his own life some years ago when his family funds were threatened. He is represented in the Yale University Library of American Authors, with his own works and his letters to Lawrence Conrad and his wife in the collection, as well as a copy of Van Vechten's *Going Somewhere*.[39]

Carl E. Gehring. Of the University vintage of Frost's first year in Ann Arbor, Gehring was both music critic and composer. He set

to music the poetry of Edna St. Vincent Millay, as well as that of
Frost, and—in a different vein—composed two band marches, "The
Stadium" and "The Wolverines," performed in the summer of 1964
by the Detroit City Band on Belle Isle, and directed by Leonard
Smith. The titles and the music reflect Carl Gehring's love for the
University of Michigan and his long residence in Ann Arbor. He
had many friends among the gifted students of his time, including
those who cherished the presence of Frost at the University. At one
time the Frost family as a group heard his settings of the Frost poems,
including the grim "The Hill Wife." For years he was music critic
of *The Ann Arbor News*, in a city proud of its long musical tradition and its excellent School of Music.

Frost was a true friend of Carl Gehring, and visited him whenever
he was in Ann Arbor, including the last times in the spring of 1962.
One of his proudest possessions was a copy of the Special Edition of
Frost's *Collected Poems* (Spiral Press, 1930), with the following
inscription:

> Dear Carl,
>   I send you this to commemorate the day I received your lovely
> music to Stopping by Woods, The Road Not Taken, A Peck of Gold,
> Acceptance, The Freedom of the Moon, Acquainted with the Night,
> Tree at My Window, Spring Pools, Bereft, and The Birthplace; and
> to tell you how glad I am to live in an age when you and I can write
> together and be friends.
>
>   Affectionately
>   Robert Frost
>
> Amherst Mass
> November 27 1932

In view of the many mean and destructive remarks made about
Frost since his death, it is pleasant to recall that Carl Gehring cherished both man and poet, and even hoped at one time to move and
live in the neighborhood and ambience of Frost in New England.
Alas, it was not to be, for Frost died in January 1963, and Carl Gehring himself on 24 September 1966, still in Ann Arbor.

James House Jr. The sketches and portraits of this gifted artist
enlivened the student publications of the Frost era in Ann Arbor,
all signed with a tiny "house" and "jr" beside it. As noted, one of the

earliest portrait heads of Frost was "drawn from life" while the poet was interviewed by Edwin R. Meiss for an article in *The Michigan Chimes*, published in November 1921. Though House later published a *Book of Portraits*, this one was not included. Following a career as professional artist, he now lives in Media, Pennsylvania.

Paul Osborn. Known in the New York theater world for his plays *The Vinegar Tree* and *Morning's at Seven*, among others, Osborn knew Frost during his Ann Arbor years—he once said in an interview published later[40] that he had stayed in the University town too long, partly because of Frost's presence there—and also later while he lived in New York City. Both Frost and Louis Untermeyer were often in Osborn's company there, and one of the poet's letters to Untermeyer from Ripton, Vermont, in 1945 mentions that Osborn had "just been with us for a visit." In another letter two years earlier (October 27, 1943), Frost mentioned the full-length play he had completed—it was never published or produced—and mentioned that "Paul asked if he might drop a hint in the right quarter, but I positively forbade it."[41]

Clement A. Smith, M.D. One of the many friends of Frost who kept in touch with the poet from the time of his Michigan years until his death was Clement Smith, a Michigan graduate, later a distinguished pediatrician. In the first year of the publication of *Whimsies* he won the competition for the best poem, "Mallards in February," published in May 1921. He was later elected to the editorial board of *Whimsies*, but resigned the post when he entered Medical School, before serving. His literary gift came naturally, for he was the son of Shirley Smith, long on the administrative staff of the University, one of whose stories was dramatized by Valentine Davies (q.v.). Strangely, the family were neighbors of Robert Frost when he lived on Washtenaw Avenue in Ann Arbor—Dr. Smith remembers that Frost was in their home at least once when his father's club met there—and later, when Frost lived in Cambridge, Dr. Smith and his own family were again the poet's neighbors for years.

Dr. Smith writes: "I can't help but think of taking the daughter of one of my Boston friends and her family to his Cambridge home a year or so before he died so that he could autograph the child's book. Even later than that I remember talking with him after an evening of readings for the benefit of the *Harvard Advocate*, and finding him—a tired old man—politely and interestedly receiving a large portrait of Tagore from a confused Indian girl in a sari. Through it all there went that same old receptiveness of people as individuals which never left him." [42]

Clubs Known to Frost in Ann Arbor

Was it becoming a "social lion" in Ann Arbor that kept Frost from maintaining the seclusion necessary for the production of poetry? Perhaps it was instead his own habit of seeking out company, as he often did, both by day and by night, for purposes of exchanging ideas and talking. In general, the press—very active in reporting on Frost in his years in Ann Arbor—was prone to make it appear that the fault, if there was one, lay with the University community. As often with Frost, perhaps the truth faced both ways. In any event, it must be remembered that his first two years were spent in houses on opposite sides of handsome Washtenaw Avenue, more or less in the heart of the University community, with faculty residences and fraternity houses near at hand.

He certainly knew of the existence of both faculty and student clubs which escaped the knowledge of many in the diversified and culturally abundant life of those times. One that came to my attention was the club called Indipohdi, taking its name from a drama by Gerhart Hauptmann, as suggested by a popular professor of German, Jonathan Hildner—who had probably been known as well to Jeanie Frost. (Hauptmann was at that time riding high, for he had won the Nobel Prize in Literature in 1912.)

Warren Bower, a member of the club, describes it as bringing together at its weekly meetings a group of kindred spirits—were they called "kinsprits," as Christopher Morley would have it?—with Hildner the only faculty member, and otherwise such students as Lawrence Conrad, Max Ewing ("who influenced us all in subtle ways and introduced us to new writers"), Paul Osborn, Halsey Davidson, Carl Gehring, and once at least Tom Dewey, of later fame. As the list suggests, all knew Frost, who came to at least one meeting, "but was much more a spirit of whose presence we were aware than he was an active participant."[43]

As the list indicates, all members were men, with the exception of the late Roberta Conrad, then the wife of Lawrence—at whose house the club often met. That it was so—when many of these members were also active in *Whimsies*—suggests the spirit of the University for many years, since men students predominated and the faculty was almost exclusively made up of men. (The fact is stated without prejudice.)

One of the most distinguished of faculty clubs at Michigan was the Quadrangle Club, whose meetings Frost attended, as Carlton F. Wells of the faculty remembers. *The Quadrangle Book*[44] lists the names of many members, some still there while Frost was in Ann Arbor, though it was published in 1914. Among them is Isaac Newton Demmon, Professor of English and Rhetoric, 1881–1903, whose house—across the street from the D'Ooge house on Washtenaw—the Frost family occupied in 1922–1923. Among the members as well was John R. Brumm, Professor of Journalism, genial mentor of many newspaper men and women, who lived on beautiful Cambridge Road, as Professor Louis A. Strauss did. As was his way, Frost no doubt visited both in their spacious homes.

There is no question that both Indipohdi and the Quadrangle Club have gone their way into oblivion, except in the memories of some and the dwindling records they left, some probably in the archives of the Michigan Historical Collections. But some still living remember that a poet named Frost used to attend meetings of the Quadrangle Club, as they have told me.

Faculty Members Known to Frost

Frost was brought to Ann Arbor chiefly to create a richer cultural climate for students, but sometimes it appears that the faculty and townspeople and even the city of Detroit—which gave Frost a tremendous coverage in the press—were the chief beneficiaries. The other side of the picture is equally apparent, for Frost could not have been happy without the friendship and hospitality of the many faculty members known to him. After all, the faculty is the stable element in a university town, indispensable as the student body may be.

Many of those faculty members have been mentioned, but those best known should be named again. First of all, since he was earliest known, was Morris P. Tilley and his family of Ferdon Road, who knew Frost first at their summer home in Franconia, in the White Mountains—where the Frost home has recently been turned into a living museum as the summer home of a "poet-in-residence,"[45] the first appointed in 1977.

It was the Tilley family who were the earliest and most continuous of Frost's Michigan friends. The earliest of Frost's famous Christmas cards, titled "Christmas Trees," in the poet's own handwriting, and illustrated by Lesley with a row of evergreen trees, was sent in 1915—it was written on Christmas Day of that year, according to Thompson[46]—to "Miss Tilley and her mother." The original, along with other Frost letters addressed to Professor Morris Tilley, is now in the University of Michigan Library. Even at that early time Frost, as one line reads, was aware of the "Trial by market that all things must come to." It was during that same Christmas season that Frost wrote to "My dear Tilley" from Franconia, thanking him for "trying to make the professors out there like me"—all of six years before his first fellowship at Michigan was to materialize. It is sad to read in the same letter of "all sorts of sickness" in the family, and that Frost himself was "very much down" and did not see how he was "going to get into shape for all the lecturing I have ahead."[47]

As was true of the Dean Joseph Bursley family, Frost became the friend of the younger generation, and then of their children, with the Tilleys. Of Frost's well-known friendship with apple orchards and apple picking and his advice, "Good-by and keep cold" (p. 228), George Tilley—son of Professor Tilley, and a Detroit attorney well known in the city—once said that "Robert Frost could tell from smelling an apple what variety it was."[48] Frost must often have dined at the Tilley home, for one of Tilley's assistants recalled that once, when the Tilleys were entertaining the famous Wordsworth scholar, Ernest de Selincourt, Mrs. Tilley was somewhat flustered when Frost also appeared.[49]

Roy W. Cowden, long Professor of English Language and Literature at Michigan, was among those who had a long and continuous friendship with Frost. In fact, he was one of those who greeted the Frosts when they first arrived at the house on Washtenaw in the autumn of 1921. It was at the Cowdens' home at 1016 Olivia Avenue that the student writers and editors of *Whimsies* and *The Inlander* met from first to last, and it was there the famous poets and dramatists and novelists also gathered—usually with Frost in the foreground and background, as he chose.

Cowden's good statement of the impact and influence of Frost at the University was published in Elizabeth Shepley Sergeant's biography: "The periods during which he lived here were high lights in the lives of the students he came to know. He not only influenced their writing, but he was a great force for good in their lives. A great and good human being only needs to walk the earth, to be a help to mankind."[50]

Incidentally, for all the talk of being set among fraternity houses and other causes of interruptions to the writing of poetry, Frost somehow managed to write, "in his very first term," that wonderful poem "The Witch of Coös,"—and, as evidence, to show it to Witter Bynner.[51] He was to mention the circumstance in his talk in Ann Arbor in April 1962.[52]

Of the warm hospitality of Roy and Mabel Cowden in those years of Frost's fellowship, the often quoted essay by Frances Swain—daughter of George Swain, University photographer who recorded some of the Kelsey archeological expeditions—provides a lasting record.[53] So aptly and poignantly do they recall those times of long ago, and the Cowdens with them, that they deserve—those pages from *The Inlander*—a full report.

The Robert Frost of the Whimsies Evenings

BY FRANCES SWAIN

"WHIMSIES Evenings," for those who do not know, have been at the Cowdens'. Beforehand we always set a big wicker chair directly under the reading lamp for Mr. Frost, then he comes and selects some unpretentious, dim corner far distant from the throne, and we are ready to begin—talking, and more, listening to him talk. Although he speaks lightly enough, with a whimsical, skipping surface over his comments, there is a lasting tang of significance in the

stuff of them that puts one remotely in mind of that earlier luminary, Dr. Samuel Johnson. Except for that note of rugged sincerity,
however, the two are extremely unlike. The most trivial remarks
of Johnson have the reputation for a quality of inkiness even though
they escaped formal print; the conversation of Frost sparkles, more
lightly, more elusively, and is at its best in the pauses—when it is in
his eyes, between words.

His talk proceeds so deliberately and informally that you might
wonder, were you not too absorbed for wonderment, where it was
leading anyway. When he was still a newcomer and a curiosity
here, he launched his bolt against the academicians with the statement, "I like to see a woman take a sixty-foot dive in the Hippo-
drome—and break her neck. . . . I like to be at a football game where
five men are carried out on stretchers." There are successive strata
of illumination. Rambling he interpreted: "I like to see the literary
artist dare to risk his whole literary *life* just to say what he wants"
—audacity, sincerity, tenacity! Then after an interval, his trick of
making a clean breast of things forced him to add, "I know you're
not all in sympathy with me. I'm glad—because I don't mean half
of what I say." You conclude that he would perhaps not enjoy
severed necks then, but as for the rest, his severity may be earnest.
He makes you do the testing.

He is humorous and ruthless. Occasionally he mentions profes-
sorial days at Amherst. Once he spilled an entire lot of themes
heartlessly into the waste-basket without glancing further at them
because when he had inquired of the class whether anyone wanted
his composition saved for him not one student had valued his work
enough to ask the favor. Fearlessness and conviction and honesty—
I seem continually to be having to enumerate for him those virtues
that are really most "bark and steel." Of free verse he remarks that
the *difference* of it as a whole from the verse that preceded it is obvious, but that critics need hardly make much over eccentricities
in its individual writers, because when they enter the ranks as verse
librists they assume an obligation of non-conformity. "Let's be
honest with ourselves!" He is guilty of trifling statements that you
suspect of hyperbole or irony, but his actual sturdy intent is seldom
obscured.

When you first meet him he appears to be quite a middling citizen—his build the least bit taller and stockier than the average, cos-
tume unostentatious (it has been a tweed suit this past season),
greyish hair kept too short to swagger very temperamentally, and
eyes nondescript except for their eminent kindliness. Only his fore-
head, broad and majestic, marks him for an "intellectual." How he

would despise the term! He is all antagonism toward "the academic," but therein is simply a token of kinship with his fellow poets, and as a matter of fact he is friendly everywhere. You comfortingly forget the frequency with which his name appears in print, and take Frost at just the valuation of a *man*—one to be characterized by his epithet of "nice person" pronounced in the genuine tone of Frost's own nice, homely, earnest moods. Indeed, he is so very comfortable that he induces all the *Whimsies* in their private talk of him familiarly to call him plain "Robert" or "Frost." If I describe the affection that in our hearts we think into that "Robert" he would accuse me, unjustly, of verging into sentimentality. His tenet is that only occasionally does the best of men lapse into sincerity. He quite persuades you.

He furthers ease. He scorns an atmosphere of stiltedness. And—long-suffering godfather!—he has had his tussles to enliven us at times when a stifling formal silence has descended subsequent to the reading of an indifferent manuscript; but he bragged to Padraic Colum that on need he "could *make*" us talk! His blunt candour, turned genial by the twinkle in his fatherly eyes, is enviable. Once in the process of criticizing a "nice obscure poem" (he is a master in subtly discriminating between his *nices*, this one being strongly derogatory because coupled with the *obscure*) he said meditatively, "You know—there is a difference between fetching and farfetching. . . ." He will often help tide over an emptiness thus, although he would much prefer to be exempted from the criticizing, and does manoeuver so as practically to obviate the impression that he is doing a thing.

But, before sufficient temptation, he can be frail. (If ever "we" transgress in what is to follow, you are to blame the spokesman alone. *Whimsies* collectively would court the unrestricted approval of the man who by his intimations really launched us on our rather unique, altogether pleasurable Evenings some months back. To soothe this most famous of its friends, the plural *Whimsies* would even go so far as to refrain from advertising his endearing humanness—but I am less scrupulous.) I recollect that when our Evenings were impending we discussed the advisability of refreshments. Mr. Frost was opposed to them; then we tried them despite him, and he countenanced and disposed of ** glasses of punch and ** cookies. I suppress the numerals out of appreciation for the hazards of his position. For one thing, there would have been Mrs. Cowden to propitiate had he refused. But we chortled in private. As for *his* laugh, he has a contagious chuckle mellowed into semi-dignity.

After he moves the chair out of the light, and we begin to limber up, he chats about all sorts of things, and people, in his offhand, reminiscent way. We like to hear of the world of poets, and Frost is an excellent gossip, safely. Once he repeated an anecdote that he had heard about Amy Lowell. At a poet's banquet in Chicago, Miss Lowell was seated next "a poetess of the old school." At the close of the evening, she sputtered of this companion, "That old thing complimented me on my dress!" "Don't," Frost advised us, "compliment Amy on a dress when she's just given a speech."

He told us of his first call on Miss Lowell, in Brookline. A precocious lad who shared his seat in the street-car volunteered the information that to pass in safety Amy's guard of pedigreed dogs a visitor must gather up imaginary stones from the walk and fling them with hardihood and speed. Robert Frost is a grown man, "but I pretended with all my might when I saw them! . . . And they did almost kill one poet once!"

There are trains to be made a laughing-stock of always. "But if you miss yours at one station you may be able to catch up with it by the next. I did once. How? Just ran like everything!" We chuckle breathlessly with him, then as an afterthought he hints that maybe automobiles might have helped some in this prodigious tale; but always he waits a bit before clearing the mystery so as not to spoil the fun. He is deliciously funny.

We have liked watching Frost with the other poets who have been here—or they with him, perhaps I should say, for he keeps pretty stubbornly in the background, just suggesting in an undertone to Carl Sandburg that Carl impart such and such a folk song to us young people next, or trying inconspicuously to engender a more sober mood for the reading of a poem of Jean Starr Untermeyer's by telling us, who had been revelling in drollery, "Let's change the mood now"—as if that could solemnize things! So insistent was he on keeping backstage the evening the Untermeyers were with us that he refused almost tartly Louis' request to read a poem . . . and it was someone else's too! (I refuse to interpret my own last phrase more specifically. To me, a poem of Frost's should be best suited to vindicate Frost: but he would prefer slander to praise where he himself was concerned.) However, the appeals of Padraic Colum, coupled with an embarrassing muteness on our part, did induce him to break his rule. Small wonder! Padraic had treated him with peculiar deference, and he Padraic with an intimacy that savored of mild, pleased patronizing. Padraic had read some dainty verses of his own. "Are they obscure, Robert?" he had begged. "Are they so mysterious?" "Oh no! Just your pronunciation is a bit mysterious." There were two hours of winning banter. But although with Mr. Untermeyer Frost was more stern, he was hardly less kind underneath. When the guest poet rued comparison with Tennyson, Frost told him, "You can stand it, Louis." In his more earnest veins he can bestow bouquets meaningfully. He and Mr. Colum together eulogized Harriet Monroe's industry in her editing of *Poetry*. For years she has been broad-minded and fair to the best of her ability, almost never making an incorrect prophecy. True, she had underestimated Mr. Frost's early work. She had been firm in that refusal—only, unfortunately for her, the opinion of England was the reverse. Robert could not help rallying her gently on that score, out of a sense of the sport involved in making folks squirm— but fundamentally Harriet was "all right."

He is such a genuine man that even if he were not the honest writer he is, he could not but influence toward a greater sincerity everyone with whom he comes in contact. Out of modesty and generosity he wishes you to take initiative for yourself in circumstances where he might, less beneficially for you, over-exert his influence. So he has kept assiduously in the rear in the series of lectures by the five poets, but we wish we *could* thank him publicly, somehow slyly, for the encouragement given us by his bare, staunch interest.

The lovable character of him is irrepressible in his own story concerning himself and a minister who had written him testifying to eternal respect and admiration, and would not Mr. Frost just please criticize the enclosed original epic frankly? The servant of God would be grateful beyond words if the great hero among mortals would but condescend to give him the truth about this one piece of literature. The epic, by the way, had for a title some abstraction. Mr. Frost obliged replying that in all probability the clergyman's sermons surpassed his poetic compositions. Then current periodicals began featuring invectives against the adored and admired luminary, suffixed with the name of the minister. "Well, finally," Mr. Frost confided, "I sat down and wrote that chap a letter that simply finished him—just the littlest, meanest letter you ever read"—and after a sufficient number of minutes had elapsed for us to have finished picturing the worst—"but I never sent the letter."

That early portrait of Frost as he was in the spring of 1922 remained a reasonable facsimile of man and poet as he was through all the years that followed. One adjective stands out, however, as revealing a quality never far from him. *Ruthless* is the word. He could be and was ruthless in his opinions of others, especially of contemporary poets, often seen as his rivals for public acclaim. Only in his later years, when so many of those same poets were gone, and his own position was paramount, was he able to forget his early and *ruthless* opinions.

Still, his very ruthlessness could be regarded as a compliment and an admission of quality in his adversary. He did not waste his verbal weapons on those who would fall by the wayside without the Frostian thrust.

But one of his curious and long-held complaints, which he did not fail to repeat during his Michigan years, was against his Grandfather Frost. After hearing him presented several times as an old skinflint who had done his best to stifle his grandson's desire to be a poet, I was astonished to learn that it was his grandfather's annuity that had permitted the family's relatively easy life on the Derry farm—bought for them, at Elinor's suggestion, by the first William Prescott Frost—and later in England.[54] It is entertaining to recall the observation of Ezra Pound in a letter to the Editor of the Boston *Transcript*, after he had seen the paper's praise of Frost for making it on his own in England. "No, sir, Frost was a bloated capitalist when he struck this island, in comparison to yours truly, and you can put that in your editorial pipe though I don't give a damn whether you print the fact."[55] They did, as it turned out. It should not be overlooked, however, that Pound was one of the first promoters of Frost's poetry. As Mark Van Doren wrote: "He knew *The Waste Land* was a classic before anyone else did; he knew Robert Frost was one. . . . The art was all, whether living or dead men practiced it."[56]

"The art was all," and so would have said Roy Cowden, who sometimes took Frost's place at his Seminar; for Frost was often absent, as the record shows. Cowden certainly knew Frost's shortcomings as well as anyone, but I never heard him mention one of them. And in view of Cowden's precept that to dwell on the negative aspects is to cause the reader to forget the positive side of the portrait, it may be wise to quote here an early celebration of Frost's great gift, his speaking voice, in which his poetry and his theory of poetry were implicit.

And there is with us still Robert Frost, of whose voice one could almost say that it is the man himself. There is no photograph of him that conveys the fulness of personality and along with it that touch of remoteness and mystery of the poet which one senses in his presence. No picture quite succeeds in showing the man who has looked up often, if by chance, at the constellations; who has been acquainted with the night; and who is one of the lovely who shall be choosers; and who has chosen not to go in harness to bring in someone else's social millennium.

No disk can record the full music of his voice. It is a voice that can be wise, ironic, witty. Its wine can be spiced with malice and mockery. It is the voice of a man versed in country things, who knows much about inner weather and the sigh we sigh from too much dwelling on what has been. It is tuned to the sounds made by phoebes and spring thaws, the brooks and leaves of New England. When I read that it has been heard in the halls of New York I find it hard to believe that its owner has allowed himself to be whisked through those foreign canyons of masonry and steel, which echo the roar and scream of urban life, to stand at last on a platform and speak to a thousand ears or more versed only in city sounds.

Writing in *Le Temps* not long ago, Edmond Jaloux spoke of encountering Yeats during the war of 1914–18 in a 'bureau très strictement administratif,' where, nevertheless, he brought with him 'la poésie et le mythologie irlandaises et l'océan, et les nuées du ciel, et Cuchulain qui se battit contra la mer.'

I have seen Robert Frost, too, in predicaments which made poetry seem a little beside the point—at the counter of a little butcher-shop, buying provisions for his family; clinging to the running-board of a car as we fetched him home from the little post office of South Shaftsbury—but he had with him even then that look and voice of the poet which come from somewhere in the mysterious world of man's spirit.

His is one of the voices I would not have missed hearing. Now that Edison has lived, those of the future can hear it too, however fragmentarily. But Shakespeare, Milton, Shelley, and Keats—we shall never know exactly how their voices sounded unless those amateur and somewhat mystical physicists are right who hold that all sounds ever made still move somewhere in the world's envelope of air and sometime will be retrieved.[57]

It was Professor John L. Brumm, later chairman of the University's Journalism Department, who was laughing at Frost's sallies when I met them at the butcher-shop in Liberty Street, Ann Arbor. Frost was speaking about hearing himself bellowing—or someone he later realized was himself—from the platform of a woman's club. It sounded funny, but I recall hearing Frost for the first time at the old Woman's Club in Lansing, Michigan, and finding it memorable.[58] As for Professor Brumm, that genial mentor of hundreds of the nation's newsmen and women, he was a member of the Quadrangle Club and doubtless knew Frost well enough to sense when he should be taken with or without a grain of salt.

Among others of the faculty who knew the poet especially well were Campbell Bonner, Professor of Greek, and his charming wife Ethel, both originally from Tennessee. At one time, so Mrs. Bonner said, Frost had a standing invitation to dine with the family—I believe on Fridays—with Lesley included when she was present. The invitation was, one would guess, extended during the absence of Elinor Frost, though she was doubtless there on occasion. At one reception when Frost was present, after England's Poet Laureate, Robert Bridges, had departed from Ann Arbor after spending some time there as Fellow in Letters, the voice of Frost was lifted in protest against Bridges's theory of quantity in English verse. It was not the only time he was to expostulate on the subject, but that reception at the Bonners' home may have been the occasion when he had the best and most polite audience for his view.

Another memory concerns visiting the Bonners' home on Martin Place with Sue Grundy Bonner—probably in 1926—and finding there, as a guest at tea, Gorham B. Munson, who was interviewing Mrs. Bonner about Frost for the biography he was then writing, published as *Robert Frost: A Study in Sensibility and Good Sense.*

Mrs. Bonner was to be a guest at that final luncheon in Ann Arbor for Frost in April 1962, and, after his death, attended the special showing of the Frost film at Dartmouth College in 1963 as one especially invited by the publisher, Holt, Rinehart and Winston.[59]

A large file of correspondence and many conversations with Professor Carlton F. Wells of the University of Michigan (now retired) prove his intense interest in and knowledge of all things Frostian. With his wife Cecilia he entertained Frost and chauffered him to the homes of his still-living friends in the spring of 1962, when he twice revisited Ann Arbor. Wells, co-author of *The Recognition of Emily Dickinson,*[60] who visited the Amherst of Dickinson and Frost in that connection, is a staunch memorizer of

Frost poems, and has spoken before many faculty and student groups about the poet. Wells is one who cherishes some rare Frost books presented to him by the poet.

A Few Necessary Reservations

Tempting as it is to expound upon the wide and deep influence of the poet Robert Frost at the University of Michigan, it is nevertheless essential to place a few bounds on the subject. After all, the University is an old one, with many schools and colleges, and with students from all over the world, as well as many parts of the country. Moreover, there were problems of funds and plant in the 1920s, some characteristic of the years following World War I.

If President Burton inspired the gifts of Chase Osborn and Horace H. Rackham that made the invitation to Frost and his stays in Ann Arbor possible, it is also true that the creative presidency of Marion LeRoy Burton was in the main concerned with wresting from the State Legislature the tremendous sums needed to provide new buildings.[61] He was successful in doing so, as the handsome Angell Hall on State Street and other buildings still witness.

At the same time, however, funds for faculty salaries were not at their best, while student enrollment continued to climb. In an Ann Arbor where fine homes and evident wealth, much of it from private and family sources, would impress the Frost family, that scarcity would not be evident to the Poet in Residence, as the Sergeant biography shows. However, many a faculty member, fully qualified, sought greener pastures at that time—some in advertising, as I later learned—some in western universities. They were by no means the "drones" that Lawrance Thompson labeled them,[62] but often men with families to support and careers to be made. Was it strange if they occasionally looked askance at the poet in their midst, not yet as famous as he would become, and amply rewarded for his presence?

Remembering a time when law students were recruited to teach freshman English, and remembering as well that the distinguished Fred Newton Scott was the one reduced to that stratagem, one understands why no word about Robert Frost was forthcoming from that source.[63]

Of course one could recall a galaxy of bright stars among the faculty at that time who attracted students to the University of Michigan, even in the departments closely allied to the creative arts —poetry among them—quite apart from the presence of Robert Frost. Among them were Oscar James Campbell, Shakespeare scholar; James Holly Hanford, Milton scholar, Clarence D. Thorpe, Keats scholar, and somewhat later, Warner G. Rice, notable in seventeenth century English literature scholarship.

When I inquired of my fellow students, who became teachers, scholars, and authors in English language and literature, whether they remembered the presence of Robert Frost, I drew a blank from some, from others a rather sheepish admission that they had indeed known he was there, but had never been close to him. The answer, in view of the unquestionable and lasting influence of Frost upon both faculty and students who knew him, is that the University is a large one and the pursuit of learning arduous and demanding.

Let one or two graduates who were not "close to him" have their say. Thus John M. Russell, President of the Markle Foundation in New York City, writes in 1964: "The only thing I remember about Mr. Frost in Ann Arbor is that occasionally we invited him to the Fraternity (Trigon) for dinner, and we always enjoyed sitting around listening to him talk and tell anecdotes. On one of these occasions, I remember that he autographed a copy of *North of Boston* for me, but unfortunately this has now disappeared." [64]

During Mr. Russell's student years at Michigan (1921–1924) Frost lived on Washtenaw, among the fraternity houses. What a deluge of memories would flood upon the inquirer who could find all those fraternity men of long ago!

A warmer appraisal, from a newspaper editor and writer, Martin A. Klaver, who was a member of a fraternity housed in a stately residence on the corner of Hill and South State, is of more recent vintage. He writes: "Yes, I remember Robert Frost at Michigan, how he looked, how he read his poetry, how he talked, even though I was not among those who got to know him well. I met him, attended a seminar, heard him read—that was all. But he made a lasting impression on me and I still get out some of his poems now and then to read again some of those I know and read others I don't know. I've been convinced of the value of the 'poet in residence' idea ever since. I guess I'm evidence that a man like Frost doesn't have to be close to a large number of people, or to try to be, in order to make a difference of some degree in the lives of a good many. Maybe I should add that I don't recall that there was much interest in him in the fraternity and I have a feeling that the circle of his influence was rather limited. Not that that would be strange!

"Congratulations on being engaged in the Frost enterprise. Be sure to make him alive, tolerant, warm, and penetrating, with a quiet humor!"[65]

The Frost Portrait of 1923

Among many portraits painted by Leon A. Makielski of Detroit and Ann Arbor shown in a Retrospective Exhibition at the then-famous Anna L. Werbe Galleries in Detroit, in June 1963, perhaps the one that aroused greatest interest was one of Robert Frost. The death of Frost in January of that year was still of recent memory, and of many Frost portraits in oils and sculpture this one was perhaps the least known, or even unknown, to the general public.

The portrait by Makielski, painted in 1922–1923 during Frost's second year in Ann Arbor, when he was in his forties—but looked younger—took nearly a year to paint. It was done while Frost visited the artist in his studio at the University School of Architecture, at that time an easy walk from Frost's home at the former Demmon residence on Washtenaw. Then, as later, Frost had a keen interest in the work of painters and sculptors, and often purchased their work—as he bought two landscapes from Makielski.

Frost, said Makielski, "dropped in" his studio about once a week —mainly to talk. "You can tell from the portrait that he's talking," the artist said,[66] and so you can. Then, as during most of his life, Frost was a marathon talker, who not only could "tire the sun with talking, and send him down the sky," but cause the same sun to rise again the next morning, as some old friends said.

If Frost laughed when the artist first asked him to pose, he was obviously pleased with the result. On May 2, 1922, he wrote to Louis Untermeyer: "And now dear Louis I want to ax you something privileged behind closed doors. Please don't give me that pic-

Leon Makielski portrait of Robert Frost, 1923, in Harlan Hatcher Graduate Library, University of Michigan, Department of Rare Books and Special Collections

ture by Leon Makielski as being too expensive a gift, Elinor thinks, for your means when you are leaving business."[67]

Obviously the generous Untermeyer heeded this request, for the portrait was still in the artist's possession forty years later, when it came to public notice through the Werbe Galleries exhibition and the reviews in the press.[68]

By early December of 1963 the University of Michigan had purchased the portrait as a memorial to the poet who had often spoken of Ann Arbor as his second home. A Robert Frost Portrait Fund was set up and monitored by faithful Erich A. Walter[69] of the President's Office, and no doubt brought in the necessary funds, in view of the general admiration for the subject. The portrait was exhibited for a time in Alumni Memorial Hall—in which there is some irony, in view of Frost's bitter comments about the widow of the distinguished Professor D'Ooge; for Alumni Hall, handsome and classical of architecture, was once called "D'Ooge's Palace," since the Professor was influential in the style it presented.

The Frost portrait is now in an honored place—the Department of Rare Books and Special Collections of the Harlan Hatcher Graduate Library of the University, as a letter from Janet F. White, Head Reference Librarian, informs me.

A Few Side Issues

While pursuing the ins and outs of Robert Frost in Ann Arbor the author of this essay heard insistently of a bookshop in which Lesley Frost, daughter of the poet, had a share. However, when I mentioned it to Lawrance Thompson in 1963, with the idea that his research assistant might have learned the facts, he shook his head. But a friend of mine who recalled visiting the shop was right, as long inquiry revealed—though Thompson had his reasons for doubt, since it all happened while Lesley was operating "The Open Book" in Pittsfield, Massachusetts.

A letter from Anna Lloyd Jesse of Downers Grove, Illinois—daughter of Dean Alfred Lloyd of the graduate school, onetime interim President of the University, gives the facts: "Lesley Frost was a partner with Lee Harris and me for a while. When she heard that Lee and I were starting a shop, she asked to join us. I think Lee was not as enthusiastic as I, but because Lesley had a bookshop of her own in Pittsfield, Mass. and knew so much about what books to stock, we agreed to let her join us. I am sure it was fortunate for us that she did, for we were innocents in the business. She helped us launch the venture and came to A. A. occasionally, but before the first year was over, she wanted to sell her share, so Lee and I bought her out. The shop was called 'The Print and Book Shop,' was on the corner of Jefferson and Maynard Sts., was opened in the autumn of 1927 and went out of business in late March or early April of 1930." [70]

How quickly all changes and vanishes, even in a university city, is proved again by the disappearance of the very site on which the bookshop stood—evidently now a big Student Activities Building stands there. But the association also proves that Lesley Frost, like her father, had many friends in Ann Arbor. She also kept them, as her many visits to Detroit and Ann Arbor in the coming days were to show.

A Great Year for Frost in Ann Arbor: 1925–1926

By that peculiarly Frostian legerdemain of which he was past master, the poet already knew by the autumn of 1924 that he would return to Ann Arbor for the year 1925–1926. Once again he would turn the tables on Amherst College and return to the University of Michigan. Later he would turn them again, though he never entirely gave up either the Michigan or the Amherst connection.

The years between his earlier Michigan fellowships (1921–1922 and 1922–1923) had been given to Jesse Lynch Williams (1871–1929), author and playwright, and Robert Bridges, the distinguished Poet Laureate of England, from 1913 until his death in 1930. Frost evidently felt no challenge from Williams, who had made his presence felt on the Michigan campus, but did not lecture or—if memory serves—meet with "the Whimsies," as Frost called them. With Bridges it was a different matter, and Frost never ceased to decry the Bridges theory of quantity in poetry.

As for Bridges himself, who had also come to the University in 1923–1924 as a guest invited by President Burton, his theory of poetry suited his own poems no less than Frost's theory suited the poems of the American poet. One must allow each his own differences, and it is doubtful whether Bridges cared a whit about Frost's protests.

Bridges was elderly, in his eightieth year, when he came to Ann Arbor, and his energies were flagging. Still, he gave of his best, and I recall him, papers in hand, making his way down Olivia Street from Hill to the Cowden house. Like Frost, he looked the part of poet, and no one could fail to be impressed by his distinguished head and figure. His address of 1917 on *The Necessity of Poetry*,[71] sold in pamphlet form through the noble bookstores of George Wahr, must have met with approval even from Frost. Classicist as Frost was, he must have enjoyed the quotation from Sir Isaac Newton "of blessed memory": "The Greek Antiquities are full of Poetical fictions, because the Greeks wrote nothing in prose before the conquest of Asia by Cyrus the Persian. Then Pherecydes Scyrius and Cadmus Milesius introduced the writing in prose."

A backward step, no doubt, as Frost would have thought—excellent as his own prose was, when he set himself to writing it. As for Bridges, he would say, "The claim of prose is obviously high, and I could say more to exalt it" . . . as he later did, but at the moment poetry was his cause. And ample reason he had for exalting poetry, as the pages devoted to his own poems in the *Oxford Book of English Verse* prove, including the beautiful "A Passer-by" with the memorable opening line:

"Whither, O splendid ship, thy white sails crowding. . . ."

No doubt Frost knew the poem, wide as his knowledge of poetry was, and desirous as he was to be represented in that noble anthology.

Frost had met Bridges during his stay in England, soon after Bridges became Poet Laureate in 1913. They had met at the home of Laurence Binyon, famed poet of "The Fallen"—

> They shall not grow old, as we that are left grow old:
> Age shall not weary them, nor the years condemn,
> At the going down of the sun and in the morning
> We will remember them.

As Frost would no doubt know, Binyon—after forty years with the British Museum—came to Harvard in 1933 as Charles Eliot Norton

Professor of Poetry. In that earlier time he had happened to call at Binyon's home just as Bridges was expected to come for a luncheon engagement at the Vienna Café, and was invited to join them.[72] Nothing if not combative about poetry, Frost began arguing on the subject before the luncheon was over, and had a good time elaborating on the meeting in a letter to Sidney Cox.[73]

It was typical of many coincidences in Frost's life that he should be in Ann Arbor in April 1924, when a reception was being held for the Poet Laureate—at the beginning of his two-month stay as Poet in Residence—and Mrs. Bridges. Thompson notes[74] that President Burton may have scheduled Frost's week-long visit, with Mrs. Frost, with a view to a meeting of the two poets. Whether the President knew of Frost's earlier meeting with the Poet Laureate seems doubtful, for even the choice of Frost's biographer was fifteen years in the future.

At any rate, it may be that President Burton first broached the possible return of Frost to Ann Arbor at that time. Certainly Frost knew of it by the fall of 1924, as a letter to Roy Cowden, dated from Amherst, November 12, 1924 confirms.[75] And it would seem that the house on Pontiac Road had already been chosen for their home. He wrote:

> Dear Cowden
>
> It's the thought of you and the likes of you that's bringing us back; so see that you treat us with compassion when you get us there. . . .
>
> Remember me to Whimsies, both society and publication. I am wondering who now among you shines in verse, who in prose. I dont feel that it doesn't concern me now, but pretty soon it will concern me more. I shall be getting after every body in Michigan University who doesn't write something. I don't mean I shall get after them all at once in a drove. I shall take my time to it. But——
>
> Well I am going to live in a cot (with water and a crust) this time where people can scarcely find me with the naked eye. Won't it be lovely? Isn't it a lovely provision for a mighty State University to have made for one small poet? Burton is a noble giver.
>
> It doesn't seem long since I saw you and it won't be long before I see you again.
>
> > Our best to you and your family,
> > > Ever yours
> > > > Robert Frost

Frost had of course seen Cowden and many other friends during the visit of March-April 1924, when he and Elinor Frost were guests of the Bursleys, as many times before. When the visit was announced in *The Michigan Daily* of March 27, or perhaps in an earlier letter to Professor Tilley, it was suggested that Frost should make a public reading of his poems. Though he wrote to say to "Dear Tilley" that he saw "no great need of my reading again so soon at Ann Arbor"— "Neither I nor the University will have changed enough to make me a novelty to it. Why do you bother to try to get me an audience?"—it is certain that he gave a reading of his poems (or did he "say" them?) on the afternoon of April 2 at Sarah Caswell Angell Hall. In the year 1977 it is amusing to reflect upon the smallness of the hall that was sufficient to hold a Frost audience in 1924 as compared with the overflow audiences of 1962 in Ann Arbor and Detroit, both in the largest halls available.

"Of course I must sit with the Whimsies an evening" Frost had written to Tilley in that letter of February 20, 1924[76] and of course he did. After the reading in the afternoon, there was an evening performance by the Ann Arbor Playmakers "in the Dodo Playshop," of Frost's one-act tragedy, "A Way Out," in honor of the poet's visit. The audience, by invitation, was composed of members of Whimsies and the Writer's Club, and guests, and after the play Frost met, as promised, with the Whimsies and others at the Cowdens' home.[77]

How closely the Michigan and Amherst "residencies" of Frost sometimes overlapped is illustrated by that particular visit to Ann Arbor, when Frost was teaching in Amherst. Just after the notes on Frost's visit, Lawrance Thompson introduces a delightful page in which the departing editors of the Amherst *Student* published a parody of one of Frost's classes there, while Padraic Colum—visiting Frost in Amherst as he was later to visit him in Ann Arbor—impersonated a bartender and Frost "recited amid salvos of applause" a poem entitled "Shopping in Woods on a Snowy Evening."[78] Strange to find *The Michigan Daily* and the Amherst *Student* quoted in close proximity, but so it was with the facts of Frost's own life.

The visit and reports of it and the meetings held with students also help to explain the memory of an almost continuous relationship of Frost and Michigan, which the chronological tables seem to deny. It must have been so for Frost as well, who wrote to Tilley in the letter just quoted: "I got to be a good deal more Ann Arboreal than I should suppose I could have at my age. A few people and streets and a lot of the outlying landscape are pretty well incorporated in me."

It is unfortunate that Frost's biographers, who never visited Ann Arbor, had no understanding of what those "people and streets and a lot of the outlying landscape" meant to him and to generations of students who sing that song:

> I want to go back to Michigan,
> To dear Ann Arbor town. . . .

The House on Pontiac Road

If Frost was worried that the house at 1223 Pontiac Road, in the first settled part of Ann Arbor, was too far from the campus to meet with University approval, it was to prove otherwise. It was an old house, of Greek Revival architecture—which Frost called "hen and chicks architecture," perhaps echoing his years as a poultry farmer. He would spread his arms to show what he meant—the mother hen spreading her wings to shelter the newly hatched chicks. If that idea was expressive, it did not altogether satisfy the description given by architectural experts.

But for Frost the idea was to find a family home, far away from the fraternity and faculty purlieus of Washtenaw Avenue. After all, when he returned for the year 1925–1926, he came for the first time—not on a one-year appointment as Poet in Residence, as he had in 1921–1922 and 1922–1923—but on a permanent faculty basis. Not that he would accept it as such, either in anticipation, as his letters showed, or in actual performance, but on what was his usual Frost performance basis, at both Michigan and Amherst.

Was it too far away from the center of University activities, as he asked both Tilley and Bursley in letters, after the place was chosen? Today, when the University has an extensive North Campus apart from the old Main Campus, and Ann Arbor itself announces to all travelers by road its proud reputation as a Research Center, the question seems absurd. But even then the house, which

looked so Frostian—and still does, out in Henry Ford's Greenfield Village—proved near enough for all practical purposes, for both students and the poet himself. Over the big bridge that spanned both the Huron River and the railway tracks carrying the main traffic between Detroit and Chicago, that was the way to go. It was traversed many times by students and Frost, who could walk many miles without tiring, as those who knew him well have attested. That walking tour on the Long Trail, when he faltered from tight shoes and the fatigue they brought on, was an exception to the rule.

At that time a picture was taken of Frost at the side of the house, with the entrance to the Michigan cellar shown at his side. The picture was taken by his neighbor, Jean Paul Slusser, of whom more presently. It shows the poet as he liked to be, dressed like any countryman. No doubt he knew that cellar well, as he knew every house in which he lived—all its nooks and crannies, both inside and out.

But one question I long to ask him, though I never thought of it at the time, and now it is too late forever. No one else ever asked it, so far as I know. Though the remarkable analytical indexes in Lawrance Thompson's biography answer many questions, they neither ask nor answer this one. It concerns the poem titled "In a Disused Graveyard," published in *New Hampshire*. Knowing well those many little abandoned graveyards so common in the older States, I had thought the poem referred to one in Frost's New England. Then I recalled that the house on Pontiac Road was bordered on its northern side by an old graveyard, long disused by the townspeople in favor of the big Forest Hills cemetery. Was that the one Frost had in mind when he wrote:

> The living come with grassy tread
> To read the gravestones on the hill;
> The graveyard draws the living still,
> But never any more the dead (p. 221).

Only after I had "come with grassy tread" to visit the old graveyard with my friend Mary Cooley, Ann Arbor born and bred, was I to ponder that question. Certainly Frost was inclined to turn the other way, toward the "One luminary clock against the sky" (p. 255), to visit the living. But at some time or other he must have visited the

"The Ann Arbor House," residence of Robert Frost at 1223 Pontiac Road, Ann Arbor, 1925–1926, photo courtesy of the Collections of Greenfield Village and the Henry Ford Museum, Dearborn, Michigan.

old graveyard so near his abode, and studied the "verses in it" (p. 221). It could be so, for the volume in which it appeared was published in his Michigan years.

The House on Pontiac Road in its original setting witnessed many comings and goings, and is alive in many a memory still. As for me, I shall never forget the time when Frost, sitting in the stairway of that house, inscribed my copy of *A Boy's Will* with his poem "Fiat Nox," later to be titled "Once by the Pacific," and published in *West-Running Brook*. The date was April 2, 1927, and Frost was still there.

The Frost Seminar

The notable and greatly anticipated Seminar 186 given by Frost in 1926 was heralded by several letters to University faculty members. Two days earlier than the one to Roy Cowden, already cited, Frost wrote to Professor Louis A. Strauss, then head of the English Department, from Amherst, on November 10, 1924, showing that plans were already in an advanced stage. If Frost was capable of writing an uncharacteristic letter, this was not one of them. "Dear Strauss," he wrote:

> Handsomely was the way to do this thing if it was going to be done, and handsomely you have all certainly done it. I am still dazed with the pleasure you have given me. I begin to wonder if I shall be able to wait till next year to take up my desk in your office. I may have to come out for a special desk-warming beforehand. My mind is already out there with you.
>
> As you know, I have a weakness for ideas, particularly in education. The idea of the Fellowship rouses the very teacher in me. Moreover I am not averse to a great big gift once in a lifetime when it comes my way. And I rather like honors. But what exerts the main attraction in Ann Arbor is simply friends. You don't need to be told it, but I'm telling you just the same.
>
> My best to you and your family—and believe me
> Ever yours
> Robert Frost[79]

It is strange and wonderful to think back through the years to all the preparations for that Seminar—preparations that, it seems fair to say, were more elaborate from the University and departmental and student points of view than from that of the poet and teacher. There were notices in *The Michigan Daily* and announcements in various courses, and applications from those who hoped to attend. In the end, no doubt after winnowings in the faculty offices, printed course cards were issued to those fortunate enough to be chosen. Though only one division was expected, with not more than a dozen students enrolled, there were two groups finally, with a total of about seventeen students. Someone may have known the basis for dividing the groups. I do not, except that my special friends Mary Cooley and Sue Bonner were in one group and I in another. Moreover, the content, as presented by Frost, was obviously different, as reported to Thompson.[80]

If, as Sue Grundy Bonner said, Frost's teaching methods were "nonexistent" in the Seminar: "He merely talked about poetry; sometimes he talked about the technique, sometimes about fashions in poetry," she did recall that he introduced her to the "fresh images" in Humbert Wolfe's poems—"The Grey Squirrel," "Tulip," "The Lamb," and "Iliad"—that "she had never read them before—they still sound like pure magic to me." If the "teaching methods were nonexistent" it would hardly seem that what was learned was worthless! Obviously much of value was remembered from the Seminar. Frost himself must have valued two lines from Wolfe's "Iliad":

> The word, and nought else,
> in time endures.

Mary Cooley and Sue Bonner, two of the Seminar students, recall walking Frost home—or nearly so—the long way to the house on Pontiac Road, only to have him turn the trip around and walk them both home.

As for me, though the years between are many, an image remains of Frost at the end of a long table in a Seminar room of the Main Library. The time is early evening, but his seated figure, with the undeniable poet's head, is always radiant with light, though the many student figures around the table—most of them men—become shadowy, except that they listen always to what the poet has to say. They did produce manuscripts, as they were required to do, some of them prose, in which the teacher was perhaps less interested. Poetry was the thing.

What did Frost say in all those sessions? If memory serves, he spoke most often of the writers, especially poets, he had known in England, an experience at that time only some ten years in the past. He spoke not only of Humbert Wolfe, but of Lascelles Abercrombie, Rupert Brooke, W. B. Yeats, Walter de la Mare, and especially of Edward Thomas, whose death at Vimy Ridge in 1917 was one of Frost's great sorrows. His poem, "To E. T.," published in *New Hampshire*, beginning "I slumbered with your poems on my breast," salutes Thomas as one "Who died a soldier-poet of your race" (p. 222). Since Frost is credited with inspiring Thomas to become a poet, it is probably only natural that he considered his prose works as "hack work," as Untermeyer states.[81] The poems by this Welshman of the beautiful visage are to be cherished, certainly, but much is to be said for the biography of Richard Jefferies, published in 1909, and dedicated to W.H. Hudson of *Green Mansions*.

Frost had been in England during a period of literary awakening, and in one way or another had known many of those who were bringing about the dawn. It was delightful and memorable to hear him talk of them in his Seminar. Of Yeats, who had spoken well of Frost's own poems, he always spoke with admiration, and warned the students against imitation of any leading writer. "Yeats is in the van, the others are only in the procession," he said—though, after studying the Irish poetry of the time, notable for individuality, I am not certain which ones Frost regarded as in "the procession." Of Alfred Noyes—who, at Princeton, had such stars as Scott Fitzgerald and Edmund Wilson to conjure with—Frost held no high opinion, it would seem. Others, however, were not of that opinion, and in that very year the Oratorical Association Lecture Course of the University brought Alfred Noyes to Hill Auditorium on November 5.[82] It must have been in that same year that Walter de la Mare lectured at the University, to the delight of many. Both lectures were independent of the Poet in Residence or the literary group represented by *The Inlander*.

Of the stories Frost told about the poets he had known in England, one that remained vividly in my mind concerned W. H. Davies

(1870–1940), the vagabond poet discovered by Shaw in 1905, and author of some of the loveliest lyrics in the language. He was a frequent visitor to Dymock in the time when Frost was there, no doubt brought there by *New Numbers,* the periodical issued by Abercrombie and the other Georgian poets. Perhaps Frost had heard the story at first hand from Davies, but I was to read it years later as Davies himself related it in *A Poet's Pilgrimage.*[83] There I learned that the story had its setting—not in America, where Davies lived the life of a "super-tramp" for some years—as I supposed from Frost's story, but in Newport, in Monmouthshire, the town of his birth and boyhood. At any rate, Frost related the incident in a way that struck home almost more vividly than the story told by the poet to whom it happened. As a small boy, Davies relates, an old woman of the town who always "wore a soft cap made for a man," aroused his curiosity so much that one day, finding her asleep before the fire, he removed the cap gently and found—"first to my surprise and then to my horror, that two curled horns were sticking out of her head." She woke with a screech—though he had replaced the cap—and made a grab for him. He escaped the evil one, however, and lived to tell the tale years later. Obviously, Davies was not Frost's favorite poet among those he had known in England. Still, as he said in a letter to Sidney Cox, "No one at the present time can get those flashes in a line as he can. His note is Elizabethan."[84] Frost was always willing to recognize quality in the poetry, though he might not like the man who produced it. Not far away, in Nailsworth, Davies was to die, married then to the wife addressed as

> Sweet Stay at Home, sweet Well Content,
> Thou knowest of no strange continent. . . .

It was a happy coincidence that the poem "The Golden Room," by Wilfrid Gibson, was published in the *Atlantic Monthly* of February, 1926,[85] just as Frost's Seminar was beginning. It recalled the days in Gloucestershire in the "Old Nailshop," when the friendly companionship was at its best, though the war clouds were on the horizon.

> Our neighbors from the Gallows, Catherine
> And Lascelles Abercrombie; Rupert Brooke;

> Eleanor and Robert Frost, living awhile
> At Little Iddens, who'd brought over with them
> Helen and Edward Thomas? In the lamplight
> We talked and laughed, but for the most part listened
> While Robert Frost kept on and on and on
> In his slow New England fashion for our delight,
> Holding us with shrewd turns and racy quips,
> And the rare twinkle of his grave blue eyes.

Is there a hidden reproof in that "kept on and on and on," in the manner so well known to the friends of Frost? At any rate, those days were still remembered in Frost's Ann Arbor years, and he would revisit those scenes in 1928, and would see the old friends still living, including Wilfrid Gibson. Elizabeth Sergeant notes that "There is no evidence of children in Gibson's 'The Golden Room!' "[86] though they were ever-present, and Frost's four kept many records of the time.

Angus Babcock's Portrait of Frost

Angus Babcock, a fellow student who attended the Seminar, remembers an evening when the men students—and only the men—were invited to the Frosts' home on Pontiac Road, ostensibly for a session of the Seminar. Some of the women students were willing to forgive their exclusion as one of Frost's "quirks." Is that a kind name for traits that some of his enemies are now ready to call by meaner words? Reading the book of Acts recently, it seemed to me there were comparisons to be made with Frost and his true disciples I have known. There were women disciples, to be sure, but not quite of the same degree of loyalty or privilege.

As a member of the Frost course, Angus Babcock, long a resident of California, remembers "one or more classes on the campus, followed by several at his house. . . . At his home poetry, as such, was hardly mentioned. We chatted, drank tea, and ate cookies while sprawling around the fireplace. There was a dreamy-looking lad who went in and out and did not mix with us. . . . To me, still, a mystery."

The "dreamy-looking lad" was the poet Wade Van Dore, a frequent visitor to the house on Pontiac Road. Though he was well known to the Frost family and Lawrence Conrad, he did indeed remain a mystery to most students of the time, as I discovered later. Frost encouraged him and offered assistance toward the publication of his collection of poems, *Far Lake*, published in 1930.[87] As the Thompson volumes show, Van Dore was associated with Frost for some years at the Gully Farm in South Shaftsbury, Vermont.

As for the handsome profile portrait of Frost that was published in *The Inlander* of January 1926, opposite Frost's poem, "The Minor Bird," Angus Babcock provides this story of how it was produced: "Before Frost got seduced into holding a class I made a sketch of him at a lecture. It was one of those afternoon lectures, announced in *The Michigan Daily*. I used to attend many of them and was impressed by the audience—usually mostly white-haired town folk, a few students and a few faculty. I usually made a sketch or two if I could see the speaker and the light was right. When I was asked if I could produce something for that *Inlander* issue, I knew our meager budget...so I whittled out that linoleum block....I have always felt a bit of pride in that issue and have found the true Minor Bird in California. It tweets once and follows with a descending note that ends on a distinct minor note. I have often wondered if Frost had not written that around San Francisco or remembered the plaintive call after he went east."[88]

Tale of a House

If Frost's house on Pontiac Road was usually free of students and the neighborhood had neither fraternity houses nor faculty homes, in general, he was the more appreciative of having Jean Paul Slusser, artist and faculty member, within visiting distance. Living then in "a huge ground-floor apartment in the Fremont Ward house, itself a mansion dating from about 1846"—diagonally across from the Greek Revival house of 1830 where the Frost family, or sometimes only the poet, were in residence until May 1927—Slusser was often visited by Frost, both in the daytime and on the poet's night rambles.

"My apartment had a tall French window giving on the front porch of the Ward house," Slusser remembers, "and this—lighted at night—could easily be seen from the sidewalk. Occasionally, in the middle of the evening, there was a tap on the window, and there was Robert Frost, glad to come in for a few minutes' conversation before continuing his ramble. He never stayed long, but I saw him frequently, either on my premises or on his." Frost also liked to watch the progress of Slusser's paintings, either on the easel in the big kitchen studio or while the painter was out sketching "the little vernacular houses which solidly filled the older streets on this side of town—Broadway, Wall Street, and Maiden Lane in particular . . . which I am sure that Frost in his endless and probably daily walks came to know equally well. This was almost the counterpart of a small New England village."

Though the old courthouse is there no longer, its lighted clock tower—clearly visible from the hill where Frost's "cot" stood—was the one "luminary clock against the sky" (p. 255) of his poem "Acquainted with the Night."

As Professor Slusser writes, "My nephew Edgar was a kind of bond between us. Edgar had shown literary aspirations and was one of Frost's student protégés, or had been, for he had left college without graduating, to marry and go to work."

Frost was not alone in regarding Edgar W. Slusser—nephew of the artist—as gifted. Though he was not a member of Frost's Seminar, and perhaps had left before it was held, I recall that he had the very look of an artist. So Frost must have thought, for he wrote one of his characteristic letters to Edgar, then in Fort Dodge, Iowa, with a gypsum refining company, "by way of recouping finances for a return to Michigan, which didn't materialize," as he wrote in 1963. In his letter Frost inquired about "that novel, or has it boiled down into a short story? Don't let me make you cry. All I mean is when you get round to some more of that easy prose and fresh insight, remember here's your first audience—outside of your family." [89]

Evidently there was no reply, for Frost, writing to Jean Paul Slusser from South Shaftsbury on September 29, 1927, enclosing a check for paintings sent to him, continued: "Edgar hasn't answered. I'm afraid he takes things too hard. Why don't some of his relatives back him to the rest of his education? He hadn't much more to go had he? He seems to be one who is going to feel it if he isn't admitted to the society and occupations of the educated. It's made hard in America for the intelligent but uncolleged." [90]

Head by Angus Babcock, from *The Inlander*, January 1926, accompanying original publication of "The Minor Bird," University of Michigan

THE MINOR BIRD

by Robert Frost

I have wished a bird would fly away
And not sing by my house all day;

Have clapped my hands at him from the door
When it seemed as if I could bear no more.

The fault may partly have been in me.
The bird was not to blame for his key.

And I own there must be something wrong
In ever wanting to silence song.

Robert Frost's poem "A Minor Bird," published in the volume *West-Running Brook*, was given first publication in *The Inlander*, University of Michigan, in the January 1926 issue. (The title was changed from "The Minor Bird," as taken from the poet's notebook, and the last line was later revised to read: "In wanting to silence any song." See Lathem for variants.)

In Frost's long career of railing against the importance of higher education, even while teaching in colleges and universities, this letter may be the only admission he ever made that there was something to be said on the other side of the question.

If Frost was grateful in his retreat that he could more or less choose the times when he saw faculty and students, as Jean Paul Slusser remarks, "of course he saw them in plenty when he went to the campus." There was his English 186 in the second semester of 1925–1926, and all year and on his later visits he was accustomed to meet with *The Inlander* staff at the Cowdens' house. During that year the staff consisted of Angus Babcock, Sue Grundy Bonner, Mary E. Cooley, Dorothy Tyler, and Marie van Osenbruggen, with a junior staff including Theodore Hornberger, Marian Lipson, William Mullin, Wanda Rendtorff, and Lucile Walsh.

An earlier issue shows the names of both Arnold Gingrich, later well known as publisher of *Esquire* and of books famous among anglers, and Montgomery Butchart, who served as both writer and artist, as well as editor on *The Inlander*, and whose name appears several times in *The Letters of Ezra Pound 1907–1941*.[91] All knew Frost, as he knew them. (Gingrich died in July 1976.)

But that sometime retreat of Frost at 1223 Pontiac Road (later Street) in Ann Arbor was to have a strange if happy history. Both the D'Ooge and Demmon houses, where he had lived in 1921–1922 and 1922–1923, had been razed to make way for churches on Washtenaw Avenue. The house on Pontiac, where the Frost family had really taken possession—had he not written to Jean Paul Slusser in the fall of 1927 "You'll see me or my ghost back haunting Pontiac St. . . . Your address stirs me to a pleasant melancholy"—that, too, was to vanish from its site.

But not to be lost forever, like the other two. For Henry Ford, with his love for the American past, was to cast an eye on the house as an excellent example of Greek Revival architecture, built for Thompson Sinclair in the period 1830–1840. Henry Ford was to purchase it in 1935—Jean Paul Slusser had watched him studying it from across the street—[92] and had it erected in Greenfield Village in the summer of 1937. It is still called "the Ann Arbor House," although, as the archivist Kenneth N. Metcalf wrote in 1964, "the Frost association has no doubt been given greater prominence in recent years."[93] Whether known for its architecture and furnishings or its association with the poet, the house is now visited by throngs of people from all over the world. Among them, shortly after the death in January 1963, of Robert Frost—who had visited Russia in 1962—was a group of Russian visitors, guided by a daughter of White Russians, attached to the Ford Museum staff. In their tour of Greenfield Village, it was reported, they were most interested in "Edison's laboratory and the house in which Robert Frost lived when he taught at the U. of M."[94]

In the handsome history and guide, *Greenfield Village and the Henry Ford Museum*, an illustration of the house appears on page forty-four, with the note: "Robert Frost (1874–1963) served as 'poet-in-residence' at the University of Michigan and lived in this sophisticated home where he wrote several of his best poems."[95]

Frost was proud of his house at Greenfield Village, and mentioned its presence there in several talks in Michigan, including the one in Ann Arbor in April 1962.

What the fate of the house was between Frost's departure in May 1927 and the Ford purchase in 1935—a full eight years—I do not know, though others may. It is well known, however, that after its removal Jean Paul Slusser had a modern house built on the site, with the same address that Frost knew so well. All the more occasion, then, for the ghost of the poet to haunt the premises, as it would not dare to haunt the public grounds where his old house now stands.

Of the many notable and quotable occasions on which Frost came to Michigan in later years—and I have written about his three last visits in this series[96]—one that occurred during the presidency of Alexander Ruthven (1929–1951) may stand as representative of his qualities. In *Naturalist in Two Worlds*, published in the year of Frost's death, Ruthven remembers that time:

> An old friend, a distinguished poet, and a lovable man discovered after dinner and just before his public reading that he had forgotten copies of the poems he proposed to recite. Did I have a copy of his collected works? I did. 'To repay you for the use of this book I will read first the poem of your selection.' Naturally, I chose 'The Morgan

Colt.' In announcing the poem he remarked to the audience that it was a favorite of mine, and he was reading from the Morgan Horse Edition of his poems. As the audience was leaving the hall after the talk, I was stopped by two instructors in English. They told me they had thought they knew all of the editions of Frost's poems, but they had never heard of the Morgan Horse Edition. I could only tell them that I was not surprised for only one copy had ever been printed and I had it. I have often wondered for how many years this bit of misinformation was passed along to students.[97]

However mythical the "Morgan Horse Edition," it would certainly please Frost's Vermont, for the Morgan Horse is the State animal, and just as certainly it pleased Ruthven, who raised Morgan horses in Michigan.

Epilogue

As with the final word of the Gospel of John, so one might say of writing about Frost, even in relating his Michigan story: "Now, there are many other things that Jesus did. If they were all written down one by one, I suppose that the whole world could not hold the books that would be written."

Of late the whole world does seem to be threatened with a deluge of books about Frost, with more to come. And the man himself, to say nothing of his poetry, assumes the proportions of a mythical or biblical character, of Joblike nature, complete with "miserable comforters." For the Book of Job was probably his favorite book in that Bible he so often carried in his pocket.

Even so, the Lord blessed the latter end of Frost, as he blessed that of Job, with both acclaim and this world's goods. Whether it made up for the earlier sorrows and struggles, who knows?

Notes to *Robert Frost in Michigan* by Dorothy Tyler

My thanks are due especially to Mary E. Cooley and Sue Bonner Walcutt, who shared with me many of these experiences at the University of Michigan; to Lois Tilley Lewis, daughter of Morris P. Tilley of the faculty; to the late Roy W. Cowden, Louis A. Strauss, and Erich A. Walter of the faculty; to Jean Paul Slusser, artist, and Carlton F. Wells, both Emeritus members of the faculty; and especially to Robert Frost himself, man and poet, who lives forever in many memories.

1. From *Who Was Who 1943–1956*, p. 533. Tilley (1876–1947) is remembered chiefly for his *Elizabethan Proverb Lore* (1926). He was also an editor of the *Early Modern English Dictionary*.

2. In Franconia, N. H., Dec. 29, 1915. University of Michigan Library; gift of Tilley family.

3. Robert Frost: *The Trial by Existence* (New York: Holt, Rinehart, and Winston, 1960). Elizabeth Shepley Sergeant (1881–1965) was the sister of Mrs. E. B. White, who, with her husband, was for many years associated with *The New Yorker*.

4. Lawrance Thompson, II, 127, 551. (These letters were doubtless among those considered too personal for release by Lois Tilley Lewis.)

5. These letters were shown to me by Lawrance Thompson when I visited him in Princeton in 1963.

6. *The Inlander* was published at the University of Michigan 1890–1907 as a literary magazine whose contributors were evidently both faculty members and students. In 1903 it was placed under the control of the Quadrangle Club. In 1905 it was made a biweekly Sunday supplement to *The Michigan Daily*. It was revived as an independent periodical from 1916 to 1918, during which Professor Tilley's "Notes from Conversations with Robert Frost" (November 1917) was published. In 1924–1925, mainly at the suggestion of Professor R. W. Cowden, the name of the student literary magazine *Whimsies* (1920–1924) was changed to *The Inlander*, and under this name the literary magazine continued publication until 1930. (From *University of Michigan Encyclopedic Survey*, Part IX.)

7. Poet Laureate Robert Bridges (1844–1930) was not to begin his magnum opus, *The Testament of Beauty*, until 1926 (published 1929), and thus some time after his Ann Arbor stay. His arrival by ocean liner in New York in 1924, with his wife, was made famous by the headline of a ship reporter who was not able to extract a story: "King's Canary Will Not Chirp."

8. A graduate assistant to Professor Tilley at the time told me that while Ernest de Selincourt, the Wordsworth scholar, was a guest of the Tilleys, Frost "turned up" to dinner and Mrs. Tilley "had the whole group on her hands." Frost was often left stranded by his family and was obliged to seek hospitality where his friends offered it.

9. Details received from Erich A. Walter of the University.

10. The Sinclair Lewis address was reprinted in *An American Primer*, edited by Daniel J. Boorstin (New York: Mentor Books, 1966), with an introduction by Mark Schorer.

11. The "far from munificent funds" of the University at that time perhaps explained the failure of the distinguished Fred Newton Scott (1860–1931), then head of Rhetoric and Journalism, to say any word, pro or con—so far as can be learned—about the presence of Frost. If, as Thompson (II, 176) reports, RF "heard of resentments on the part of certain drones who disapproved of paying a mere poet $5,000 to sit around and do nothing all year while they slaved in classrooms," their feelings are perhaps understandable. I spoke later with faculty members who had left for greener fields at that time. (At that time Frost's stay was paid for by donors. It was when University funds were involved, in 1925–1926, that there was difficulty about Frost's frequent absences.)

12. Chase Salmon Osborn (1860–1949) also gave the University of Michigan other gifts from his properties in northern Michigan.

13. Sidney Cox, *Robert Frost: Original "Ordinary Man"* (New York: Henry Holt & Co., 1929).

14. Reported by Floyd Dell in "The Gossip Shop," *The Bookman*, March 1922, p. 91.

15. *The Letters of Ezra Pound 1907–1941*, edited by D. D. Paige, preface by Mark Van Doren (New York: Harcourt, Brace, Harvest Book, 1950), pp. 98–100.

16. In June 1926 I purchased at Wahr's Bookstore a first American edition of

A Boy's Will, in which Frost inscribed for me his poem "Fiat Nox," on April 2, 1927—while sitting on the stair of his house on Pontiac Road, Ann Arbor.

17. Conrad's essay was published in October 1930 in *The Landmark*, a bimonthly published by the English-Speaking Union from January 1919 to May 1938, at 37 Charles St., W.1, London. Thanks are due the Detroit Public Library for bringing a reprint of the essay to my attention and to the New York State Library (Mr. Siple) for bibliographic information.

18. Padraic Colum, who had long been an American citizen, died in New York in 1972.

19. Lois Elizabeth Whitcomb, later Mrs. Bohlig, corresponded with Lawrance Thompson on the subject. (See II, 578.)

20. Martin A. Klaver, letter of March 10, 1977 to DT, cited later. (It was probably Alfred Kreymborg who had the "mandolute," while Sandburg always carried a guitar.)

21. *Michigan Daily, Sunday Magazine*, "Tea with Padraic Colum," by Lois Elizabeth Whitcomb, April 12, 1922. A portrait of Colum by the Hungarian artist, Willy Pogany, illustrated the article.

22. Halsey Davidson, then living in Lake Orion, Michigan, in letters to DT, 22 November and 6 December 1963. (Davidson, artist and writer, in 1977 lives in Scottsdale, Arizona.)

23. Thompson gives the year of Amy Lowell's lecture as 1921 (II, 181); the correct year, 1922, is cited in the Notes (ibid., p. 735).

24. Ruth Lechlitner (Mrs. Paul Corey), now living in Sonoma, California, has published four books of her poems.

25. S. Foster Damon, *Amy Lowell: A Chronicle*, New York: Houghton Mifflin, 1935. A recently published book, *Amy: The World of Amy Lowell and the Imagist Movement*, by Jean Gould (New York: Dodd, Mead, 1975), has many interesting stories about the relationship of Frost and Lowell.

26. This excerpt from Mary Cooley's Diary was given to DT on February 14, 1965.

27. Charles Horton Cooley, *Life and the Student* (New York: Knopf, 1927), p. 93.

28. Bower's tribute to Frost, published in the March 1963 issue of *Pleasures of Learning*, New York University. The passage quoted was reprinted in *NYU Notebook* (vol. 7, no. 5), February 1964, in which the gift of Frost's personal library to NYU is announced, and Frost is portrayed with the caption that he received the first NYU Medal in 1956.

29. Letter of October 12, 1964 from Forman Brown to DT. The following excerpts are also from this letter.

30. Sonnet published in *Whimsies*, vol. II, no. 4, May 1922, p. 9.

31. See note 29.

32. *Richard Jefferies: His Life and Work*, by Edward Thomas. Boston: Little, Brown, 1909. (Dedicated to W. H. Hudson.)

33. See note 12. Both Governor Osborn and his second wife, Stella Brunt Osborn, are well represented in the Michigan Historical Collections, Ann Arbor.

34. In a letter of April 15, 1964, the late Arthur Krock of *The New York Times* informed me that Delbert Clark (1900–1953) at the time of his death was Eastern representative of the Fund for Adult Education, though he had been on the New York staff of *The New York Times* until October 1951. While with the *Times* he contributed to the Sunday *Michigan Daily* (May 23, 1937) a long article on the life and times of Eaton, who died in 1930 in New York. The title, which would have interested Frost, was "G. D. Eaton—A Neo-Menckenite; Colleague Recalls 'Daily' Rebel."

35. *Letters of Robert Frost to Louis Untermeyer* (New York: Holt, Rinehart & Winston, 1963), p. 145. (See note 21 for Whitcomb.)

36. Wade Van Dore gave this information to DT. However, the aid Conrad gave RF is described in some detail in Thompson, II, 245. *New Hampshire* (1923) was awarded the newly established Pulitzer Prize for poetry.

37. Quoted by Thompson, II, 225–227.

38. A copy of the letter reached DT from Mary E. Cooley, who had been visiting Elizabeth Strauss Davies in California. It is not among the *Selected Letters* published by Thompson.

39. Information about Max Ewing reached DT from various sources, including Carl E. Gehring of Ann Arbor and a letter from Donald Gallup, Curator, Collection of American Literature, Yale University (14 September 1964). The Collection was described originally in the *Gazette* of the Library, July 1943.

40. Interview with Paul Osborn, "A Superior Writing Talent," *The Michigan Alumnus*, June 7, 1958. (Illustrations included a portrait sketch of Frost by Wilfred B. Shaw.)

41. Untermeyer, pp. 333, 341.

42. Letter to DT from Clement A. Smith, M. D., October 29, 1963.

43. Letter to DT (one of several) from Warren Bower of New York University. (See note 28.) Jonathan Hildner (1868–1952), who inspired the Indipohdi Club, was born in Washtenaw County, Michigan, and received two degrees from Michigan and his Ph. D. from Leipzig. He was the author of several books, some in German. The Indipohdi Club had a publication, according to Warren Bower.

44. A copy of *The Quadrangle Book* (Ann Arbor: Privately Printed, 1914) was lent to me by Carlton F. Wells in 1964. Edgar H. Ailes, Detroit attorney, also recalled that Frost attended the "Q" meetings.

45. The dedication of the Frost home in Franconia, N. H. was given wide coverage in the press, with the first to come to my attention in *The Times Record*, Troy, N. Y., May 28, 1977.

46. Thompson, II, 540. (Contrary to the note that Untermeyer received the only completed copy of the Christmas card, the Tilleys also received one.)

47. Letter RF to Morris Tilley, Franconia, December 29, 1915; now in the University of Michigan Library.

48. Remark to DT by George Tilley.

49. As told to DT by Harry Hoey, for some years Headmaster of Cranbrook School, Bloomfield Hills, Mich. (See note 8.)

50. Sergeant, p. 246. (See note 3.)

51. Sergeant, p. 246.

52. Reported in letter to Witter Bynner (1881–1968) by DT dated Detroit, April 5, 1962. His reply of April 17, 1962 from Santa Fé stated: "It is pleasant of you to have written me the note about Frost's reference to those old days. I wish I were seeing him these new days."

53. Frances Swain, "The Robert Frost of the Whimsies Evenings," *The Inlander*, vol. 5, no. 4, April 1925. (Written spring 1922; publication deferred at Frost's request.)

54. William Prescott Frost (1823–1901). See Thompson, I, 261, 275.

55. Pound, *Letters* (London, August 1915), p. 62.

56. *Ibid.*, Preface, p. vii.

57. Dorothy Tyler, "The Sound of a Voice That Is Still," *The English Journal*, vol. 29, no. 2, part I (February 1940). (Translation of French passage: "Writing in *Le Temps* not long ago, Edmond Jaloux spoke of encountering Yeats during the war of 1914–18 in a 'bureau very strictly administrative,' where, nevertheless, he brought with him 'the poetry and Irish mythology of the ocean, and the clouds of heaven, and Cuchulain who fights against the sea.'"

58. Dorothy Tyler, "Remembering Robert Frost," *Among Friends*, No. 29, Winter 1962–63. The Friends of The Detroit Public Library, Inc.
59. Campbell Bonner died in 1954; Mrs. Ethel Howell Bonner in 1969.
60. By Caesar R. Blake and Carlton F. Wells. University of Michigan Press, 1964.
61. See Wilfred B. Shaw, *The University of Michigan Illustrated*, January 31, 1949, who states: "President Burton . . . called upon the State for $19,000,000 to finance a building program—at that time a sum beyond the wildest dreams."
62. Thompson, II, 176. (See note 11.)
63. Fred Newton Scott (1860–1931) was widely recognized for the quality of his teaching of the craft of writing and his many publications. (See especially *The Fred Newton Scott Anniversary Papers*, Chicago: University of Chicago Press, 1929.)
64. John M. Russell, letter to DT, April 21, 1964.
65. Martin A. Klaver, Kennett Square, Pa., letter to DT March 10, 1977. (See note 20.) The unidentified quotation following is from William (Johnson) Cory's translation of an epitaph on Heraclitus by Callimachus. See *Oxford Book of English Verse*, No. 759.
66. Thanks are due Leon Makielski for the photograph of his portrait of Frost and for conversations concerning it, including the comment that the poet was talking at the time the portrait was painted. For an interview with Makielski about the portrait see *Ann Arbor News*, December 30, 1963; the *News* of December 9, 1963 reported the purchase of the portrait by the University of Michigan.
67. Untermeyer, p. 147. Untermeyer brackets the date.
68. Joy Hakanson, "Festival Exhibition; 50 Years of Portraits," *Detroit News*, June 23, 1963. (Illustrated by Frost portrait.)
69. Erich A. Walter (1898–1977), who held both faculty and administrative positions at the University, was co-author (with Harlan Hatcher) of *A Pictorial History of the Great Lakes* (New York: Bonanza Books, 1963) and editor of the anthology, *Our Michigan*, 1966, published by the University. For information concerning the present location of the portrait thanks are due to Janet F. White, Head, Reference Department, University Library.
70. Letter to Mary Hays of Ann Arbor, March 1965, relayed to DT by Mary E. Cooley.
71. *The Necessity of Poetry*, by Robert Bridges, Oxford: At the Clarendon Press, 1918.
72. Thompson, I, 442–443.
73. Letter to Sidney Cox, Beaconsfield, 19 January 1914. Thompson, *Selected Letters*, pp. 107–108. (Quoted in Thompson, I, 443–444.)
74. Thompson, II, 608.
75. Quoted from holograph letter (copy). Ann Arbor source, perhaps from Roy W. Cowden.
76. Letter RF to Morris P. Tilley, Amherst, Mass., Feb. 20, 1924. (From letters now in University Library, Ann Arbor.)
77. Information chiefly from Notes, Thompson, II, 608. He cites reports in *The Michigan Daily*. (Also from memory of DT.)
78. Thompson, II, 608–609.
79. Original in University Library, Ann Arbor. (Professor Strauss, whose graduate assistant DT was in 1926–27, was a Browning scholar.)
80. See Thompson, II, 619–620, for different impressions of Frost's Seminar 186.
81. Louis Untermeyer, *Modern British Poetry* (New York: Harcourt, Brace, 1930, 3rd ed. rev.), p. 450. (See also Thompson's excellent account of Thomas in I, 461–468.)
82. A full-page announcement of the lecture by Noyes appeared in *The Inlander*, November 1925.

83. W. H. Davies, *A Poet's Pilgrimage* (London: Jonathan Cape, 1929), pp. 132–133.

84. Sergeant, pp. 134–135.

85. "The Golden Room," by Wilfrid W. Gibson (1878–1962), was published in *The Atlantic Monthly*, February 1926, pp. 204–205. In the poem he misspells Elinor White's name. (For some reason Thompson (I, 601) gives as reference, not *The Atlantic*, but *Dymock Down the Ages*, by the Rev. J. E. Gethyn-Jones, H. Osborne: Gloucester, 1951.)

86. Sergeant, p. 132.

87. *Michigan: A Guide to the Wolverine State* (New York: Oxford, 1941), p. 149 describes Van Dore as "a protégé of Robert Frost."

88. Letter of Angus Babcock to DT from San Carlos, California, May 4, 1977.

89. Letter of E. W. Slusser to DT from Oakland, California, June 11, 1963, enclosing photocopy of letter from RF to Edgar Slusser (as he was known to me and RF) dated Dec. 28, 1926, from South Shaftsbury, Vermont.

90. To Professor Jean Paul Slusser my grateful thanks are due for letters of Nov. 20 and 30, 1963, from Ann Arbor, and other materials about Frost. The artist, who attained the age of 90 in December 1976, is represented in many important collections.

91. See note 15 for Pound Letters.

92. Frederick L. Luddy, "A Recollection of Robert Frost in Ann Arbor on the 100th Anniversary of His Birth," *Detroit* (Sunday Magazine, *Detroit Free Press*), June 23, 1974.

93. Letter to DT, August 18, 1964. (Sad to relate, Kenneth N. Metcalf and his wife Margaret died in an automobile accident in September 1965, as reported in *The Detroit News* of Sept. 19, 1965.)

94. Jane Schermerhorn, *Detroit News*, March 20, 1963.

95. New York: Crown Publishers, 1972.

96. Dorothy Tyler, "Frost's Last Three Visits to Michigan," *Frost: Centennial Essays*, edited by Jac Tharpe, et al. pp. 518–534. Jackson: University Press of Mississippi, [1974].

97. Alexander Ruthven (1882–1971) writes of Frost on pages 31–32 of his *Naturalist in Two Worlds*, Ann Arbor: University of Michigan Press, 1963.

Robert Frost at Bread Loaf

CHARLES H. FOSTER

I am not going to attempt to tie together tag ends of memory, for I have discovered that I can remember nothing so accurately as the statements and events I have put in writing soon after their occurrence. My evidence for a report on Robert Frost at Bread Loaf is a diary I wrote in 1938 when I was twenty-four and Robert Frost was sixty-four.[1] But the diary was written not only on the heel of events; it was also written when I was too busy to make more than hasty notations of what Frost had left vibrating in my mind. I had no time to spoil reality by distorting it with speculations and explanations.

Some passages from the diary have appeared recently in Theodore Morrison's *Bread Loaf Writers' Conference: The First Thirty Years (1926–1955)* and in Lawrance Thompson's and R. H. Winnick's *Robert Frost: The Later Years 1938–1963* as proofs of Frost's lack of reason and his self-hatred following his wife's death from cancer in March 1938.[2] But in 1938 when I arrived at Bread Loaf as the first Elinor Frost Fellow, Mrs. Frost's recent death was, so far as I was concerned, simply a tragic loss.[3] Though I had known her, possibly, better than most Amherst undergraduates, I actually knew nothing of the deep conflicts which had agitated the Frosts' marriage from the start. To me, Robert and Elinor Frost were only slightly idealized in the charming and witty lovers of "West-Running Brook," and it simply never occurred to me that they might also be dramatized in "Home Burial" where the man and wife are darkly rather than brightly contrary in their relations. Frost's startling song of experience, "The Subverted Flower," which might have helped me understand, would not be published until 1942, and even further in the future was that record of Frost's multiple selves, Kathleen Morrison's masterly *Robert Frost: A Pictorial Chronicle* (1974). When, therefore, on my first night at Bread Loaf on August 17, 1938, Frost indulged in blasphemous self-denunciations, I did not

70

know what to make of them.[4] It was only as he made other dark references to his marriage, in the days following, that I understood that he was horrified by his vision of himself as a completely unforgiveable, selfish husband and sought relief in exaggerations which he was sure no one would accept.

But "the agitated heart" was no make-believe. As Theodore Morrison has shown in an essay with which all mature study of Frost should begin, recognition of the poet's "agitated heart" in his relations with his mother and his wife is fundamental in coping with Frost as man and artist.[5] My diary of 1938 confirms the Morrisons, however, not only on their insight into the agitated heart but also on their awareness of the agile mind. Though in August 1938, Frost was both an outraged and outrageous man, he still retained his wit and wisdom and power in aphorism which had made him a famous public figure. At the bottom of his emotional fortunes, his intellectual vigor was undiminished, and this fact helps us realize why he could in his later years confirm his reputation with new poems and prefaces and take rank as T. S. Eliot said in a toast in 1957 "as perhaps *the* most eminent, the most distinguished . . . Anglo-American poet now living."[6]

Here is my evidence of an undiminished Robert Frost in eight selections from my diary written in 1938:

1.

Last night Frost gave the best lecture I have ever heard him give. His mind was seething and rolling with metaphors and humor, and he was exhausted when he was finished. He seemed to feel it was his last talk at Bread Loaf. He said that like a drowning man he could remember everything in his life, and to hear him, one believed it.

He said he would follow his usual custom and make up some poems on the spot. It was the most remarkable performance I have ever seen. He talked on in the direction of an idea, all around it, and then said, "Here is a poem," and very slowly, changing a few words, but for the most part going ahead as one would on paper, he made his poem, and it was a good poem. He called it "Dark, Darker, Darkest." Life is *dark* because life, this bright foam that catches the light, is flowing forever and ever into insanity, into poverty. Life is *darker* because man doesn't know how to play the stops on mankind well enough to change the situation. We must advance in a broad front and we don't know how to turn to the poor and the insane. Life is *darkest* because, perhaps, we're not meant to do anything about it. Frost said he wanted life so much he hadn't time to play with dead things; man hasn't time.

Frost then talked about poetry as it had been to him during a life time. What he had wanted, he said, was not money for money's sake but money, enough of it, to show that he was wanted. A poet would be wanted, he said, if he knew how to draw across the quick, scrape across the quick the way James Stephens did in "The Snare."

> I hear a sudden cry of pain!
> There is a rabbit in a snare:
> Now I hear the cry again,
> But I cannot tell from where.
>
> But I cannot tell from where
> He is calling out for aid!
> Crying on the frightened air,
> Making everything afraid!
>
> Making everything afraid!
> Wrinkling up his little face!
> As he cries again for aid;
> —And I cannot find the place!
>
> And I cannot find the place
> Where his paw is in the snare!
> Little One! Oh, Little One!
> I am searching everywhere! [7]

Frost lingered on the last line [which I recorded in my diary as] "I cannot find him anywhere." [8]

But his own way was not to hurt. He recited the first stanza of "Ode," by William Collins:

> How sleep the brave, who sink to rest,
> By all their country's wishes blest!
> When Spring, with dewey fingers cold,
> Returns to deck their hallow'd mould,
> She there shall dress a sweeter sod,
> Than Fancy's feet have ever trod. [9]

That he said was drawing across the quick in a nobler way. Poetry is saying what you don't mean, putting a veil between yourself and the rawness of life.

Another matter poetry considered was saying one thing and meaning another, the whole business of metaphor. Suppose, he said, I want to tell you about Lytton Strachey. I could tell this story. A boat put forth from port with a clean-looking crew—all except one tough-looking individual. At Key West, a wild woman came on board and spent the night with this tough fellow, and next morning, as she left him, she gave him a present of a cigar box. Every day Strachey drew a beautiful suit of clothes, a pair of shoes and a good hat out of the box, and one by one he dressed all the crew—all except himself. On the last day of the voyage someone put a Bible in the box, there was an awful explosion and everyone stood naked.

Poetry was much the business of being demure. Women were demure, and men made demure poetry, "demure" being "not saying what you're full of."

Frost then told another story to show what he meant by metaphor. It was, so a girl told me at breakfast, one of Grimms' fairy tales, and Frost, she said, told it word for word.[10] It was the story of a man who noticed the strange way a troll fished. The troll used to get in a boat with his wife before supper and row around the lake. He would ask her, "Are my eyes green yet?" and when she finally said they were green, he would dive overboard and come up with armsful of fish.

The man thought this was a pretty good way to fish. He was like a lot of poets: he didn't want so much to write as to be told that he wrote. When he came home, he tried to fish the way the troll did. He rowed around and around the lake with his wife and asked her again and again if his eyes were green yet. "Why should they be?" she asked. Finally in desperation, the man said, "Say my eyes are green!" She said, "Your eyes are green," and he dove overboard and was drowned.

2.

Frost began his talk by remarking that there are two continents he has always plied between. The first of these is experience, everyday experience. Writing starts with him, he said, in remembering something he didn't know he knew about experience. But he never seeks experience. "I never went anywhere to get anything." He told about an English poet he went to a race with, who said as they came away: "I didn't see anything I could use. Did you?"

Of the other continent he said: "I've built another continent of the place to go, the continent of Over-there." He wants, he said, to have this continent wild country, as wild as the region here that is laid strata on strata. It scares him to have people find a definite form in his Over-there. He wants it to be as inexplicable as this world.

Unlike the college people, he has no knowledge that isn't emotion. It's that kind of knowledge that makes poetry. But you mustn't know where you're going. He never knew even in the long poems where he would end but supposed it was implied in the logic of the first line. No surprise in the writer; no surprise in the reader. No tears in the writer; no tears in the reader.

He recited a good bit of "Lycidas" from memory. He showed how Milton's art lies in the slight displacement of a word. He said the line, "Weep no more, woful Shepherds weep no more," made him suspicious and he saw that poetry's business is to play expression tones across the jingle. He recited Shakespeare's sonnet, "Let me not to the marriage of true minds,"[11] as another example of playing expression tones.

3.

Last night after Gorham Munson's lecture I bought Frost two bottles of gingerale to "wash out," as he put it, the remarks about A. R. Orage, [whose theories about ancient Greek dancing and ancient Greek poetry infuriated Frost.] As soon as people began to gather, Frost whispered that he wanted to get out, and we walked a couple of miles up the road toward Bread Loaf Mountain. He pointed out the stars and constellations and talked about the unity the Platonists and Transcendentalists sense. Things, he said, are not so dual as Norman Foerster would have them be,[12] nor are they so unified as the Platonists maintain. It is like marriage. You make a tight bargain with someone and your spats are attempts to get over that something that keeps you two persons. You want to be one, and you almost are but never so completely.

A few minutes ago I saw Frost and he said Jesus and Freud are the great humanitarians, but God is better than both. One must not be too much of a Christian.

4.

Robert Frost spoke this morning of the poet's use of words. He came without a tie and without notes. He quoted from memory various words that had, as he put it, "made a dent in the human mind no garage man can take out." Keats was his text. First there was the word "alien" in "Ode to a Nightingale":

> Perhaps the self-same song that found a path
>   Through the sad heart of Ruth, when, sick for home,
> She stood in tears amid the alien corn. . . .[13]

Then there was "surmise" in "On First Looking into Chapman's Homer":

> Or like stout Cortez when with eagle eyes
>   He star'd at the Pacific—and all his men
> Look'd at each other with a wild surmise—
>   Silent upon a peak in Darien.

In the opening of *Hyperion* a fine example of "denting" words was

> the Naiad 'mid her reeds
> Press'd her cold finger closer to her lips.

Another, to turn once more to "Ode to a Nightingale," was

> Charm'd magic casements, opening on the foam
> Of perilous seas, in faery lands forlorn.

Then there was the "Hymn to Pan" in Book I of *Endymion* which showed Keats "doing it as no one else can." The trick was to fetch words just enough—to fetch them but not make them far-fetched. Frost thought that the way any author, prose or poetry writers, should work was in envy of such high things. Frost said he had three translations of the *Divine Comedy*, those of Carey, Fletcher and Charles Eliot Norton, but that none of them had come so close to

Dante as had Keats in his sonnet on where he didn't go in hell but how finally he was with Paolo and Francesca,

> Where 'mid the gust, the whirlwind and the flaw
> Of rain and hail-stones, lovers need not tell
> Their sorrows. Pale were the sweet lips I saw,
> Pale were the lips I kiss'd, and fair the form
> I floated with, about that melancholy storm.

Frost recited many, many more lines of Keats, for he wanted to show the "denting" words in context. "The Eve of Saint Mark" showed, he said, Keats putting by the fever and trying to be cool. It was good—but not so good as were the other poems.

The question is how slow can you move and still be moving. Force is all there is to it. Go it as hard as you can with a flourish of feeling. Be like a butterfly who is so full of life that he can't go straight.

5.

About five minutes ago I listened to Frost talking to the Communist poet Florence Becker.[14] Frost said that when he met a revolutionary, he always hoped he would meet someone with fresh ideas but usually he met someone with slogans. "Have your old revolution but spare me the slogans." All there was to poetry was innocence— sufficient innocence so that you never rested in a truth till it became dull and untrue. Frost said he stood for the deepest of all revolutions: the revolutionary activity of the mind. That was what he liked about Emerson, his freedom and his bidding us to freedom. He recited the final stanza of Emerson's "Ode":

> For He that worketh high and wise,
>   Nor pauses in his plan,
> Will take the sun out of the skies
> Ere freedom out of man.[15]

6.

In his lecture this morning—or in what grew into a lecture from a discussion of Florida Watts Smyth's poetry—Frost said that the writer is he who notices what's going on inside or outside him and has the power to nail it. You luxuriate in little physical items, and you've got to be able to remind people of things they wish they had thought of. The question is "Have you enough emotion to use words describing such things so that they will be vivid?" Frost recited a poem about the dragon fly and how when he has shed his skin, his husk, he looks like a sapphire.[16] Frost said his ambition was to tear the husk off words. You've got to love things so much that you become aggressive on words. You don't have to think of method —T. S. Eliot's or anyone else's. You've got to be near things and get to the quick about them.

The way to begin either life or literature is at the pleasure end. Trust society and your friends to keep you out of trouble. Pray to God if you wish your pleasure to be innocent, but be happy. If you're happy, you'll be good; good-good not bad-good.

Poetry is like smiling. It is best when it comes from being happy. When it occurs under order, it is a disgusting thing, and a man who indulges in it becomes false all the way through. Some poets are like the bull frog who could swell in his throat and hoped to be as big as his friend the bull—to swell into a Milton or a Dante.

But it isn't just happiness. Like the beer song, "It's 'I'll be happy; I'll be sad.'" Be sad-happy like a billiard ball with English on it that's coming and going at the same time. You begin not at the wisdom end but at the personal end. Frost said that when he was young, people were allowed to fall in love without knowing the consequence of babies. He said if he was a young poetess today in one of these submarine courses, he would faint and be carried out. All women know how to faint. Poets likewise should faint when they were taught Aristotle. The best time to read Aristotle would be when you are too old to see whether you had come to his conclusions.

7.

Last evening Archibald MacLeish read a lecture built on a pronouncement of Stephen Spender's that the new poetry believes first of all in literalness, the transcription of the world not as the poet would find it but as he does in fact find it. This program, MacLeish suggested, rests upon a belief in this world and a turning away from the absolutes which have oppressed poetry in the past as *The Oxford Book of English Verse* testifies. MacLeish read his long poem with pictures, *The Land of the Free*, and a sequence of love poems from *Public Speech*.

Frost did not take kindly to Archie's talk I found when I met him in the kitchen of Treman Cottage.[17] He was fixing himself a tumbler of whiskey with a piece of ice in it. Ted Morrison asked him to be good, and he said he'd be all right when he put what he had in his hand where it should go.

When we went into the living room, everyone felt the tension, and Benny DeVoto was pacing around the room like a captain on the quarter-deck. I asked him when we'd reach port, and he said, "God-damn it to hell, Charlie. Robert's acting like a fool. Archie wasn't talking against him. He knows Robert is at the bottom of the new literalness."

Under pressure from Ted Morrison, Archie read a new poem called *Air Raid*, written for radio rather than the stage. He gave through the voices of women and men an experience of the bombing of a mountain town. The women thought war was childish and that the enemy was not interested in killing them but rather in killing the generals and captains. The women could not be persuaded to take shelter.

Benny wondered if there weren't archaic phrases in the poem that ought to come out if the spirit of modernity was to be preserved. Frost said that that wasn't the point and he stopped the quarrel over it, punctuated with "God-damns" and "shut-ups" that had arisen between two of the others. The point to judge the poem on, Frost said, was its literalness. How true is it that modern armies want to kill women and how true is it that women like to spread their skirts to protect themselves? Not only that. We were asked to imagine a town in which women were so used to the old idea of fighting that they did not suspect that they themselves might be killed. Where was such a town? Archie took it all in the nicest way and said that he based his poem on happenings in Spain and on his own memories of air raids in France.[18]

The conversation shifted from this talk across the room into little
eddies, and I went over to see how Frost was stirring the waters. I
sat next to him on a davenport and after a time Archie came over
and sat on the arm of it. Frost had one arm around me, and, as more
drinks were drunk, and discussion arose, Archie balanced himself
with an arm around my shoulder. With Frost's arm around my back
and Archie's around my neck and with both arguing and almost
meeting before my nose, I felt—at least physically—in the center of
American poetry.

Frost said it made him mad when a young squirt like Spender
gave what he had worked on all his life a phrase and tried to take
the credit for it. "I'm going to England and spank Spender." "Jesus
H. Christ, Robert," said Archie. "You're the one who ought to be
spanked. You're the foundation and we all know it." "I'm an old
man. I want you to say it, to say it often. I want to be flattered."
Archie said, "It isn't that you want flattery. It is perfectly natural
to want to get recognition for what you had started."

Archie then tried to make the conversation less personal, and
Frost said, "God-damn everything to hell so long as we're friends,
Archie." "We are friends, Robert." Archie then wondered what
could explain the fact that poetry which had been in the ivory tower
so long had suddenly gotten literal about 1910. "That's *my* date,"
Frost said. "Of course it's *your* date."[19] "The literalness is nothing
new," said Benny DeVoto. "It's as old as Abelard, as old as the dispute between Thomas Aquinas and Abelard; it's older than that
even." Charles Curtis wondered if Shakespeare didn't use the same
technique, beginning with things and ending in a meaning. "Sure
he did," said Frost. "*Macbeth* is a two-for-a-cent story but Shakespeare made it have all kinds of meaning." At this point I wondered
out loud if a poet didn't come to meaning by realizing the symbolic
character of the world; I was trying Emerson out. "I never thought
of it that way," Frost said, "but it sounds right."[20] "It's something
like that," Archie said. But nobody liked the word "symbolic" for
some reason.

"It's in meaning we go wrong," Frost insisted. "We go wrong
in having meanings and then finding things to prove them, and we
go wrong in the meaning we trip into at the end of our description,

our toying with physical things." The best way, Frost said (this
repeated what he had said to me in the afternoon), is not to have
anything settled. When you rested in a truth, it became an untruth.
Turning to me, Frost stated: "You know what's wrong with your
poetry? You read it as if it all had one tone and that means it had one
tone in your mind. There are all kinds of tones and here he recited
[and sang] a dozen or so snatches of Elizabethan song to show how
many, many tones there are to poetry. Archie, I could see, got the
point. It was not only me Frost was talking about. He hadn't in fact
called my name and, as he looked into my face turned toward his,
he could also see Archie's looking straight ahead. He did mention
my name at the end of his little monologue, but everyone knew that
the criticism was not meant just for me. But I knew it was meant for
me as well as for Archie as Frost punctuated his remarks with hugs.

8.

Robert Frost came back to Bread Loaf tonight after a considerable
absence to speak the final word of the Conference. He said he always
carried a thorn in his pocket to remind him that it is from the realities, physical, mental and spiritual, that poetry springs. After the
talk he explained to me and another friend that he went away as a
woman does to let people know how badly he felt about everything. Over in Treman Cottage he was drinking only gingerale,
and he said he was off drink. He looked and acted like his old self.

Notes to *Robert Frost at Bread Loaf* by CHARLES H. FOSTER

1. This essay was read as a lecture sponsored by the English Department at the
University of Minnesota, May 18, 1977. In copying my diary I have corrected my
spelling, made definite the reference of pronouns and padded out a few half-
expressed phrases. But I have changed nothing in those sentences and phrases
quoted from Frost or attributed to him.
    For further information concerning my relations with Frost, see Edward Con-
nery Lathem and Lawrance Thompson, eds., *Robert Frost: Poetry and Prose* (New
York, Chicago and San Francisco: Holt, Rinehart and Winston, 1972), pp. 313–328.
    2. Theodore Morrison, the Director of the Conference, quotes selection 7 in
Bread Loaf Writers' Conference: The First Thirty Years (1926–1955) (Middlebury:
Middlebury College Press, 1976), pp. 69–70. Lawrance Thompson and R. H. Winnick quote the second paragraph from selection 1, a portion of 7 and use other
portions of the diary, such as the self-denunciation in which Frost told me he was
"a God-damned son-of-a-bitch," not here reprinted, in *Robert Frost: The Later*

Years, 1938–1963 (New York: Holt, Rinehart and Winston, 1976), pp. 7, 8, 371, 372.

3. Frost wrote to Theodore Morrison, who summarized his message in inviting me to Bread Loaf: "I'm going to let you give a scholarship in her name this year and ask your permission to give one myself in her name next year. Then there will be two boys to go forward with thoughts of obligation to her. I have in mind for the benefit this year a boy whose work in verse she has long had special hopes of. In writing to see if he can accept it, please make him realize that it is as good as if he were her personal appointment. His name is Charles Foster. . . ." See Thompson and Winnick, p. 370.

4. Thompson and Winnick, p. 8. Kathleen Morrison, who in 1938 began her long and indispensable career as Frost's secretary and general manager, reports Frost's self-denunciations during this troubling summer in *Robert Frost: A Pictorial Chronicle* (New York: Holt, Rinehart and Winston, 1974), p. 18.

5. Theodore Morrison found the phrase "agitated heart" in Frost's early poem "Revelation" in giving title to his profound disclosures in "Robert Frost: The Agitated Heart," *The Atlantic Monthly* (July 1967), 72–79.

6. Thompson and Winnick, p. 244.

7. James Stephens, *Collected Poems* (New York: Macmillan & Co., 1935), p. 23.

8. There is a puzzle in the discrepancy between Stephens's final line in the printed version and the line I recall Frost's quoting. The error is probably mine, not Frost's. He possessed an extraordinary verbal memory and seemed to carry accurately in his memory literally thousands of poems.

9. Frost also admired Collins's "Ode to Evening"—that is through stanza four. The succeeding nine stanzas seemed to him to detract rather than add to the poem, as he told me in one of our sessions at Amherst College.

10. The girl at breakfast was in error. The story is not one of the folk tales collected by Jacob and Wilhelm Grimm. Rather, it is a Danish folk tale, "I Know What I Have Learned." Frost probably read this story to his children from the version translated by W. A. Craigie and anthologized by Andrew Lang in *The Pink Fairy Book* (London and New York: Longmans, Green Co., 1897), pp. 148–153. In his retelling at Bread Loaf Frost limited himself to the third and climactic adventure of the father with troll sons-in-law and told the tale, to judge from the summary in my diary, in his own words rather than in Craigie's unexciting phrases.

11. Sonnet 116.

12. Frost returned again and again in talk with me at Bread Loaf to Norman Foerster, Director of the School of Letters at the University of Iowa, and his bad influence in leading me, as he had indeed done, to an interest in Aristotle. But Frost was not simply down on Aristotle; he was quite as critical of Plato. As an Emersonian-Jamesian pragmatist, Frost ranged himself against all thinkers who in his view imposed prefabricated systems on reality. These included the New Humanists, Babbitt and Foerster.

13. There was nothing surprising to me in Frost's using Keats as his text in discussing the poet's use of words. In my one-man class with him at Amherst College, Frost, I recall, once spent almost a whole afternoon pointing out to me the excellence of Keats's "To Autumn," particularly the excellence of the second stanza, with which he thought the poem should end.

14. Mrs. Florence Becker, later Mrs. Florence Becker Lennon, won the poetry prize at the Bread Loaf Writers' Conference in 1938. She was "a Communist poet" in that she shared the then widely held belief that Russia was a fountainhead of economic and social justice. Her latest book, *The Good Green Footstool* (1976), issued in her eighty-first year, indicates a larger affinity with Lewis Carroll and Emily Dickinson than with Karl Marx.

15. R. W. Emerson, Concord Edition, *The Complete Works of Ralph Waldo Emerson* (Boston and New York: Houghton Mifflin Co., 1901), IX, 200.

16. I have been unable to find the poem on the dragon fly which Frost recited.

17. In *Bread Loaf Writers' Conference* Theodore Morrison describes Treman Cottage as "a club lounge and refuge for the staff and the Fellows" (p. 36).

18. It is possible that this discussion of *Air Raid* on August 27, 1938, led MacLeish to some revisions of his poem. In the conclusion of an article on *Air Raid* in *Time*, October 31, 1938, p. 30, is the remark, "Poet MacLeish began it in the spring, rewrote it in August."

19. Nothing noteworthy regarding Frost and literalness took place precisely in 1910, but *about* 1910, specifically in 1913, Frost published his first book, *A Boy's Will*, in London.

20. Frost's saying he had not thought about a poet's coming to meaning through realizing the symbolic character of the world is odd to say the least. As early as 1923, he was making observations of the kind he made to Rose C. Feld in an interview for *The New York Times Book Review*: "What's my philosophy? That's hard to say. I was brought up a Swedenborgian. I am not a Swedenborgian now. But there's a good deal of it that's left with me. I am a mystic. I believe in symbols. I believe in change and in changing symbols." Edward Connery Lathem, ed., *Interviews with Robert Frost* (New York, Chicago, San Francisco: Holt, Rinehart and Winston, 1966), p. 49.

Per Ardua ad Astra

ROBERT FROST literally lived by the stars. The most vivid symbols in his verse, stars also flashed in and out of his conversations and added brilliance to his correspondence. They were his personal guideposts, for reasons both stated and unstated. It is said that, in all his travels in this country and abroad, he never went to sleep without first looking into the night sky for the North Star.

Our title, "Per Ardua ad Astra" (through troubles to the stars), is a tribute not only to Frost as a great classical scholar who loved Latin but also to him as a towering human being who never gave in to defeat. Although tragedy dogged him from infancy, he never lost sight of the stars.

Trouble followed Frost even to the grave. In the summing up period that follows the death of any public figure, the clash of sabres over Robert Frost was heard around the literate world. Critics, scholars, thinking people everywhere—personal friends of Frost and others who knew him only through his poetry—felt the need to take sides, to stand up and be counted.

Curiously, they were not quarreling so much over Frost's work or how to place him on the scale of poetic greatness (which must have been what Robert Frost meant when he predicted the "clash of sabers over my grave"[1]) but over his worth as a man, a husband, a father, a human being.

An aura of near holiness enveloped Frost in his lifetime. When he died (January 29, 1963) at 88—only weeks away from 89—leaders from all parts of the world joined in praising the best-loved poet in the United States and his work, recalling his four Pulitzer Prizes, his many honorary degrees, and how he had added something infinitely fine to our world.

The self-styled literate farmer had become a national treasure, a folk hero, everybody's grandfather, a kind of intellectual teddy-bear. School children for the past couple of generations grew up knowing lines from his poems, remembering them when they couldn't recall any others. Even those people not acquainted with his poems remember with affection the craggy old man who appeared to read his poetry at John F. Kennedy's 1961 inauguration.

Millions watched on television as Frost took a great bard's ancient place beside the leaders of his world. We all winced with him as a chill twenty-mile-an-hour wind smarted his eyes and whipped the typewritten sheets from his hand. But he never lost his dignity, only —momentarily—his composure. A few minutes later, we rejoiced at his courage as he said "The Gift Outright" from memory.

The next time Frost was in the public eye was in 1962 when President Kennedy asked him to go to Russia as an ambassador of culture and good will. When Frost met with Nikita Khrushchev, the nation held its collective breath, knowing Frost's forthrightness, wondering what impact he would have on the Soviet Premier.

Later, we gasped when Frost described Khrushchev as a "ruffian"[2] at a news conference. He later explained that he meant it good-naturedly and that it was a northern Vermont kind of praise for a rough-and-ready man with energy and courage. That explanation satisfied nearly everybody. Those who read more deeply about the trip[3] realized that Frost had done his best to initiate an atmosphere of détente before it became the "in" thing to do.

But apparently President Kennedy did not understand. Perhaps he could not forgive Frost for utter frankness with the press without first consulting with him. Frost waited in vain for word from the courageous young president he so admired. But official thanks never came from the White House for Frost's strenuous trip in behalf of the nation. At Frost's death, Kennedy made his statement to the nation. "The death of Robert Frost," he said, "leaves a vacancy in the American spirit."

On October 26, 1963, at the dedication of the Robert Frost Library at Amherst College, John F. Kennedy spoke again of Frost, calling him "one of the granite figures of our time. . . . In America, our heroes have customarily run to men of large accomplishments. But today this college and this country honor a man whose contribution was not to our size, but to our spirit; not to our political beliefs, but to our insights; not to our self-esteem, but to our self-comprehension.

"In honoring Robert Frost, we therefore can pay honor to the deepest sources of our national strength. That strength takes many forms and the most obvious forms are not always the most significant.

"The men who create power make an indispensable contribution to the nation's greatness. But the men who question power make a contribution just as indispensable, especially when that questioning is disinterested.

"For they determine whether we use power or power uses us. Our national strength matters; but the spirit which informs and controls our strength matters just as much. This was the special significance of Robert Frost.

"He brought an unsparing instinct for reality to bear on the platitudes and pieties of society. His sense of human tragedy fortified him against self-deception and easy consolation.

" 'I have been,' he wrote, 'one acquainted with the night.'

"And because he knew the midnight as well as the high noon, because he understood the ordeal as well as the triumph of the human spirit, he gave his age strength with which to overcome despair. . . ."[4]

The nation again honored Robert Frost in 1974 on the 100th anniversary of his birth (March 26, 1874, in San Francisco). A U.S. commemorative stamp was issued in Derry, New Hampshire, where he farmed and wrote in the early 1900s.

In Washington, D.C., the Library of Congress offered special ceremonies and public readings of Frost's work. Newspapers and magazines all over the country carried the impressions of many who had known him. Cities and hamlets staged programs where his poetry was read and music set to his verse was played and sung.

The adulation was so effusive and so widespread that one could not help hoping that somehow Robert Frost was looking down through the stars he loved so well and enjoying what was happening as the world celebrated his centenary. Perhaps it would make up a bit for the potshots some were beginning to take at the poet following publication of the second volume of Frost's official biography by Lawrance Thompson.

With publication of the third volume, Frost's inner struggles and their ultimate effect on his family and friends became the target of critical interpreters who made headlines if they were controversial enough to tear into the image of the super saint and beloved grand-father. Frost was accused of being outrageously sly and dishonest, egotistical, arrogant, vindictive, self-pitying, vacillating and even lecherous and adulterous. In perhaps the most widely read of the critical reviews (New York *Times*, January 16, 1977), David Brom-wich, throwing professionalism aside, steps out of the role of re-viewer and into the role of judge. He calls Frost a "successful liar" and a "hateful human being" and concludes that "standing in the same room with a man about whom one knew a quarter of the things one now knows about Frost would be more than one could bear."

I did stand in the same room with Robert Frost and bore it very well. Loved it. Loved him. The brief meeting probably influenced my life more than any other before or since.

For many years, there was anger mixed up with my memory of Robert Frost. I had a "lover's quarrel" with him as much as he had one with the world.

Our meeting happened in April 1944, when one of Frost's famous "barding trips" around the nation included the University of Cin-cinnati, where I was a coed.

It was war time at U. C. The campus was partially a military en-campment with thousands of Army Specialized Training Corps and Air Force students living there and attending classes.

As Frost spoke, his audience was divided between teenagers in uniform and those in sloppy Joe sweaters and de rigueur dirty saddle shoes. I was in the latter category.

I had come to hear Frost because it had been recommended by my creative writing instructor, Dr. Victor E. Reichert, a close friend of Frost. I was an English major but was studying art too. My sketchbook went everywhere with me. As I listened to Frost's deep sonorous voice, I also was struggling to capture his likeness in charcoal.

His hair was pure white and as unruly as a poet's should be. His piercing blue eyes seemed to search for truth. They also searched out distractions in the audience. And I was one of them. I was uncomfortable, knowing that Frost was very much aware that I was sketching him.

The sketch was not going well. Frost's powerful head would remain surprisingly still for a long time, his penetrating voice moving on steadily. Then the voice would drop to a whisper or stop intermittently for long pauses, coming back suddenly with a shake of the mighty white head or an emphatic gesture of a powerful hand. The angle of the head and the body—the entire mood—would be changed.

Dismayed, I put the sketch pad down. I found the intense blue eyes upon me. Purposely, he caught my eye, and pursed that lower lip of his into a half smile, continuing all the time with saying his poems.

A flash of Frost personality had come through to me. And an idea that had presented itself earlier—that it would be interesting to talk with him—became stronger. The thought grew in me that I must find some way of talking with him alone.

I studied him. He was as plain and as full of power as his verse. The way he moved, it was obvious that he disliked the dark business suit, the stiff collar and tie, and was itching to get into something more in keeping with the man he was—an open sports shirt, slacks, or perhaps even a pair of comfortable overalls. Yet, glancing around at the faces of the audience, eager to the point of adulation, I mused that the most appropriate attire for Frost would have been the flowing robes of a biblical prophet.

Inspired anew, I started a new sketch, working on it rapidly as Frost finished the program by saying "Birches" and "Mending Wall." The last strokes of my sketch were completed as students and faculty crowded around him, eager for a word or an autograph. Most of the books thrust at him for signing were *The Witness Tree*, which had earned him his fourth Pulitzer Prize the year before.

After most of the crowd dispersed, I approached him. There was no book in my hand, just a sketch. I thrust it upon him. A small pleased smile lighted his face as he autographed it and returned it to me.

"Stick around," Frost said sotto voce, "and we'll talk."

He had anticipated my desire to talk with him. He was indeed a prophet! "Where?" I asked.

"In the hall—in twenty minutes," Frost said. He smiled briefly, then dismissed me with a nod and turned to talk to another student who had been waiting for his attention.

In the hallway, I opened my notebook, checking to make sure I had brought some of my own verse and wondering if I really would have the courage to show it to this great man. I wanted his opinion, but I was scared.

As Frost walked out of the auditorium with a faculty member, he motioned to me to come with them. The two were deeply involved in conversation as I followed them down the hall. Then the professor indicated a room where the interview could take place and disappeared.

"Good to get away from crowds. They always scare me," Mr. Frost confided to me. He went directly to a window, forcing it open to let in the cool spring air.

The scene in that room nearly matched the most dramatic of Robert Frost's poems, I thought. The great poet and the teenage girl sat on two straight hard chairs, no table or desk between them. The room was barren except for us two and a delicate spray of yellow forsythia in a coffee jug on the windowsill. As I look back on old photographs of myself now, I can see that I was fragile and pretty and, with long dark hair, a contrast to the sturdy figure of the white-haired poet.

Through the open window came the vigorous voices of Air Corps boys singing as they marched to classes—and, eventually, to war.

While we waited for quiet, I noticed that Frost's large loose frame seemed to relax, now that his work was over. I could see the tension going out of him. But it was building up in me.

As soon as the singing had faded, I said simply, "Here are some of my poems." My voice sounded nervous, squeaky. I placed several typewritten pages in Frost's hand, gently, for the poems were my children, the product of painful hours of conception and labor.

He must have realized that creativity is more anguished for a teenager than at any other time of life, for his treatment of me was gentle, *very* gentle.

Frost read the top sheet silently, running his hand restlessly through that white thatch of hair as he read. I searched his face for a revealing glance and found nothing.

A bee buzzed around our heads slowly and headed out the window. Tension left the room with the bee. Then an incredible thing happened. Mr. Frost sat back and started reading aloud from my "Melancholy Walks," a long and tragic poem about the death of love.

I sat entranced, listening to Robert Frost reading my poem with a slow deliberation in that fabulous, famous voice of his.

Quite seriously, and without a trace of a smile, that dear man read such labored lines as

> When Phoebus reclaims the rays
> That illuminate the earth,
> The bleeding sky bewails
> The death of mortal mirth . . .

and on and on and on.

I was puzzled at first, then desolate. My overly dramatic, anguished lines stood bare in the light of Frost's reading. I hadn't fooled anybody by searching for "artistic" ways to say simple things, by using Roget's Thesaurus again and again to change plain words to long complicated ones. I was a phoney.

"It's not real—It doesn't ring true!" I burst out, pronouncing my own judgment.

My poem was an impressive nothing.

I sat and stared, too shocked to cry. Shivering, I clasped my arms around me, feeling naked. My own words had revealed me as a fake before Robert Frost.

Then I felt his arm was around my shoulder, warming me.

"We writers have to be honest with ourselves and with everybody else," he said.

"Read the good writers, the good poets. Then, have the courage to be new.

"You have known dark moments in your life, haven't you?" he

asked and went on, answering his own question. "And you are not afraid to write about them. That's good.

"But it's *how* you write that counts. You don't plan it. You let the emotion find the words. You start out and you let the poem take you. You believe it in."

He folded the typewritten pages carefully in their original creases and placed them in my hand with finality. "Do you have anything else?"

I dug down further into my large handbag and brought out battered clippings of some of my feature stories from Cincinnati and Covington (Ky.) daily newspapers. Some were about service men I had met as a hostess in the USO doughnut center, one about department store Santa Clauses, several about a trip out West I had made with other teenage girls.

As Frost read these, intently and with wrinkled brow, there was in that room a deeper quiet than I had ever known. And the suspense was greater, too.

"These are real," he pronounced, nodding. "They show originality—iniative—freshness."

Noting that writing for a newspaper is basic training we all need, he then provided the shocker: "What you *don't* need is to stick around this school.

"You'll be all right. You'll make it. You have two skills—writing and art—and versatility is important. If one skill goes out of fashion, or doesn't buy the bread, you have the other. Like poetry and farming."

I protested that I was a little too old to "run away from school," but he said I wouldn't be running *away* from something but *to* something—my future.

"Education is just hanging around until you catch on," he insisted. "There isn't much connection between what happens here and in real life. A writer has to season a little outside the ivy-covered walls."

His eyes twinkled ". . . but don't tell the college officials that I told you to quit. After all, they brought me here!"

This incident is an example of the sort of thing I believe Robert Frost meant when he so often called himself "bad."

Periodically, he felt chagrined after taking what he felt was too much responsibility upon himself in advising others about their lives. We know that he wrote with "troubled conscience" to at least one other student whom he had counseled to quit school and later was delighted to learn that the young man had achieved fulfilment and great success in life (*SP*, p. 117).

His dismay at his own "meddling" was far more tragic when his 38-year-old son, Carol, took his own life. Frost blamed himself and his own failure as a father.

In a letter to Louis Untermeyer, October 26, 1940, shortly after the tragedy, Frost wrote, "I took the wrong way with him. I tried many ways and every single one of them was wrong. Something in me is still asking for the chance to try one more. That's where the greatest pain is located.... Two weeks ago I was up at South Shaftsbury telling Carol how to live. Yesterday I was telling seven hundred Harvard freshmen how to live with books in college. Apparently nothing can stop us once we get going. I talk less and less however as if I knew what I was talking about" (Untermeyer, pp. 322–23).

In the four years that intervened between the time Frost wrote that letter and our meeting, he apparently recovered his own sense of worth and the belief that he could contribute to the life of another. His advice to me was in no uncertain terms.

Leave school, he had said. And leave school I did with the exuberence and blind self-confidence that can come to a novice in any field when he or she acts on the authority of the great.

It was a kind of twisted comfort to be able to blame Robert Frost in my own mind at times when things did not go well in the years that followed. Yet I knew that Frost had given me the advice in good faith. He had been a college dropout (from Harvard and Dartmouth) and ultimately had achieved all that any poet could dream of. He had given me his own success formula.

I told myself that I would have felt more secure with at least a bachelor's degree. But, looking back, who can say if I would have accomplished more?

It was not Robert Frost's fault that my concentration upon my career was diverted by a disastrous wartime marriage followed by rearing a son single-handedly. But forged into my unconscious was a certain buoyancy born of the comaraderie that Robert Frost and I had shared in our brief talk at U. C. He had treated me very much like an equal; "we writers" he had said. This, and the fact that he had assured me I could "make it," sustained me in adversity as much as the practical advice on writing that I received from him. He "believed me in."

I realized my debt to Frost only after many years of being angry with him. These were years of spending my "spare time" (while I was paying baby sitters) earning credits at the University of Michigan, the State University of New York at Buffalo, the Cincinnati Art Academy, and Northern Kentucky University as I moved about the country working at various writing jobs.

The last year of my studies was more difficult than all the others. Suffering a severe back injury, I attended classes at Northern Kentucky University for several months with the use of a walker, then with a platform cane. In the summer of 1976, with the aid of my cane, I took my place in a long line of other students in cap and gown and received my bachelor's degree (in art) from NKU President A. D. Albright. In that moment I forgave Robert Frost.

That night, I lay awake reflecting on my life and in particular the influence of Robert Frost upon it.

In the thirty-two years since my talk with Frost, I had been successful at newspaper and public relations work and as a freelance writer—and also had begun to build a reputation as an artist and photographer. I had reared a son who was a fine editor and professional photographer—a good man with the kind of courage that Robert Frost admired. I was a community leader. I had won several national honors. And all this was documented in the *Dictionary of International Biography* and *Who's Who of American Women*.

It all had been done the hard way. Would I have learned less, been a different kind of person, if I had not followed Robert Frost's advice—if I had not experienced "trial by existence" and "trial by market" (Thompson, III, 46) in much the same way that Robert Frost had in his own life? [5] Was this all part of what I was supposed to learn in "taking the road less travelled by"?

It was a question that had been festering inside of me for a long time.

When Frost died (1963), I felt compelled to sort out my thoughts about him and did it in the usual way of a writer—by writing. The Buffalo (N.Y.) *Courier-Express* published my brief account of my meeting with Frost.

Following publication of this article, I began hearing from others who had known Frost, including Howard G. Schmitt, a wholesale grocer of Hamburg, New York. In its Sunday magazine, the *Courier-Express* published my article on Frost's friendship with Schmitt and his young daughter. It was the story of a quiet man with few interests other than Frost. His whole life revolved around his collection of some three hundred Frost items—autographed books, photographs, handwritten letters and poems, and even a brilliantly colored patchwork quilt made by Schmitt's three aunts from twenty-eight hoods presented to Frost when he received honorary degrees from universities in the United States and abroad. An identical quilt from the same hoods was presented to Frost.

At Chautauqua, N. Y., that spring, I met the poet and critic John Ciardi on tour. He was then director of Bread Loaf Writers' Conference at Middlebury, Vermont, and urged me to enroll.

In August, I did go to Bread Loaf. I was happy to be in Frost Country even though Ciardi had forgotten me by then and few were eager to talk about Robert Frost. It was just a few months after Frost's death, and his loss was not easily accepted at Bread Loaf where he had been the guiding spirit. I consoled myself with a visit to Middlebury College where a kind librarian allowed me to make photocopies of some of the library's choicest original, handwritten Frost letters.

Most of the students at Bread Loaf that summer were promising beginners; I was one of the few published writers among them. But it was not boring.

The star attraction was Nelson Algren, author of *The Man with the Golden Arm*. Algren provided the most earthy advice I got that summer. At the end of his session, I wrote in my notebook: "Do not write prostitute. Write whore." I wondered how Frost would have felt about this. He believed that

> Earth's the right place for love:
> I don't know where it's likely to go better (p. 122).

But, as Radcliffe Squires pointed out: "Frost always looks the other way when nature is breeding."[6] He defends Frost's poetry on its "legality of language, its relevance to life, and above all its truth and honor of concept—the philosophic muse that speaks in the center of his poetry, giving, in the final analysis, intensity and endurance. . . . His poetry has carried the day, just as it will carry the centuries."

Squires is one who feels quite strongly that Frost hid his personality in his poems and that the poet's "worldly face" was seldom cast aside. "That is why I must distrust most of the anecdotal 'biographies' of Frost," writes Squires. "They are true lies."

True lies? What was the truth?

The question was to haunt me for the next ten years after Bread Loaf. I thought about it often, at odd moments when I was not earning a living or going to school or attending to family obligations.

The true character of Frost—and his impact upon the lives of us all—was something that fired my imagination. Was Frost's "lovers quarrel with the world" one-sided? How did the world feel about him? . . . his life? . . . his work?

My son and I packed notebooks, tape recorders and cameras and went in search of answers.

Eighty miles away, in Lexington, Kentucky, we talked with Thomas B. Stroup and William S. Ward. Both friends of Frost, they shared their memories with us in separate interviews high in Patterson Tower at the University of Kentucky, where each has the title Professor of English Emeritus.

Said Dr. Stroup: "I met Frost in perhaps the most difficult time of his life. It was at the University of Florida in Gainesville where I was on the faculty. He was supposed to be doing some lecturing but, when his wife died in 1938, it changed everything for him. He couldn't do anything; he was crushed. A couple of years later, his son committed suicide, followed by his daughter Irma's being placed in a mental institution.

"Read his poem 'Come In,' written about that time and you'll understand him better. He refuses suicide in that poem; it expresses the utter despair he reached.

"Lawrance Thompson in *The Years of Triumph*, claims that Lesley said Frost was impossible to live with and gave the feeling that he had treated his family miserably. I don't give much credence to that. The odd thing to me is that Frost designated Thompson as his official biographer, but that was done long ago.

"There is much talk, too, about Mr. Frost's ego. In his later years, he developed an old man's pride in what he had accomplished and reveled in the adulation people had for him.

"I don't know that there's anything wrong with that. The students loved him always. They sat around him on the floor, as you know, and he would pontificate and enjoy himself immensely. The adulation that he brought was charming—enjoyable.

"About 1948, we brought him to U. K. to lecture and he stayed at my house then and many times afterwards. Before a lecture he would have no dinner; he was busy marking his book. He never prepared notes.

"He was devoted to my wife. After a lecture, he would come home with us and would say, 'Anna Mary, will you get me a glass of milk?' And she would say, 'Surely you want something else.' And he'd say, 'Can you find me a cold boiled potato?'

"He could be made angry by people, you know. And he could tell people off—but *only* those whom he loved. People who took exception to this didn't understand him or his sense of humor.

"Although Shakespeare still is the most popular in U. K. classes, students enjoy Frost because he is easier to get into. And you can remember Frost's quotes. His poetry calls upon you for a great deal if you let it. You are stimulated and you reach back for what he has to state.

"My favorites of Frost are 'Come In,' 'The Death of the Hired Man,' 'After Apple-Picking,' and the masques. I don't go along with them necessarily, but he is getting into some extremely important things. Job faces the issue; this is affirmation.

"For Frost to have been invited to speak at the Kennedy inaugu-

ration—for him to have been in the 'Kennedy camp'—was particularly interesting because, politically, he was not the liberal that the
Kennedys were thought to be. But Frost appreciated Kennedy, a
political figure who had gumption enough to recognize him. Courage is a dominant theme running throughout Frost's poetry. It's a
theme everybody can understand. And it's one of the reasons Frost
is the most influential American poet at the present time."

Professor Ward had this to say:

"At least three times during my thirteen years as chairman of the
English Department here, we had Robert Frost at the University
of Kentucky. He stayed at my house on one of these occasions and
was a wonderful guest. There are stories that he could be a nasty
old man, and that's possible. But I saw nothing of this sort while he
was here save on one occasion. This was very shortly after a lecture
began and a lady for reasons unknown to me arose from near the
front of a large auditorium and made her way to the exit. When she
started her long trek, Mr. Frost stopped his reading and followed
her with his eyes until she disappeared through the door through
which she had entered. But this was the one exception.

"In general, he was kindly and considerate, and loved chatting
with my two daughters and with the students who came to talk with
him informally in McVey Hall where, everyday he was here, we
would 'hold court' for all who wished to come to Room 205. Whether it was a roomful or one person, he could chat.

"But on the day of a lecture he didn't want to see anybody or do
any talking after the noon hour. He would go to his room and remain there till about 5:30, at which time he would ask for a cup of
strong tea and sugar—lots of sugar—and a one-minute egg. After
that, he would take a walk, declining to see anybody until time to
go to the lecture.

"On his way to the lecture, he would be tense, and his mouth
would crackle as he spoke. The dryness was usual before a lecture,
he said, and was due, he thought, to the fact that each lecture (or
reading) was a creative performance rather than a prepared speech
or a certain set order of poems to be read. He used no notes—only a
copy of his 'complete' poems; and until he had been on stage a few
minutes, he would not know whether the performance would go

right or not. Once he was settled in and the tone set, however, the tenseness quickly left him.

"We felt it was important for each generation of students to be exposed to Frost because, by this time, he not only was recognized as a good poet but he had become a highly esteemed representative of poetry, a good salesman for poetry—poetry for people who might otherwise not to be exposed to it. Whatever disapproving sense of poetry they might harbor, they were disarmed by liking Mr. Frost. And he had drawing power. Many came because he was a celebrity, not because they liked poetry, but they often left liking it. He neutralized the indifference to poetry."

We interviewed famed ballad singer John Jacob Niles[7] at his rugged Boot Hill Farm on a bend of Boone's Creek, Clark County, Kentucky. Mr. Niles was eighty-two and "tired of reporters and photographers" but he agreed to talk to us about Robert Frost.

"I met Frost at Bread Loaf when we both were appearing there," said Niles. "It was one summer in the early sixties. I remember how the females hounded him. One time he grabbed me as I was going by and pleaded: 'Please, for heaven's sake, sit here by me. Look like you're taking notes. I'm tired of these females who keep asking me where I get the idea for a poem.'

"Robert Frost was fed up when I knew him. And he seemed worn to a frazzle. Maybe he didn't feel well. I thought: Why can't this nice guy go back to the woods—wherever he lives—and whittle a stick or fish or talk to his family and quit this rat race? But he didn't. He may have had to make money—and he loved being in the public eye, just as I do.

"Frost is an example of a man who could not be defeated—the American ideal—though he had plenty of trouble in his own life. He had a difficult childhood. Then there were long years of his life when he was snubbed. Professional recognition didn't come until he was near forty. He had children who died young, a son who shot himself, a sister and a daughter in mental institutions, and finally the death of both an adult daughter and his own wife. He had a lot of illnesses of his own too. But he kept on going.

"Frost knew the earth, worked with the earth, literally worshipped the earth. He seemed to understand that the earth produces a kind of thinking that is near nirvana."

Before we left, Johnny Niles and his beautiful Russian-born wife Rena gave us some corn and tomatoes, grown of their own love of the earth. We ate the Niles's tomatoes up the road a piece. It was a hot day and they were juicy, rich, and refreshing.

Good farmer you picked for a friend, I said silently to Robert Frost. Enjoyed meeting him. Thank you.

There were to be many other occasions to bless Robert Frost for new friends we made in pursuit of the dream. We found a common bond of awareness—sensitivity—in those who had known Frost or who knew him only from his poetry.

Usually those in the latter category enjoyed finding fragments of Frost's life hidden within his poems. Knowing about his years of sorrow and frustration, they found, as I did, some sense of rapport with the poet whose life has been described as Jobian.

One who recognized that Frost used his own acquaintance with the night as a starting point, building his philosophy from there, was Celeste Madeleine Colatrella, age seventeen.

Following the advice of Celeste's high school English teacher, I contacted the young girl at her home—just five miles down the Dixie Highway in the little village of Edgewood, Kentucky—and found her eager to talk about Robert Frost.

Celeste and I sat in her mother's bright kitchen having tea while she told me calmly that her experience with Frost's poem "Home Burial" had helped her prepare for and accept the death of her brother Ralph, fifteen, who had died of a brain tumor just one month before our interview.

"I tried to find a poem I could identify with to learn for a speech contest," Celeste explained. " 'Home Burial' was that poem. I knew that Ralph was going to die very soon and the poem really hit me.

"Frost's 'Home Burial' depicts misunderstandings which can cause rifts between those who love. It taught me the consequences of a lack of communication and I learned that there is more than one way to accept death.

"Amy, the wife in the poem, stands on the stairs looking out a window onto the family graves. In her own grief, she is blind to her husband's feelings. All the way through the poem she wants to run away, to get her hat and run out the door.

"This taught me to prepare myself—that running away is not the right answer. You have to stand there and face problems. I guess Mr. Frost knew this because of all the troubles in his own life.

"I could sit around here wearing black, but we have to go on with life. That was the husband's philosophy in the poem and I have tried to develop that attitude.

"Even to write about death so vividly takes a very strong person like Frost, don't you think?"

I didn't answer immediately. I was too busy thinking that strength was no stranger to Celeste Colatrella—the slight girl who, I am told, comforted the mourners at her brother's funeral, then gave the valedictory address for her graduating class only two weeks afterwards.

Only a few months later I was glad to hear that Celeste had acknowledged the strength in herself and was expressing her affirmation of life in the best possible way. She had begun studies (under a scholarship at Thomas More College) that will make her a medical doctor about the year 1984.

John A. Ruthven, the famed wildlife artist, told us of the influence of Frost's "The Road Not Taken" on his life.

We talked with Ruthven in his home studio on his 165-acre farm and wildlife sanctuary in Georgetown, Ohio. It was easy to imagine that Ruthven and Frost would have been friends if they had met in Frost's lifetime—both intensely masculine, handsome men—both with a rare sense of humor and a passion for independence, coupled with a love for God's creatures.

Sitting at his "painting desk," Ruthven talked in an easygoing manner, occasionally emphasizing an important point with the staccato sound of the blunt end of his pencil.

"Every blade of grass or tiny feather is important to the design of a painting, just as life is made up of influences that happen along the way," he said.

"And some of them are major influences, as Frost's poem 'The

Road Not Taken' has been for me. I read the poem early in my life. And I thought about it and felt it deeply. It inspired me when I needed it most.

"It's a *daring* poem, a very American poem. America offers freedom to be yourself and to work for yourself, the greatest experience I can imagine, and one I appreciate even more now, having spent some time in the Soviet Union where people can't even realize what freedom is.

"But even some Americans tend to follow the leader in every aspect of their daily lives. If they would take the road 'less travelled by' that would make 'all the difference,' as the poem says.

"I believe what Frost means is: stand up and be counted as an individual; seek a different way.

"Most of the great people in the world—the ones who have been able to create beautiful things—have taken the unbeaten path, not for the sake of being different but because that's where you find more opportunity, more inspiration.

"Even being an artist was a radical thing for me to do; there were no artists in our family. I was a city child—a Depression child—who didn't even realize that a person could make a living painting birds and animals. I needed somebody like Robert Frost to tell me about the natural world, the meaningful things, and give me guideposts for living."

One of our most significant interviews was with Professor Walter Havighurst.[8] He was on the Miami University faculty for nearly forty years before he retired in 1969, and still has an office on the Oxford, Ohio, campus.

Professor Havighurst and his late wife met Frost at their vacation home near Ripton, Vermont, and continued the friendship when Frost came to Miami University to lecture. We heard more about Frost and his famous love for raw eggs, his delight in talking with the common men he saw in walking about campus and town, and his recurring visits with people like an Oxford shoemaker who had come from Lithuania, reared a family in the back of his shop, put two children through college, then bought a farm where Frost visited him whenever he could, calling him "an American dream being lived and fulfilled."

But it was Professor Havighurst's discussion of the poetry that was most revealing of Frost, the man:

"Frost's poetry contains the essence of the man—both simple and profound. His subject was the world that is so familiar and that no one can ever understand.

"In many of his poems, one can find the soul-and-body scars that living cost him. Yet only a few—'I Could Give All to Time,' 'Two Look at Two,' 'Love and a Question,' 'Happiness Makes Up in Height for What It Lacks in Length'—were so personal that he declined to read them on the platform.

"He was the great maker of metaphor—or, as he would have preferred, the *finder* of metaphor—writing so simply that none could miss his meaning, though few could find it all.

" 'Stopping by Woods' contains only two words of more than two syllables, *promises* and *evening*. Simplest of all vocabularies, but there is no end to what is implied by that darkness, that road, those promises.

"In Frost's 'Cabin in the Clearing,' the clearing is a little area of human order that man has made at much expense in the universe, the penetration of nature by human thought and effort.

"From solar energy to basal metabolism, to the mind's own reaching, said Frost, it is all expenditure. Life is a giving out.

"Hemingway saw the measure of character in one's ability to die well. *Frost said that to live wholly in this world takes brains and bravery and belief.*"

That simple statement of Professor Havighurst summed up what Robert Lee Frost—and his poetry—are all about.

It nullified all those "true lies" of some of the recent controversial biographies containing interpretations of those who could not understand a man who often spoke tongue-in-cheek and declared "I'm never serious except when I'm fooling," who was so honest that he readily admitted to behind-the-scenes maneuvering and did not know he would be judged for it, who cared desperately about the opinion of his fellow man but far more about how God would receive his poems and whether "my best offering would not prove acceptable in His sight" (Thompson, III, 401).

Truly, only the Secret who sits in the middle knows the real Frost. The nearest we can come to resolving the question is by examining his work. In doing so, we are taking a clue from him. "I don't like to read about a man. . . . I'd rather read the man himself" (*SP*, p. 9).

To many readers, Frost and nature are synonymous. He has come to be associated with symbols such as stars, trees, snow, brooks, horses, cows, butterflies. These are the symbols that make his poems shimmer with beauty. His words are simple and stark. Even an untutored person can understand them and most likely agree with them, saying, "Ah, yes, that's true. I have felt that way myself."

Looking a little deeper, we find an amazing variety of ideas and themes in Frost. There is wisdom for survival in his words, the searching wonder of a child combined with the knowledge of a scientist, the most awful puns and thorned humor yet the deepest tragedy accepted with dignity and the least amount of wailing at the wall.

There are some who declare Frost to be a poet of darkness. And certainly there was a dark part of his life that shows in his work if you know where to look. But the closest he ever came to self pity in print was a little gem called "Lodged."

> The rain to the wind said,
> "You push and I'll pelt."
> They so smote the garden bed
> That the flowers actually knelt,
> And lay lodged—though not dead.
> I know how the flowers felt (p. 250).

Throughout Frost's poetry there is an affirmation of life, though it's not often said in those words. His people carry on because it is their sacred duty to endure. Perhaps it is most clearly seen in the last poem of *In the Clearing*.

> In winter in the woods alone
> Against the trees I go.
> I mark a maple for my own
> And lay the maple low.

At four o'clock I shoulder ax,
And in the afterglow
I link a line of shadowy tracks
Across the tinted snow.

I see for Nature no defeat
In one tree's overthrow
Or for myself in my retreat
For yet another blow (p. 470).

Frost's brand of courage can be a strong force for unity in a badly fragmented land. Whether we find it in his life or in his verse, it is ours to use.

Robert Frost looked squarely into our future when wrote "Take Something Like a Star." The poem closes with these lines:

It asks a little of us here.
It asks of us a certain height,
So when at times a mob is swayed
To carry praise or blame too far,
We may take something like a star
To stay our minds on and be staid (p. 403).

Notes to *Per Ardua ad Astra* by LUELLA NASH LEVEE

1. Quoted in the *Christian Science Monitor*, January 30, 1963. A similar remark was in a letter of June 18, 1959 to Lionel Trilling (just after the famous talk in which Trilling termed some elements in Frost's poetry "terrifying"). See *SL*, p. 583.

2. Associated Press account in Buffalo *Courier-Express*, September 9, 1962.

3. A vivid account of the Russian experience is given by Franklin D. Reeve (who accompanied Frost on his journey) in *Robert Frost in Russia* (Boston: Little Brown, 1964). The significance of Frost's trip is explored in Jac L. Tharpe, "Afterword: Frost as Representative of the Eidolons," in *Frost: Centennial Essays*, ed. Jac L. Tharpe (Jackson: University Press of Mississippi, [1974]), pp. 596–606.

4. New York *Times*, October 27, 1963, p. 87.

5. Frost expressed himself to his good friend John Bartlett about his theory that hardship developed character in young people. "My best wish," he said, is "that in success they wouldn't be too excited by it, or in failure too crushed. Young people should have a long life . . . and full of trouble. You can't have life without trouble." Margaret Bartlett Anderson, *Robert Frost and John Bartlett: The Record of a Friendship* (New York: Holt, Rinehart and Winston, 1963), p. 178. The following quotation in the text is from "The Road Not Taken."

6. *The Major Themes of Robert Frost* (Ann Arbor: University of Michigan Press, 1963), p. 14. The next quotation is from the unpaged preface, the next from p. 19.

7. Celebrated for his compositions "Black Is the Color of My True Love's Hair,"

"Go 'Way from My Window," and "I Wonder as I Wander." Also famed for books of ballads he has collected since boyhood in the Appalachians and for concerts he has performed, accompanying himself on the dulcimer, in the United States and abroad.

8. Perhaps the best known of Walter Havighurst's books are *The Long Ships Passing, Voices on the River, Signature of Time*, and *The Heartland*.

The Robert Frost I Knew

VICTOR E. REICHERT

W̲ʜᴇɴ January 29, 1977 rolls around, it will be fourteen years since Robert Frost, at the age of eighty-eight, breathed his last. He died, still creating poetry, at the Peter Bent Brigham Hospital, where he had gone with raging reluctance. He thus died in Boston, Massachusetts, at the other end of the continent from San Francisco, California where he was born on March 26, 1874.

Had Frost lived on to March 26, 1963, he would have been eighty-nine. That is an impressive number for most of us. But Robert Frost was aiming at one hundred. He wanted his life to span half of our country's history.

You might have thought that Frost would have shown signs of earthly weariness as he neared his eighty-ninth birthday in the Peter Bent Brigham Hospital in Boston. But there are those who were at his bedside who can vouch for the amazing vitality of the man. Louis Untermeyer is one. And Anne Morrison Gentry, daughter of Kathleen and Ted Morrison is another. Anne too was at his bedside in those last days.

She has told me that Frost was composing a poem based on the Book of Daniel in the Bible. Some of that poem he had dictated to Anne. The third and final volume of Larry Thompson's official biography of Robert Frost is not yet out as I write this piece. This last volume, scheduled to appear late in 1976 or early in 1977, will bear the name of Roy Winnick as well as Lawrance Thompson, who died before he could complete his work. Roy Winnick was a Princeton graduate student of Thompson's. It will be interesting to students of Frost's literary achievements to see if the poem he was composing on what was to prove to be his deathbed appears in this final volume. I hope so because it will provide evidence of Frost's tenacious hold on life and of his invincible creative thrust. (The Thompson-Winnick volume *Robert Frost: The Later Years 1938–*

105

1963 reached me in late February 1977. On page 442, in note 21 Anne has some rough notes that include this:

king says to prophet youre a real prophet
a wonder, what's your name?
he says my name is Daniel, call me Dan.
I am the author of the famous letters
from Dan to Beersheba)

There is danger, so I have been warned and even admonished, that the portrait I will offer of the Robert Frost I knew will be so prettified in sweetness and light as to be glamorized far from recognition by others, still alive, who also knew Robert Frost as a living person. One of my severest critics said to me: "When you write this essay for Professor Jac Tharpe of the University of Southern Mississippi, don't rely only on your memory. You know that memory often plays the best of us tricks. With your great love for Robert Frost, you are apt, without being aware of it, to paint such a rosy picture of the poet that the real man will be lost in all your embellishing colors. So what you should do is look through your books and diaries and see if you do not find things jotted down, at the time they actually happened. If you do this you may escape the danger of going overboard in excessive praise."

I remember telling this adviser of how to proceed with this assignment, something to this effect: "You see, Jonathan," I said, "from the very beginning of my friendship with Robert Frost, which goes back to the fall of 1938 when Frost came to Cincinnati to give a talk and 'say' his poems before a group called Talaria and the Ohio Valley Poetry Society—from the start of our first meeting, I resolved never to exploit this friendship. I never took notes of what he said. I never jotted down confidences of his personal life that he let me share."

"This may be true," said Jonathan. "Yet," he persisted, "I'll bet if you make a search, you will find you did in fact, on occasion, write down things at the time they happened that will give rock bottom reality to the warm robe in which you now wrap your Frostian memories."

I decided to take Jonathan's good advice. And do you know, as luck would have it, the first random National Diary I opened did in fact have an entry that I had completely forgotten.

> Memorable evening with Robert Frost. I called for Robert at the Homer Noble Farm, in his snug Cabin back of the Farmhouse. First knocked in there and found Ted Morrison, his brother, and Stafford Dragon sitting about the fire-place. I have contracted with Stafford Dragon for a full cord of wood for next August . . .
>
> Robert was just dressing. "Where are we going?" he asked.
>
> "Waybury Inn."
>
> He had a hard time with matching pants and coat. I sat in quiet while he dressed.
>
> One of his schnauzers (Kathleen Morrison corrected me when I read her this page. She said it was *her* schnauzer)—I guess Mark— climbed up and licked my hand in friendship. Down to the School-house for a rum drink. Louise in her deep maroon dress waiting for us.
>
> A grand evening—delightful supper of Roast Duckling at Waybury and wonderful talk—we mostly listening.
>
> At one point, speaking of how he'd been slighted, Frost said to me: "You know, you haven't been a Jew for nothing."
>
> Robert told us he was to receive a Gold Medal from Congress— probably from the President himself!

Strange that making this entry of Sunday, 4 September 1960 should have completely vanished from my mind. And yet, stumbling upon it in this random way only encouraged me to keep rummaging further in my disordered study.

The Sunday, 4 September 1960 diary entry throws light on several important things about the character of Frost.

There is no doubt that Robert Frost had experienced in his own life many slights and rebuffs. He was highly sensitive, as perhaps most of us are, to disparagement and criticism. Those early years, before I knew him, had been filled with hardship and difficulty. Not until Frost had reached thirty-eight was his first public book, *A Boy's Will*, published in England.

When he gave his college readings and talks, he needed and usual-ly received the rapt attention of his audience. But he could be ter-ribly upset when this didn't happen. Brendan Gill, in *Here at The New Yorker*, speaks of one such occasion at Yale University.

I remember another time—it must have been in 1954 when the

University of Cincinnati conferred an honorary LL. D. upon Frost, that a distinguished professor of philosophy who shall be nameless sitting up in front, perhaps to hear better, suddenly got up and walked out of the auditorium. You must bear in mind that Frost went through agonizing, solitary preparation before every public appearance. In this instance, when the philosopher abruptly left the hall, Robert Frost was visibly upset and later spoke to me of the incident. Perhaps the professor actually meant to insult the poet by deliberately walking out on him. They were miles apart in their philosophy. But it is also possible that the professor was only responding to the call of nature.

Hewette Joyce has told me of the time that Frost came to the Joyce home in Dartmouth and brought with him the still unpublished manuscript of *A Masque of Mercy*. He was going to read it to the Joyce family and some friends. Professor Joyce's daughter, sitting opposite the poet, had started knitting as he was about to begin, when she had the presence of mind to ask:

"Does this bother you, Mr. Frost?"

"Yes, it does. Any motion in front of me like that bothers me."

She put her knitting back in the bag.

The Joyces knew they were highly privileged to have Robert Frost, The George Ticknor Fellow in the Humanities, in their home giving a private reading of *A Masque of Mercy*.

"We knew that we had heard something great in a way all its own."

One of the slights that perhaps, as Frost grew more famous, amused more than annoyed him was to have some captain of industry say condescendingly to him after an introduction:

"Oh, you're the poet, Robert Frost. My wife reads your stuff."

The Sunday, 4 September 1960 diary entry lit up for me another side of Robert Frost's soul, where, after speaking of how he had been slighted, he said to me:

"You know, you haven't been a Jew for nothing."

Actually, as I think back through the years, especially my years as rabbi, I find it hard to remember personal slights because of being a Jew.

But of course my personal fate should not blind me to the tragic fate of my people. And Frost, intuitively, was thinking of the long martyrdom of the Jewish people when he said to me:

"You know, you haven't been a Jew for nothing."

Perhaps he was remembering those powerful words of Mark Twain:

"The Jew has made a marvelous fight in the world, in all ages; and has done it with his hands tied behind him."

Mark Twain wrote that in 1898 when the Zionist Movement was in its infancy and Herzl seemed a quixotic dreamer.

But it is to Robert Frost, with his large grasp of history, that I owe much of my present appreciation of the immense importance of the fact of Israel in the fight for Jewish survival.

Frost, like Longfellow and Emerson, had a warm feeling for the Jewish faith and the Jewish people. Frost loved the Old Testament. The Hebraic prophetic teaching is omnipresent in his poetry and prose. The two great *Masques—Reason* and *Mercy*—rest solidly upon Job and Jonah in the Hebrew Bible, and the Sermon on the Mount in the Gospels.

Frost was pleased to speak in the old Jewish cemetery in Newport and to recall George Washington's words "to bigotry no sanction, to persecution no assistance." He gladly went to Jerusalem to speak at the Hebrew University. He numbered Jews among his close friends—like Louis Untermeyer and Joe Blumenthal.

On more than one occasion, he spoke of his friend, the Cincinnati rabbi who summered in Ripton and who preached and taught in the little white-framed United Methodist Church. He thought of it as an act of magnanimity. Perhaps that is an added awareness of what he meant when he said:

"You know, you haven't been a Jew for nothing."

In the spring of 1960, the Hebrew Union College—Jewish Institute of Religion was honored to bestow upon Frost the degree of L. H. D.—Doctor of Humane Letters, honoris causa. Samuel Sandmel, then provost of the seminary, asked me to sound out Frost about accepting the degree and to arrange for the date of the ceremony. With Frost's heavy speaking schedule, there were some rearrangements to be made. But we managed it, and Frost finally came. Nelson Glueck, famed archaeologist, president of our Hebrew Union College, bestowed the degree, saying of the beloved American poet that he was a "true interpreter of the soul of America whose sensitive portrait of life's vast mystery and of man's efforts to comprehend it is in the highest tradition of our prophets and of our rabbis."

Robert Frost's last stop before coming to Cincinnati early in April 1960 to receive the degree of Doctor of Humane Letters was at Delaware, Ohio, the Ohio Wesleyan University. I took my sons, David and Jonathan, with me to bring him to our home where he was to be our house guest.

It was at two o'clock in the morning, one of those days of his visit, that Robert astonished me by tearing out of his ledgerlike note book a page of the original manuscript of the poem "Pod of the Milk Weed." He signed it over to me. "Pod of the Milk Weed," two years later, appeared as the lead poem in Frost's last book, *In the Clearing*. I tried to match that gift with a rare book of Psalms, in Hebrew, on vellum that dated from 1520.

But it was the night that Robert came to The Literary Club and the way he began his talk at the HUC Chapel—these two things, that I wish to recall here.

Let's take the second first.

On his way down from Delaware, Ohio, Frost had carried on a vigorous dialogue with Jonathan. They enjoyed crossing swords about science. David, always more reserved, was content to listen. Frost was enormously interested in David's experiences in the army and of the rigors of camp life. But Jonathan, more verbally outgoing with Frost, was defending science against some of the sarcastic sallies that Frost made against its claims to answer all the questions. The dialogue had come to an inconclusive end when we reached our Red Bud home.

But imagine Jonathan's surprise, when at the convocation called to confer the honorary L. H. D. on Frost at the Hebrew Union College in Clifton, Frost at the outset of the talk that followed his hooding, with only Jonathan, in all that great assembly that packed the chapel and overflowed into several other buildings of the College campus—only Jonathan aware of what Frost was saying, as he took up the theme they had been considering before arrival at our home the day before.

"I want to speak about the king," said Frost. "The king is the one I am speaking of. Who thinks he's above the ruler? I have to remind the young scientists I know that they are not to think that they are greater than the ruler of this country. Poetry is posted on the brink of spiritual disaster. One of the dangers of our time is that science shall think that it can do what it pleases with the future of the world. But it can't! It doesn't have to worry about itself. It will be taken care of by the king. The same as everything else."

This matter of keeping something in his mind, of turning over and playing with an idea, the way you might turn a diamond or a star sapphire to see how the light danced from it—this was characteristic of Robert Frost.

He liked to alert you to the difference between a happening and an occurrence. Happenings from the outside come to us all. But few have the intellectual tenacity to hold on to something that happens to us and make of it an occurrence—to entertain a notion to discover whether any truth or substance is in it worth welcoming into our minds and hearts.

That day at the Hebrew Union College, with the chapel filled to capacity and loudspeakers rigged up in numerous class rooms and the gymnasium so that the large overflow might hear President Nelson Glueck's citation and Robert Frost's talk, the powerful snow-haired poet with clear resonant voice convulsed the receptive audience by saying again the naughty couplet asking the Lord's forgiveness for Frost's little jokes on Him with the promise that if He would forgive, then, said Frost, "I'll forgive Thy great big one on me" (p. 428).

I had heard the audience at Ohio Wesleyan explode with laughter on hearing this. The same thing happened in Cincinnati. What was it about this daring mischievousness that provoked such spontaneous mirth? In the long literary, prophetic tradition of the Jewish people, there have been bold challengers of the Lord. The patriarch Abraham does not hesitate to challenge the Divine:

"Shall not the Judge of all the earth do justly?" The prophet Jeremiah dares to challenge the Lord about the prosperity of the wicked: "Wherefore," says Jeremiah, "does the way of the wicked prosper?"

And that perfect man in the land of Uz whose name was Job, ravaged by incurable disease and despoiled by catastrophic loss, flings this bitter word at Heaven:

> Wilt Thou harass a driven leaf?
> And wilt Thou pursue the dry stubble?

The Talmud knows of one of God's pets, Honi, the Circle Drawer, who, like an indulged and spoiled grandchild, tells the Lord that he will not stir from the circle he has drawn on the ground about himself, until he gets the right kind of rain from the heavens, neither too violent nor too gentle and inadequate to stay the drought.

We have a tradition that can tolerate bold familiarity with the Holy One, Blessed be He. And perhaps Americans of all denominations or none have learned to take sauciness about the sacred, remembering Mark Twain's immortal *Adventures of Huckleberry Finn*.

Yet, whatever it is, Robert Frost knew he was naughty that Sabbath afternoon, and the audience seemed to enjoy his now celebrated couplet. It is possible that some of the gossip, untrue, that Frost was an atheist, derived from this kind of Frost's Yankee humor. The two masques are full of such fun. At all events, it was during Frost's stay in Cincinnati that week early in April 1960 that I felt moved to write the following fantasy. You will find it in my *Tower of David*—1964—Vermont Books, Middlebury, Vermont.

A FANTASY

ROBERT FROST AND KING SOLOMON MATCH WITS BEFORE GOD

Robert Frost Speaks First:
  Forgive, O Lord, my little jokes on Thee
  And I'll forgive Thy great big one on me.
King Solomon:
  I did most my sinning when I was young and gay
  That I might live saintly now I am old and grey.
The Lord, on high, laughs in thunder, and then, in gentle reprimand, speaks in a still, small voice:
  Holy Smoke, dear Robert, I forgive and glad you do,
  But I was bored with angels, and I had no choice but you.

And as for reformed sinners, you naughty Solomon,
Tell it not in Gath, but remember I am one!

And now for the second remembrance of Frost's visit to Cincinnati in the early days of April 1960.

On the Monday night following the Sabbath afternoon bestowal of the L. H. D., Walter Beckjord telephoned me to ask if Robert Frost would accept his invitation to have supper at the Bankers Club and then we would adjourn to The Literary Club, our beautiful home at 500 East Fourth Street, for the literary exercises and the feast of food and drink and friendship that always followed.

Our historic Guest Book at The Literary Club preserves this record of Robert Frost's visit. It reads:

4/4/60
I never dared be radical when young
For fear it would make me conservative when old (p. 308).

Frost wrote those two lines into our Guest Book of The Literary Club and then signed *Robert Frost*.

He was given an ovation that night by the members. And though I felt that he went at first out of friendship for me, he enjoyed the warmth of the reception he received. It pleased him to write in our historic Guest Book. Long before, one of his great admirations, Ralph Waldo Emerson, had visited our Literary Club.

Louis Untermeyer, in his *Makers of the Modern World*, tells us in his essay on Frost, that there were detractors of the poet who deplored this teasing jibe about never daring to be radical when young for fear it would make him conservative when old. To my knowledge, none of these could be numbered in The Literary Club. They looked upon Robert Frost with the highest regard and knew that his place, despite all the calumniators who might arise, would always be a niche of triumph in America's Literary Hall of Fame.

At one point at Walter Beckjord's party for Frost at the Banker's Club before The Literary Club meeting, as I now clearly remember through the mist of seventeen years, Robert said:

"The other night I got to thinking about my friend Rabbi Victor Reichert and how he differed from Saint Jerome. So you know how I am. I could not sleep, wondering. So I got up and checked with my books. Then I saw I was right. I went back to bed and fell asleep easily, having satisfied my curiosity.

"This is the way it is. Saint Jerome studied the Old Testament to show how much you need the New. But Rabbi Victor Reichert studies the Old Testament to show how easily you can get along without the New."

I nearly fell off my seat. But I have never forgotten how he startled me that night.

Frost liked to call himself an Old Testament Christian.

The poet Daniel Smythe, in his book *Robert Frost Speaks*, in part corroborates what I have just described happened in Cincinnati, April 4, 1960 at the Bankers Club. Dr. Smythe had gone to visit Robert, taking along his wife, Ruth. This was at the Homer Noble Farm in Ripton. It was the month of July 1959. They were talking about prejudice.

"Did I ever tell you," said Frost to Smythe, "about the 'summer Methodist' we have near here? He is a rabbi, and he comes from Cincinnati, and he preaches in the Methodist church. After listening to one of his sermons, a lady said to me, 'Just what is the difference between him and us?' She was baffled. This rabbi is an interesting man who has a habit of dropping in on me once in a while and discussing religious matters. He knows the New Testament as well as he knows the Old, and he maintains that all the material in the New can be found in the Old. He has intimated that it is foolish and futile for two religions to have differences, since they study the same book.

"Once I preached in a synagogue. I didn't know what I was going to talk about until I was introduced. As I was waiting in my chair, I thumbed through the Jewish Bible and I noted these words, 'You don't say to God, What do you think You are doing?'" [Actually, Frost saw in our Union Prayer Book that festival morning these words: "Thou art our God in this life, and Thou art our hope and refuge in the life to come. Creator of heaven and earth, of the sea and all that is therein, Thine alone is the power in the heaven above and on the earth below, and none can say unto Thee: What doest Thou?" The words, "You don't say to God, What do you think You are doing?" are Robert Frost's paraphrase of our Jewish Prayer

Book.] So I used this as a text and preached a sermon. One of the examples I used was that of a woman whose best friend's child was killed in an accident. She said to me, 'I resent that.' I answered her, 'At whose feet are you going to lay your resentment?' " (p. 136). (Whatever may account for the difference, Frost says explicitly in the sermon that he was thinking of "the death of a young doctor in Bataan.")

In chatting with Daniel Smythe that July day in 1959 in Ripton, Vermont, Frost was alluding to the now celebrated sermon that he preached from my pulpit, the Rockdale Avenue Temple, at the corner of Rockdale and Harvey Avenues, in Avondale, Cincinnati. It was the first day of the Feast of Tabernacles (Sukkot in Hebrew) October 10, 1946. Historians of Robert Frost's life will look in vain for the beautiful Greek structure that was the home of our congregation, K. K. Bene Israel, founded in 1824 when Thomas Jefferson and James Madison were still alive. We worshipped in that magnificent edifice from 1906 until late in the 1960s.

The building was desecrated by the riots in the black ghetto that by that time completely surrounded our temple. We are presently on Ridge Road and Cross County Highway in the village of Amberley, Cincinnati. The name Rockdale Temple is retained as part of the name of our oldest Jewish congregation west of the Alleghenies.

Thompson and Winnick, in *Robert Frost: The Later Years*, devote two pages to this event in Frost's life. There are two errors in their account. It was not the "eve" but the morning of Succoth. And there were not two sermons preached that morning. I threw mine away.

The sermon that Robert preached with little immediate awareness that I would ask him to preach fortunately is not lost. Without upsetting Frost by telling him in advance that we had a way of recording what was spoken from the pulpit, we did in fact succeed in getting a faithful transcription of Frost's remarks.

By present standards, our recording machine would seem old-fashioned. There were green disks, flat, like a phonograph record. Harvey O'Connor, our custodian, watched the record from the library in back of the pulpit.

Often, when I was asked for a copy of my sermon, if there was something controversial that I had said, and played it back, there might be little or nothing that could be heard from the disk. That day, happily, we got Robert Frost's words accurately. Bill Clark, head of the English Department of McMicken College of Arts and Sciences of the University of Cincinnati, a former Amherst man and a great admirer of the poet, and myself, who had taught at the University since 1921, played back the disk.

My Methodist secretary, Caroline Romer, carefully typed the manuscript. Joe Blumenthal, head of The Spiral Press, beautifully printed the sermon as a lovely brochure (October 1947). When we told Robert what we had done, he was not displeased. It was his intention to send out his 250 share of the 500 copies that were printed under my copyright with Frost's knowledge and consent, as Robert Frost's Christmas gift that year (1947), in place of the usual new poem.

Then something happened. We discovered that we had misheard one crucial word toward the end of the sermon. We thought we had heard the word "worry." We were wrong. The correct word was "mercy." Frost was thinking of God's "mercy." In preaching that morning, he had suddenly seen a way to end his *Masque of Mercy*. The dramatic poem had been much on his mind. But resolving the play had given him great difficulty. That morning, preaching without notes as was his custom whenever he talked in public, he suddenly saw his way out.

When I called Robert to tell him of our mistake, he said that he had decided not to send out the sermon as a Christmas gift. There were living persons alluded to in the sermon. They would recognize themselves. Their feelings would be hurt. Frost did not wish to add to their grief over the loss of someone they had loved.

Robert, over the long-distance phone, said he would destroy his own copies of the sermon. He did not ask us to do the same with our copies. Bill Clark and I had already sent copies to family, friends, and some rare book college libraries. I know of at least one copy that Robert autographed some years later in Tallahassee that sold for a fabulous price in San Francisco. On March 11, 1970, Ed Latham, Head of Libraries of Dartmouth, surprised me with a call from

Hanover to tell me that Kathleen Morrison had found fifty copies of the sermon. I suggested that they be given to friends of Frost or to college libraries that would value them. I have never sold any of the copies I possess.

All Frost's friends who are still alive will bear witness with me to Robert's warmth of heart and brilliance of mind. More than once he absolutely astonished me by the treasures it contained and upon which he could draw as from a bottomless well with effortless ease.

Professor Hewette Joyce of Dartmouth has told me of the time when Robert took over for an hour Joyce's class in Milton. Joyce had opened the text to "Lycidas." But Robert did not need the book. He had that poem treasured up in heart and soul.

"If you really like a poem," he told Joyce, "you remember it."

Frost closed the book and said the poem by heart, commenting on lines as he went along, holding both professor and his students spellbound. He played with Milton's "Hence with denial vain, and coy excuse . . ." by saying, "Don't be coy now, Muse. You can't back out of this."

Hewett Joyce several times told me how he wished he had had a tape recording of that wonderful hour. The brilliance of that performance has lived forever in the memory both of the professor and of his open-mouthed students.

Here at the University of Cincinnati, Bill Clark once told me of meeting Frost at the train station to take him up to the campus in Clifton. "Mr. Frost," he said, "would you be willing to speak to my honors class who will be assembling within the hour?"

"What are they reading?" asked Frost.

"They've been reading the *Odyssey*," said Clark.

"Yes," said Frost.

That was all the preparation Robert had or needed. He walked into that class and electrified those U. C. honors students with his intimate and loving knowledge of the immortal Greek classic. And Frost could read Homer in the Greek.

"Sit on top of it," Frost would often tell me when I spoke of my difficulty in holding on to names and dates. Frost could amazingly sit on top of endless facts. He held in his grasp a university of learning in all branches of literature, philosophy and science to thrill and delight you into the wee hours of the morning.

Many are the books in my personal library that I bought because Robert Frost talked to me about them and alerted me to their importance or interest. As I write this, I stopped long enough to take one from its place and look at it again.

It is Butler's book. A pretty fat book it is, going to 1154 pages. It contains the autobiography and personal reminiscences of Maj. Gen. Benjamin Butler. Now I like to think of the vigorous way in which Frost first introduced me to this colorful, controversial figure of the Civil War.

Robert, as you can sense from a dramatic masterpiece like "The Black Cottage" (*North of Boston*—1914) had a keen, searching awareness of the spiritual significance of the Civil War:

> He fell at Gettysburg or Fredericksburg,
> I ought to know—it makes a difference which:
> Fredericksburg wasn't Gettysburg, of course.
>
> .   .   .   .
>
> Whatever else the Civil War was for,
> It wasn't just to keep the States together,
> Nor just to free the slaves, though it did both.
> She wouldn't have believed those ends enough
> To have given outright for them all she gave.
> Her giving somehow touched the principle
> That all men are created free and equal.
>
> .   .   .   .
>
> That's a hard mystery of Jefferson's.
> What did he mean?
>
> .   .   .   .
>
>   the Welshman got it planted
> Where it will trouble us a thousand years.
>
> .   .   .   .
>
>   why abandon a belief
> Merely because it ceases to be true.
> Cling to it long enough, and not a doubt
> It will turn true again, for so it goes.
> Most of the change we think we see in life
> Is due to truths being in and out of favor.
> As I sit here, and oftentimes, I wish

I could be monarch of a desert land
I could devote and dedicate forever
To the truths we keep coming back and back to (pp. 56–8).

Thirty-two years later after the publication of "The Black Cottage," Frost makes use of a Civil War memory. It was in that sermon spoken on the first day of the Feast of Tabernacles at the Rockdale Avenue Temple, Cincinnati, Ohio, Thursday morning, October 10, 1946. How spacious, original and searching is Frost's awareness that religion is "a straining of the spirit forward to a wisdom beyond wisdom. . . . the fear of God always has meant the fear that one's wisdom, one's own wisdom, one's own human wisdom is not quite acceptable in His sight. . . . That, I take it, is the fear of God, and is with every religious nature, always. . . .

"A little while ago I visited with friends in Cambridge, Massachusetts. The lady of the house was from the Deep South. I knew all about her. She was from Mississippi. She was married to a well-known, a very well-known, reformer, advanced thinker. She's a reformer herself. With us was a man whose father's picture hung on the wall—small picture—in officer's uniform.

"I didn't know much about it, but I said: 'What was he?'

"The son said: 'He was a commander in the Union army of Negro troops. It is death to be caught—hanging to be caught—in command of Negro troops, you know. That's far away now. We didn't weep or anything. He got through it apparently. He didn't get hanged.'

"Then here was this lady from the Deep South, the reformer, friend of people high up in these new movements in the world. I said to her: 'Now I've got you two where I want you. I'm going to find out which side God was on in the Civil War.' I said: 'The lady speaks first, courtesy.' The lady from the Deep South, mind you, whose father had been an officer—he'd been a fighting bishop, been fighting on the southern side as a bishop—you know some did.

"I said: 'Which side was God on in the Civil War?'

"We were making a little light of wisdom, you know, so she just spoke right up and said: 'My father was a Methodist bishop, southern, and a bishop ought to know, and he thought God was on the southern side.'

"And I said: 'That settles it!'

"I didn't give the man a chance! But that was, you see, the way. All of us know better than that. But anyway all of us knew that beyond the wisdom that clashed there—the two wisdoms that clashed there—was something of God."

Among the treasured Frost books in my library is one of only ninety-four pages called *You Come Too*. The subtitle reads *Favorite Poems for Young Readers*. Robert Frost. Henry Holt is publisher and Thomas W. Nason did the wood engravings. The book bears this inscription in a strong, upright hand:

> To Victor and Louise
> particularly whats
> new in it
> > Robert and
> > Hyde
> Crow Island
> Oct. 12 59

Below this, Hyde Cox, who wrote the beautiful foreword, has signed his name.

The people who have been reading poisonous things about the personality of Robert Frost had better take another look at Hyde Cox's illuminating foreword. Hyde was a close friend for twenty years. "To me he has seemed wiser and wittier than most men—and braver. I have never seen in anyone else such a mixture of toughness and tenderness. He has seemed bigger than most men but he has never, somehow, seemed older. Few men as they grow old possess so many of the attributes of youth: zest, charm, and curiosity. He holds people dear perhaps for the ancient and basic reason that man is made in the image of God. And perhaps also because, as he says, 'Earth's the right place for love. I don't know where it's likely to go better.' "

Read what Doc Cook has to say of Robert Frost as both poet and person. Reginald L. Cook was for years Director of the Bread Loaf School of English of Middlebury College. Frost was a commanding influence on that Green Mountain campus within easy walk of the Homer Noble Farm.

Any fairminded critic looking for the truth about Robert Frost had better add to his reading list Reginald L. Cook's *Dimensions of*

Robert Frost and *Robert Frost: A Living Voice*. These two books from the pen of Middlebury's revered Professor Emeritus of American Literature and former Director of the Bread Loaf School of English will be a wholesome corrective to the myopic maligners of the good name of America's beloved poet who is not now alive to defend himself from his foes.

> Woe unto them that call evil good,
> And good evil:
> That change darkness into light
> And light into darkness:
> That change bitter into sweet
> And sweet into bitter (Isaiah, 5:20).

Robert Frost never aimed at being a saint. But he did aim at Truth. The remarkable fact about him was his spiritual intactness. As James Reston said of him: "Every time the old gentleman comes to Washington, the Washington Monument stands up a little straighter."

Fortunately, these puny, self-assured peddlars of poison will soon perish. But for those of us who loved him, both as friend and poet, and for all Americans to whom he bequeathed his literary legacy, this will endure for the ages.

On a hot, muggy, humid afternoon last August 28, 1976, we dedicated the Robert Frost Interpretive Trail in Ripton, Vermont, near the Breaf Loaf campus, not far from our Schoolhouse Home. Hyde Cox gave the dedicatory address. I gave the dedicatory prayer.

I close with this prayer, since it best expresses for me and my family the Robert Frost I knew:

"Almighty God, our Heavenly Father, in whom we live, and move, and have our being, how manifold are Thy works; in wisdom hast Thou made them all. Man goeth forth unto his work and to his labor until the evening.

"We rejoice that we who were blessed with the living presence of Robert Frost and who often heard him say his poems in his resonant voice may now share in dedicating this Interpretive Trail, where the generations to come may pause to read, reflect, and be moved by his creative vision.

"Let the youth of tomorrow, as they saunter here, in these Green Mountains Frost loved, find in this sampling of Frost's poems a faithful portrayal, not alone of Nature's woods and brooks, of flowers and song of thrush; but the subtler and deeper implications of the meaning and mystery of life. May they not miss the wisdom and the mirth, the playfulness and the sorrow, as well as the quiet and often devastating irony and scorn directed at human pretension and vanity. And above all, may they be aware of the hidden springs of love and beauty that like the flowery waters and the watery flowers of spring pools stir the mind with their delicate imagery and quicken the heartbeat in poem after poem.

"For this, his legacy to us, of sight and insight, of affirmation and dedication, of refusal to go into the dark and lament, of courageous but not vaporous optimism, as one 'who had a lover's quarrel with the world'—may these hard-won lessons endure to strengthen us upon our way.

"For this we now pay homage to his genius and gladly dedicate this Interpretive Trail to Robert Frost. Amen."

Robert Frost in Context

REGINALD L. COOK

1.

ROBERT FROST in Context" aims neither to explore the psychology of creation nor the nature of art, but to focus on statements, episodes, and stories revelatory of how Frost regarded his world and times. This essay covers a period of forty years. It taps the resources of Frost's private conversations as well as his public statements. Secondly, it establishes their context. Thirdly, wherever appropriate, it relates them to his poetry. And lastly, it documents them.

I have quoted only what I heard viva voce, which implies that I have had no alternative but to exclude some eloquent statements too lengthy to retain wholly in memory. I have resisted paraphrasing these statements, for, once indulged, paraphrasing only too often encourages a writer to assume a surrogate role for the protagonist. In movement the essay proceeds from the personal to the interpersonal, and from the intrapersonal to the suprapersonal. The method, illustrative and allusive, aims to be cumulative and suggestive in effect.

Several caveats are in order. First, these contextual statements are presented as heard on the lips of Frost. Thus, in the absence of the communicants with whom he exchanged views, they are usually presented from his point of vantage. Yet examples in which other people than myself are present will be cited in order to anticipate a criticism that Frost aimed his comments at a friend whose reactions might be taken for granted.

Invariably Frost appears to be the master of the riposte, humanly exulting in superior feats of wit. We often miss the background but can ourselves imaginatively supply the quizzical cross-questioner who rationally tests the validity of Frost's position. Let me illustrate. As a participant in a panel discussion on "The Future of Man," sponsored by Joseph E. Seagram and Sons in the Waldorf-Astoria on September 29, 1959, Frost recounted how he conjured the phrase "passionate preference" (*Interviews*, p. 208) at a strategic point in the discussion and used it to cap an inquiry by Julian Huxley. The question had arisen concerning what operative natural force thrusts homo sapiens forward in the long evolutionary climb. Agilely Frost, with a poet's felicity of phrase, had rejoined: "Wouldn't it be possible to say that it was passionate preference?" Deferentially, Huxley thought there was "some sort of an upward lifting," but he insisted that it was "*accidentally* upward" (italics added).

Frost's wit is pretty sharp in this significant verbal encounter. Certainly the sexual impulse, euphemistically described as "passionate preference," has been a powerful determinant in racial proliferation. Yet Huxley also has his point, dimmed only, so to speak, by Frost's alliteration. In context, the occasion had been like a medieval tourney at which the 72-year-old biologist and the 85-year-old poet had jousted for the prize. But, as he told it, Prosperolike, Frost was a little overanxious to exult in "some vanity of my art." Later, he incorporated the coveted phrase effectively in "Accidentally on Purpose."

Secondly, we realize a compelling necessity to be on guard when a poet offers an opinion on how he thinks a particular poem should be taken, a statement construed, a story viewed. A subtle and sophisticated ironist in his quirks and crotchets, Frost could throw dust into the eyes of the ingenuous and unguarded. And yet, how salutary it is to have his own words as correctives for any tendency to misread or overread. I recall a statement Frost made about "Into My Own," the important introductory poem in *A Boy's Will* (1913). The key lines are:

> They would not find me changed from him they knew—
> Only more sure of all I thought was true (p. 5).

Nearly fifty years after their first publication Frost remarked that the key lines only meant he wanted to be true to the things he saw as he continued to experience life. No intention of ascribing fixity was in his mind. On the contrary, he opposed stiff-necked intractability and mulish obstinacy. The resilient Frost not only marched to a different drummer, he kept pace with an irregular drumbeat. There is little indication in his life that he was ever locked into a rigid position. Speculative and protean as a poet he was concerned about being true to whatever position he found himself in as he followed shifting psychological states, and the twists, turnings, and hazardry of chance in the processes of life. Consequently his revisionary tendency has given some critics an awkward time. What they fail to grasp is that being true to himself in the process of becoming is altogether different from the fixity of an intransigent stance.

And thirdly, as in marksmanship on a firing range, some allowance must be made for windage. In this case, the windage is not rhetorical ebullition, but variance in Frost's changing attitude. Although not a prevaricator, he was conscious of the occasion and the person to whom he addressed himself. In word or phrase he might readily alter the implications of a view or statement. The various phrasing of repeated statements, a shifting angle of vision, the confusion time plays with the memory of specific facts significantly altered meanings. Only a variorum would attest to how many people Frost told the same story and how many different versions are extant.

Professor Wilfred E. Davison, dean at the Bread Loaf School of English on the Middlebury College Mountain Campus in Vermont, once quoted a Frost aphorism. In the summer of 1921, during Frost's first appearance at the School, he said: "Observation covers sight and insight." It was a shrewd unelaborated Frostian aphorism. Nearly fifteen years later, when it might be assumed that his aphorism had long been forgotten, I was a little startled during a personal conversation to hear Frost not only casually repeat the aphorism but explain it. *Covers* was the key word. Insight was like seeing into an invisible world with a clarity and intensity similar to the sight of specific objects, like birds or flowers in the visible world. Observation thus *covers* both kinds of seeing: seeing into the world of specificity as well as into the psychological world. But I have no way of being sure that in the fifteen years interval Frost had not earlier amplified what weight of association he had intended the aphorism to carry. Nevertheless, in time, his aphorism had lost neither its terse vigor nor its speculative breadth.

"There are not many things," I once heard Frost say revealingly, "I have got over thinking that I have thought." If I had been previously skeptical, I was now prepared to believe him. Time and again I heard him tug at early ideas, a bit more of which he pulled out each fresh time. I also learned that the thrust and snick of an epigrammatic phrase was not always as spontaneous as one might suppose.

To these three caveats—Frost's influential dominance, the protean aspect, and the exfoliation of thought or story—in considering the contextual relationship, should be added two equally relevant, correlative ones. First, what does a statement or episode show of Frost, and secondly, of what relevance is it to his poetry? Since the two aspects are inextricably intertwined, I have not thought it necessary to insist on a point of connection. After all, some ingenuity becomes a reader. Something must be left to a lively imagination. And something there is about Frost that doesn't lend itself to programming.

Commonly the magnetic needle of his compass settled in the neighborhood of personal experience in writing. Here he was on home ground, as he surely was in his familiarity with the great tradition of British verse, quoting memorably and in total possession from Shakespeare and Milton, from Sir John Davies and Christopher Smart, from Keats and Browning, or whomever. A notable difference separated these quotable poets from his own experience. Rarely explicating what he quoted from the great tradition, he was provocatively explicative about his own experience. His writing, so often the result of self-surprise, was a constant source of speculative interest and eloquent comment in the conversational interludes of writing. He mused and talked indefatigably—some would add interminably—on the peculiarities and ramifications of that surprise.

For a long time to come we shall have those—and I am no exception—who listened to him, pinching off little bits of Frostiana and holding them up to the light as all the law and the prophets. He said things memorably as in an italicizing light. However, in this discussion I am not Frost's Boswell or, rather, I am not a Boswell for Frost's Johnson. I only happened to have heard him talk at generous length about all kinds of things, talk that was streamlike, eddying on the surface but always following the slow forward thrust of its current. The pull of the current was impressive. So too were facial expressions, the nod of the head, the dexterous movement of the hands, the timbre of the voice, the teasing, ribbing, joshing, baiting words, and the sometimes testy and bristly, sometimes amiably chortling rejoinders. He was most effective vis-à-vis.

I doubt that in the one-to-one sessions the relaxed Frost ever exhausted himself. On the contrary, the occasions served a unique purpose. They enabled him to refine and clarify ideas in the multiple expression of them. His language, ready to hand in phrasing, was often felicitous. *Mother Goose*, who must have been his early jump rope and mumblety-peg, he cherished with a life-long affection. So too were the *Odyssey*, *Walden*, *The Voyage of the Beagle*, and Palgrave's *Golden Treasury* warmly regarded. It was great to hear him on any topic, and none better than poetry and science, especially the latter when he eloquently described the structure and significance of Niels Bohr's atom, or on historical parallels when he reflected speculatively on the modern application of Thucydides's cycle of history (despotism to oligarchy to democracy and back again). To be with him was always pleasurable. He always seemed to know the third verse of poems, reveled in studying good maps, say topographical ones like the U. S. Geological Survey maps, hummed a lot to himself and, like a doughty Hellenist, celebrated "the fine point of daring" in the thrust of science, and, like a humble Hebraicist, sought acceptability of *Complete Poems* as a kind of sacramental offering of a poetic gift, had good provocative titles like "The Road Not Taken," rather than "The Alternate Plan," and wrote characteristically, "Something there is that doesn't love a wall . . ." (p. 33) rather than "Something there is that doesn't love archaic barriers." A fervent nationalist, he was not a militant one; a self-declared conservative, he was not an iconoclastic one.

Although my earliest intimate meeting with Frost did not take place until 1925 at the Bread Loaf School of English, later I met him frequently. I did not formulate any rationale concerning the approach in our relationship, but instinctively I adopted a theory of priorities. That is, I deferred to his spontaneous initiation of topics. Any more formality or any insistent probing would, I am sure, have led to an abrupt end of our meetings. Even though I listened closely

and jotted down notes afterward, it never occurred to me to trespass on his sensibility or encroach on his good will by bringing lists
of questions in my pocket. Such a manipulative device struck me
as precisely not the approach to make to Frost. The pleasure was
being with him and not in affronting him by inquisitional exploitation. The latter did not work out well as we know from the constraint in the meetings between Elizabeth Shepley Sergeant or Lawrance Thompson, official biographer, and Robert Frost.

What surfaced most prominently in the talks was the craft of
poetry. I mention this fact particularly because it is often assumed
that he was reticent about discussing his poems. Certainly he was
wary if the approach was like a confrontation, but at the Bread Loaf
School of English—from 1921 until 1962—he rarely talked about
anything else than poetry. However, there must be a qualifier even
here. The discussion of his poems hinted and intimated, it did not
tell the listener what to think. Touchy when an incautious public
statement sometimes bounced back in print, he tended in private to
be voluble and revealing. In view of the caveats already noted, a
discussion of Frost's statements is of the first importance. But the
discussion makes no pretense of definitiveness. There are too many
variations in the oft-repeated versions. For example, I have heard
him define poetry in at least twenty different ways.

Candor also characterized a great deal of his talk. Once when referring to a president of Harvard University who had lost touch
with his faculty, Frost pointed out shrewdly that the Board of Over-
seers was likely to stick by the president so the proud institution
would not sacrifice its prestige. Pride, not expediency, motivated the
institution's defensive policy. Or, when he anticipated—as it turned
out, prematurely—a severe criticism of my Passage to Walden
(1949) by a mutual professional acquaintance, he thought such hostile criticism was, in a forceful figure, like a tearing of one's flesh.
This, he seemed to be saying frankly, is the way he felt about some
recent negative criticisms of The Witness Tree (1942) and Steeple
Bush (1947) as well as the two masques.

Frost's generalizations could be immensely notional, especially, I
should think, his concept of historical progress in terms of a north
by west impulse, originating in Egypt and Sumeria and moving in

the direction of Italy, France, Germany, and England. The theory ignores the migratory impulses and counter currents moving from Asia toward North and South America. He liked parallels to illustrate the way human nature operates. Human nature was motivated, he thought, either by the voice of fraud, as in Cicero's case, or by the fist of force, as in Caesar's case. He took a dim view of programmed education, resisting the tendency in France to harden up the educational process, or as in Russia to speed it up. He advocated toning it up. He talked engagingly about myths and miracles and "ultimates." When he said that "the big essence of all history" was in Browning's "Protus," I hastened to read it to see how it could be so. When he referred to Arnold's "Mycerinus," I wondered why, and found posed there the age-old problem with which he wrestled: why good leaders are fated and unjust ones spared.

One midsummer evening when we were having a happy social party with lots of good talk and drinks up in the Bread Loaf community, Frost contended that Socrates had been justly condemned for his teachings by the judges in the Athenian court. At once Professor Theodore Morrison of Harvard and I rallied to Socrates' defense. There was a lively give and take among us, and Frost, who himself was sipping wine, laughed off his vulnerability, accusing us of drinking too much. The episode was like a spin-off of Plato's *Symposium*. When I said, "Well, this gave me a good laugh," he replied affably, "You can't laugh too much for me." At these times it was hard to think of a more pleasurable companion than Frost. All the fun was in the play of ideas. If it was not always easy to match his comebacks, it was possible to share the freemasonry of an exciting camaraderie. It was like Rinaldi and Lt. Frederic Henry in Hemingway's *A Farewell to Arms*. There were even signs and countersigns in Frost's camaraderie. When a reference was made to "the small rain," he quoted from the wonderful poem of the Middle Ages: "O Western wind, when wilt thou blow/ That the small rain doon can rain?" He stopped abruptly and challenged me: "Can you finish it?" "Too risqué," I bowed out in the mixed company. Then he quoted Burns's "To a Mouse"—"A daimer icker in a thrave," and remarked that knowing what Burns meant by the reference was the password. In Frost's company the important thing was to be able to pick up where he left off and go along with it, or to go him one better in a trial by recognition. Once when I put him off, he scoffed: "Oh, you only read *American* literature."

Idiosyncratically, he would startle his auditors with unusual twists of thought. He would say, cryptically, "self-consciousness makes us terminal," which was like an explosive spark in lint. How, I wondered, by any stretch of the imagination, could human self-consciousness make mankind terminal. However, there was, I discovered, a clarifying context. He was visiting at my home a week following his participation in the panel discussion on "The Future of Man." Still trailing clouds of reactions—spinoffs as it were from the heady interchanges with Julian Huxley, Ashley Montagu, Bertrand Russell, Hermann J. Muller, and others—he continued the speculation on man and his destiny. No other living thing, he conjectured, had anything like man's spiritual, intellectual, and moral self-consciousness.

Despite the fact the talk turned in other directions, doggedly Frost refused to relinquish his assertion on terminal self-conciousness. Glancing across the room at well-stocked bookcases, he underscored his epigrammatic assertion. "Look at what man has done," he said, "written it all down," thus implying that man's self-consciousness had taken the unique dual form of inventing words to communicate ideas and in making books the repositories of those ideas. His own *Complete Poems* was a personal testimony to self-consciousness as Frost was using the compound. And I recalled how, at a formal lecture in 1950, he had exultantly brandished a copy of the green clothbound *Complete Poems* before a collegiate audience, boasting, "I have a thrust of power that comes out in the book." There is nothing far-fetched in associating this exuberance with his epigram, for Frost always gave the impression that his personal experience was held in solution and condensed under favorable conditions in a sudden insight.

Now, in this room on this particular evening, after glancing at the books, Frost analogized. "The ants," he explained, "had only their eggs." They might reproduce themselves but man not only reproduced his species, he produced ideas. But how was this analogy connected with a self-consciousness that made human beings terminal? In the physical sciences, after several centuries of remarkable human enterprise, he still found the scientists unable to answer three fundamental questions: where we came from, where we were going, and what our steering principle was. In effect, on the evidence of the great feats of science, scientists can still only ponder and not as yet answer the important questions. And it is equally apparent that nothing else in the world—as far as we know—is able to supersede us or supply answers to the ultimate questions which challenge us. Our fate's in that, he seemed to be saying; our own self-consciousness therefore makes us terminal.

I have lingered on these preliminaries in order to stress how careless the mistake would be if we attempted to separate the poet from the man. We can no more take the man out of the poet with impunity than we can take the poet out of the man. I only contend that it is of the utmost importance to point out the contextual complementariness of Frost's foreground statements with the background.

Each of the four categories—the personal, the interpersonal, the intrapersonal, and the ultrapersonal—will consist of representative illustrations which reflect further light on Frost's temperament and habits as a poet. My primary aim, restated, is to show the importance of quoting Frost in context. *Statements quoted out of context compromise literal truths, and nontextual references certainly lead to serious misrepresentation of the poet.*

In the following discussion of the first of these categories—the personal—I have drawn directly upon my memory and specifically upon two notable meetings with Frost late in his life. There were many other meetings, not all of course as personally noteworthy and as full of typical rejoinders, but nevertheless memorable. What I shall attempt mainly is to set up the background for the vis-à-vis conversations in the expectation that Frost's image will break through clearly in the spectrum of the talks.

2.

Only two points need to be underscored in this section on a personal relationship with Frost. First, in view of the negative reaction to Frost as a man, so prominent in the official biography, an important question must be raised: Whatever happened to the image of the quick-witted, sportive Robert Frost, jesting and teasing, ebullient and artful? I think we need to take another look at a poet who, despite the harrying daemons, or, as he identified them, the Eumenides, was incredibly gifted in his quicksilver aperçus. And, secondly, I was enabled to keep a psychic distance from Frost, the failure of which affected some of his other personal relationships. I was preoccupied as a teacher of American literature at Middlebury College and, later, as director of the Bread Loaf School of English. Because I did not trespass on Frost's privacy, our relationship remained a lively and amicable one.

Although I was privy to many intimate disclosures, Frost's resolute wisdom and rascally ironic wit always seemed to be in requisition. In his own figure, he could "swing [his] wit." One Saturday morning toward the middle of May in 1952 when I drove up to Ripton to fetch him to my Middlebury home, I found him sitting on a sofa in the cold Homer Noble farmhouse, apparently nodding, his legs stretched out. In no hurry to leave, he began to talk about Albert Einstein. Then he turned to his children, emphasizing solicitously how hard they had all tried. But something, as he implied, had gone dreadfully wrong. Like his sister Jeanie, his daughter Irma had broken down mentally, and Carol, his son, had killed himself. He talked about the plight of the stricken children in considerable detail and, as he spoke, the dispassionate tone of his voice only pointed up emphatically but undespairingly the sadness of the familial situation. I sat silent, listening disquietedly. A dozen years earlier, I had heard the story of Carol's suicide in similar detail. On both occasions it had been an unsettling experience. I have heard it said and found it written that Frost was a reticent man. For all his gregariousness, I think he was more reserved than reticent and had a natural dignity not to be encroached on. The scars, like those of Hawthorne and Melville, were on the soul. Only on occasion did the exposed fractures show lines of stress.

Mostly the personal meetings were anything but melancholy. I would meet him in the log cabin on the Homer Noble farm just as I had earlier in the 1930s met him at the Stone Cottage and the Gully farmhouse in South Shaftsbury, Vermont, and on Sunset Avenue in Amherst, or at 35 Brewster Street, Cambridge, and, of course, frequently at my home, first in Middlebury and later on the Pulp Mill Bridge Road in Weybridge. I heard him talk publicly at Harvard, Dartmouth, and also in Santa Fé, New York City, and Washington, D.C. And for nineteen consecutive years, Frost appeared before crowded audiences at the Bread Loaf School of English, saying his poems and delivering sotto voce the celebrated asides.

At the Homer Noble farm were open fields for pasturage, good soil for gardening, hard woods for selective cutting, and stunning views of the upper range of the Green Mountains, between Worth Mountain (el. 3300 ft.) to the south and lordly Bread Loaf Mountain (el. 3823 ft.) to the north. The lower range, rising modestly southward, over Goshen way, enclosed the farm in a bowl. Frost's cabin commanded an eye-filling view, and when, at first, the trees were shorter, the Adirondacks could be glimpsed on clear days, standing up boldly twenty miles to the west.

Inside the cabin a sitting room extended the entire south side of the building, a wide comfortable fireplace occupied the central portion of the northerly wall. Windows opened views southward. An old battered Morris chair stood at the east end of the room, a tall light standard at its side, a writing board propped up against the wall, a typewriter on a small table on the west side of the fireplace and beside it a pile of folders, letters, and manuscript. A couple of easy chairs and an equal number of hard-bottomed ones accommodated visitors. Against the east wall stood a table with books, mostly Modern Library editions, and against the table was a large chest. From the wall hung a snapshot of Ripton, two bird drawings, and, above the fireplace, a little woodcut—not a J. J. Lankes—of a snow scene.

The built-in bookshelves on the northeast wall were filled with "tattered veterans," like George C. Coulton's *From St. Francis to Dante*, George Ticknor's *Life, Letters and Journals*, Walter Havighurst's *Long Ships Passing*, William A. Percy's *Lanterns on the Levee*, Louis Madelin's *French Revolution*, Donald Davidson's *The Tennessee*, Weber's *History of Philosophy*, Victor Von Hegen's *Maya Exploration*, Lt. Colonel Whitton's *Moltke, Great Sea Stories*,

Thomas Peacock's *Works* (in three volumes), Henry Bugbee Kane's *Walden*, Britton and Brown's *Illustrated Flora* (in three volumes), the Bible, Robert Herrick's *Poems* (illustrated by Edwin Abbey), A. J. Miller's *The West of Alfred Jacob Miller*, Viking Portable copies of Shakespeare and Blake, Marjorie Rawling's *The Yearling*, Stegner's *Mormon Country*, Audie Murphy's *To Hell and Back* (a Frost favorite), Rachel Carson's *The Sea Around Us*, and two of his father's books—Adam Smith and the fourth volume of Mommsen's *History*.

A doorway at the west end of the room led to the kitchen, pantry, washroom, and bedroom. In an inner alcove bookshelves supported copies of an extensive Modern Library collection, a gift of Frost's publishers.

His talk-spiels were legendary; marathon nocturnal sessions, continuing from two to four or five hours. He could talk anywhere, anytime, and with the greatest of ease. Yet the length of the talks was hardly more remarkable than the range. Once he launched into a diatribe on doctoral dissertations, shifted key to the reading of poetry, alluded to prize fighting, and reacted vigorously to the current popularity of the anti-Keynesian Adam Smith. Another time— October 4, 1952—he covered the spectrum, talking about baseball, the presidential campaign, education, poetry, language, the Greeks (notably Herodotus), Shakespeare's songs, Russia, slavery, loyalty, and writers (Jesse Stuart, Robert Penn Warren, Ernest Hemingway, William Faulkner, and Earle Stanley Gardner). After a formal lecture, he unwound in the house of a stranger, talking about witches, politics, great Americans, and words with three n's in them, like *noumenon*. Following another formal lecture and reception, he talked from eleven o'clock until three in the morning, discussing en route Morgan horses, psychiatry, Catullus, politics, Tung oil, spunglass fishing rods, philosophy (categorizing philosophers into two groups—the annalists and the analysts), education, Generals Lee and Grant, the Imagists F. S. Flint, T. E. Hulme, and Ezra Pound. He wrapped up the nocturnal session, expressing a preference for Immanuel Swedenborg's "Heaven" to Dante's "Hell."

I have chosen as complementary, reenforcing illustrations two meetings with Frost to indicate his indefatigable mental energy.

Both meetings occurred late in his life, which makes them all the more remarkable.

On a bright, clear, late September afternoon—September 28, 1957—my wife and I drove up to Ripton from Middlebury to pick up Frost and take him to the Bristol Inn for dinner. At the appointed time—5:30 P.M.—we arrived at the Homer Noble farm, and the schnauzers, Mark and Sheba, came out barking fiercely. Frost's top coat was lying on the grass near the front-lawn flower beds. So we looked around and waited, first going to the cabin on the rise above the farmhouse, but he was not there. A strong ray of light scoured the lip of the mountain bowl to the southwest, and beneath it shadows deepened.

As we returned to the farmhouse, the 83-year-old poet sauntered across a pasture, a white ash pack basket with adjustable webbing harnessed on his back. In it was a young tamarack and its root system. Frost, looking sheepish, inquired repeatedly: "What time is it?" "Only quarter to six," I told him. He slipped out of the harness, crouched down and crawled under the fence, and hastened into the house to change from blue jumper and khaki trousers into a dark blue suit. He was ready by six o'clock, but we paused to look over the horses, the hay barn, and to watch the squirrels gather coddlings for their winter granary from the nearby apple trees. Robins and jays were numerous.

We drove over the dirt backroad from Ripton to Bristol, and en route crossed a plateau that reminded me of the Brontë moorland country. Entering the outskirts of Lincoln, we followed the west ridge with its magnificent view of the valley below and the Lincoln range above, which appropriately Frost called a "balcony view." He noted that among the surrounding peaks only Mt. Abraham (el. 4052 ft.) "came to a point." A slant of light still raked its upper flank. We were driving slowly. "I went all over England during May and June and I didn't see anything as good as Vermont," he said approvingly. As we descended the gradient into Lincoln village, he described the cluster of white farmhouses as an "innocent view."

Business was brisk at the Bristol Inn, but when the lady in charge looked up and saw Frost she waived the long line ahead of us and set about preparing a table. As we waited, Frost told how he had tried to help one of the families in Ripton, securing for them a decent house in the village center. But at once the housewife had torn her kindlings from the shed, stripping it from bottom to top until the building had become a central eyesore to the proud little community. The befriended housewife was now resentful of her obligation to him.

While dining on roast beef and chicken in the privacy of an inner room, Frost referred to poems of his which had been found in the Huntington Library in San Marino, California. Some of them, he asserted, were not his but when he asked to see them, the library officials would not let him have them. "I should have torn them up right then or stuffed them in my mouth and made pellets of them," he said rather morosely and vindictively.

On his recent trip to England on a "good will mission" supervised by the U. S. Department of State, he had received honorary degrees from Oxford and Cambridge universities during the latter part of May and early June. "Was England in for bad days?" we asked. In view of the self-assurance and self-containment he saw, he thought it was not. There was not the slightest indication that the English had encountered headwinds in recent years. Maybe, he suggested, England will sign a pact with Russia and go clear to the top again. England's ambitions were not unlike Germany's in the last war. It wanted a position at the top where it could "recline" and indulge an "air." When he said that England had retained "an air," I thought how true it was that England could be beaten only on its own terms. "You go across to Europe to learn how to behave at home," he said significantly.

Elizabeth Shepley Sergeant, who was at the time writing a book on Frost (*Frost: Trial by Existence*, 1960), was giving him a bad time by her insistent demands on biographical data. "I don't want to write my own biography," he said flatly. The conversation switched. When I told him I had heard the Tunbridge Fair was one of the real ones, he said emphatically: "No, it's not. The fair grounds are nice but the honky-tonk is wicked."

After dinner, we drove to Middlebury, and Frost, as he so frequently did, talked about family—his grandfather, employed in the big Pacific Mills in Lawrence, Massachusetts, his mother's influence, and his early schooling. He did all of his high school work in a year and a half, studying algebra, English, and geography on his own. In Lawrance high school he edited the school paper, and once, he said, prepared the copy for the whole issue: editorials, sports, and social items, and then resigned. He did not explain why. Poems like "The Trial by Existence" had first appeared in the literary magazine.

At the house Frost sipped a cointreau and reviewed his impressions of England; notably, on a trip to Durham, its university, cathedral, and circuiting river; on the calmness of the Jonathan Cape publishing house in Bloomsbury, so different from the frenetic air in an American publishing house on Murray Hill; and on a visit with my̅ old don, Nevill Coghill, at Exeter College, Oxford, then Merton Professor in Literature at Oxford—a "saintly looking man," in Frost's words, who looked as though he had lived through a lot.

Although the state department had sponsored "the good will mission," it did little about the planning except place a car and a woman secretary at his disposal. "I didn't go on errands," he explained, and he didn't try to impose anything on anyone, but he did stop to sign in at the embassy in Grosvenor Square where Ambassador John Hay Whitney, as Frost commented, sat on the edge of his chair. "So I didn't talk," added Frost dryly. Mrs. Whitney offered to arrange a tea for him but he would have none of it. "Remember Eakins," Frost quipped, "when someone asked him had he received any honors, he said, 'Yes, I was given a tea by a woman in Lancaster, Pennsylvania.' " The showiest affair on the tour was at Cambridge where his honorary Doctorate of Literature was given during a degree-awarding exercise at the end of Trinity Term. Sir Arthur Tedder, formerly chief of the British air staff in World War II, was chancellor, and conferred the degree, and, in passing, lauded President Eisenhower for patience, courage, and faith. What, thought Frost, of the opposites of these virtues. Wasn't there a time to be impatient, a time to run, or a time to be skeptical? I inferred Frost thought Sir Arthur Tedder a little shallow.

When he talked about "the contemplation of stand-offs," I asked him what side he was on in "The Egg and the Machine." "Oh," he said, "it's a stand-off between vitality and machinery." And he launched into an interesting theory of stand-offs—the stand-off between those who help themselves, that is, the self-helpers (e.g., Emersonian self-reliance) and those who consider themselves their brother's keeper (e.g., Christian morality). Then there were believers in tools and believers in weapons. For example, one of his recent talks was entitled (after Emerson's phrase in "Berrying") "Fraud or Force"—the fist of force and the mouth of fraud. Consider Brutus, shall we take him as Caesar's betrayer, he inquired rhetorically, or as the noblest Roman of them all? How, he wondered, did Shakespeare intend that we take him? "Isn't there a scene in *Julius Caesar* where Shakespeare indicated his intention?" I asked, "Isn't there a scene where the playwright shows that he was divided in his viewpoint?" "No," Frost said, "I don't think so in spite of some of my friends who think otherwise. Shakespeare was still following North's *Plutarch*. But Dante—think of it—puts Brutus in Inferno with Judas and Cassius." Dante, he thought, overdid it. Still, the interpretation of Brutus was a "stand-off." Julius Caesar, he opined, was the great one, an enlightened and benevolent dictator.

Once again Frost alluded to the north-by-west theory (prominently incorporated in "Kitty Hawk"), that civilizations started in the midst of "the fertile crescent" along the Euphrates, giving us the alphabet and mathematics and all the rest, and moved directionally through Europe to Great Britain and then to the United States. He wondered about the blacks who for over ten thousand years had lived in the midst of "the fertile crescent" and had failed to "take fire."

"What was in the Christian religion?" he asked rhetorically, and immediately answered musingly: "To make us believe." Believe in what? "Why, to make us believe in belief." "It's [i.e., Christianity] the nicest religion," he said. "Why? Because of the Gospels, the stories." While he was teaching philosophy at Amherst College for two years (1923–25), the professional academics reacted against him. "What philosophy did he teach?" they asked, with only routine courses in Aristotle and Plato in mind. "I taught my own philosophy," replied Frost. "The first thing in philosophy and in religion is to find the thing to say to the thing said." The professional academics, he implied, always thought one had to have a formal course in something in order to teach. "They think Emerson is unsound but his penetrations go right through things," he remarked. Frost's chronic unhappiness with academic rigidity and myopia surfaced. Why did everything have to be programmed? He rebelled at the institutionalization of what should remain free and adventurous. Excessive planning deadened innovation. Even the humanities program at M.I.T. was all wrong, it seemed to him. It was introduced "like an ingredient" in bread; it wasn't, as it should be, the essential part of education. "The past," he asserted, "is the great book of Worthies."

I had long wanted to ask Frost about "A Winter Eden."

"Is it a two-layer poem?" I asked

"They're all two-layer," he replied, tongue-in-cheek.

"Is it meant to be ironical?"

"No."

"How, then, is it to be taken?" His reply was vintage Frost.

"The poet," he said, "expects to have the poem more felt than said." In writing poems, the real thing was when he felt "the mischief (or daemon) of it in me," not when the poet tries to write all the time. Browning, he thought, in the last years of his career was a victim of the impulse to write.

The evening talk, typically fragmented but uniformly revelatory, exhibited range if not exhaustive deliberation. For example, Frost, in reacting to Neil H. McElroy, formerly a Proctor and Gamble executive, who replaced Charles Wilson as Secretary of Defense (1953–57) and who served under President Eisenhower from 1957 until 1959, thought McElroy did not answer questions at the senatorial confirmatory investigation with any degree of sharpness. When he was asked about the Proctor and Gamble Soap Operas and their educational value to the American television public, he should have insisted that whatever he did, whether as a business executive or as a public servant, was done because he loved it and not because he was trying to entertain or educate people. By way of contrast with the obtuse McElroy, Frost, who liked the sharp comeback, told how he met Allen Tate, a Catholic convert, talking with Father Lynch at Smith College. Frost looked at Tate and shook hands with Father Lynch, saying mischievously: "I trust you're not a convert."

When Frost referred to Tom Paine, he asked quizzically: "Who's Tom Paine? How do we know him? As Jefferson saw him or Washington or Gouveneur Morris or Monroe or Madison? Only the latter stuck by him and treated him decently." Frost was reminded of Henry Wallace, another maverick like Paine. At a celebration over in Plymouth, Vermont, for Calvin Coolidge, Wallace, an invited guest, approached, asked for, and was given permission to speak briefly. All the previous speakers had spoken confusedly as mixed-up Republicans, but Wallace told the group what Coolidge and he had in common. In Washington, D. C., he had attended a party where he felt pretty solitary. Spotting another man seemingly unattached in a corner, he went over to him and started a conversation. It was Coolidge, and right there began an enduring friendship. "I must write to Wallace," added Frost, reminded of some social obligation.

The talk, just before it broke up for the evening, turned to books, and I showed Frost my blue clothbound Frontenac Edition of Francis Parkman, purchased in Los Angeles and toted clear across the continent. He was thoroughly interested. "I would like to have one, too," he said. We also browsed through Rutherford Platt's *American Trees: A Book of Discovery* (1952), looking up tamaracks and maples. How were they defined? he inquired. Was the tamarack really an American tree? What was the strongest wood? The browsing reminded him of a yellow birch which he had discovered while out walking and which he had replanted in a damp place. He planned to fetch it in his big shoulder basket.

On the way homeward up the mountain, he returned to our earlier discussion on "stand-offs." There are also "ultimates," he qualified, not all "stand-offs." In human and racial relations he agreed that magnanimity was the great thing.

Had we seen the comet in August? Yes! And the tail? Yes! He hadn't, and missing it disappointed him.

Between Sand Hill, out of East Middlebury, and Ripton, we stopped by the South branch of the Middlebury River to let two young coons get safely across the road from where they had been fishing in the gorge. When we reached the Ripton farm we saw a brilliant display of Northern Lights. I waited at the fence by the old barn while Frost took some things into the farmhouse. Inside the house, the two restless schnauzers were barking at a great rate. "Wait little doggies," said Frost, as he fumbled with the key in the lock. Over his shoulder, he warned: "Stand back until they satisfy their appetite for excitement or they may bite."

When he returned from the house, we stood by the fence under the stars in the cool night, the dew thick in the grass, and gazed raptly at the flaring Northern Lights. "Hold out your hand," he urged, "and you'll see it in the light." So both of us stood there holding out our hands, and, in the light of the streaming aurora, they had the same paleness as in daylight. Then, directing me to look upward in the light of the marvelous illumination, he said: "There's the Heimdal bridge, see?" And he pointed out a dark band of light soaring above the northern horizon. "That's where the gods went," he added.

As we stood there looking skyward, he pointed out the constellations—Taurus, Cassiopeia's Chair, Orion's Belt, the Pleiades. Then he named separate stars: Aldebaran, Vega, Capella.

Frost had not, of course, seen the lights the way a scientist would see them. The scientist would undoubtedly see more "in" the lights. A poet, however, would see all that he could see of all that he wanted to see rather than all that he wanted to see of all that he could see. So, as a poet, Frost saw the Northern Lights in a wide imaginative context; in short, in the evocative frame of reference of Old Norse mythology. There was the Heimdal bridge—the rainbow bridge called Bifröst, of which Heimdal was the guardian against marauding giants, over which the Norse gods passed from the earth to the Heaven of Asgard. Frost had reminded me: "That's where the gods went," when he had pointed to the dark bank of light extending above the horizon.

But while Frost had seen the Northern Lights in the perspective of Norse mythology, I was seeing the Northern Lights and the stars in the perspective of the poet. Although neither of us heard the sound of Heimdal's mighty warhorn, nor witnessed the trembling of Bifröst, the rainbow bridge, at least for me, at this exceptional moment joined poet, place, and time together in a rare attachment.

The second illustration is drawn from a meeting on an early June day in 1959, when Frost was eighty-five. He had invited my wife and me to dinner at the Bristol Inn. We picked him up at the Homer Noble farm in the late afternoon, and apprehensively he urged: "Now go slow." Driving at about thirty-five mph, we took the secondary road from Ripton to Lincoln so he could see the mountains. En route, we frequently spotted cottontail rabbits, and once a wild animal resembling a bobcat crossed the road very deliberately but a distance ahead. We passed several bedraggled shacks in a lonely back country. When we first raised Mount Abraham, he said feelingly: "That's my mountain." We again took the high road and from Frost's "balcony view" looked up at the lordly Green Mountain range and down into the scenic Lincoln valley with the outlying farms set in close to the dark hardwood stands. Frost eyed the abandoned farmsites wistfully, and guessed there would be a day when these would be bought up. He had tried to buy one, but the occupants wouldn't sell. He didn't indicate which one.

He talked a good deal about people—John Ciardi, Archibald MacLeish, Lionel Trilling, Ray Nash, and Arthur Jensen at Dartmouth, and the 85th Birthday Dinner held in New York City on March 26. He talked about being misinterpreted. George Whicher had, for example, been wrong in thinking he had ever worn celluloid collars, and Lawrance Thompson was wrong in implying in the *Saturday Review* (March 21, 1959) that his father was "a gambler." ("What were his own chances," wrote Thompson, "when he played as a boy in the streets of his native San Francisco while his father, having failed as a gambler, was dying of tuberculosis?") If Larry Thompson had meant that his father was a gambler with fate, he would have been correct, but his father had never been a *professional* gambler.

After a steak dinner at the Bristol Inn, we walked on the village green, listening to the local band, stopping to look into the quaint Town Hall ("Where else," Frost asked, "would you see one like this?") On this pleasant evening kids were active, playing tag, riding bicycles, ganging up on the friendly musicians in the covered bandstand. It was a setting for a Norman Rockwell *Saturday Evening Post* cover, and Frost enjoyed it immensely. He bought two bags of old-fashioned, pink-striped peppermint drops, handed one to my wife, saying: "One for you and one for me," and popped a candy in his mouth. In the southeast, Jupiter blazed away, and, in the west, Venus rose brilliantly.

En route back to Ripton by the valley road to East Middlebury, he asked if I had read Howard Nemerov and what I thought of his poetry? He referred to Robert Lowell's *Life Studies* (1959), expressing dismay at one of the poems on Delmore Schwartz, subheaded "Cambridge 1946." He told of a party to which he was invited by Lowell, which he assumed would be small. Instead the party was a large one and Lowell took Frost into another room and began to disparage the poetry of Richard Wilbur. Upon returning to his guests he sat down in the middle of the room and poured wine over his face. A woman guest turned to Frost and said: "You don't want any more of this, do you?" After Frost left, he heard later that Lowell was removed that night in a strait jacket. "He's back in the asylum," he said ruefully, adding uncommiseratingly, "and how these maniacs talk about *their* misery!" Once he overheard Ted Roethke and Lowell, while visiting him at the Homer Noble place (early in August 1947) address each other, while stopping to pick blackberries: "Come on, you manic." Frost described Lowell harshly as "a terrible diseased ego," and wondered how Boston University, where he was teaching, handled him during the periods of manic depression.

In one of the swank hotels of Phoenix, Frost had recently encountered a ghost from the past. It was the well-dressed son of Thomas Bird Mosher, "the little man with the black cap" who pirated the British poets of the "Yellow Nineties," publishing their poetry in his Bibelot. Mosher paid the poets but by-passed the publishers. The kind of verse Mosher published was what he called "blue-china poetry," that is, teacup stuff, like Lionel Johnson, Ernest Dowson, John Davidson, and the early Yeats. How strange, Frost thought, to meet in Phoenix the ghost of the past in Mosher's well-to-do son, now a part of the automotive industry in Detroit.

When I contended that if the Nazis had not suffered from a lack of oil, they would probably have beaten the West, Frost disagreed. "Oh, no, they wouldn't have. We were just getting going. We're slow to do anything but when we get going we're hard to stop. We have to have an issue and it takes us a long time to get one."

Earlier in the spring, he accepted an honorary degree at Syracuse University because Frederick Melcher was to receive one. On Sunday next Tufts was to honor him. No speeches, just the degree, he added. He thought colleges ought to pay if they asked him to speak.

When we returned to the farm, he unlocked the door, quieted the excited schnauzer, Mark, then carefully pulled the curtains of the windows in the living room. "It always seems cozier to shut the night out," he remarked.

The best of the talk began right then. The three of us were alone and two kept silent. He said that all he had aimed at in life was *not* to be a farmer. He only wanted to be the one who didn't miss a trick. When he read the page, he wanted to read it and know he wasn't missing anything. If someone said something to him, he wanted to be able to hold his own. He wanted to be able to tread metaphor, by which he meant he wanted to be ready to come up with his own metaphor. Nothing conclusive, you know, just waiting to meet the next emergency with a ready answer. He illustrated how very early in life the apt response had become idiosyncratic. When he was fourteen his Swedenborgian mother had said, "God made man of mud," and with Darwinism in mind, he rebutted: "You say, God made man of mud, and I think God made man of *prepared* mud."

"What's wrong with poetry today? Why are there so few poets?" he inquired. He dismissed Paul Engle's *West of Boston*. "What's lacking?" I asked. "No phrase, force, distinction, penetrations." When he was Consultant in Poetry in the Library of Congress (October 1958–May 1959), Miss Armstrong, the secretary, had screened fifty poets and let in two to see him. One was a 45-year-old Navy man with a Harvard background and a friend of David McCord's, and a writer of humorous verse. The other was a woman with a book of sonnets and she came in with tears streaming down her face. But neither had the root of the matter, so far as he was concerned.

Then Frost deliberately, as if to illustrate the penetration, distinctions, and force of poetry, quoted as rapidly as they came to mind five short passages from Matthew Arnold. "And they're all in one small book," he exclaimed. I recall two: "A voice oracular hath peal'd today" (written in Emerson's *Essays*), and "Business could not make dull, nor Passion wild" (cf. Sophocles in a "Sonnet to a Friend"). And he also mentioned Arnold's "Mycerinus."

Had he enjoyed the post as Consultant in Poetry at Washington? Oh, yes, he had very much. But he had wanted to be consultant not only in poetry but also in religion, philosophy, and politics. He hadn't wanted to routinize the post. He mentioned his successor, Richard Eberhart, and, during the late evening, spoke well of John Crowe Ransom's influence on a few prospective poets.

When the talk turned to the sight of terrible things, Frost told movingly of the visits with his father to the slaughterhouse in San Francisco when he was a small boy. In those days it was thought that tuberculosis could be treated effectively by drinking hot blood. At the slaughterhouse a cow would be lassoed in a corral and a portcullis dropped, the cow slugged, its throat cut. Father and son visited the slaughterhouse twice a week. Recalling Robert Lowell and Delmore Swartz, to whom he had referred earlier, Frost said ruefully: "It was a terror equal to any they could invent." This seemed to me a curious way to match psychological scars by exhibiting them publicly, but the remembered incident helped me to understand why Frost had reacted earlier to Robert Lowell's painful affliction.

He spoke of subjects for his talks and said amusingly: "You know I'm like a dog with bones buried under shrubs. I dig up a bone and gnaw it for awhile." As we parted, I asked him if John Ciardi had taped the interview reported in *Saturday Review* (March 21, 1959), entitled "Master Conversationalist at Work." The reportorial accuracy was striking. It had been done vis-à-vis, without a tape recorder. However, on two other occasions, tape recordings had been made and Mrs. Kathleen Morrison, who had heard them, praised both. The first was an interview with Randall Jarrell, and the second, with Robert Penn Warren and Cleanth Brooks, was included in "Conversations on the Craft of Poetry," to accompany the third edition of Brooks and Warren, *Understanding Poetry.*

Directly after both visits, I jotted down notes and then prepared working copies. Irrelevant details were omitted but the statements appear as spoken. What is missing of course is the tone of voice, whether ironic or mocking, exultant or melancholy, petulant or teasing, bitter or compassionate. Although his voice in conversation was invariably low in pitch, almost gruff, there were the slight intensities to accommodate the causticity or harshness of an acerbic mood, as there were, similarly, the vigorous thrusts in a perky phrase. I didn't detect any false drama, either in insisting on a point or to emphasize quizzicality. The difficulty was quite the opposite. Often his voice diminished in pitch to a murmur. It is also hard to communicate the ironical play in some of the statements. Two things Frost said he always kept in mind were: (1) being taken in the right way; and, (2) that what he said in passing was often to be taken as only off the top of his head and therefore transient. But any listener to Frost over the years is in a position to catch variations in vocal tones, match repeated references, evaluate the validity of statements, and weigh the worth of incidents, as well as cancel out the trivia from the deeper certainties.

A further variation in the representative categories is interpersonal. What is stressed in this category is not the direct vis-à-vis relationship of the personal category. In the interpersonal the stress in the context is on Frost's thoughts and reactions as they grow out of one-on-one relationships. If the context of the personal is conditioned by Frost's relaxed friendliness, the context of the interpersonal focuses solely on the provenance of the poet's thought.

3.

One day in May 1931, I heard Frost define poetry, in one of his many definitions, as "the renewal of words," a definition he was to repeat in the presence of others. But what did he intend by it? He meant, I inferred, that poetry had to do with the etymological association of words and that in writing, words were twice born when freshly used.

To illustrate what he meant by renewal, Frost once used the phrase "poring over" and called attention to its verbal similitude to "pouring over." The phrases had a common origin in Middle English. The source of *pour* is in the Middle English *pouren, poren*; and, as W. W. Skeat notes, it is especially used with *out*, thus *pouring out*. In its original sense, it meant to purify and clarify by pressure and squeezing out. The *Oxford English Dictionary* indicates that *poring over*, a phrase of obscure Middle English origin, derived from *pūren, pouren, puri*, signifying to look intently or fixedly into a book, "to read or study earnestly or with steady application." When a reader pores over a page, does he not therefore, figuratively speaking, pour over it with his eyes and ears?

Literally, an absorbed reader does pour his mind over what he reads, not only by steady application but as well by a clarifying pressure that squeezes out the essential content. Or so I think Frost conjectured; and so I surmised I saw a little deeper into the contextual meaning of "the renewal of words" where, in poring over a page of poetry, we pour the head and heart over it in the renewal of words. Numerous examples of the renewal of words in his poems spring to mind: "A *leaping* tongue of bloom" in "The Tuft of Flowers"; "Water came to *rebuke* the too clear water" in "For Once, Then, Something"; "What to make of a *diminished* thing" in "The Oven Bird"; and the brook in "Directive," "Too *lofty* and *original* to rage" (italics added).

Another illustration of the importance of background to fill out an interpersonal reaction occurred in July 1949, following a lecture by Mark Van Doren on *Don Quixote* at the Bread Loaf School of English. Frost was present. Afterward, at an informal social gathering, the talk turned on translations, and Van Doren said he read *Don Quixote* in the Pierre Motteux translation (probably in Ozell's revision). While he chatted about reading foreign books in the original, Frost told Van Doren: "I'm a great deal happier in my own language." Yet he always speculated as he read a translation what the precise meaning was in the *original*. Van Doren, reminded of the closing line of "The Wood-Pile"—"With the slow smokeless burning of decay"—wondered how a translator would succeed in translating this in a foreign language. The magic, Frost thought, was in the phrase "smokeless burning." It was, he added, one of "the lucky snatches," and he continued, elaborating felicitously, "The magic of the thing is the lucky snatch you take as you go."

He had snatched it at the time from a firearms advertisement for smokeless powder then in a current magazine. (*The Literary Digest* for August 25, 1906 on page 257 has an advertisement for Laflin and Rand's "Infallible Smokeless" powder. The advertisement appears also in subsequent issues. But smokeless powder, no new thing, was of course first invented in 1863 by the German Schultze.) The phrase was "the lucky snatch," and, as Frost said about the things a writer picks up from here and there and uses in his own writing, he "steals them to new uses." Frost borrowed the firearm company's alluring phrase for a haunting line of poetry, and Mark Van Doren's pressing him on translations evoked the remembrance of the phrase's provenance.

In view of Frost's reading of George Santayana, I have also wondered whether he had unconsciously "lifted" a favorite phrase "passionate preference" from page 113 of the Modern Library edition (1955) of *The Sense of Beauty* (1896). Santayana is discussing the writings of Walt Whitman in which he finds the charm of uniformity in multiplicity profoundly impressive: "Everywhere it greets us with a *passionate preference* . . ." (italics added). On September 29, 1959, when participating in the symposium on "The Future of Man," previously mentioned, Frost had used the phrase "passionate preference" to indicate the force of the sexual impulse and affections in the onward thrust of human society. In the last two lines of his poem, "Accidentally on Purpose," in *In the Clearing* (1962), Frost boldly declares:

> Our best guide upward further to the light,
> Passionate preference such as love at sight (p. 425).

Surely, if the phrase had been encountered earlier—and forgotten—Frost has put it brilliantly to "new uses."

Another example of the interpersonal context illustrates a trait of independent thinking deeply ingrained in Frost's character. *Walden*, a greatly favored book of prose, was, he once told a collegiate audience, "one of the greatest books ever written." Remembering his wholehearted approbation of *Walden*, I reminded him that in the second chapter "Where I lived—" Thoreau had declared for the "free and uncommitted life." He had written with typical Thoreauvian urgency: "But I would say to my fellows, once for all, as long as possible live free and uncommitted." Let me try this Thoreauvian declaration on Frost, I thought, and see what his reaction will be. In education, in poetry, in politics, he had so often stood up for the unorthodox, so often against routine and the systematic, certainly he will favor Thoreau's spirited belief. I was wrong, for I had not taken into consideration the difference between Frost's leveling tendency and his tendency toward elevation. He would have none of Thoreau's "free and uncommitted life," but argued that whatever freedom we enjoyed originated in commitments—to our friends and family, to our town, state, nation, and to the vocations to which we had been called. He was, as we see, not rejecting freedom, he was interpreting freedom under the restraints of human society within the civilized community. I saw demonstrated recurrently the trait in Frost to take a normally assumed position and with a show of common sense call in question the impracticalities of the theoretic and notional. Sometimes it would be done with a quip as quick as an eyeblink. Once, after a fine evening performance of the two masques and "The Witch of Coös" at Bread Loaf School of English when interpersonally he was commending the performers, I said: "They worked hard at the evening program." He replied almost in the same breath: "You think there's a virtue in work? I think there's more virtue in imagination." He responded to a commonplace reaction neither politely nor weakly.

The one-on-one interpersonal context is also illustrated by an interesting occurrence. In May 1936 at Middlebury Frost inscribed a personal copy of *A Further Range*, which had just appeared, with an improvised couplet. It read:

> They say the truth will make you free.
> My truth will chain you slave to me.

The question is: how does a reader take the couplet? Obviously there is something ambiguous and a little enigmatic in it. Is "the truth," as Frost refers to it, to be taken abstractly or humanly? Moreover, is the statement to be taken as the counsel of a partisan or simply as the pronouncement on a fact of life? What is the poet's tone of voice? If it is resigned in tone, then the couplet would imply that

in the scheme of things this is the way of the world. It is also possible to infer, if the reader considers Frost's "*my* truth" as a counter-
statement to a vague abstraction "*They* say the truth," that his truth
is a designed, hence forceful, statement of avowedly enslaving one
to a *human* ideal rather than to a vaguely abstract truth (italics
added).

What was I, a New England Yankee who am voluntarily no
man's slave, to infer? (I had heard Frost once identify a slave as "a
man who doesn't ask why he does what he does.") Should I take
Frost's enjoinder straight and capitulate to his personal views no
matter what their consequences and consider these preferable to a
historically acceptable truth? Granted the couplet is puzzling, but
also granted it is meant to be. If I recognized in Frost an imperious
egotist, I would then read the couplet as a straight enjoinder and
solicitation to submission. But if I knew Frost and had found out
how to take his play in paradox, I would find the couplet not an example of arrogant egotism, but rather an example of teasing irony.

As I have already pointed out, there are background contexts for
the reading of a sophisticated, elusive, and subtle poet. Yet, if I
think the couplet means something different from the above possibilities, what supports a less direct reading? What validity is there
in contending Frost meant otherwise than the surface reading?
Only the knowledge that in his art he was much subtler than early
critical exegetes intimated. I once heard him tell a college audience:
"You can talk by opposites and contraries with certain people because they know how to take you."

Later in the same month in which Frost's *A Further Range* (1936)
was published, he appeared before my classes in American literature
at Middlebury College and casually quoted the couplet to the students. Then he hinted what his own position was by urging the
students to seek the freedom of their own thoughts. He declared:
"Having thoughts of your own is the only freedom." Bearing this
recommendation in mind, apparently the intent in his paradoxical
couplet was to encourage assuming a position diametrically the opposite of the verbal statement. There is nothing at all surprising in
this inference. First, Frost wanted his readers to be sure they knew
how to take his poetry. "I have written poetry ever since I was fif-

teen years of age and there come to be quite a number of people who know how to take me in my wry way," he once explained, "in my twisted way with the words cocked a little like a cocked hat, like a cocked feather—that is poetry." And he elaborated: "The large strain of poetry is a little shifted from the straight out, a little curved from the straight." He recognized, if not self-consciously at least self-understandingly, the implications in a highly personal idiom and attitude. And secondly, he did indeed have a rationale for his poems. At Amherst in the early 1930s, he had asserted that poetry was "the one permissible way of saying one thing and meaning another." He explained: "People say, 'Why don't you say what you mean?' We never do that, do we, being all of us too much poets. We like to talk in parables and in hints and in indirections—whether from diffidence or some other instinct" (*SP*, pp. 36–37).

In a poet of such paradoxical wisdom as Frost, it isn't unusual to find reactions so incisively relevant they expand horizons in speculative thought. I think this is the nub of the couplet, and I think, further, there are several reasons why the poet preferred the method of indirection. Neither quirky nor whimsical as it might be supposed, it was in reality one way to avoid the banality of the oversimplified commonplace. In addition to eliciting the possibilities in different views, simply phrased, it also exhibited a deep-dyed reluctance to the closed doctrinaire, definitive statement; and, by implication, it indicated a preference for the speculative over the dogmatic assertion.

When, for example, Frost counseled the students at Harvard: "Don't work, worry," what was he trying to do? Was he trying to rally a generation of feisty student revolutionaries against the orthodoxies of education? Or, was he, like Whitman, inviting the students to loaf at their ease and observe if not a spear of summer grass at least their immortal souls? When Perry Miller, professor of American literature at Harvard University, heard Frost's motto generally quoted, he wondered immediately what present form of educational subversion Frost's "one-man revolution" was about to take. Learning of Miller's reaction, Frost explained disarmingly, "I meant worry about ideas." Students "were too prone to worry about busy work," planned hours and programmed careers. I am sure such busy work was as much a bête noire to Miller as it was an institutional abhorrence to Robert Frost. Superficially trivial, Frost's explication of the motto points up the need to be understood correctly.

In correlation with the necessity to clarify the ambiguity of a simple motto is another demonstrable contextual quotation. By way of preface, Frost was one of the most unorthodox, and, at the same time, one of the best teachers I have ever known. Like Socrates, he was a great stimulator of ideas. Excessive scholarship, which he found dominating some scholars, prompted him to type them like Casaubon in *Middlemarch*, the erudite man who is mastered by his material. In *Steeple Bush* the type is recognized in The Dean of "Lucretius versus the Lake Poets." Frost stood against personal and institutional pretension of any kind. One should, he thought, at least know how to swing one's load, feel free with his knowledge, and express it imaginatively. In his opposition to the scholar-type, Frost was biting and testy. John Finley, Jr., professor of classics at Harvard, had lectured on "What is Classicism?" at the Bread Loaf School of English on August 1, 1949. Frost had not attended the lecture, and several who had attended summarized Finley's position. Frost listened and then somewhat tartly proposed and answered his own proposal. "You know what a classicist is?" he asked, rhetorically. Then he quipped acerbically: "He is one who knows all the Greek irregular verbs." We laughed at the quip, but not at Dr. Finley.

It would be natural enough to pause here and accept this as one of Frost's characteristically perverse witticisms. Yet once again there is more here than meets the ear. Back of his jibe at excessive scholarship, there was an interpersonal context, just as there had been in my misapplication of Frost on Thoreau and in Professor Perry Miller's misconstruing Frost's motto. Finley had sent some poems to Frost, and the latter had not responded favorably. A constraint had grown up between the two. So Frost had purposely absented himself from Finley's lecture the evening before. Yet there was more to this constraint than Frost's reaction to Finley's poems. In June 1950, Frost heard Finley contend that the only difference between the student and himself was in "learning." "The students," Finley argued, "have got all we've got but the learning." If this is true, Frost thought, how little the teacher must have. As if learning was any *great* distinction or even *the* great distinction. The important thing to Frost was what one had more than learning. In more senses than one, Frost's point of contention is a strong one. It was a conviction with him, and it would seem that he could not forgive Finley's "softness," a fact which, in Frost's judgment, compounded his limitations as a poet, if not his scholarship as a professor of classics. Surely these interpersonal relationships are of the most delicate texture, and as in the Frost-Finley context, we have only the apparent fullness of Frost's side as objectively noted above. We do not have John Finley's side, which might greatly modify but not extenuate the rudeness of Frost's quip on a classicist.

In the intrapersonal category which follows, the emphasis will be placed on the psychological, or on what might be more precisely described as Frost's reaction to rivalry in the practice of his vocation. The text for this section of the essay is a statement of his view on artistic rivalry. The context consists of his intimate reactions to it over the years. A good deal has been written of the relationship of Frost to those among his peers whom he considered to be rivals. Some of this comment is mere hearsay, and perhaps most of it has no further validity than casual or trivial anecdotes. However, the intrapersonal aspect remains unusually important. In several ways it mirrors not only Frost's temperament and struggle, but also the plight of the poet in modern American society. A highly competitive capitalistic society encourages a vigorous give-and-take between its writers in order that they might survive. Unfortunately a struggle that should rest on the basis of excellence more often is judged on the basis of news publicity and public recognition.

4.

In an important statement Frost made in June 1948, we have reliable testimony of the intrapersonal in his commitment to poetry. "When I write," he carefully pointed out, "I must be free of all sense of rivalry, away from it all and a part of the life of the spirit where it is non-competitive." This revealing statement has a considerable context, only the contours of which can be indicated here. Consequently, I shall explore a few of the contours in Frost's attitude. A good deal has already been written and said about his sensitivity to criticism and his implacable resentment of actual or imaginary rivals, both in the official biography and elsewhere.

On the evidence, is there the slightest doubt that he had strong, antagonistic feelings about the success of foreign intruders in the American dust of the early Poetry Movement in this country? Wilfred W. Gibson comes to mind. In the United States, Masters and Sandburg appear as "hostiles," and in Europe, the applausive recognition of the expatriate Eliot especially galled him, and Ezra Pound represents a whole case in itself. Undoubtedly Frost's animus originated naturally enough in an anxiety whether he would truly win the acclaim he thought he justly deserved on the merit of the poems. This anxiety had been prolonged almost past human endurance, from the high school days at Lawrence, Massachusetts until the breakthrough in 1914. It was a long foreground of effort, obscurity, denial, and anonymity. The effects of this prolonged period—about twenty years—lingered throughout his life like a chronic low-grade infection, which surfaced often in bitter memories of "back in those long, lonely days."

Frost's acute sense of professional rivalry, especially with his peers, surfaced in 1949 in a dismaying context. He cited the locale of the incident as Philadelphia and it involved Wilfred W. Gibson who—and the occasion was apparently in 1917—was visiting in this country on a lecture and reading trip. Frost had known Gibson while living at Little Iddens in the Dymock region of Gloucestershire. Gibson lived for awhile close by in a thatched cottage, called the Nailhead, outside the town of Dymock. Frost's feelings about Gibson were ambivalent. Although Gibson had been friendly toward him abroad, Frost resented Gibson's failure to help Edward Thomas when the latter was unestablished as a poet. Socially, Gibson lacked breeding—"no breeding, low-class English" is the way Frost described the Northumberland poet. And he regarded him as only facile and slight as a poet.

Gibson and Frost had been invited to share a lecture engagement in Philadelphia at which each was to read from his poetry. Gibson, introduced first, made a strong favorable impression upon his audience with his North Country accent. Then, as Frost explained, after Gibson's sweeping victory, there was an interlude during which a pianist played for a half hour. Frost was to follow the pianist. After listening to Gibson's vigorous performance, he was emotionally disturbed. During the piano recital he left the room and soused his neck in cold water to restore composure. When he read his poems they did not receive the pouncing approval of the Northumberland poet's and this galled him.

Afterward, the two poets were asked to share the same bedroom. While preparing for bed Gibson approached Frost and drew a check out of his inside pocket, saying, "Let us see who got the larger check." Of course Gibson's check proved to be the larger amount. "But," complained Frost justifiably, "wasn't it rude of Gibson? It was humiliating—the whole evening—and I was resentful." Frost added tersely, "Haven't seen Gibson since. Suppose he's still living." The frustration of Frost's ordeal by nonrecognition is encapsulated in this bitter and nagging recollection. However, if the date of the appearance in Philadelphia in 1917 is correct, then Frost did see Wilfred Gibson once more, in 1928, when he revisited England. The other details are viva voce and their accuracy hardly disputable. For over thirty years Frost had carried the scars of this recrudescent wound.

In the duration and severity of Frost's long period of nonrecognition, his resentment toward fellow poets of equal or lesser stature intensified. Despite his praise of Pound's "Doria" or Robinson's "Mr. Flood's Party," the latter of which he read with delight close to tears, or the last stanzas of Eliot's "The Hollow Men," the specific poems of his contemporaries which he praised were few and far between. When he quoted it was almost unexceptionally from the great tradition of Raleigh and Shakespeare, Campion and Shirley, Davies and Herrick, Cowley and Milton, Smart and Burns, Keats and Tennyson, Browning and Landor, Patmore and Dowson.

Not only was he stingy in praise but his withheld approval suggested littleness. He also exercised selectivity and discrimination. Both discernment and causticity appear in his criticism of Sandburg. He deprecated, probably with justification, Sandburg's "awful sentimentality" which tended to blur the effect of an enlight-

ened social vision. And he referred to Sandburg with excessive scorn
as "all bubble, bubble, bubble." Yet in 1951, when Sandburg received the Pulitzer prize in poetry for *Complete Poems*, published
in 1950, Frost readily admitted that Sandburg deserved the prize.

Of Vachel Lindsay, the second of the Mid-American poets, Frost
always spoke well. The Illinois poet of "the higher vaudeville" and
an exponent of romantic primitivism was hardly a rival. Frost's reaction to Edgar Lee Masters, the third poet in the Mid-American
triumvirate, was another matter. Once, when Jesse Stuart, the interesting and original short-story-teller of W-Hollow in Eastern
Kentucky visited with Frost on a midsummer day in 1953, Frost
described Masters as a "dark, somber person," who was "hostile" to
him. Frost did not elaborate. What had happened between the sensitive Frost and Masters? Was it some affront? A failure in communication? Another unhappy sharing of a lecture-reading? His reserva-
tion about Masters had early roots. While living in Franconia in
1915, the Frosts had been invited to a dinner party at the home of
some wealthy people, recently settled in the vicinity. Throughout
the evening, as Frost told it, there had been nothing but praise for
Masters, who wrote *Spoon River Anthology* in those moments he
could snatch while fighting injunctions against a waitresses' union
struggling for the right to picket and get an extra day of rest each
week. The book, published in 1915, was an immediate sensation. It
sold 80,000 copies in 1915 and 1916.

During the evening someone mentioned that Frost had written
a book, entitled *North of Boston* (England, 1914; U. S. A., 1915),
but no more was said of it. "I had a hard time," admitted Frost un-
abashedly, "trying not to show resentment at praise of Masters and
neglect of *North of Boston*." He added, not as a non sequitur, that
one reason the Frosts moved away from Franconia to South Shaftsbury, Vermont, was so the children wouldn't be brought up exposed
to these insensitive, wealthy people.

The impression Frost's relationship to other poets, notably American, had on his writing might lead one to wonder when he ever
found, in Melville's words, "the calm, the coolness, the silent grass-
growing mood in which a man *ought* always to compose." In the

intrapersonal context, there were his differences with the energetic and combative Amy Lowell, the constrained relationship with the retiring and meditative Edwin Arlington Robinson, and the less than cordial meetings with the snobbish and arrogant William Butler Yeats when he visited this country.

When Professor David Daiches, then at Cornell University, lectured on "Modern Poetry" at the Bread Loaf School of English in the summer of 1951, it was arranged that Frost would meet him the day following the lecture. During the daylong meeting in which we met at the cabin, then drove to East Middlebury and lunched at the Waybury Inn, circuited the Vermont countryside in the afternoon, driving from East Middlebury to the Homer Noble farm in Ripton via Bristol and Lincoln, Daiches pressed Frost on the Imagist poets. Frost declared it was not T. E. Hulme (*Speculations*, 1924), whom he described as "a big brute, jovial, and a great scoffer," or Ezra Pound, or Amy Lowell, who was the important influence on the Imagist Movement in modern poetry. The most influential force was the timid, learned F. S. Flint, master of two languages and translator of works on Lenin and Gandhi as well as French and Latin poetry. Frost, praising Flint's *In the Net of the Stars* (1909), asserted that the brilliant Flint had influenced all the others. Daiches listened quietly. "Nothing could have happened," said Frost later, in 1952, "had it not been for F. S. Flint." But when, on another occasion, Frost acknowledged voluntarily the early support which had been given him, he did not forget Dr. William Hayes Ward, editor of *The Independent*, and his sister, Susan Hayes Ward. Frost's only qualification was that Ward wanted him to be like Lanier or Milton. When Frost dropped out of Dartmouth College in 1892, Ward thought it was the end for Frost. Ward's idol, John Milton, had learning, and the young Frost was apparently turning his back on it. In passing, Frost conjectured interestingly that if Ward had at the time shown him Lanier's "The Revenge of Hamish" he might have gone along with his advocacy of academic learning.

Deliberating on Frost's statement that he must be "free of all sense of rivalry"—a statement that nearly amounts to a cri de coeur or paranoia, is it not only of the utmost interest but certainly important to establish the context of his intrapersonal relationship with Ezra Pound and T. S. Eliot, two of the major poets in modern American literature? How seriously did Pound and Eliot affect the flow of Frost's writing and his rise to prominence?

Frost described Pound as a man "jet-propelled by hate from country to country." Often he openly disaparaged this central figure—so central that Hugh Kenner entitled a major critical book *The Pound Era* (1971)—by such unsparing epithets as "a slasher," "bossy," "bullying," "conceited." Yet Frost also took pains to make correctives which neutralize and modify an ambivalent attitude toward Pound. Frost pointed out that Pound had "aesthetic courage" and that generously he had given anything his friends required, provided of course that he remained the boss. In an unmistakable show of approbation rather than a patronizing attitude as might be inferred, Frost, as already noted, remarked not grudgingly of Pound: "He's done enough poems to earn a place in the story of American literature."

Frost did describe Pound as "fascinating" and "like an elf." More frequently he was caustic, and derogatorily called Pound "a buncosteerer" who had gone "from ancients to antics." I mentioned to Frost that Ezra Pound claimed he had "discovered" him. In March 1913, for example, Pound had written Alice Corbin Henderson: "Have just discovered another Amur'kin," and, in another letter, this one to H. L. Mencken dated February 18, 1915, Pound had written: "Frost is in America, dull, perhaps, but has something in him."

"Did Pound discover you?" I asked Frost.

"No!" he replied. "F. S. Flint discovered me."

F. S. Flint had first met Frost at Harold Monro's Poetry Bookshop at 35 Devonshire Street (now Boswell Street) in London where he had gone on the opening night of January 8, 1913 when John Drinkwater read. Flint, sitting on a staircase, had looked at Frost's shoes, and asked:

"Are you an American?"

"Yes," said Frost.

"Are you a poet?" asked Flint.

"I accept the omen," Frost replied.

Then Flint inquired: "Do you know your countryman, Ezra Pound?"

"No!"

"Well, then, you better not let him know it."

Soon after the evening at Monro's Poetry Bookshop, Frost received a card from Pound inviting him to stop in for a visit at Church Walk in Kensington. Characteristically, Frost didn't do so immediately, but while wandering around the streets of London, he came upon Church Walk and, recognizing it as the street in which Pound was living, stopped in and Pound urged him to let him see his poems. This story is well known. After reading Frost's poems, Pound wrote favorably of *A Boy's Will* in *The New Freeman*, London, in September 1913, and, in December 1914, reviewed *North of Boston* on its publication in *Poetry* V, 3. Frost's account so casually told, and so often repeated with variations, must have been the way word of his "discovery" became linked with Pound's name. Yet what Frost meant by being discovered was not that Flint had "discovered" his *poetry*; only that he had discovered *him*.

There is another important glint in the shifting light of Frost's intrapersonal relationship to Ezra Pound. "Old Ez," as Pound familiarly called himself in *The Cantos*, always a controversial figure, dramatically entered the political world of international affairs during World War II. Living in Italy from 1924 until he stood trial for treason in Washington, Pound had held an official post in the Italian Fascist government of Mussolini and broadcast anti-Allied propaganda over the Rome radio. When Italy surrendered in 1945, Pound was brought to the United States and indicted on the charge of high treason. He was adjudged insane and committed to St. Elizabeths Hospital. Consequently, in 1948, when he received the Bollingen Award for the *Pisan Cantos*, the honor was protested stormily in and out of the news media. In 1950, Archibald MacLeish published *Poetry and Opinion*, which is not so much an apologia for Pound's receiving the prize, given by the Mellon Foundation under the sponsorship of the Library of Congress, as an intelligent rebuttal to an intransigent editorial comment which appeared in *The Saturday Review of Literature* on June 11, 1949. *The Saturday Review* contended that "if Pound is not to be shot as a traitor, at least let him not be festooned with quasi-official prizes and laurels." MacLeish's *Poetry and Opinion*, fundamentally concerned with justifying Pound's right to the award, based its justification on Pound's right to the prize on the central conviction that "loyalty to the art of poetry has not been synonymous . . . with loyalty to the society and the values it accepts." MacLeish separated the art of poetry, an aesthetic matter, from its social role, just as the purely aesthetic art for art's sake view would separate art from moral responsibility during the fin de siècle of the 1890s.

It helps to have both the charge of high treason and the Bollingen affair in focus when we consider Frost's further relationship to Pound. For indeed the details represent a rather ironic commentary on Frost's desideratum of a freedom from all rivalry. It requires no act of the imagination to realize (a) that a fervent but not militant nationalist like Frost ("I'm a terrible nationalist"), and (b) one who tardily received the Bollingen Prize in Poetry on his deathbed, on January 5, 1963, would be reluctant to assist an expatriate. On the record, Pound appeared not only to have committed treason against a country for which Frost felt strongly, but Pound ("Lord of his work and master of utterance") had also received an award long before him.

On January 14, 1957, Archibald MacLeish who, together with T. S. Eliot, was indefatigable in trying to get Pound released from St. Elizabeths Hospital without having to stand trial, prepared a final draft of a letter in Pound's behalf, and sent it to Attorney General Herbert Brownell, Jr. It was typed on the letterhead of the American Academy of Arts and Letters and signed by Eliot, Hemingway, and Frost. The attorney general's office acknowledged receipt of the letter on February 28, 1958.

> It is our understanding, based on inquiries directed to the medical personnel at St. Elizabeth's Hospital, that Pound is now unfit for trial and, in the opinion of the doctors treating him, will continue to be unfit for trial. . . . Under these circumstances, the perpetuation of the charges against him seems to us unfortunate and, indeed, indefensible. . . . We cannot but regret the failure of the Department thus far to take steps to *nol pros* the indictment and remit the case to the medical authorities for disposition on medical grounds.

On April 1, 1958, the new attorney general, William P. Rogers, who had replaced Herbert Brownell, Jr., indicated to the press that the Department of Justice had taken under consideration dropping the charges against Pound. In the Washington District Court on April 18, 1958, Judge Bolitha J. Laws dismissed the indictment—exactly twelve years, eleven months, and two weeks after Pound was taken into custody at Rapallo. He was officially discharged from St. Elizabeths Hospital into the custody of his wife on May 7, 1958, lingered in the United States for a couple of months, then sailed for Italy on June 30, and reached Naples on July 9.

To a reporter, when reminded of Frost's efforts, Pound said: "He ain't been in much of a hurry." When later those words were quoted to him by Harry Meacham, a poet and businessman from Virginia, Pound, more gracious, said: "Frost's debt was paid when he published *North of Boston.*"

How does this relevant prefatory statement fit into the context of Frost's reading of "the Pound case"? On the evening of June 3, 1958, a year after cutting the Gordian knot of Pound's incarceration, Frost invited my wife and me to dinner at the Waybury Inn, in East Middlebury. We had no sooner become seated than he launched into the Pound case. Successful in securing the release of Pound from St. Elizabeths Hospital, he was exuberant with the outcome and his prominent part in it. How was it done? Well, he got the best legal counsel he could, and Thurman Arnold, of Arnold, Fortas and Power, on April 14, 1958 had asked that the 1945 indictment against Pound be dismissed. The smoothness of the operation after last year's stalemate appealed to Frost. He had gone to the attorney general, William P. Rogers, and said: "What's your mood?" Rogers replied: "What's yours?" That was that, I gathered. Nothing was said about the interest of Senator R. L. Neuberger or Rep. Usher L. Burdick in the case, or of the long report prepared by H. A. Sieber of the Library of Congress on "The Medical, Legal, Literary and Political Status of Ezra (Loomis) Pound." Nothing indeed about Dr. Gabriel Hague (President Eisenhower's Advisor on Economics) and Sherman Adams (President Eisenhower's influential assistant). Adams asked for and got the President's permission to go forward with the legal aspects of the case.

Rogers and Frost, according to the latter, had pushed the case right through the federal district court in Washington, and Judge Laws dismissed the indictment against Pound. Once more he was free to return to Italy. Only—Frost hoped that the United States government wouldn't become too apologetic. In Frost's opinion Pound had been paid by the Fascists for the broadcasts, although Pound had denied this to be so. Throughout the Pound affair Frost had not seen Pound, but the latter had written him a note of thanks: a tiny message at the top of a sheet and a big bold E. P. inscribed on the rest of the sheet. He was, Frost thought, still crazy as a coot. Later in the evening when we were at the Homer Noble farm, Frost again referred to the Pound case, and said self-approvingly: "I'm a pretty damn shrewd politician." None who know Frost would doubt this for a moment. He also added that he was working on James Laughlin of New Directions, Pound's publisher, to arrange some financial assistance for "Old Ez."

Frost, a week later—on June 10, 1958—in the company of a collector of his memorabilia, appeared at my home on the Pulp Mill Bridge Road. He brought up the Pound affair, still vividly on his mind. The Library of Congress Fellows in American Letters had wanted Frost to let Pound make some new records to take back with him into his self-exile in Italy. At this time Frost was the recently appointed Consultant in Poetry in the Library of Congress, a term that began in October 1958 and ended in May 1959. Frost thought this suggestion ill-advised, and, as the new consultant, he didn't want to permit it though as he saw it, he had just been chiefly instrumental in getting Pound freed from the charge of treason. Frost argued that Pound would use the grant of permission as a total exoneration and claim he had been put in St. Elizabeths Hospital by mistake, which was not the case. He had been indicted and convicted of treason, Frost argued; now he was free but there should be no attendant reparation, no forgiveness for his treasonable acts during World War II. Those treasonable acts stood, but mercy had been shown in the dismissal of the indictment. As the newly appointed consultant, Frost did not like the idea that the old Bollingen group, including Randall Jarrell, were trying to put something over by getting him to accede to the maneuver of making the records.

How relentless Frost was in his tough-mindedness surfaces in the context of this reaction, especially in view of one who wrote *A Masque of Mercy* (1947) and told the premier of Russia, Nikita Khrushchev, in a talk with him at Gagra on the Black Sea on September 7, 1962 that the great thing was "magnanimity."

The T. S. Eliot-Frost affair, now a common subject of literary gossip, has its variations and proper context. However, I shall make no attempt to deal with it comprehensively or exhaustively. Eliot and Frost were poets of different aims and methods as well as different influences, generations, antecedents, and temperaments. We probably know more of Frost's side since he seems to have been the more self-consciously aggrieved party. Certainly, he was jealous, belittling, and voluble.

It is hard to recognize in Frost's hostility toward Eliot anything more than a jealous rivalry at Eliot's phenomenal success. *Prufrock* had appeared in England in 1917, and the American edition, including other poems, was published in 1920. But it was the publication of *The Waste Land* in 1922 that fixed a powerful image of a whole epoch. A year later, in 1923, Frost published *New Hampshire*, his fourth book, and although it won the Pulitzer Prize, Eliot's "difficult" poetry took the play away from him. What really troubled Frost about Eliot, excluding the expatriate stance and the elegant snobbery, was the praise Eliot's poetry received for its exegetical quotient. Eliot required close reading, and his reputation grew with the footnotes. The dismayed Frost tauntingly deprecated Eliot and the epigones. "They're all infected with their own criticism," he remarked testily later in life.

In context, one of many stories illustrates the tenuous relationship between the two. Frost made a point of describing the incident. In 1939, Ferris Greenslet, a highly respected editor-in-chief at Houghton Mifflin Company, invited several prominent people to meet Eliot at the elite St. Botolph Club in Boston. At the dinner, Eliot, the guest of honor, read from his poems. Frost, who was also there, listened, and, at the close of the reading, in a fit of bravado, challenged Eliot to improvise a poem on the spur of the moment, a not untypically aggressive Frostian reaction. Eliot was evasive. Frost, gathering up some scraps of menus, wrote out "A Record

Stride" as though freshly conceived. Actually, it had been earlier written at his home in South Shaftsbury, Vermont, and disingenuously he was trying to diminish Eliot. If Eliot felt chagrined at or simply indulgent of Frost's aggressive show of equivocal manners, I don't know.

Frost loved to tell the story as though he was the champion of this field of prowess, the implied point being, at any rate, that Eliot's poems might lend themselves to careful explications de textes, but hardly to memorization. And what was poetry if it wasn't memorable? During the evening Frost was also miffed when Eliot asserted that no worthwhile poetry had been produced north of the Tweed. Frost countered with Burns. Eliot sniffed at Burns as *only* a songwriter, though he did condescend to grant William Dunbar words of slight praise.

In Frost's presence, I witnessed a remarkable and completely unrehearsed putdown of Eliot as a poet when, one late May day in 1943, I stopped in to see him at the Homer Noble farm. We were conversing in the front room of the farmhouse, and on the table in front of the sofa was a copy of Eliot's *Four Quartets*, freshly cut. He asked me to read from it. I demurred, and he picked it up, and reading here and there, but especially in "East Coker," analyzed the texture of the line, word usage, and content in an unforgettable, unsparingly close examination of Eliot's poetic art. It was an exciting tour de force, and at the conclusion of this voluntary object lesson Eliot's skill as a verse technician appeared to me greatly diminished. I had heard previously that Frost had, in a classroom at Amherst College, exposed Robert Bridges's much-praised *The Testament of Beauty* (1929) to a similar close critical examination. The dual impression I had was, one, that Frost was distinctly a poetic craftsman, but, two, that he was a knowledgeable verse critic, acute in reading the poetry of his peers. Elizabeth Shepley Sergeant reminds us in *Robert Frost: The Trial by Existence* (1960) that Frost had met Bridges and listened closely to the latter's views "on the application of classical prosody and quantities to English metrics" (p. 105), and that he had disagreed with what he heard, as he mentioned in a letter to his friend Sidney Cox, written from Beaconfield, Buckinghamshire, January 19, 1914. Frost opposed Bridges's argument for fixed quantities in English verse, and, in turn, proposed his own theory that "the living part of a poem is the intonation entangled somehow in the syntax idiom and meaning of a sentence" (*SL*, p. 107). What troubled Frost in *Four Quartets* was not dissimilar from what troubled him in *The Testament of Beauty*. He missed the natural intonation of the speaking voice entangled in the syntactical idiom and sentence meaning.

There was another fundamental difference between the two poets. Eliot was a poet's poet who had progressed from an articulation of post-World War I demoralization and despair to religious devotion. His pious call for a return to the faith of the fathers after 1927 followed the brilliantly subtle portrayal of the waste land and the hollow men, from 1909 until 1925. In the voluntary restraint of impulse and the subordination of the individual to an aesthetic and ethical order, he represents the believer in classical discipline, a countertendency to the view of the Rousseauistic epoch. And in his insistence on Christian discipline in the moral and spiritual realm he represents a believer in the religious tradition. So, when, on an early June day in 1958, Frost talked about "taking things as they come," he underscored the difference between Eliot and himself. Although the witty distinction Frost made has been bandied about as though it was a wisecrack, Frost was serious. "T. S. Eliot," he said, "is a Christian pessimist; I am a pagan optimist." Or the variant: "What's the difference between T. S. Eliot and myself? Eliot's churchly, I'm religious." He continued: "Eliot divides his talks into four parts: Heaven, Hell, Purgatory, and this world. I divide my talks into two parts, both in this world. First, there is the basic animal faith which leads me to believe in playing to win. And, secondly, at a higher level, there is a lift or crest where you hope that what you do will be acceptable. But whether you win or lose you hope you don't make too much of a fool of yourself in the eyes of *It*." Despite the rivalry, Frost respected Eliot. Yet as a human being, it was not easy for Frost to see the international accolade of a Nobel Award in November 1948 go to an expatriate. What galled him most in the following years was to have to take in stride the withholding of the courted prize, not only because of pride, but certainly because he felt he had let down those who believed stoutly in him.

In approaching the suprapersonal context, the discussion will focus entirely on the transcendent religious aspect. There is, of course, no intent to go into all the ramifications of this complex subject. I have been content to try to place in context some of Frost's statements, especially the prevailing assertion concerning acceptability which became an important part of the sermon he gave at the Rockdale Avenue Temple in Cincinnati on October 10, 1946.

5.

Frost's particular religious belief represents a suprapersonal relationship. What, for example, did he mean to imply when he called himself "a pagan optimist" in contradistinction to Eliot's Christian pessimism? In what context shall we read his self-identification? I find a clue in a favorite story to which he often alluded publicly and privately. When I mentioned that he had referred to himself as "an Old Testament believer," what had he actually intended? The Old Testament was, he explained, "full of good things." "Oh, I see," I replied, "it was the literary content you liked." But he added clarifyingly that it was the monotheism which had attracted him, saying: "You know, I think Jewish monotheism comes from the Egyptian Akenaton [Amenhotep IV], the first Unitarian." "Once," he continued, "I used the phrase 'free thinker' in my mother's presence and she murmured and was troubled, but I didn't use it as she thought. I simply meant free to think in all ways, not as a religious doubter." He explained further: "And I thought quite awhile before I made that quip I used over at Hanover [at the Commencement exercises on June 12, 1955] about the difference between mud and prepared mud." Frost was alluding here to the oft self-quoted incident previously noted when, as a boy of fourteen, he had countered his mother's pious orthodox view that God made man out of mud. He told her, with Darwinism in mind, "You say, 'God made man of mud,' and I think God made man of *prepared mud.*"

As a monotheistic "Old Testament believer," he was early exercising his right to think (after the Darwinists) in a new-fashioned way, and his mother was exercising her right to think (after the conventional orthodoxy of the time) in an old-fashioned way. What is significant is the essential fact of belief. In a revelatory statement at an open discussion at the Bread Loaf School of English, no one in the crowded audience could very well have mistaken his position. At 86, he was sure of his stance. It was not the atheist, like Julian Huxley, whom he reproached, it was the agnostic. "My greatest prejudice," he said emphatically, "is against an agnostic. He doesn't believe either way. He's just afraid to believe—afraid to disbelieve, and afraid to believe." Yet Frost's defense of Huxley's status, and Frost's scorn of agnosticism, doesn't tell us with any assurance whether Frost was (a) a believer, or (b) what inclination his belief took.

To understand the answers to these inquiries, we have to consider exactly what constituted belief in his mind. He was a hard man to pin down. When discussing the two masques with the students who were to perform them at the Bread Loaf School of English (on the evening of July 22, 1957), he was asked: "What do *you* really believe?" "Oh, don't ask me that," he answered evasively. "I go around the edges of it. Historically, I'm a Congregationalist. My ancestors were so independent we sang different songs in church. We were not Cromwell and Milton." On another occasion when we drove past the lovely old New England Congregational Church at the top of Main street in Middlebury, Vermont, he looked up and said slyly: "I don't go to church but I look in the window." Hardly a churchgoer, he knew, I am sure, what was going on with the ecumenical thrust of the times. "What's in Christian religion?" he once asked rhetorically, and answering his own question, he replied: "To make us believe. Believe in what? Why, to make us believe in belief. It's the nicest religion. Why? Because of the Gospels —the stories."

Although later in life he liked taunting institutionalized religion about as much as he liked taunting *exact* science and *formal* education, I noticed that he was keenly interested in trying to define what religion meant, as he was in trying to identify poetry. Two of his definitions of religion stand out. In June 1948, he defined religion precisely as he had in a most revealing sermon which he delivered at the Rockdale Avenue Temple, Cincinnati, Ohio on October 10, 1946 at the First Day of the Feast of Tabernacles. "What is religion? When we say we can aspire to full consent." Or as he amplified in the synagogue: "Now religion always seems to me to come round to something beyond wisdom. It's a straining of the spirit forward to a wisdom beyond wisdom. . . . And the fear of God always has meant the fear that one's wisdom . . . one's human wisdom is not quite acceptable in his sight." Almost ten years later—in 1957—he redefined religion. "It's an adventure of the spirit into the material; that's religion," he said. Neither definition cancels the other; but rather, they are supplementary. In both cases, the view is not concerned with either "ineffables" or "divine visitations." It is an horizontal slant, but the highest to which a human being can rise within himself. When I said: "Well, I suppose religion has to do with the universe and our relationship to it," he replied bluntly, "Now you're getting scientific. You're looking at it from the viewpoint of matter and force. All I know is what I find to say sometimes. The highest nobility is in that."

One October day in 1959 when we were talking about religion, he asked quizzically: "Well, am I a religious man? I don't know. How can I say? I'm not sectarian, I suppose." When I said that I thought he was a religious man, he neither demurred nor asked for an explanation of terms. Then he said very provocatively: "Religion is self-hate," a statement that seemed to me enigmatic, to say the least. Yet what he meant was simple enough. Consistently with his concept of religion as presented to Rabbi Victor Reichert's congregation in Cincinnati, he meant that in loving something greater than oneself we must hate a part of ourselves. When in the Bible (see St. Matthew XIX, 19; Leviticus XIX, 18) we are enjoined to love our neighbors as ourselves, we really take the text to mean that we love ourselves a little more than we hate ourselves. Yet if we follow the logic all the way through, if we love ourselves as our neighbors, then we ought also to hate our neighbors as ourselves. And what it amounts to is our hating our neighbors a little more than we hate ourselves. As for original sin, he had no truck with this medieval concept.

If, in the context, Frost is a pagan because of his nonsectarian view, he is a pagan only in the literal etymology of the word—a countryman (L. *paganus*), that is, a heathen because the rustic people remained longest unconverted. As for the optimist, on the same occasion when he conjectured on religion as "self-hate," he remarked about seeing the darkness of the world—and who doubts it?—but he thought, despite the darkness, it was not overwhelming. He had a sense of what the human race can do. "There are two ways of taking the awfulness of it all," he conjectured, "either laugh it off—that's comedy, or curse it out—and that's tragedy." In "The Lesson For Today," Frost wrote:

> There's nothing but injustice to be had,
> No choice is left a poet, you might add,
> But how to take the curse, tragic or comic (p. 352).

There is a fuller context for Frost's definition of religion as aspiring "to full consent" in June 1948. He had been talking euphorically about the Ionian philosophers (Xenophanes, Heracleitus, Parmenides) and criticizing sharply the Orphic and the Eleusinian groups. Of the Ionians, he had wondered where they got their stimulus to challenge the authority and hierarchy of the gods. And he recalled, by way of allusion, an Inca (probably Huaina Capac) who stood out from his people by challenging the claim of the Inca priests that the Incas were descended from a god and therefore were a god-chosen people. Frost was not attacking religion; he was only calling in question sentimentality and mysticism in orthodox belief and the superstition and dogma in ancient belief. For this reason, he commended both Epicurus and Lucretius for their intellectual boldness in daring to clear away the underbrush with the challenging counterstatements to those who seemed to be seeing things illusorily. In this band of Ionian Greeks, Frost found a wedge of doubt that split open the heart of the ancient fears. They too were pagans, and in their courageous intelligence he found a justification for optimism.

6.

Intimate disclosures surely grow out of unexpected occasions, and novelists have not been slow to prove the validity of this age-old psychological truism. In the remarkable chapter 40 of *The Portrait of a Lady* Henry James shows us how profoundly illustrative Isabel Archer is of the impact of the unexpected intimate disclosure when she suddenly recognizes in Madame Merle an altogether too familiar connection with her husband: "But the thing made an image, lasting only a moment, like a sudden flicker of light." There are times when, in James's phrasing, "the inch takes an ell." For example, quite unintentionally, I once surprised Frost at the Homer Noble farm in the late 1940s when he had a right to consider himself secure from intrusion. He was in a pasture trimming brush with a long-handled Disston hedge shears. As I approached the preoccupied poet, I spoke up but he did not at first hear me. But sensing a presence, he looked up startled and on his expressive face was a look of self-defensive anger or fear. It was hard to tell which. Immediately upon recognizing me his expression and manner changed and we turned at once to the business at hand, discussion of a mutual problem at the Bread Loaf School of English. On this occasion, where the inch takes an ell, I learned that he had grown deaf and all future references to birdsongs in his poetry would depend upon early aural memories.

In the late years I came to understand that the early private figure of the long New Hampshire background—"back in those lonely days"—had not become the public one of the New Poetry Movement without paying a scot, either economically or psychically. Just as obviously, Frost had not reached an elevated place in national recognition without personal doubts and uncertainties. As late as 1949 I noticed an insecurity even when he was "saying" his poems and amiably bantering with an audience whom he could always expect to be comfortable at the Bread Loaf School of English. After heartwarming applause, I thanked him enthusiastically. "It was wonderful," I said. A little plaintively, he replied with a slightly diffident rebuke: "That's what *you* would say, anyway." In effect, was I sincere? Had he really performed well? He showed a doubt and a hesitancy that was not attributable to modesty.

Yet he remonstrated at any attribution of frustration. In the long uphill pull he seemed to say there had been disappointments, but hardly frustration. Carefully, he distinguished between people who are defeated and those who are frustrated. The former are "the nice ones," the latter, as he said, "aren't nice." When the nice ones fail, their courage takes the sting out of defeat. Years later—in 1962—he told of a young woman who appeared after one of his lectures at Boston College, who introduced herself and said:

"Now I want to talk to you for a half hour about poetry."

"Well, go ahead," he nodded, "what do you want to know?"

"I want to know where the frustration comes in," she said.

"If that's what you want to talk about, I've nothing to say," he replied. A priest appeared, apologized for the young woman's intrusion. "She shouldn't be here," the priest explained. Frost, in relating the incident, said to me defensively: "But I've never been frustrated. Frustration isn't part of it. I picked up things from my reading." By way of illustrating what he picked up, he quoted from the witches' scene in *Macbeth*, from "Kubla Khan" ("Where Alph, the sacred river, ran"), which he discovered as an epigraph in Rider Haggard's *King Solomon's Mines*, and Keats's "magic casements, opening on the foam/ Of perilous seas, in fairy lands forlorn."

The contretemps of sorts at Boston College points up the fact that no matter how insecure and uncertain Frost might have felt in his personal relationships, he had a secure relationship to the great tradition of English poetry. And I for one do not find him unduly boastful in the letter he wrote his friend John Bartlett from England. "Some day," he wrote, on August 6, 1913, with the confidence of a skilled performer, "I will take time to explain to you in what sense of the word I am one of the few artists writing. I am one of the few who have a theory of their own upon which all their work down to the last accent is done. I expect to do something to the present state of literature in America" (Anderson, p. 59). To impose a theory of poetry upon a poet tends to load the dice. And to extract a theory from a poet's work might only be a subtle confirmation of the extractor's subconscious vision. In Frost's case we should be content with neither the imposition nor the extraction. Early he had worked out his own theory, which he continued to clarify and refine during the rest of his long life.

In view of the ascendency of technology in our culture, Frost may well have been one of the last poets of stature to play a major role in American society, when we consider his unofficial "barding around," the four Pulitzer prizes, numerous honorary degrees, trips to South America (1954), England (1957), and U. S. S. R. (1962) under the auspices of the U. S. Department of State, and, of course, his much publicized participation in the inauguration ceremonies for President John F. Kennedy in 1961. The future in poetry, like Frost's, or in any other poet for that matter, is in moving the human heart. Such a capacity is a token of the continuity which knits the present with the ongoing in a perennial solidarity.

I do not think that, like T. S. Eliot's image of the wasteland, Frost has imposed an image on his generation, or that like Milton he has influenced the great tradition by the form of what he did. But he has correlated the great tradition of the past with the varying impulses of the present. What identifies his indelibility are the shrewd and perceptive insights of an imagined reality. In the totality of his consciousness, he enforces in this imagined reality a spare and realistic but not impoverished vision of the world. It is more speculative than comprehensive, and it disclaims the prophetic and predictive. "Someone," he said banteringly but no less significantly, "wants me to do something to glorify the space age and our part of it. That's prophecy and I charge more for prophecy." The key to his vision would seem to be self-discovery, the results of the twists and turns in the process of his life. Unlike Whitman, he was not a writer of proclamations or of edicts like the Imagists, nor even of credos like Pound's "A Retrospect." I think he was content, after securing a language to express his singularity, to use trees, brooks, stars and flowers, springs and dark woods as symbolic referents to evoke a vision of the human heart. The roothold of the regional was not thereby his ultimate realm. And nature, of which he said, "It's just the background of the picture for me, just a background for human ideas," was read thematically to point up *human* ideas.

Our contemporary critics in discussing Frost continue to echo the burden of the plaint we early heard about "the dark woods." Surely "the dark woods" represent a symbolic referent of psychological depths in the poet. Yet all who read his poetry carefully must also acknowledge the sanguinity and humor to be found there. Consider his exaltation of the art of poetry ("But where does poetry come in? It's interstitial."), or the great tradition ("The past is the great book of the Worthies."), or science ("the fine point of daring in our time"), or religion ("That's what the Christian religion means—God's own descent into flesh meant as a demonstration that the supreme merit lay in risking spirit in substantiation."), or the Greeks ("I have been moved to the pleasure of tears in reading the Ionian philosophers who challenged the authority and hierarchy of the gods."). Except for poetry, I doubt that any realm—religion, or science, or politics—alone held the Ark of the Covenant for him.

The secret of Robert Frost wherever it sits tends to make some interpreters paranoic. Commonly they are valid victims, who, like Yeats, are fascinated by what's difficult. They wonder how much role playing there is, how many masks, what the postures mean, how much the Movement shaped the poetry, how much the familial background, how much the world of literary politics entered. Yet what always stands out is the struggle and the loneliness, the sadness and the courage, the refusal to capitulate to fashionable taste, either because temperamentally he could not or because intransigently he would not compromise.

Robert Frost's Favorite Poem

N. ARTHUR BLEAU

ROBERT FROST revealed his favorite poem to me. Furthermore, he gave me a glimpse into his personal life that exposed the mettle of the man. I cherish the memory of that conversation, and vividly recall his description of the circumstances leading to the composition of his favorite work.

We were in my hometown—Brunswick, Maine. It was the fall of 1947, and Bowdoin College was presenting its annual literary institute for students and the public. Mr. Frost had lectured there the previous season; and being well received, he was invited for a return engagement.

I attended the great poet's prior lecture and wasn't about to miss his encore—even though I was quartered 110 miles north at the University of Maine. At the appointed time, I was seated and eagerly awaiting his entrance—armed with a book of his poems and unaware of what was about to occur.

He came on strong with a simple eloquence that blended with his stature, bushy white hair, matching eyebrows, and well-seasoned features. His topics ranged from meter to the meticulous selection of a word and its varying interpretations. He then read a few of his poems to accentuate his message.

At the conclusion of the presentation, Mr. Frost asked if anyone had questions. I promptly raised my hand. There were three other questioners, and their inquiries were answered before he acknowledged me. I asked, "Mr. Frost, what is your favorite poem?" He quickly replied, "They're all my favorites. It's difficult to single out one over another!"

"But, Mr. Frost," I persisted, "surely there must be one or two of your poems which have a special meaning to you—that recall some incident perhaps." He then astonished me by declaring the session concluded; whereupon, he turned to me and said, "Young man, you may come up to the podium if you like." I was there in an instant.

We were alone except for one man who was serving as Mr. Frost's host. He remained in the background shadows of the stage. The poet leaned casually against the lectern—beckoning me to come closer. We were side by side leaning on the lectern as he leafed the pages of the book.

"You know—in answer to your question—there is one poem which comes readily to mind; and I guess I'd have to call it my favorite," he droned in a pensive manner. "I'd have to say 'Stopping by Woods on a Snowy Evening' is that poem. Do you recall in the lecture I pointed out the importance of the line 'The darkest evening of the year'?" I acknowledged that I did, and he continued his thoughtful recollection of a time many years before. "Well—the darkest evening of the year is on December twenty-second—which is the shortest day of the year—just before Christmas."

I wish I could have recorded the words as he reflectively meted out his story, but this is essentially what he said.

The family was living on a farm. It was a bleak time both weatherwise and financially. Times were hard, and Christmas was coming. It wasn't going to be a very good Christmas unless he did something. So—he hitched up the wagon filled with produce from the farm and started the long trek into town.

When he finally arrived, there was no market for his goods. Times were hard for everybody. After exhausting every possibility, he finally accepted the fact that there would be no sale. There would be no exchange for him to get a few simple presents for his children's Christmas.

As he headed home, evening descended. It had started to snow, and his heart grew heavier with each step of the horse in the gradually increasing accumulation. He had dropped the reins and given the horse its head. It knew the way. The horse was going more slowly as they approached home. It was sensing his despair. There is an unspoken communication between a man and his horse, you know.

Around the next bend in the road, near the woods, they would come into view of the house. He knew the family was anxiously awaiting him. How could he face them? What could he possibly say or do to spare them the disappointment he felt?

They entered the sweep of the bend. The horse slowed down and then stopped. It knew what he had to do. He had to cry, and he did. I recall the very words he spoke. "I just sat there and bawled like a baby"—until there were no more tears.

The horse shook its harness. The bells jingled. They sounded cheerier. He was ready to face his family. It would be a poor Christmas, but Christmas is a time of love. They had an abundance of love, and it would see them through that Christmas and the rest of those hard times. Not a word was spoken, but the horse knew he was ready and resumed the journey homeward.

The poem was composed some time later, he related. How much later I do not know, but he confided that these were the circumstances which eventually inspired what he acknowledged to be his favorite poem.

I was completely enthralled and, with youthful audacity, asked him to tell me about his next favorite poem. He smiled relaxedly and readily replied, "That would have to be 'Mending Wall.' Good fences do make good neighbors, you know! We always looked forward to getting together and walking the lines—each on his own side replacing the stones the winter frost had tumbled. As we moved along, we'd discuss the things each had experienced during the winter—and also what was ahead of us. It was a sign of spring!"

The enchantment was broken at that moment by Mr. Frost's host, who had materialized behind us to remind him of his schedule. He nodded agreement that it was time to depart, turned to me and with a smile extended his hand. I grasped it, and returned his firm grip as I expressed my gratitude. He then strode off to join his host, who had already reached the door at the back of the stage. I stood there watching him disappear from sight.

I've often wondered why he suddenly changed his mind and decided to answer my initial question by confiding his memoir in such detail. Perhaps no one had ever asked him; or perhaps I happened to pose it at the opportune time. Then again—perhaps the story was meant to be related, remembered and revealed sometime in the future. I don't know, but I'm glad he did—so that I can share it with you.

A Note by Lesley Frost

For many years I have assumed that my father's explanation to me, given sometime in the forties, I think, of the circumstances round and about his writing "Stopping by Woods" was the only one he gave (of course, excepting to my mother), and since he expressed the hope that it need not be repeated, fearing pity (pity, he said, was the *last* thing he wanted or needed), I have left it at that. Now, in 1977, I find there was at least one other to whom he vouchsafed the honor of hearing the truth of how it all was that Xmas eve when "the little horse" (Eunice) slows the sleigh at a point between woods, a hundred yards or so north of our farm on the Wyndham Road. And since Arthur Bleau's moving account is so closely, word for word, as I heard it, it would give me particular reason to hope it might be published. I would like to add my own remembrance of words used in the telling to me: "A man has as much right as a woman to a good cry now and again. The snow gave me its shelter; the horse understood and gave me the time." (Incidentally, my father had a liking for certain Old English words. *Bawl* was one of them. Instead of "Stop crying," it was "Oh, come now, quit bawling." Mr. Bleau is right to say my father bawled like a baby.)

ACCEPTABLE IN HEAVEN'S SIGHT

Frost at Bread Loaf: 1939–1941

PETER J. STANLIS

Yes, there you have it at the root of things.
We have to stay afraid deep in our souls
Our sacrifice—the best we have to offer,
And not our worst nor second best, our best,

. . . .

Our lives laid down in war and peace—may not
Be found acceptable in Heaven's sight.
And that they may be is the only prayer
Worth praying. May my sacrifice
Be found acceptable in Heaven's sight.

A Masque of Mercy (p. 520).

Robert Frost, on the porch of Little Theater, Bread Loaf, 1940

A Prelude to Bread Loaf:
1937–1939

THE STRENGTH OF THE HILLS IS HIS ALSO. On September 18, 1938, toward early sunset, I stood before the Middlebury College Mead Memorial Chapel and read this Biblical inscription (Psalms, 95:4) chiseled in marble across the façade of its portico. The chapel, a Greek classical structure with six marble columns across the portico, was topped by a white New England meeting house steeple reaching toward heaven. In its Biblical emblem, mixed architecture, and Vermont setting, the chapel embodied perfectly the Congregational Calvinist origins of Middlebury College in 1800, as evolved into a modern, rural, New England liberal arts college.

The chapel faced toward the east and was silhouetted on the rim of a long sloping hill overlooking the gray-granite, ivy-covered buildings of "Old Stone Row" on the lower campus. Beyond these buildings, farther downhill, lay the village of Middlebury, shire town of Addison County, largely hidden under green summer foliage, but flecked here and there by the first faint gold of approaching Indian summer. From the northeast the dark green shadow of Chipman Hill covered the village. Five miles or so farther east the low-lying Front range of the Green Mountains rose three to four thousand feet above Champlain Valley, running north and south to each horizon. At their rim against the sky the dark, unevenly shadowed ranges were touched here and there with a purple glow, a gold and maroon haze, from the sun fading below the Adirondack Mountains twelve miles to the west, beyond Lake Champlain. To the northeast, past the villages of Bristol and Lincoln, Mount Ellen rose 4,135 feet above the valley. Six miles to the southeast lay the tiny village of East Middlebury, nestled against the foot of Ripton Gorge, along which ran state highway 125, the road that wound its way four miles through the first range of the Green Mountains to the village of Ripton. Three miles or so beyond were the Bread

Loaf Inn and the Middlebury College mountain campus of the Bread Loaf School of English. The cottages of the campus lay on both sides of the road, in an open clearing of a large plateau surrounded by evergreen forests and mountain ranges. Almost directly north was the most conspicuous landmark from the campus, Bread Loaf Mountain, rising 3,823 feet high.

Standing there before the chapel steps that September evening I was almost totally unfamiliar with the geography of Vermont and the history and character of Middlebury College. I had arrived only the day before, hitchhiking up from New Jersey, to enter Middlebury as a freshman in the class of 1942. I had come up two days early, to find work so I could earn my way through college. Since the events that had finally led me to Middlebury had great bearing upon my college life, and eventually determined my going to Bread Loaf for eight summers, it is necessary to review briefly my earlier schooling and my literary experience before I met Robert Frost.

In 1923, when I was three years old, my parents had moved out of the "Ironbound" slums of Newark, New Jersey, where I was born, to the beautiful rural suburb of Nutley. I grew up in ideal surroundings and graduated from Nutley High School in June 1937. But the United States was still in the great depression, and my family had a very hard struggle to survive. Between June 1937 and September 1938 I spent months in fruitless searching for work. After making the rounds of shops and factories each morning, I usually spent my afternoons and evenings in the Nutley Public Library. In fourteen months I read several hundreds of books—much history, politics, and science, some philosophy, but particularly the fine arts and literature.

I read voraciously yet selectively in the whole range of English and American fiction, drama, and poetry. Since childhood I had had an intense and natural affinity for poetry, graduating from *Mother Goose* and Robert Louis Stevenson's *A Child's Garden of Verses* to the poetry anthologies of Louis Untermeyer used as texts in high school. I had soon discovered that when I liked a poem, often a single reading enabled me to retain it in memory and to quote it in full, almost regardless of its length. Later, when I came to know Frost well, he said my acute memory for poetry was the result of "out-of-school" and "self-assigned" readings, rather than "in-school" and "laid-on" education. However it may be explained, I read poetry in the spirit of what Frost in "A Tuft of Flowers" called "sheer morning gladness at the brim" (p. 23). Undoubtedly, Frost was largely right. The poems lodged in my mind because I read them with all the intense and spontaneous enthusiasm of uncritical youth, with an intuitional love, or what Frost called "passionate preference" (*Interviews*, p. 208), and not as a body of academic knowledge to be learned. During the fourteen months prior to entering Middlebury I read and retained in memory thousands of lines of poetry, from Shakespeare's sonnets, lyrics, and plays; from the poems of Ben Jonson, Donne, Herrick, and the Cavalier poets; from Milton, Dryden, Pope, Thompson, Gray, Blair, Young, Samuel Johnson and Goldsmith; from all the major and some minor Romantic and Victorian poets; and from the modern British and American poets in the latest edition of Untermeyer's anthology, including Frost. Among American nineteenth century poets I knew to memory many poems of Bryant, Poe, Emerson, Whitman, Crane, Dickinson, and others.

Although I did not realize it then, I was really preparing myself in the best possible manner for entering Middlebury, for my summers at Bread Loaf, and for my conversations with Frost. But because of the depressed economic condition of my family, and my inability to find work, until Christmas of 1937 I had not entertained any hope of going to college at all. Then by chance I met a history teacher I had known in Nutley High School. About the middle of December Miss Esther Byerley found me reading in the library, and with the help of one of my high school English teachers, Miss Ida Cone, who had sent several students to Middlebury College, encouraged me to apply for admission. In February 1938 I was admitted with a half tuition scholarship. Through odd jobs during the spring and summer I managed to save fifty dollars, my total financial resources when I journeyed to Middlebury on September 17 to look for work.

The next day I managed to find four meager jobs—as usher in a theater downtown; as a page in the college library; as attendance officer in daily and Sunday chapel; and as a campus mailman, delivering mail and notices from the administration offices in Old Chapel to the various faculty offices. All these jobs together were not enough to cover my room, board, and books, and beyond these expenses I still needed to raise half of my tuition. But that evening, in front of the chapel, entranced by the magnificence of the campus setting and distant mountains, I had pushed my economic problems completely out of my mind, so that for a moment I was hardly aware that a man had come out of the chapel and was standing next to me.

He was tall, white-haired, and somewhat frail; he was well-dressed and carried a black cane. He had the dignified, formal bearing of a Victorian gentleman, and looked like the very image of a picture I had seen of John Galsworthy. He smiled broadly, shook my hand, asked my name and home town, and whether I was to be a student at the College. Soon we were launched on an animated conversation about the College and various academic subjects, and particularly on the place of literature in a liberal education. Newman's *The Idea of a University*, which I had read with great satisfaction just before going to Middlebury, provided the basis for my convictions. As we talked we strolled slowly down the long walk from the chapel to the lower campus, where for about a half hour we talked within the shadow of Old Chapel as darkness descended. Then the white-haired gentleman suddenly said goodbye and walked away. I was mortified to discover that although he had probed my mind, I had neglected to ask anything about him. I hadn't even gotten his name. I was acutely embarrassed over my bad manners.

Early the next afternoon when I went to the college mail room in Old Chapel to pick up campus mail for distribution, to my surprise I found a note in my box asking me to go immediately to the office of Dr. Paul D. Moody, President of Middlebury College. I went upstairs and gave my name to his secretary. To my greater surprise she recognized my name. She ushered me into the president's office, and to my utter amazement there stood the white-haired gentleman I had met outside the chapel. He smiled indulgently at my obvious stupefaction. Dr. Moody quickly put me at ease by assuring me that our conversation of the previous evening had pleased him. He wished to continue it and discuss some matters relating to my coming year at Middlebury. In the next half hour I listened and learned a great deal about President Moody. He was the son of the famous evangelist Dwight L. Moody (1837–1899); he had been head Protestant chaplain in the American Expeditionary Forces in France during World War One; he had met such luminaries as Marshal Foch and Sergeant York; he had known intimately and was a close friend of Father Francis P. Duffy, the famous chaplain of the New York City regiments of the Forty-second Rainbow Division; he had been appointed President of Middlebury College in 1921; his daughter, Charlotte Moody, had literary talents of the kind I admired, and had published in *The Saturday Review of Literature, Harpers*, and various magazines of fiction. By an easy transition from things personal to him to things literary, President Moody steered his monologue to the main purpose of our meeting. From fragments in our recent conversation he had pieced together the facts about my economic plight. He told me that out of his "President's Purse," a fund provided by the College for use at his discretion, he would pay the balance of my tuition for my freshman year. Before I had recovered sufficiently to thank him for this startling generosity, President Moody told me he had also asked the registrar to schedule me in the freshman English class to be taught by Professor Harry G. Owen. With that, President Moody shook my hand warmly, wished me well, asked me to drop in occasionally for a chat during the coming months, and ushered me out.

On the same day that classes began at Middlebury, September 21, 1938, a devastating hurricane swept across the northeastern United States, killing nearly 700 people, and damaging property worth tens of millions of dollars. Near Middlebury the hurricane washed out highways and bridges, stranding some parents of students for days. Symbolically, this regional catastrophe, and the resulting physical damage and dislocation of human lives, was but a prelude to what the whole civilized world was soon to experience in World War Two. On our first day of classes Czechoslovakia capitulated to Hitler's partition ultimatum. Four years later almost to the day, I was to be inducted into the United States Air Corps at Fort Dix. Meanwhile, against the background of the politics and violence of approaching war, I plunged into the calm but intellectually exhilarating academic world of Middlebury and the Bread Loaf School of English, a highly civilized, aesthetically oriented, and idealistic world, peopled with scores of outstanding teachers, scholars, poets, writers, fellow students, and a variety of remarkable characters.

Soon after classes began I discovered why President Moody had steered me into Professor Owen's English class. Owen was a brilliant and highly articulate teacher, thoroughly educated in the fine arts as well as in literature. He had a catholic literary taste that included an appreciation of the best in Ancient, Classical, Metaphysical, Romantic, and Modern literature. He was intensely devoted to music and was a very accomplished pianist. Freshman English at Middlebury consisted of a year-long survey course in English literature, with reading selections from *Beowulf* through Thomas Hardy, in two large volumes. But Owen demanded much more than the rest of his colleagues. He assigned supplementary readings: a Shakespearean tragedy, comedy, and history; an eighteenth and nineteenth century novel; Boswell's *Life of Samuel Johnson*; and selected essays in literary criticism. He also required two or three brief themes each week, written on the daily assigned readings. By June 1939 I had written over forty critical papers for Owen, thus deepening, extending, consolidating, and systematizing my knowledge and understanding of English literature. Owen was a strict disciplinarian, and held frequent conferences with his students to improve their writing. Although I had entered Middlebury as a physics major, I soon shifted to English because I was more interested in people than in atoms and molecules, and Owen became my academic advisor. Before going to Middlebury I had become interested in writing, both poetry and prose. I had composed about twenty lyric poems, mostly sonnets, and had written some reflective essays. Owen provided great critical perspective for my work.

Before Christmas recess, largely through Owen's teaching and conferences, but also through the example of two other faculty members at Middlebury, Professors Vernon G. Harrington in philosophy and Reginald L. Cook in American Literature, I had decided that for my life's work I wanted to teach literature in a college and to write. But the whole course of my graduate studies in literature, and of my professional life, was to be determined by Robert Frost.

In addition to his teaching skill, Owen possessed great social charm and tact and was an outstanding administrator. In 1937 President Moody had appointed him Dean of the Bread Loaf School of English. (Several years later, after Owen became academic dean at Rutgers University, I learned from Frost that President Moody had groomed Owen to succeed him as president of Middlebury College, but that the War had destroyed this plan.) In January 1939, Owen offered me a scholarship and all expenses to attend the Bread Loaf School for the coming summer, in exchange for waiting on table. He reminded me that to teach in a college I would need M.A. and Ph.D. degrees and that going to Bread Loaf was the first step toward these academic goals. Owen agreed with the philosophy of education then practiced under Robert M. Hutchins at the University of Chicago, that a student should be allowed to proceed according to his proven ability and attained knowledge and skill, rather than through a piecemeal system of fixed earned credits. If I could handle the graduate courses at Bread Loaf, Owen argued, I should be able to earn credits toward an M.A. even before getting the B.A. He also noted that at Bread Loaf I would have an opportunity to study with outstanding English teachers from all over the United States, under ideal conditions, and that this would make me a stronger undergraduate English student. His clinching point was that I would meet Robert Frost at Bread Loaf and that after the summer school session I could stay over for the last two weeks in August and attend the Bread Loaf Writers' Conference.

But the hard-pressing facts of economics stood in the way of accepting Owen's very tempting offer. I believed it was essential to earn money over the summer for my sophomore year and to secure the B.A. before being concerned about advanced degrees. I discussed my problem with "Gramps" Harrington. He had taught for thirteen summers at Bread Loaf, from 1920, the year the school was founded, through 1932. He knew Frost well and had a very high opinion of the poet. He advised me to take the long range view, to ignore economics, live on faith, and go to Bread Loaf. I then consulted "Doc" Cook, whom I had come to admire as a man and a teacher. Cook had taken his M.A. at Bread Loaf in 1926, and he too was a good friend of Frost. He urged me to go to Bread Loaf, saying that the opportunity to know Frost was the greatest education in the liberal arts I could possibly get anywhere. President Moody reinforced the advice of Harrington and Cook and assured me that my full tuition scholarship would be extended as long as my academic record was good. He suggested that I apply to the Middlebury Inn for a job during my sophomore year; I did and secured a job that gave me room and board starting in September. I then accepted Owen's offer.

Robert Frost at Bread Loaf
1939

I

Aт the end of my freshman year in June I remained in Middlebury and worked in the college library, packing several thousands of books in large wooden crates, to ship by truck to the Bread Loaf library for the reserve shelves for the summer school courses. Four other Middlebury students were also going to Bread Loaf: Edward Hayward, a native Vermonter, who had graduated and now ran the bookstore at Bread Loaf; Norman Hatfield, a senior English major, editor of the Middlebury College literary magazine; and Charley Sanford and Bob Maxwell, my classmates. Hayward had attended Bread Loaf every summer since 1935, and Hatfield had spent several summers at Bread Loaf. On June 21, a week before classes began, we all went up the Mountain to prepare the campus for the summer session. Ed Hayward and I spent a day unpacking books and placing them on the library shelves. Then I joined the other scholarship students, including some from Vanderbilt, Virginia, and Harvard, as a ground crew working under the direction of E. H. "Al" Henry. We worked with several Riptonites, Harold

Whittemore, Milton Kirby, and a crew of boys led by Bishop McGill, to whip the Bread Loaf campus into shape. We cut the lawns, planted more bright flowers in the formal eighteenth century garden in front of the Inn, rolled the three clay tennis courts and stapled down the tapes, opened all the cottage dormitories, did minor carpentry repairs on the porches, repaired and painted lawn chairs and cottage porch railings, piled firewood at each fireplace or stove in each cottage, and did miscellaneous other tasks. Dean Harry Owen was a fanatic for neatness, and when the Bread Loaf School opened on June 28, with words of greeting from President Moody, the whole campus gleamed in the sunlight.

Shortly after classes began, Harold Whittemore, Mrs. Homer Noble's adopted son, told us that Robert Frost was staying in Ripton, having rented a small guest cottage across the road from Mrs. Noble and her sister, Miss Agnes Billings. Harold Whittemore had a small greenhouse nearby and provided fresh vegetables for the ladies and for Frost. The poet took his meals with Mrs. Noble and Miss Billings, and often had dinner with Theodore (Ted) and Kathleen (Kay) Morrison at the Homer Noble farm, about a mile west from the Bread Loaf campus, which they had rented for the summer. But Frost spent most of his day in Ripton and slept in his cottage there. Late one day after work, Ed Hayward and Norm Hatfield went to Ripton to visit Frost and arranged for a group of Bread Loaf students to return for a talk the next evening. Like everyone else who had spoken about Frost to me, they held him in high esteem and stressed his unusual brilliance as a conversationalist. Apart from such comments and slight reading about Frost's life and literary career, I knew very little about Frost's personal life and character. I had heard that his wife Elinor had died fifteen months before (March 20, 1938), that he had barely survived "a nervous breakdown," that he had behaved very badly during the previous summer, interrupting a poetry reading by Archibald MacLeish, but that with the help of his Harvard friends, and particularly the Morrisons, he was beginning to build a new life. During the summer of 1938 Kay Morrison had helped Frost restore good order in his life by becoming his secretary, answering his voluminous mail, scheduling his poetry readings around the nation, and supervising many practical details in his life. Kay had given permission for the visit by the students, with instructions not to stay past midnight.

The next evening toward sunset, loaded down with half a dozen bottles of ginger ale, a large bag of ice, and packages of ginger snaps, Norm Hatfield, Bob Maxwell, two other students, and I walked to Ripton to visit Robert Frost. The poet, aged sixty-five, greeted us warmly at his cottage door. In a quiet and gentle manner, as we filed into the cottage living room, he shook hands and asked each of us his name and where he was from. Frost settled down in an old rocking chair near the center of the room, with his back to a wall. He had just moved to Ripton for the summer from Shaftsbury, Vermont, and there were books, magazines, and unanswered letters or papers piled on a table, and additional books on the floor. We sat in a semi-circle around the poet.

In physical appearance Frost was a rugged man's man, with white unruly hair covering a large, well-shaped massive head set on broad shoulders. His thick shaggy eyebrows hid the frequent twinkle in his deep-set pale blue eyes. His eyes were his most expressive feature. They appeared intelligent, friendly, yet a bit quizzical, sensitive, and crinkled at the corners with crowsfeet. His face was tanned by the sun, and slightly mottled, with wrinkles running across his brow and around his mouth, deepening when he laughed or spoke with animation. His hands were large and sun-tanned, like a laborer's, and moved about slightly as he talked. His dress was very casual. He wore light tan trousers and a short-sleeved, open-collared shirt. His voice was deep and throaty, slightly gravelly and gruff, and inflected with a salt-tinged New England accent. His manner was most informal, relaxed, artless, sociable, warm-hearted, and touched by good humor.

Frost soon established a good rapport with each of us, and as a group, for a spirited conversation. The same effort to charm a large audience that I was to witness many times in public readings of his poetry was evident here for the first time in his appeal to his audience of five young students of literature. He first asked each of us in turn which teachers we were going to study with at Bread Loaf and what we thought we would get from our courses. I told him I was taking Donald Davidson's course in modern poetry and hoped for the opportunity to read and talk about modern poetry. I was also auditing Perry Miller's course in "Social and Intellectual Backgrounds of American Literature," to learn more about Puritanism; and Mrs. André Morize's course in Elizabethan music, because I liked madrigals. Frost praised Davidson as "a very good man" and an excellent teacher and writer.

He asked each of us to say which poem he first liked beyond nursery rhymes. He appeared pleased with my reply, Robert Herrick's "Corinna's Going A-Maying." He then asked each of us to say a poem he liked. Hatfield quoted parts of A. E. Housman's "Terence, This is Stupid Stuff," but shortly became annoyed with himself when he got bogged down in the middle of the poem. I quoted Coleridge's "Kubla Khan." Frost remarked that Kipling had especially praised the lines:

> A savage place! as holy and enchanted
> As e'er beneath a waning moon was haunted
> By woman wailing for her demon lover!

These lines, said Frost, together with Keats's lines from "Ode to a Nightingale"

> The same that ofttimes hath
> Charmed magic casements, opening on the foam
> Of perilous seas, in faery lands forlorn

were considered by Kipling to be the essence of Romanticism. Frost said the lines have a strange beautiful unearthiness about them.

Frost then remarked how lucky we were to be "Harry Owen's boys," going to Bread Loaf, where literature was treated as literature, and not as a handmaid to something else—to linguistics, or sociology, or as mere raw material to study for "busy work scholarship." He said too many schools, especially graduate schools, took all the fun out of reading literature, by insisting upon a scientific approach to it. He acknowledged that scholarship has its value, and he respected it as a way of establishing facts, but it wasn't everything or even the most important thing for literature. In its humane treatment of literature Bread Loaf provided a healthy alternative to much current scientific scholarship. The teachers at Bread Loaf, such as Perry Miller, whom he knew at Harvard, and Donald David-son, whom he had met at Vanderbilt and come to know well at Bread Loaf, were excellent scholars and writers, but they wore their learning lightly at Bread Loaf. During only six weeks, and in the relaxed atmosphere of the Mountain, teachers at Bread Loaf had to concentrate on literature as literature; they did not have enough time to spoil literature by demanding "research" from their stu-dents. It was a case of virtue by default, although most of the faculty were sympathetic with the policy of Harry Owen to escape from conventional graduate studies back into the true spirit of poetry. Bread Loaf teachers, Frost remarked, were more creative than critical and more critical than scholarly. We would get a good edu-cation by their presence, as much by talks outside class as by class lectures. Frost said the word *creative* was often abused, by being applied to a mere dilettantish interest in reading or writing litera-ture, but so were criticism and scholarship abused, and never more so than when taken most seriously by professional educators. In approaching poetry he preferred the word *amateur* in its literal meaning, a true lover of poetry. A student should never lose his "amateur standing" in literature. Frost also praised Bread Loaf for treating both American literature and creative writing with far more respect than other schools did.

The great evil was the necessity of giving grades, credits, and degrees. Young talents should be free to disport themselves without too close supervision, particularly if the supervision was only to correct errors. A teacher's chief value was as an example to a stu-dent. He could teach by his example the superiority of leisurely ease and fruitful idleness over mere "thoroughness" and conscientious "busy-work routines." He could teach by his original expression of ideas the value of ideas in fresh relationships, not only in literature but in life. In the classroom, poetry comes to be too separated from daily life.

Frost mentioned that he had recently quit Amherst College, after being on the faculty there for years, partly because its structure tended to make the machinery of the college into an end. There were good liberal arts men in all the schools where he had been, at Michigan, Amherst, and Harvard, but there was also too much

PETER J. STANLIS 193

pedantry. Frost showed something like contempt toward the air
of intellectual superiority assumed by learned pedants in having
acquired some specialized knowledge through scholarship. He contended that to make subjects departmental, or specialized through
one major interest, was contrary to the true spirit of humane learning. The very word *professor* was a kind of built-in affectation.
Compared with religious prophets and with explorers, Frost joked,
many professors had "little to profess," often nothing original of
their own. They merely dispensed knowledge at second hand, about
the original work of other writers, as book reviewers did. Even in
what they considered "original research," or scholarship, they were
merely "the first to be second." They were like the country boy
who went to the city and picked up the current jokes and returned
home and was the first to tell the jokes to other country boys.

Someone mentioned that he had read an article on Frost in an
academic journal, in which the poet was called an "anti-intellectual."
Frost asked: "What does that mean?" He objected that abstract
"labels," such as being called "pro" or "anti" anything, were mean-
ingless categories, without any substance. He asked, did anyone
ever go around calling himself "pro-intellectual"? What he objected to was better called "pedantry," which was the "pseudo-
intellectual" learning of educated fools who pretended to more wisdom than their specialized academic knowledge could support to
any practical end in life. At this point in the discussion, amidst
much pouring out of ginger ale into glasses with ice, I remembered
and quoted an appropriate couplet from Pope about learned dunces:

> The bookful blockhead, ignorantly read,
> With loads of learned lumber in his head.
> ("An Essay on Criticism," III, 612–13)

Frost nodded in agreement and asked me to repeat the lines. Someone asked whether the couplet was from the *Dunciad*. I said I
thought it was from "An Essay on Criticism." Frost remarked that
the *Dunciad* was a good guess, that there were many such lines in
Pope's satire. He added that Pope was exactly right, that he recognized it was foolish to read poetry merely to acquire knowledge—
even knowledge of the poetry. It showed ignorance of poetry as

literary art to treat it as a source of knowledge, even though, as art, poetry provided knowledge of life stripped to form. History and science could more properly be read for knowledge as information, but poetry should be read for pleasure and insight, for a sense of form, for understanding and wisdom. Poetry involved knowledge of our total nature as man, and not only of our intellect, and therefore it went beyond rational knowledge. Frost denied that he was "anti-intellectual," but admitted that he was an "anti-rationalist." He rejected the assumption that man's reason alone provided the final source, or test, or end of human knowledge. Furthermore, he asserted that reason could not legitimately claim to be the arbiter of what went beyond rational knowledge, such as religion, poetry, and the mysteries of life.

This was the first time I had encountered the distinction between an "intellectual" and a "rationalist," and I was fascinated by Frost's quick follow-up statement that there was no contradiction between being a profoundly intellectual skeptic about the claims of pure reason as the original or ultimate source of knowledge and truth, and having a deep respect for human reason as an instrument for truth. But reason was only one of many vehicles for finding truth. And it was as subject to error as any other instrument. Indeed, often people with very superficial intelligence had the most exalted faith in human reason. As "rationalists," with unbounded faith in their own reason, they were not intelligent enough, or skeptical enough, to understand the limitations of human reason, and condemned as "anti-intellectual" men of far greater intelligence whose skepticism about reason aided the understanding and acceptance of its limitations. Frost clearly favored the full use of the power of the human mind in probing any subject—science, history, politics, education, literature, and even religion—but with a full awareness of where reason was competent and where it was limited. I thought he had neatly turned the table on the critic who had called him "anti-intellectual."

Norm Hatfield asked if Frost agreed with Wordsworth, who thought too much learning out of books deadened creative sensibility. Frost thought learning from books was good, but felt it should always be combined in good proportion with learning from life, which should enforce and invigorate each other. But it wasn't a question of the quantity of book learning a writer absorbed; it was rather whether or not he could use it well in his work. Of course, no one could tell beforehand what might prove to be useful, and a poet should acquire much knowledge. Milton was a great poet with enormous learning, who didn't flout his erudition. Frost quoted some lines from *Comus* to show how casually Milton assumed his learning. Milton was a learned, well-disciplined, Christian, Puritan poet. I added—as contrasted with Robert Herrick, who was a well-disciplined, epicurean, Christian, pagan poet. That seemed to tickle Frost's fancy.

We drifted into a discussion of what is a Puritan. Frost defined a Puritan as one who was willing to put moral bounds on what he wanted, including not only pleasures of the senses, such as "wine, women, and song," but also such things as political power. To Frost a Puritan was essentially an ascetic regarding pleasure and power. Puritanism was as much a practice of restraint through temperament as a recognition of and abiding by right moral principles.

I asserted that I understood Puritanism in quite a different way, as essentially Calvinist in morality and religion, and therefore not so much ascetic as anti-aesthetic. Monks in monastaries or religious orders were ascetic, and took vows of chastity, poverty, and obedience, but they were not "Puritan" in religious worship, because the aesthetic element in their liturgy was paramount. The Mass was an attempt to teach the good through a dramatization of the true and beautiful in Christ's life, passion, and death. The Calvinist reformers in Scotland and England were called "Puritan" because they "purified" Christianity by eliminating the aesthetic from worship. Their object was to be totally good, and they assumed that the good and the beautiful were antithetical and could not be reconciled. They believed the aesthetic originated in sense appeals, which were evil because the senses gave sensual pleasure, which led to desire, which led to temptation, and on to sin and damnation. Unlike Roman Catholics and High Church Anglicans, the Puritans regarded art not as auxiliary to worship, not as a stepping stone to the contemplation of God, but as a stumbling block which came between men and God. Therefore, the Puritans sought to avoid damnation by destroying the beautiful; they had invoked Biblical passages against the worship of idols and graven images to justify their destruction of art objects in churches and cathedrals.

My remarks were a summary of what I had argued in my freshman English course with Harry Owen and with Norm Hatfield at a meeting of the English Club. On one occasion I had gone on to argue an aesthetic theory of "art for art's sake," and in favor of a theory of "pure poetry" through the perfection of form and technique, totally apart from considerations of particular content or themes. The themes of art did not have to be moral. Hatfield had interpreted my theory as denying a place for morality in literary art, which he claimed showed in the poetry I had written, and he had dubbed me "the immoral bard." He repeated his phrase, as we argued heatedly. Frost listened to our exchange with great interest.

There was much historical truth in what I said, Frost commented, for he had seen in St. Andrews, Scotland, the destruction wrought to the cathedral by the Calvinist reformers. But he objected that my understanding of Puritanism was too narrowly historical and sectarian. In his view there were "'puritans" in every age and in every religious sect. It was not something begun by Calvin or limited to Protestants. Jews and Catholics were more likely to be "puritans" than Protestants were. The opposite of Puritanism was self-indulgent epicureanism and undisciplined selfishness. That involved a moral difference, not just a difference in aesthetics. Calvinism had created a special kind of Puritan, and Frost admitted that many modern people identified the word with thin-lipped, glint-eyed "kill joys." He also objected that the Calvinist Puritans were lacking in an aesthetic sense. There was beauty in their world, but it was centered in nature and the Bible, or in simple art, rather than in the complex and ornate art of Rome and Canterbury. I referred to a comment by G. K. Chesterton on this point, that the Puritans thought it was better to worship God in a plain barn than in a magnificent Gothic cathedral. They preferred direct sunlight to light filtered through stained glass windows. Frost responded that the New England meeting house had an architectural appeal of its own; it was more than a whitewashed barn topped with a steeple. I recalled the appeal of the Middlebury College chapel and agreed.

Prudence dictated that I should have deferred to Frost's greater authority, but with the rash impetuosity of youth I plunged forward with a new argument. I conceded that Frost was right about "puritan" traits being found in all sects, but as the enemies of Calvinist Puritanism had noted, there was such a thing as selective self-denial of sinful pleasures. I quoted Samuel Butler's couplet against the Calvinist Puritans of his era, that they were inclined to

> Compound for sins they are inclined to
> By damning those they have no mind to. . . .
> (*Hudibras*, I, 213–14)

And on the matter of moral self-denial in seeking and using political power, I asked was Milton's chief, Oliver Cromwell, a Puritan? He was an usurper; he had no constitutional sanction for sovereignty; yet he had assumed a more absolute power than any but the most absolute of English kings.

Frost replied that Cromwell was one of the great bad men in English history, who accomplished much good by original means that could be criticized. He admitted that Cromwell had a lust for absolute power and that in this he was much less a Puritan than Milton, whose humane learning circumscribed his will within common morality. I questioned whether by Frost's definition of Puritanism Cromwell was a Puritan at all. I thought Cromwell's lust for absolute arbitrary power could be explained better by my view of Puritanism as essentially Calvinist. As one of God's "elect" Cromwell believed he and the "saints" had a moral right to have dominion over the godless nonelect. Frost countered that appeals to scripture and theology were common on all sides in the political disputes of that age, and although Cromwell could be explained in Calvinistic terms, his temperament and character probably had more to do with his life and rule than the theology of the Independents.

At this point, in the new context created by our discussion of Puritanism, Frost reintroduced his earlier criticism of "pseudo-intellectual" scholarship by noting that it was not limited to college professors, but that some poets and literary critics had fallen prey to the same weakness. He instanced Ezra Pound and T. S. Eliot among the poets, and their admirers among the critics, who revealed a simple faith in a highly specialized erudition in dead mythology and personal symbols. He observed that the need of being versed in country things was far greater, and often harder to achieve, than the need of being versed in pseudo-intellectual myths and symbols. These writers reduced poetry to an esoteric puzzle, an intellectual game of identifications like "button, button, who's got the button?" It was a game that critics who liked to be symbol hunters loved to play.

Someone suggested that in an age as complex as our era perhaps it was necessary to use mythology and symbolism the way Pound, Eliot, and Joyce used it in their work, even though the use of such methods resulted in obscurity in literary art. Furthermore, mythological symbolism in poetry was the best way to capture the essence of our age. Frost disagreed. He questioned whether the object of poetry was to capture the historical essence of any age. That assumed that poetry must serve a social function, and such an assumption would likely land a poet into sociology.

But even if that assumption were valid, how was the present age best captured by a heavy use of ancient mythologies? Nature and the country were common and necessary to all ages, including the twentieth century, and provided the images and metaphors by which the age could live. The twentieth century was out of harmony with itself, because it had digressed too far into the specializations of urban life and had become much too remote from nature and the country. Frost noted that the trouble with the literary art of Pound, Eliot, and Joyce was that it was fit only for a "private coterie" of specially initiated critics. This process of excluding much of the reading public had been carried to the point that now we have critics writing poems for other critics to criticize.

Viewed vulgarly, as mere communication to readers, poetry could run the whole gamut from "most public, public, less public, least public, private, and esoteric." At the "most public" end were newspaper versifiers, such as Eddy Guest, who had no skill in technique, no ability to create images and form, but only a Sunday school message or sentiment to convey. But over the centuries most good poets have been content to be more or less public. They have been able to combine meaningful content with perfection of form.

Frost was all for a poet's perfecting his technique; the more perfect the better. But craftsmanship was developed in order to be "original" in the traditional forms of verse.

He again expressed his unease about academic life, because of the ways teachers treated poetry, as something to be studied for the sake of criticism and scholarship. It was bad for students to have their intuitive, spontaneous, amateur love of poetry displaced by such rational scholarly self-consciousness. Writers such as Pound and Eliot, and their academic critics, contributed greatly to this displacement process in our colleges.

Frost dilated on the theme that poetry should be loved for itself, as metaphor and form, as a craft to be perfected by those who write it, for those who read it, and not as an instrument for changing or reforming society. Those who thought that literature should serve society undervalued art and suffered from that great modern vice —an excessive social consciousness. What such people valued was skillful propaganda, not literary art. The Marxists carried this line of thought further than anyone, with their own brand of consciousness of what society should be. But at Bread Loaf, the teachers at the School, and the staff at the Writers' Conference, were right in ignoring the popular theory that literature and writing, to be good, had to be concerned with solving social, economic, and political problems. Frost referred to such work as "mad, glad stuff." He told an anecdote about a man who had recently told him that literature was good in direct ratio to its ability to move readers to revolutionary action. To which, with mocking irony, he had replied: "How soon?" Such men valued content or theme above skill in technique. Frost believed that form and content were both important, and should always be united, but the final judgment of a poem was in its achieved form. He added that discipline in writing does not come from technical mastery alone; the theme also provided a basis for discipline.

Before Frost could develop his statements on writing someone noted that it was midnight and that since we all had to be up early the next morning it was time for us to leave. The poet tried to wave us down, to stay longer, but we were already on our feet, gathering up the empty ginger ale bottles, and moving toward the door. I was reluctant to leave and lagged behind my friends. When they had all filed outdoors I found myself alone with Frost. As we said "good night," he urged me to be sure to come again soon for "a good talk." "Come alone," he said. I was delighted and said I would.

Walking back to Bread Loaf we were all a bit intoxicated on ginger ale and the stimulating talk. I sensed that Norm Hatfield had a full head of steam over how the evening had gone. His pent up frustration and suppressed anger exploded. He said that he was disappointed because he had already heard last summer much that Frost had said; but he was especially angry with me, accusing me of talking too much, hogging the limelight, trying to upstage everyone, including Frost, and in general showing my special brand of freshman arrogance. I remained silent. This seemed to intensify his feelings. I thought he was right on both counts: Frost was reputed to repeat himself, with variations, from year to year, and undoubtedly I had talked too much. Hatfield threatened to cut me off from any future talks with Frost. I did not tell him I was to return soon alone on Frost's invitation. After all, despite our differences over aesthetics, I liked Norm, and really there was no point in making him angry.

After we returned to Bread Loaf, I spent several hours writing out the highlights of all that I had remembered of our visit with Frost, the subjects discussed, the arguments advanced, Frost's manner of speaking and appearance, and his pithy phrases. I recalled Samuel Johnson's advice to Boswell, that the important thing to record in a journal, beyond empirical facts, was one's state of mind and feeling in an experience. The chief value of keeping such a record was to note whether we improved in our understanding of life, other people, and ourselves. I recorded the evening's talk because I believed that what Frost had said, and the way he had said it, would be of great value to me in becoming a better student of literature and eventually a better college teacher.

II

On Monday evening, July 3, Frost gave a poetry reading to the students and faculty of the Bread Loaf School in the Little Theatre.

After Harry Owen introduced him, the poet put his audience at ease by talking casually about some items he had read recently in the newspapers. His manner of weaving around a subject, making whimsical, puckish, off-the-cuff comments, reminded me of Will Rogers. His subject was the relationship between the federal government, Franklin D. Roosevelt's "New Deal" administration, and the poor in America. He noted that Congress had recently voted down "the Townsend Plan," to give federal pensions to old people as a means of solving the economic depression.

Frost remarked: "The test is always how we treat the poor." Then addressing his audience he said: "For Christ's sake forget the poor some of the time!" This remark produced a mild shock wave in the audience. Then, in a softly modulated voice he asked members of his audience whether they recalled where the Bible said that. Of course, he added, it doesn't say it quite in those words, though it means just that. He paraphrased Christ as having said: "For my sake forget the poor. The poor you have with you always, but me you have not." Frost remarked that some people think Christ believed we shall always have poor people among us, but the poet disagreed.

Frost disliked judging people by their economic condition or their social status based on money. He asked the audience: "Don't you think the poor are disgusting, and the rich are disgusting—as such?" If we must judge people by their "class," why concede anything to the Marxists by using "class" only in its economic sense? Why not judge people by their emotional or psychological class? "To which class do you belong," he asked, "the neurotic class?"

Most of the rest of Frost's remarks during his poetry reading were satirical thrusts at the Marxian view of man in society, which in modified form he believed some New Deal politicians shared to some degree, in their criticism of the American free enterprise system. Frost attacked the Marxist view of labor: "What some people call 'exploitation' I call employment." When New Deal politicians condemned "rugged individualism" and politically unregulated freedom in the economic sector of American society as forms of selfishness and callous indifference to the welfare of the poor, Frost refined upon the phrase "rugged individualist" and called himself a "ragged individualist," thereby insisting that he valued his personal freedom even if it meant suffering poverty. He lamented the great stress laid upon "social security" at the expense of private freedom. To live life assertively, with audacity and courage, Frost said, man needed some "social insecurity." He was particularly critical of Mrs. Eleanor Roosevelt, whose humanitarian sympathies for the poor tended to undermine the strength of character needed by individuals to overcome their poverty and become self-reliant. Frost remarked that because of the psychology of the New Deal, which aimed at eliminating failure through competitive adversity and establishing an egalitarian mediocrity, about the only social activity in which the desire to excel still remained strong in America was competitive sports.

Frost remarked that socialism was based on the same theory as fire insurance. If everyone paid a small premium, the risk of a total loss through fire by any particular individual could be eliminated. The New Deal socialists applied the principle to the economic life of Americans, in order to take all the risk out of life.

He observed that there were advantages and disadvantages in every state or condition of life. The disadvantage in being poor was that it was damned inconvenient. The advantage was that the poor had to face the realities of life each day, to survive, and this made them realists. There were no illusions in the poor, except when they became revolutionary theorists and dreamed of the big rock candy mountain of a future Utopia. The advantage of being rich was in the power and convenience money provided. The disadvantage was that wealth often weakened character, by making what a person has more important than what a person is. Few things were worse than having too much money combined with too little character or wisdom. Today we have a unique development—the growth of millionaire socialite socialists. Some of these Utopian dreamers become socialists more out of a bad conscience because of their father's or grandfather's success than because they really like the poor.

Frost interspersed these remarks with readings of his poems, including "Birches," "Provide, Provide," "A Drumlin Woodchuck," "A Roadside Stand," "Mending Wall," and "Stopping by Woods on a Snowy Evening." When he came to the final stanza of "Provide, Provide," a truculent and almost defiant tone entered into his reading, so that the final two words, "Provide, provide!" were delivered in a snarl, drawing out the long "o" and "i" vowels. He also read "The Runaway" and commented that he hoped his audience caught the urgent tone of "moral indignation" in the last three lines:

> Whoever it is that leaves him out so late,
> When other creatures have gone to stall and bin,
> Ought to be told to come and take him in (p. 223).

Frost never commented on his poems beyond a few words on the occasion of their composition, or on how some friend "got it" or failed to "get it." Clearly, he believed his poems should stand or fall as delivered, without any critical comments from him.

III

On Monday afternoon, July 10, Frost returned to the Bread Loaf campus to discuss with Professor Hortense Moore, director of drama in the Little Theatre, the staging of his poem "Snow," which she had adapted as a one-act play. Miss Moore was directing the play, assisted in the stage settings by Raymond Bosworth. Students at Bread Loaf were allowed to sit in on their preliminary discussions, and I took advantage of this privilege, even though I was not a drama student.

Leon Drury was selected to play Brother Meserve, a preacher of the fundamentalist Racker sect, who is caught in a blizzard while returning home after preaching, and is forced to stop over at the home of a farm couple, the Coles. His insistence on going back into the blizzard, in order to reach home that night, creates the central plot and character conflict in the play. Brother Meserve's wife, an off-stage character who is contacted by telephone, wants her husband to remain overnight with the Coles, until the storm subsides. The Coles, who consider themselves intellectually and morally superior to Meserve, would just as soon not be bothered by him as an overnight guest. Mr. Cole was to be played by "Al" Henry, and Priscilla March was chosen to play his wife, Helen Cole.

After the cast was chosen they spoke sections of the play, and

Hortense Moore and Robert Frost discussing the dramatization of Frost's "Snow," on the porch of Bread Loaf Inn, 1939

there was a long discussion among Miss Moore, the cast, and Frost on whether the speeches of Meserve were too long, without sufficient interruption by the other characters, for stage drama. Frost thought not. He contended that Meserve, as a preacher, was supposed to be a rather talkative character and that if the actors spoke their blank verse lines with proper rhythm, tone, and emphasis, there would be no problem. Everything depended on the actor's skill in the timing in his dialogue. The voice tones and rhythm of the actors had to create the illusion of "natural" speech. Frost also objected to the use of a heavy New England dialect. Even though the setting was rural New England, "Snow" was not a "regional" play. Frost argued that too obvious use of an unauthentic dialect would distract attention from the characters and the dramatic situation, as had happened in an American presentation of Synge's *Riders to the Sea*. Miss Moore was clearly convinced by Frost's remarks. But when the poet left the Little Theatre, he was apparently unconvinced that the poem as play would be well acted.

As Frost walked away, I caught up to him and told him I would like to accept his invitation to visit him for an evening talk. We agreed on the next evening.

IV

Around 8:30 P.M., I walked to Ripton for my first meeting alone with Frost. I was filled with a strong sense of exhilaration and anticipation. Frost's previous talks had whetted my appetite, and I was eager to discuss poets and poetry and all sorts of subjects with him.

Still smarting from Hatfield's criticism, I began by apologizing for talking too much at our last meeting. Frost responded: "Never apologize. Never explain." He denied that I had violated "the golden mean of grace" and said that as Americans we are democrats, not courtiers. We had met to exchange ideas and to learn from each other. I admitted that I had learned to see Puritans in another light. Frost remarked that I had defended my view very well. It was a common mistake for students to hide their weaknesses and cover their ignorance from their teachers, instead of having their ideas challenged and tested. That was because they were too concerned about grades. He said that good talk, like poetry, is one of the great norms for civilization. In conflicts of ideas we should fight hard with courage and magnanimity, to win for the ideas we believed in. Intellectual virtues and social virtues can be combined. Our wit should be pleasant and disarming. Socratic irony is a form of polite dissimulation. Frost admitted that good talk lifted him out of himself. His remarks not only put me completely at ease, so that I felt I could always be candid with him, but they gave me an important insight into how he regarded conversation, and its significance in life and education.

After we were well settled in our chairs, Frost asked me for more details about my family background and upbringing in New Jersey. I sensed how genuinely interested he was in what I told him about myself, particularly in the events that had brought me to Middlebury. He became extraordinarily alert when I mentioned the great kindness and personal interest of President Moody. I told him I owed my freshman year at Middlebury to Moody and that he had established a base for my next three years in college. I mentioned Moody's high regard for him. Frost said Moody had a high respect for writing and a deep personal interest in good literature and that he had once been an excellent editor, preferring professional writers to academic scholars.

Frost remarked that his mother's family name was Moodie, spelled with an "ie" rather than a "y," and that she had migrated to the United States from Scotland after her father had drowned at sea. That gave him something in common with recent American emigrants, one generation removed from Europe, to balance off with his father's family, which had come to America early in the seventeenth century. Speaking of his mother, Frost asked whether I had ever noticed how fond the Scots were of the diminutive? His mother had used it frequently. Where the English said "lad" and "lass" the Scots said "laddie" and "lassie." Bobby Burns often used the diminutive: "bonnie," "mousie." The Scots, he said, were a remarkable people. Considering how small their population was, their achievements in history were tremendous. Their stark climate and Calvinist religion had disciplined them to work hard just to survive.

When they left Scotland their characters were strong, and they were like a spring that had been compressed by adversity but was suddenly released by opportunity. The Irish were like that in politics, and the Jews in business, but the Scots were like that in many things.

Frost advanced the theme that strongly-formed character can carry through several generations. Paul Moody had told Frost how much he owed to his father. Frost had a high respect for Moody's father as an evangelist. He liked men who held strongly to their commitments. He was not concerned much with the substance of their beliefs but with the firmness with which they held them. Life would test their ideas. He did not care for such "scoffers" as H. L. Mencken and Clarence Darrow, who had nothing to offer in matters of faith except their acid wit and private reason. He also disliked college professors who thought it their right and duty to destroy the traditional religious beliefs of their students and replace their beliefs with modern science. Paul Moody was a thoroughly admirable man. Frost was glad to see that my gratitude was not mixed with resentment. He said some people resent help from others because it put them in debt to their benefactors. I suggested that I could discharge my debt by helping others as I had been helped.

I said I was as grateful to Harry Owen for getting me to Bread Loaf. Frost expressed his very favorable opinion of Owen as a man and teacher and said he had been treated well by Owen at Bread Loaf. He approved of how Owen was running the School, and how Ted Morrison was running the Writers' Conference. Both were among the best institutions in America. They were like the state slogan: "Unspoiled Vermont." They were like a modern Brook Farm, but without the manure to shovel.

I mentioned Vernon Harrington, my teacher in philosophy at Middlebury, whom I had come to admire greatly and who wished to be remembered to him. Frost knew Harrington well, having seen him at Bread Loaf many times since the summer of 1920, when the poet gave his first poetry reading there. It was rare, Frost remarked, to find an academic philosopher who believed so much in the moral virtue derived from physical labor. This gave Harrington roots in the earth, which was lacking in his model, Plato. Harrington was also a truer humanist than Plato, Frost said, in his intense love of poetry. Frost had heard Harrington recite as a monologue the whole of Robert Browning's "Caponsacchi," a remarkable dramatic performance of almost two hours. Harrington as a Platonist who loved poetry was as good as or better in his way than Edwin Arlington Robinson, who was a poet aspiring to be a Platonic philosopher.

I also mentioned Reginald Cook as a teacher at Middlebury whom I admired. Again Frost responded enthusiastically. He said "Doc" Cook was also an old friend of his, since "Doc's" student days at Bread Loaf in 1925. Frost commented that Cook was a fine athlete as well as a superb teacher. I told him Cook still held some track records at Middlebury. Frost was pleased to hear that I was active in sports. I told him I had broken the freshman cross country course record at Middlebury by two seconds, but had still finished second to an Indian runner from McGill University, who had broken it by twenty seconds. Frost said that Cook by his enthusiasm created enthusiasm for literature in his students and that for those who already were enthusiastic he helped to create disciplined enthusiasm. This was the true function of a good teacher of literature. A better appreciation of better literature would follow in time. Frost also approved of Cook's policy at Middlebury of teaching American literature separately from English literature.

Frost said there were at least five things a good teacher could have students do with a poem in the classroom: read it out loud; reread it; memorize it; write it down in an anthology of poems; apply it to life in a story or analogy with something students already know. People underestimate the importance of simply reading a poem. A good reading is as much a performing art as playing music or acting on the stage. If we miss too much the first time, we should read a poem again. The one thing a teacher should never do is analyze a poem scientifically. Never "study" a poem. Never put it under a microscope or magnifying glass. That is horrendous. It is like explaining a joke. That kills the poem.

Frost observed that I had done very well in my friendships at Middlebury. Four such men as Moody, Owen, Harrington, and Cook were rare in any college, and I was lucky to have found such friends. He remarked that along with religion, love, and poetry, true friends were among the best things in life. Next to poetry he valued and enjoyed "good talk" with friends above almost anything. It had not always been so with him. Early in life he had been very shy and fearful of making friends.

For the next several hours Frost talked about his parents and his early life and literary career, from his birth on Nob Hill in San Francisco through his return to America from England early in 1915. All he said, and a good deal more, was to be described in far greater detailed thoroughness by Lawrance Thompson in *Robert Frost: The Early Years, 1874–1915* (1966); and other biographers, such as Elizabeth Sergeant, also were to write about many of the points he made. But in July 1939 everything about Frost the man was new to me, and I found his reminiscences of the highlights of his life completely fascinating. I let him talk and interrupted only occasionally to ask questions on points he made, or to probe something further.

He described his mother's Scottish background, and how she had migrated to Columbus, Ohio; how she met his father, William Prescott Frost, Jr., when she came to teach at Lewistown Academy in Pennsylvania; how after their marriage his father went to San Francisco, where she joined him; how after their troubled life in California, when his father died, she took him and his sister Jeannie across the continent to Lawrence, Massachusetts, on "the saddest and longest train ride I ever took;" how his grandparents treated his mother badly, and forced her to resume teaching school, until her health declined and she died of cancer in 1900. Frost particularly emphasized his mother's growth into religious mysticism, from her original Presbyterianism to the Swedenborgian faith she finally embraced. He learned to love poetry from her. He remembered with great sadness his mother's stoical courage in facing the great tragedies in her life. Frost clearly loved and admired his mother.

Frost described his father as "a rebel," at sharp odds with his Calvinist New England inheritance, and a religious skeptic. While a student at Harvard his father gambled and drank. Frost said: "He was a wild one." In politics his father was a Democrat and sympathized with the South in the Civil War, not because he accepted slavery, but because his theory of political sovereignty favored "states' rights." Later, he named his son Robert Lee Frost, in honor of the Confederate general.

One of his father's favorite themes about America was the westward movement of civilization since the time of Columbus. He was fond of quoting a line from George Berkeley's "Verses on the Prospect of Planting Arts and Learning in America": "Westward the course of empire takes its way." The settlement of the American continent by the pioneers was so rapid, the poet's father contended, that it was "like unrolling the map as they went West." Frost's father was convinced that the geographical extent of the United States was too vast for it to be one nation. He thought it would split up into six or seven regional independent nations. Frost recalled that when he was about nine years old his father once spread out a map of North America and drew out the approximate boundaries of his hypothetical future nations. Although his father's political vision of the future never materialized, the poet observed, his regional concept of sovereignty was sound and consistent with the maximum of freedom for individuals in a democracy. Frost still believed in 1939 that for democracy to be effective the political unit of society and the nation should not be too large. As a "states' rights, free-trade Democrat," Frost called himself a "sep-a-ra-tist." He accepted fully the federalism of the United States, but he interpreted federalism to include a strong emphasis upon territorial democracy, retained on the state and local levels.

During the first presidential election of Grover Cleveland, Frost's father ran for a city office, and the poet recalled that he often went campaigning with his father through the saloons of San Francisco. He would put a tack through his father's political cards, and use a silver dollar to impel the card upward to impale it on the ceiling for advertising. Frost remarked that there was much "old fashioned political corruption" in San Francisco, in which an office holder pilfered public money. It was different from "modern political corruption," in which office holders waste untold millions of dollars of tax money on wild schemes, which they justify by claims of social consciousness. Instead of being condemned, as were the old fashioned corrupt politicians, the modern politicians were praised and reelected. Frost said he preferred the old fashioned political corruption; it was "more honest."

Frost's father greatly admired athletic prowess, and on one occasion he accepted the challenge of a champion long distance walker and won a walking race that extended over six days. But he weakened his already ravaged body, and his "consumption" and heavy drinking soon brought on a serious illness. The poet recalled that because his father thought swimming would help him recover his health, he swam out into San Francisco Bay, until his head was barely visible among the waves, while the son stood "forlorn" on the beach, in dreadful fear, until his father reached shore and crawled exhausted into his tent. Frost also remembered how his father would go to a slaughterhouse and drink the warm blood of steers, believing it would help cure his tuberculosis. When his father came to die he discovered he really did not hate New England, that at heart he was still a Yankee, and he asked to have his body returned to Massachusetts for burial.

Frost also spoke about his grandfather, William Prescott Frost, toward whom he had ambivalent but mainly negative feelings. His grandfather was the living symbol of the popular image of a Yankee Calvinist, stern and unbending in character and temperament, without humor, penurious, sometimes downright mean, and with no appreciation of literature or the arts.

Even when his grandfather did a kindness, Frost remarked, he always attached conditions to it. The poet recalled two such events. Once his grandfather offered to support him for one year while he wrote poetry, provided that at the end of the year if he had not succeeded in poetry to the point that he could support his family, he would give up poetry for good and take a "practical" job. Frost responded by assuming the stance of an auctioneer selling an item and chanted over and over: "I have one! Give me twenty! Give me twenty!" And, he added, it was almost exactly twenty years later when he published his first book of poems. When his grandfather bought him and his wife the farm in Derry, New Hampshire, it was on condition that he would live on it and not sell it for at least ten years. To insure this his grandfather kept the title deed until his death.

The most remarkable thing about Frost's personal reminiscences was not what he said about his mother, father, and grandfather, but his almost total omission of anything about his wife and children. In July 1939 it was still too painful for him to speak about his immediate family.

After Frost had skimmed lightly over his schooling in Lawrence High School, and at Dartmouth College and Harvard, and his years on the farm in Derry, he described how he and his family had gone to Britain in 1912, in his great final effort to become recognized as a poet. I asked him whether he had met any poets during his stay in England. He began his story with an account of his visit early in January 1913 to Harold Monro's poetry bookshop in Kensington, London. Monro's bookshop was "a gathering place" for clannish Scotsmen living in London, and a magnet for young would-be poets. Monro edited and sold copies of a poetry review, as well as books of poetry and criticism. His shop was also a forum for poets to read their poetry in public. Frost first went there out of curiosity. He arrived late and barely found room to sit on the stairs. Sitting next to him was a pleasant young Englishman who identified Frost as an American. Frost asked him how he knew he was an American. The Englishman replied, by his square-toed shoes. The Englishman introduced himself as Frank Flint. He asked Frost whether he wrote poetry and was pleased to learn that *A Boy's Will* was about to appear. Flint asked Frost if he knew his fellow American poet, Ezra Pound. Frost confessed he had never even heard of Pound. Flint laughed heartily and cautioned Frost never to let Pound hear him say that. Flint had recently published a book of poems, and he knew Pound and his "imagiste" friends Hilda Doolittle, Richard Aldington, and others, yet he was quite independent of them. Frost took an immediate strong liking to Flint. He told his new English friend that in his poetry he put far more stress on "cadence and metaphor" than on images alone, and he admitted to a strong dislike of vers libre, preferring traditional stanza forms and rhyme. Flint told Frost he would tell Pound about him and would arrange for them to meet.

Robert Frost's cabin, near Bread Loaf, 1941, the first summer of the chickens

Very shortly Frost received through the mail a postcard with Pound's address printed on it and a scrawled phrase, "At home sometimes." He put the card in his wallet and deliberately forgot about it for almost a month. One day while walking through Kensington he noticed a street sign and remembered it was the street where Pound lived. He went to Pound's apartment and found him in. Frost said he had expected an old and patriarchical man, because Pound had already published four books of poetry; he was established as an important literary figure in London; and he was known to be the European editor of Harriet Monroe's *Poetry: A Magazine of Verse*, established just three months earlier, in October 1912, in Chicago. Therefore, Frost was surprised that Pound proved to be his junior by eleven years. Pound was by nature and art a kind of wild, Goliardic, modern Bohemian poet; this was reflected in his reddish hair, blooming unkempt, circumscribing the fine frenzy of his luminous eyes and neat red beard. At his first meeting with Frost he wore an oriental kimona.

The two outstanding qualities of Pound, according to Frost, were his sharp mind and his great ego. Frost referred to Pound as "the great I am, the perpendicular pronoun." Yet he respected Pound's complete devotion to poetry. Pound was clearly miffed that Frost had taken his own sweet time to call. When he learned that *A Boy's Will* was being bound at David Nutt's, he insisted on going to the printer's office immediately. They returned to Pound's apartment with a copy of the page proofs of Frost's poems, the first the poet had ever seen. He was embarrassed by Pound's reading his poems in his presence. At one point, Frost recalled, Pound looked up and said with relish, "You don't mind if we like this?" He used the editorial "we." Pound then gave him copies of his two most recent books of poetry, dismissed him curtly, and told him he had to write a book review. The review turned out to be of *A Boy's Will*, and appeared in *Poetry* in May 1913. It was the first important review by a major American writer in the United States of a book of poems by Frost. On the strength of that review, Frost remarked, Pound always claimed afterwards that he had "discovered" Frost as a poet.

But then and thereafter Frost clearly took exception to Pound's claim. Despite Pound's generous interest and apparently good intentions, Frost was more appalled than pleased by portions of the review. It contained a gratuitous attack on the boorish stupidity of American editors of serious literary journals for their neglect of Frost. Since the poet was then taking pains to cultivate the good will of such editors, he did not relish Pound's comments. Also, apparently taking his cue from something Frost had said, Pound painted his grandfather and his uncle as misers who had neglected him for writing poetry. Finally, Pound had clearly misunderstood Frost's character and his work. He thought Frost was a simple American farmer with a motherwit knack for rhyming, a kind of artless and undesigning primitive poet.

Even before the review appeared, Frost said, he perceived that Pound wished to "expropriate" him for his own literary interests, by sponsoring him among literary people in London. Through Pound he met William Butler Yeats, whose poetry and plays Frost had long known, and whom he regarded as the greatest living poet in Britain. Pound and Flint told him that Yeats thought *A Boy's Will* was the best book of poetry to come out of America in many years. But Frost found Yeats was almost as vain and egocentric as Pound, and as "daft on spiritualism" as Pound was on wild experimentation in verse techniques. Frost saw Yeats several times, but always in the presence of a crowd of admirers of his poetry, or of other spiritualists, and they never became friendly. Years later, Frost remarked rather tartly, after the Irish Republic was established, Yeats became dissatisfied because he was made a mere senator, when he expected much more, and he spent his later years anxiously maintaining his various "masks" as a public man, rather than writing poetry. In describing Yeats's attempts to attract admirers late in life, Frost compared him to a piece of sticky candy left in the sun, drawing flies.

In several meetings with Pound, Frost recalled, they discussed the state of poetry in America. Pound considered the United States a cultural wasteland and was already a permanent expatriate. Since Frost was American to the marrow of his bones, even though his country was far from being aesthetically oriented as he wished, he differed strongly from Pound in his affection for America. Pound praised William Carlos Williams as the best poet in America and urged Frost to look him up when he returned. Frost also remembered how he and Pound chortled heartily over Robinson's lines in "Miniver Cheevy":

> Miniver thought, and thought, and thought,
> And thought about it.

The fourth "thought," Frost said, was the marvelous excess that overflowed and made the lines leap beyond prose into poetry. Even in retrospect, while quoting the lines, Frost laughed with glee.

But Pound's character and erratic temperament were not congenial to Frost. He remarked that when Pound's son was born he named him Homer Shakespeare Pound, "for the crescendo effect." Once when the two poets had dinner together in a London restaurant, Pound quoted his poems so loudly, and used such vulgar language, that their waiter placed a tall screen around their table. Frost also repeated a story told him by some English literary friends —that after Pound published *Personae* his friends gave a party to celebrate the occasion, and as guest of honor Pound arrived very late, dressed in an old sloppy sweater, and insulted his hosts. Pound would do anything to be "the center of distraction." Pound thought of himself as not only the foremost poet of his age, but also as a sponsor of young writers, with wealthy people he knew as patrons to provide the money for publishing books and journals. But Pound's literary enthusiasms were like fads in fashions. When Frost knew him, he was about to chuck free verse and imagism for another experiment called vorticism. Frost recalled that when Pound once asked him what he thought about a poem in *Ripostes*, and he made some favorable remarks about it, Pound expressed haughty disdain toward his own poem, and claimed he had far outgrown it. By indulging in increasingly esoteric experimentation in techniques, Frost remarked, Pound eventually reduced his reading public to "a couple of fat English duchesses." Pound went into rages against the conventional sentimental and mellifluous lyric poetry of Swinburne and A. E. Housman. He was "full of Pound and fury" against them. To a large extent Frost agreed with Pound's strictures as they applied to meter and rhyme, but he defended the traditional forms of poetry against Pound's free verse.

But their differences were not literary; they were personal. Frost was not ungrateful for what Pound had tried to do in promoting him, but he was determined to remain true to himself and to his own conception of poetry. For this and other reasons there was soon a cooling off period between them. Shortly afterwards, when Frost came to know some of the "Georgian poets," such as W. W. Gibson, Lascelles Abercrombie, and Edward Thomas, he moved to "the west country," in Gloucestershire, and he and Pound drifted apart.

When Frost had completed describing his return with his family to America from England, I suddenly realized it was past midnight and I feared I had overstayed my welcome. Without apology or explanation I said I should go back to Bread Loaf. Frost waved me down. He asked if I wrote poetry. I told him I had written some lyrics but that my ambition was not to be a poet but to teach in a college and to write. I had submitted a dozen poems in a poetry contest last fall at Middlebury and had won a prize of $25 for two sonnets. To celebrate I had spent $10 on a barrel of beer for the students in my dormitory. Frost smiled and asked me to say the poems. He remarked that my sonnets were smooth, too smoothly facile; the lines were too regularly iambic and run-on, without sufficient compression through rhythm breaking across the meter. He said that developing as a poet was like playing a game of "He can do little who can't do that." When he taught English at Pinkerton Academy he once asked his students to write on something they once believed but no longer believed. One student, who Frost thought was rather dull, without imagination, wrote that when he was around nine years old he used to think the trees along the shore of a nearby pond were palm trees along the shore of Florida. That was the most original thought this boy ever expressed in Frost's class. "He can do little who can't do that." Another boy once described a stoical schoolmate: "He's the kind of boy who wounds with his shield." Said Frost: "He can do little who can't do that." Thus it is with poetry. It begins with very simple analogies or metaphors, like those contained in Mother Goose, and it grows and becomes extended into more and more complex metaphors, until it includes the most profound philosophical thought that human nature is capable of reaching.

Frost went on. As metaphor, poetry consists of saying one thing in terms of another. The highest human thought among our greatest poets consists of saying spirit in terms of matter. That is the greatest attempt that ever failed. I asked, "Must it fail?" Frost replied that it must fail because men are imperfect, because the conditions of human life are too imperfect, and because language as a vehicle for saying spirit in terms of matter is inadequate. He said: "I'm always looking for a poem I didn't write." Frost added that his favorite figure of speech was synecdoche, because he most loved figures in which a part stood for the whole, or the whole suggested a specific part. As a poet he was "a synecdochist." New England was for him a synecdoche for the whole world. That was why critics who referred to him as "a regionalist" were talking nonsense. Wordsworth's poetry was not limited in its significance to the English Lake Country. Faulkner's fiction was not limited to the South. The concrete-particular suggests the general-universal. To illustrate this quality in the synecdoche as a figure of speech Frost quoted the first four lines of William Blake's "Auguries of Innocence":

> To see a world in a grain of sand
> And a Heaven in a wild flower,
> Hold Infinity in the palm of your hand
> And Eternity in an hour.

But a synecdoche doesn't merely compare two things, such as a part and the whole; it illuminates things, by saying the unknown in terms of the known. In saying spirit in terms of matter, the strange and mysterious are drawn within the orbit of the familiar and common, so that in writing and reading poetry we go "from sight to insight, from sense to essence, from the physical to the metaphysical." To illustrate this principle and power of poetry, Frost quoted the second quatrain of Shakespeare's sonnet CXVI:

> O, no! it is an ever-fixed mark
> That looks on tempests and is never shaken;
> It is the star to every wand'ring bark,
> Whose worth's unknown, although his heighth be taken.

The final line, said Frost, is one of the triumphs of English poetry. It describes the guiding star in its mystery as value, the star in heaven as seen by lovers and poets; and it qualifies this by seeing the star in the sky as precisely measured matter in space, as seen by physicists and astronomers. The line is one of Shakespeare's most profound insights, combining spirit and matter, and also separating spirit as value from matter as measurable quantity. Shakespeare understood the limits of science in penetrating matter. Poetry is more inclusive than science because it can deal with both spirit and matter.

Speaking of the human spirit, Frost quoted a line from Shakespeare's sonnet XXIX, "With what I most enjoy contented least," as perhaps the harshest line of self-criticism of the spirit of man in all English poetry. He remarked that it has "all the animus of Housman" in it, but it is directed against the self rather than against the world, and is therefore on a much higher moral level than anything found in Housman's poems.

Frost concluded his examples of how the synecdoche works in poetry by quoting the speech of Jaques in act II, scene 7 (ll. 139–66), in Shakespeare's *As You Like It*, beginning

> All the world's a stage,
> And all the men and women merely players.

It was a perfect example of saying a part for the whole, of saying the stages in the life of man in terms of the drama. Frost particularly relished the line describing the infant, as "Mewling and puking in the nurse's arms," saying that in one line Shakespeare had captured the first year of everyone's life.

We got into the subject of the creative process of the poet or artist, and I mentioned that Sheldon Cheney was speaking that night at Bread Loaf on "Expressionism in Modern Art." Frost objected to the popular idea that the artist is primarily concerned with "self-expression." That was a one-way street from the writer's ego, just as "communication" was a one-way street to the reader. I suggested that if writing is not centered in "self-expression," or in "communication," then it must be primarily concerned, as Aristotle had said, with "an imitation of life." Frost responded that the *product* of art might in some ways "imitate" or "reflect" life, though he doubted whether that was an adequate concept of its nature or function, but the *process* of creating poetry was better described as "a correspondence" between the poet and his reader. Creativity involved response in the writer and counterresponse in the reader, eye to eye and mind to mind. It was a two-way flow between poet and reader of sensations, impressions, images, associations, ideas.

Frost added that the writing process involved both the conscious mind and the unconscious mind. Poor writers are unconscious when they should be conscious, and conscious when they should be unconscious. Edgar Allen Poe had put forth a theory of creativity that was totally conscious. He reduced the creative process to a rational and scientific formula that applied to mathematics but not to poetry. Poe was dead wrong. In contrast the Freudians make the creative process wholly unconscious. They are wrong also, because to a certain extent, a writer should be aware of what he is doing; it is not just a matter of letting the unconscious mind take over, although in fact, when the going is good a poem should write itself. A good writer, while writing, should concentrate on his theme or content, on what he is saying. When he is finished writing, the only thing he has a right to boast about is his technique and form, how well he has said it.

We talked for another half hour or so, and when I suggested again that I should go home, so Frost could get a good night's sleep, he again waved me down. Shortly after two o'clock I felt I should leave for my own sake, since I had to get up at 6:30 to work and attend classes. Finally, after my third attempt to say good night, Frost said he would walk a way with me toward Bread Loaf. We crossed the bridge at the east end of Ripton and plunged into the dark, tree-shaded road leading back to the campus.

The night was pitch black, with dark clouds obscuring the stars. We could hear the flow of water of the branch of the Middlebury River rushing by over boulders to our right. We guided our steps by the sound of our feet on the road and the touch of the grass at the edge of the road. Frost's voice came out of the darkness like a disembodied spirit. He quoted what I recognized as a deliberately modified line from Milton's *Samson Agonistes*: "O dark, dark, dark, amid the blaze of stars," changing Milton's last word, *noon*, to *stars*. I was startled at the dark, ominous, brooding tone in his voice. I remarked that the philosophy implied in Milton's line reminded me of Thomas Hardy's in his poems and novels. But Frost objected to having the word *pessimist* applied to himself. He preferred *meliorist*. He even referred to himself as "a one percent optimist." He justified this positive term because, despite the sadness of the human condition, as a member of the human race he shared in the extension over the centuries of knowledge as revelation, and therefore in humanity's control over life and nature. As Tennyson had said, man moved from precedent to precedent into an open-ended future. Despite the cosmic darkness that surrounded him on the tiny planet earth, there was reason for man to hope. But Frost said the idea of progress as understood by some historians and sociologists, of mankind moving toward a Utopian state, was pure illusion.

On the walk back toward Bread Loaf Frost did most of the talking. He seemed intensely restless. I had not sensed this while we had talked in the circle of light within his cottage, but it was very evident in the dark out of doors. After we had gone about a mile, we stopped by an open area and Frost talked on the laws of compensation in nature and in human affairs. His theme was that many things which appeared as contradictions were really only contraries that needed to be balanced out. Contraries showed themselves in the contrasts of apparent opposites, such as good and evil in life, and of comedy and tragedy in drama. But the contraries were each real in themselves. They were not merely the absence of their opposites, as philosophical monists and Platonists thought.

We walked on, and less than a mile from the Bread Loaf campus we came to a country churchyard on the south side of the road. We talked about death as the contrary of life, whether it was "real" in itself, or only the absence of life. The great unresolved question was whether death applied to the spirit as well as to the body—the problem of immortality. Frost said it was normal to love life and fear death. To relieve the Gothic atmosphere of the dark night, and Frost's dark mood, I punned on the popularity of country churchyards, saying that people were just dying to get in. Rather grimly Frost joined in the punning, saying that death is a grave matter. We talked about the "Graveyard poets" of the eighteenth century, Blair and Young, and especially William Cullen Bryant's "Thanatopsis" and Gray's "Elegy in a Country Churchyard." We agreed that none of these poets, except Bryant in the final lines of his poem, took death with courage and stoical dignity. They all wallowed in their miseries and wept sentimentally because there was such a thing as death. I suggested that the Graveyard poets were rather too fond of crying in their bier. That did it. Frost roared with laughter. And almost as if to confirm the change back to a lighter mood, the clouds broke to the north over Bread Loaf Mountain and Burnt Hill and revealed patches of blue sky, and some faint stars became visible. As we stood there silently we could see each other's features in the eerie soft gray light encircling the road and the cemetery.

We walked on in silence the short distance to Billy Upson's place, where on our left, parallel to the road, was a long stone wall. Frost remarked that "the caterpillar tractor man" would not mind if we sat on his wall. We talked and quoted poetry until the first rays of dawn became visible to the east over Middlebury Gap. I offered to walk Frost back to Ripton, but he insisted that he preferred to return alone. We shook hands and said goodnight, and I hurried back to my room and spent the time until called to work writing down the highlights of our night's talk.

I felt more exhilarated than exhausted. I knew I had taken part in some of the best conversation I had ever heard. Because of Frost's associative method of moving from subject to subject it was easy to write out the matters discussed in the order of their occurrence and to note the themes he had expressed. I made an anthology of his most pithy phrases and noted especially his distinctions in diction in making points during an argument. Our talk had been both dialogue and monologue, but it was not Socratic dialectic talk. Frost was a naturally brilliant nonstop talker, a raconteur, with a deep love of words. He relished and savored well-turned phrases in the way a gourmand savors delicious morsels. He believed in words as deeds. He was highly sensitized to every nuance in the shades of tone in ordinary animated original talk, and in responding he took his cues with an intuitive grasp of both the immediate and the implied meaning in a statement. He was almost compulsive in his energetic need to grasp life through language. Neither in 1939 nor later did I ever believe that Frost's talk flowed because he wished artfully to impress people (though he did impress them), nor as some critics suggested because he was a compulsive neurotic who feared being alone at night. Far from being artful, his talk was naturally unaffected, though reflective, because his mind was full to overflowing with ideas and images. This made his character and temperament extremely attractive to me. Although I was only nineteen and Frost was sixty-five, because of his enormous zest for living I never thought of him as an old man.

V

On Friday, July 21, Frost's poem "Snow" was produced as a one-act play at the Bread Loaf Little Theatre. "Al" Henry, dressed in his working man's clothes, looked most authentic to both life and art. The play was quite somber, but the audience laughed at Mrs. Cole's description of Meserve, "With his ten children under ten years old." One of Frost's great themes in his poetry, that in a dark and cold universe humanity can create a microcosm of light and warmth by which men give some response to life, was captured by Meserve in these lines:

> You make a little foursquare block of air,
> Quiet and light and warm, in spite of all
> The illimitable dark and cold and storm . . . (p. 148).

I noted a similarity in these lines to the theme and dramatic situation in "An Old Man's Winter Night," which Frost had read several weeks earlier at his poetry reading.

After the play Professor Perry Miller congratulated Frost and remarked of the acting: "Wasn't it well done!" Frost agreed and expressed his warm approval to Hortense Moore of how skillfully the actors had delivered their lines.

VI

During the rest of the summer school session Frost seldom came to the Bread Loaf campus. He played tennis several times, once or twice with Kay Morrison, but generally doubles against friends, with Kay as his partner. He played badly, being slow in his reflexes and heavy of foot, but his opponents were as inept as he, and they generally divided the sets between them.

Late one afternoon when I was running cross country on the road between Bread Loaf and Ripton I saw Frost as he was going up the side road leading to the Homer Noble farm. We waved a friendly greeting to each other, but I did not stop to talk. Late in July I saw Frost outside the Ripton community house, when a group of students from Bread Loaf came down for a square dance, but again there was no occasion to talk, beyond social chit chat.

One afternoon early in August I walked past the Little Theatre and heard Frost's distinctive voice floating out to the West Lawn. He had been invited by Professor Lucia Mirrielees to talk to her class on methods of teaching English and poetry in high school. I sat in the back of the room and listened. Frost's theme was what poetry suffered in being taught badly in the classroom. He admitted that perhaps poetry could not be taught at all in school. He defined three kinds of "accountability" in classroom teaching. In their order of importance they were: The accountability of a teacher to himself. Every teacher should take great pains to enjoy literature and thus make himself as educated as possible in poetry. As with the Ten Commandments in religion, all other accountabilities in teaching depended upon fulfilling the first one. Unless a teacher was himself well educated in literature, he could not hope to teach poetry well to his students. The first requisite was mastery of the subject. The second accountability was to the literature itself, to treat it as important, with love and enthusiasm. Teachers should show by their example to students how much poetry means to them. Frost warned against treating poetry too rationally, by critical analysis, or as a subject for scientific research. High school was no place for scholarship. The final accountability was to the students. Frost remarked that he differed strongly from departments of education which taught that students were most important and that a teacher's first duty was to stimulate or motivate students to "express" themselves. Many students "have nothing to express," and those who do don't need a teacher to stimulate them.

VII

Summer School ended on August 13, and one day was allowed for the students to leave the campus and for the conferees to arrive for the second Bread Loaf session, the Writer's Conference, which ran from August 15 to the end of the month. Although Harry Owen administered Bread Loaf for the entire summer, the Writers' Conference was wholly under the direction of Ted Morrison. Owen's policy for scholarship students at the Bread Loaf School included an arrangement for those who wished to stay over and attend the Writers' Conference. In exchange for waiting table, students received room and board and were permitted to audit the various clinics in nonfiction prose, fiction, and poetry. For six summers, 1939 through 1944, I stayed over for the Writers' Conference, thus satisfying my dual interests in preparing myself academically to teach in college and to write.

The Bread Loaf Writers' Conference was born during the fall and winter following the Summer School session of 1925, and it was the joint creation of President Paul Moody, Professor Wilfred Davison, Dean of the Bread Loaf School, and John Farrar, an editor and publisher. The first Writers' Conference was held during the final two weeks of August 1926, with John Farrar as director. Ted Morrison was director from 1932 to 1955. The Writers' Conference was a natural outgrowth of the great emphasis placed on both creative writing and American literature at the Bread Loaf School during President Moody's administration.

The Writers' Conference differed greatly from the School of English in its personnel, purpose, methods, and atmosphere. The academic faculty and high school English teacher graduate students of the School, filled with Victorian respectability, were replaced by nonacademic professional writers and editors and by amateur would-be writers, tinged with a cavalier Bohemian spirit. The pedagogic purpose of the School, with its structure of scheduled courses, lectures, assigned readings and papers, final exams, and credits leading to a degree, was totally absent from the Writers' Conference. Instead, there were informal talks on writing problems and techniques, tutorial conferences and clinics in which a short story, poem, essay, or play, submitted by a conferee, was discussed in open meeting. The academic, aesthetic, and literary atmosphere of the School was largely replaced by a concern with practical problems in writing. Many of the staff, such as Bernard DeVoto, Fletcher Pratt, Edith Mirrielees (sister of Lucia), Louis Untermeyer, and Frost, had been coming to the Writers' Conference for years, so that the last two weeks of August at Bread Loaf was like an annual reunion of friends in a mountain retreat.

Robert Frost was much more in evidence at Bread Loaf during the two weeks of the Writers' Conference than he was during the six weeks of the School of English. Clearly, the Writers' Conference appealed to him far more than the School of English. He played tennis quite often, singles with Louis Untermeyer or Kay Morrison, or doubles with Kay as his partner against Untermeyer and various other players, such as Lesley Frost, or in later summers with Richard Ellmann. Frost's tennis matches with Untermeyer were a popular comedy of errors. He played with quiet, stolid determination, remaining planted like a mountain and moving only when he had to go after a ball that was already over the net. By contrast Untermeyer played as in an hysterical frenzy. With his pince-nez perched precariously on the top of his classically Jewish hooked nose, his receding hairline arched broadly in a halo of thin frizzy hair floating over his head, his swarthy brown arms flailing like a windmill, he was in constant motion all over the court. He would stand flatfooted at the back of the court, his brown spindly legs protruding like broom handles under his baggy shorts. When the ball was served he would rise on his toes like a ballet dancer, and rush in short, quick, jerky, erratic leaps in the direction of the ball. This sports comedy was played with intense dead-pan seriousness, because of Frost's intense passion to win. The poet was so competitive that when he or his partner missed a shot he would become surly. On one occasion, in 1941, when I chided Dick Ellmann on playing poorly and losing, he winked and smiled, and confided to me that it was understood by him and Untermeyer that if they won the first set they were expected to lose the second. Otherwise, Frost was not fit company for a day.

Very early during the Writers' Conference Frost gave a poetry reading. President Paul Moody came up to hear him, and it gave me a peculiar pleasure to see them talking together as friends. That evening I learned that Frost's private talks with friends were a kind of dress rehearsal for his public readings: he repeated with slight variations in expression several of the themes we had discussed in Ripton. He called himself "a synecdochist" and said that all poetry, and even all thought, is essentially metaphorical, in which a part stands for the whole. He identified "synecdoche" as derived from the Greeks.

He remarked that poetry is at once "self-discovery and discovery of self." That is why it is simultaneously so private and so public. "Self-discovery" could come best by treating poetry as a craft, through mastery of technique and form, and not through inspiration and "self-expression." He thought the terms "creativity" and "self-expression" were being badly abused. They led young poets to "sunset raving." Young would-be poets would watch a sunset, and instead of describing it they would express how they felt about it. "It's all oh's and ah's with them and nothing more." After a while they wouldn't even look at the sunset, but would continue to express their feelings. This was "sunset raving." A good poet would so master his technique that he could describe the sunset in a way that made his readers see and feel it. He would never state his abstract emotions about his subject. "Sunset raving" was often found in modern novels, those huge, shapeless, sprawling expressions of raw creativity. Frost was very critical of modern literary critics who praised "the Russian novel" in order to justify condemning American fiction.

Frost read several of his poems, including "The Bearer of Evil Tidings," and remarked that it had been inspired by a friend of his, to whom he gave that title, because the friend often told Frost all the bad things others had said about him, in order to be able to tell him what he had said in his defence. (Later, in a private talk with Frost, I learned he was referring to Sidney Cox). Frost read "The Witch of Coös." He described the woman in the poem as "an old style witch," in contrast to "a young new style witch," such as he had met at a dinner party recently in Boston, wearing a low cut gown and sparkling earrings.

Frost made the cryptic remark: "You can't talk about the wisdom of having children until you have had them." He went on to say there are two kinds of children: those who receive every advantage from their parents and society, by having everything done for them, and end up hating their parents and their country; and, conversely, children who are neglected by their parents and society and are allowed to grow like Topsy, yet despite every bad treatment stick through thick and thin and remain loyal and loving to their parents and country. The first type of child is weak and unhealthy; the second is strong and normal. The theme seemed to be that the soft life destroys character and adversity builds character. He applied his theme to politics. The New Deal politicians in Washington did not understand that their humanitarian policies were undermining the character of the American people. Frost concluded his argument by saying that the great drift toward the common brotherhood of man does not take into account the individual differences in men and that he would hate to live in a wholly "homogenized society."

Except for a loose associative connection, there was almost never any logical relationship between Frost's preliminary rambling remarks and his reading among his poems. A poetry reading by Frost was not a lecture but a performance, in which a theme or two ran like a thread through his comments. He would weave around his subject, seem to digress from it, then return to his subject, carrying new materials to it from his digression, by which he enriched his theme. He often gave the impression that he was thinking out loud and improvising as he rambled on from point to point, even from phrase to phrase, with pauses between points and phrases, while he visibly probed his mind, fishing out from some dim recess an original idea, image, or analogy, which became reflected in his face and gestures, as the idea, image, or analogy welled up inside him and spurted out of his mouth in a voice that also seemed to be searching for exactly the right word and tone to convey it directly to each listener.

After Frost's poetry reading he and the Writers' Conference staff and a few guests went to Treman Cottage for refreshments and some social talk. The Treman Cottage continued to be the social center for the Writers' Conference until at least 1944, just as the large common room in the barn was the gathering place for the conferees.

During the day, between sessions of the writing clinics, there was often a good deal of light bantering about writing and politics between Frost and his friends. He enjoyed teasing them about their latest political enthusiasms. Bernard DeVoto came in for some good-natured ribbing, and on one occasion, when Archibald MacLeish visited the campus, "Archie" was criticized more seriously as "a true believer" in the New Deal. In all these exchanges Frost exemplified completely what he meant by "education by presence." He dominated everyone by his personality, including his critics and detractors. He was always treated with a special formal yet friendly deference, not only by conferees who talked with him, or asked him to autograph a book of his poetry, but even by his friends. While he referred to "Benny," or "Archie," or "Ted," or "Wally," or "Louie," they always called him "Robert." Frost was so obviously *the* literary presence on the Mountain that in response to someone's complaint that too much attention was being paid to him Untermeyer conceded that Bread Loaf was "the most Frost-bitten place in America."

Frost was a friend of most of the Writers' Conference staff, but he was particularly close to Ted Morrison and Louis Untermeyer. Morrison was a good poet, an excellent prose writer, editor, and teacher of writing, and an ideal director of the Conference. He was an affable, kindly, sensitive man, and knew well how to handle Frost's volatile and moody temperament. Since his wife Kay was Frost's secretary, scheduling the poet's lectures and even managing his domestic needs, Morrison and Frost were very close throughout the year at Harvard University, and not merely during their summers together at Bread Loaf.

Frost's unique friendship with Louis Untermeyer reached back to 1915. By 1939 they knew each other's character, beliefs, and idiosyncrasies so well that they could take each other for granted as friends who could be perfectly candid with each other. Despite their very serious political differences they clearly liked and respected each other. Frost chided Untermeyer about his Marxian economics and politics, and Untermeyer endured Frost's defence of individual freedom and American capitalism. During the Writers' Conferences of 1939 to 1944 they formed a team in running the poetry clinics. Untermeyer did all the legwork with the conferees, but Frost attended the poetry clinics four or five times each week. During the sessions of 1939 President Moody and Harry Owen also attended several clinics.

At the poetry clinics Untermeyer would read a poem submitted by a conferee. The author remained mercifully anonymous, and everyone was free to criticize the technique, form, and content of the poem, with no holds barred. While reading a poem Untermeyer's voice occasionally sputtered out, but his wit and humor generally managed to put everyone at ease for a good discussion. He referred to the conferees as "a nest of singing birds," although he and Frost were well aware that many of the birds sang badly, that some were sentimental or crabbed, and that even the old birds were sometimes more concerned with staying snugly in their nest than in singing or flying. Much of the poetry read at the clinics was wretchedly conventional.

On one occasion Untermeyer read a sonnet and everyone tore it to shreds. It was full of clichés, sententious sentiments, high-flown rhetoric and inflated diction, and was in every way a poor imitation of conventional love lyrics. This time, Untermeyer said, he would break the rule of anonymity. He was sure the author wouldn't mind. The poet was William Shakespeare. Untermeyer had read one of Shakespeare's lesser known sonnets. There was a stunned silence. Someone asked to have the poem read again. Then the conferees gradually retreated from their severe criticism. They found many little literary gems they had missed with the first reading. Afterwards Frost and Untermeyer chuckled over how easily people can be intimidated by established literary reputations.

On another occasion Untermeyer read a poem about nature which was so poor, so filled with "sunset raving," devoid of images, and with so much jerky meter and forced rhymes, that Frost could not contain himself, and growled out some very harsh remarks. In an attempt to soften the blow to the conferee's feelings, Untermeyer was kind and compassionate. Later, Untermeyer remarked to a group that lingered after the clinic adjourned that his and Frost's responses utterly demolished and reversed their stereotyped public images. Here was Untermeyer, the supposedly smart-alecky, hard-boiled, New York Jew, being nice as apple pie about the wretched poem, and here was Robert Frost, the epitome of old New England, the sweet old man and most loved and popular poet in America, being utterly nasty and hard as nails about it.

One other event occurred during the poetry clinics of 1939 which revealed one of Frost's most important convictions about poetry. A woman came up to him after a clinic in which "meaning in poetry" was much discussed, and said: "Mr. Frost, what do you mean by 'Fire and Ice?'" Frost looked her steadily in the eyes and recited his poem, then said: "It means that." The woman looked baffled. Frost responded in conclusion: "If I had wanted to say anything more I would have included it in the poem."

One of the social highlights during each Writers' Conference was the soft ball game played in an afternoon on the boulder-strewn meadow on the lower end of the Homer Noble farm. The staff, the conferees, famous visiting writers, and occasionally guests at the Inn, divided into two teams. Great care was taken that the best players should be on Frost's team, thus increasing the odds that his team would win. Frost disliked having women players, so they were not chosen for his team. Conferees with cameras recording the occasion called forth his silent ire and wrath. Fletcher Pratt, who was reputed to have been a prize fighter, was generally the plate umpire, and his gestures in calling strikes and balls, and in declaring base runners out or safe, were histrionic, and provided many hot arguments and witty comments.

Benny DeVoto and Frost were generally the two outstanding players. DeVoto's rambunctious character came out sharply during the softball games. He would lay down a bunt along the third base line. Then, after reaching first base ahead of the ball, counting successfully on the ineptitude of the fielders, he would keep running to second, then on to third, always a few strides ahead of the ball, then in a mad dash home, climaxed by a slide that began a good ten feet before he reached the plate, with the cheers of supporters and the jeers of opponents ringing him around the bases. Thus, on several occasions he turned a soft bunt into a home run. Once in his slide to the home plate he tore his trousers from ankle to knee and had to play the rest of the game with safety pins holding his pants together.

Frost was always in his pristine glory during the Writers' Conference softball games. He played with the same wild and reckless audacity as DeVoto, as though he were an enthusiastic rookie trying to make his favorite big league team, the Boston Red Sox. Softball was much more Frost's game than the genteel games of tennis at Bread Loaf. He would have preferred to play with a hard ball, so he could emulate his favorite ball player, the rookie Ted Williams, starring in his first year with Boston. But in the fiercely aggressive way Frost threw himself into hitting, running bases, and fielding, a dimension in his character became very clearly evident: the game was played to win, not just for fun.

One incident humiliating to Frost occurred, which illustrated why he did not like to play softball with women on the teams. Frost hit a liner into left field and tried to stretch it into a double. The outfielder threw the ball in a long arching fly back to the second baseman, Laura Brooks, a hefty, solid girl, who stood in the base path between second and first, blocking Frost's path to the bag. As he ran toward second base Frost saw her standing with her gloved hand outstretched waiting for the ball to descend. He stopped, perplexed by how to get around her to second base. She caught the ball with one hand, turned around, and casually tagged Frost. Fletcher Pratt had run out almost to the pitcher's mound, and with elaborate gestures he shouted Frost out, waving him to the sidelines. Sheepishly, Frost left the field. To be tagged out thus by a mere girl was almost too much for him. Had the second baseman been a man Frost would undoubtedly have knocked him over to reach the bag. It was very difficult to play to win when women players required chivalrous behavior by their male opponents.

The Writers' Conference of 1939 ended on a very ominous note. Despite the almost fairy land kind of isolation of Bread Loaf from the rest of the world, we were aware that all during August a war crisis had been brewing between Nazi Germany and her European neighbors. Like other scholarship students I stayed over after the Writers' Conference to help Harry Owen wind up the Bread Loaf campus for its three seasons of hibernation. On August 31 the Nazis invaded Poland, precipitating World War Two. A group of us, including Frost and Untermeyer, gathered around a car radio and listened to an account of the invasion, described by the Nazis' propaganda as "a counter attack with pursuit." The ultimatums of Britain and France against Germany indicated a major war. Untermeyer was very disturbed. He appeared more concerned about the fate of Soviet Russia than the imminent destruction of Poland. He hoped that in the coming war the United States would not remain neutral. Frost remarked that regardless of its sympathies the United States would have to remain neutral until we had a serious grievance against Germany involving our self-interest. On that political difference between Untermeyer and Frost ended the summer of 1939 at Bread Loaf.

Robert Frost at Bread Loaf
1940

I

AFTER the death of Elinor Frost on March 20, 1938, a fellowship in her memory was established by Middlebury College for a young writer to attend the Bread Loaf Writers' Conference. In 1938 Frost awarded the Elinor Frost Fellowship to Charles Foster, a graduate student at the University of Iowa. In 1939, at the suggestion of Lesley Frost, the fellowship was given to Mrs. Lois Squire, to attend both the School of English and the Writers' Conference. Her inability to handle the academic work resulted in a revision of how the fellowship was to be awarded. During the fall of 1939 Harry Owen and Frost worked out a plan by which students at the Bread Loaf School and Middlebury College who wished to apply for the fellowship were invited to submit poems in competition. These were screened by Harry Owen and submitted to Frost, who made the decision. I submitted a batch of poems, and in April 1940

Harry Owen informed me orally that Frost had awarded the Elinor Frost Fellowship to me for 1940. Owen confirmed this by letter on May 14, in which he referred to the award as "the Robert Frost Fellowship."

Late in June I went up to Bread Loaf and settled in at Gilmore Cottage. Frost had bought the Homer Noble farm at the end of the summer in 1939, and came up the Mountain in May 1940 for the summer. One evening after work at Bread Loaf, before classes began, I went to Frost's farm to thank him for the fellowship. He invited me back for "a good talk" the next night. I arrived around sunset, just as Frost and the Morrisons were finishing their dinner, and they invited me to join them in dessert and coffee, after which the poet and I went to his log cabin, about a hundred yards up the trail beyond the farmhouse. Frost's new dog, a small black collie with a white muff around his collar and nose, ran ahead of us to the cabin. The poet said his name was Gillie, which was Scottish for the servant of a Highland chief.

Frost's rustic cabin, built of large, smooth, pine logs, had a cobblestone chimney and a screened-in porch facing west and south toward the farmhouse and meadow below. From the porch we entered a living room with a fireplace to the left in the center. The walls were of rough tan beaverboard. To the left of the fireplace a door led to the kitchen, bedroom, bathroom, and utility room at the back of the cabin. On the right wall of the living room was a bookcase half filled with books. Directly in front of the fireplace were two lounging chairs; on the seat of one was a copy of William Cowper's *Complete Poems*, turned face downward in the middle of "The Task." A half empty jar of strawberry jam lay within easy reach of a large Morris chair to the right of the fireplace. The floor by the chair was surrounded by cracker crumbs. The fireplace showed the charred ashes of previous fires.

I sat in one of the chairs and glanced at Cowper's poem. When I looked up Frost was gone, and a few moments later he returned with an armful of split logs which he set in place over the iron bars. He crumpled up a few newspapers and thrust them under the logs. As he put a match to the paper he looked up and said: "Out West they think a man's a tenderfoot sissy if he lights a fire from the bottom,

Interior of Frost's cabin near Bread Loaf, 1974.

and a dude if he uses paper." He saw me looking at Cowper's poem and said that Cowper lacked what we were about to have—"fire." Cowper was too thorough; a little sensationalism wouldn't have hurt him.

Frost settled down in the Morris chair with Gillie at one side. He asked me which courses and teachers I had elected at Bread Loaf. I was in Reuben Brower's "The Classical Tradition in English Poetry." Frost was delighted and said Brower had been the best student he had ever had at Amherst College, and was acquiring an excellent reputation as a classical scholar. Also, Brower had strong intuitive feeling for poetry as a living art. His course, said Frost, was mainly in the poetry of Dryden and Pope, our two best poets in English in the Horatian vein. I couldn't have chosen a better teacher or course.

I also had registered for two courses with John Crowe Ransom, one in "The Seventeenth-Century Lyric" and the other in "Analysis of Poetry." Ransom had rented the Schoolhouse Cottage along route 125, between Bread Loaf and Ripton, Frost informed me, and he was looking forward to a renewal of friendship with Ransom, whom he had known at Vanderbilt University. Frost expressed confidence that these two courses would provide me with good occasions to read and talk about much good poetry. But he expressed extreme skepticism about the analysis of poetry. We murder to dissect. Frost expressed the hope that Ransom would stick to writing poetry and forget criticism. As a poet, Frost said, Ransom had a fine ear for sounds. In the long run he would be remembered longer for the poems he had written than for any and all the criticism he had written or would write. His poetry had much dry wit, but was too "hard," that is, unemotional, for popular consumption.

I asked whether it was possible to be both a good poet and a good critic. Yes, Frost said, one could be both Dr. Jekyll and Mr. Hyde, at least for a while, but it was an unhealthy condition. The critical faculty is too rational and academic, and no scientific analysis can do justice to a poem. Criticism, as such, is largely a waste of time. If there is anything more to be said about a poem after it is written then it is a bad poem. If the poet had wanted to say anything more he would have said it himself in the poem. Ransom would make a serious mistake if he were to shift from writing poetry to criticism; he would be in danger of allowing himself to become dominated by modern science and the academic life. Frost thought writing criticism could drain Ransom's creative power and imagination and ruin him as a poet.

Frost asked me whether I knew Mark Twain's story, "The Celebrated Jumping Frog of Calaveras County." I confessed I had not read it. Fred Lewis Pattee, a faculty member at Bread Loaf for ten years, up to 1936, had sent Frost a copy of an anthology, *Mark Twain: Representative Selections* (New York: American Book Co., 1935), and Frost had reread Twain's story. As an editor, Frost said, Pattee was "a mouse in a waste basket." Frost remarked that Twain's jumping frog story was the most perfect short story of its kind in all American literature. It was a poem in fictional form. The voice tones and sense of sound in the style were lyrical: "The prose sings." The timing was perfect and there was "punch in the punch lines." Frost summarized Twain's plot, of how the jumping frog leaped free and far, like a true champion, until the city slicker filled him secretly with buckshot, after which he was heavy and ponderous, anchored to the earth, and incapable of leaping.

Frost did not analyze Twain's story, but treated it as a parable. Before the frog was filled with buckshot he was like a poet, light and imaginative and capable of great leaps by a command or the slightest stimulus. But after being filled with buckshot the frog was like a scientific critic or scholar, weighted down, stuffed with ponderous logic and knowledge, but useless in the art of jumping. No amount of prodding could get him to budge. The chief virtues of the poet—imagination, fancy, audacity, courage, wit and humor, which created his originality, were lost. "No performance, no form." The chief characteristics of the scholar are a love of facts for their own sake as knowledge, thoroughness, accuracy, and systematic scientific method. Most scholars lack imagination and spontaneity and are "humorless and witless." Scholars are "too thorough, too specialized, too fastidious, too proud." In summary, Frost said the scholar sticks to his subject until he is stuck to his subject. He exhausts everything about his subject until everything about it exhausts him and everyone else. His knowledge clings to him like burrs caught in crossing a field. But the poet allows his subject to stick to him as long as he wishes, and while it is attached to him he shoots out leads from it which he is free to follow. The poet keeps up a fastmoving interest in his subject while getting the maximum benefit of what his subject has to offer. This is the difference between the scientist and the artist. There were dangers in absorbing knowledge beyond one's capability to use it well. But Frost conceded that the scholar was decidedly superior to shallow readers who merely skim a work.

Frost compared a poet to a man standing at the edge of a Vermont boulder-strewn field, trying to reach the other side of the field by leaping from one boulder to another, without touching the ground. Since the boulders are scattered he cannot cross the field in a straight line, as a scientist or expository prose writer would, but must use metaphors, analogies and figures to zig-zag his way across. Through his imagination the poet must leap from one boulder to the next and the next; only with audacity, courage, and skill will he reach the other side without falling to the ground or finding himself stalled with no boulder to leap to, never to arrive at his destination. And, Frost emphasized, there is no way to retrace his way once he has made his first leap or two. He will either cross the field or not. The poet is like God, who writes straight with crooked lines. He follows Shakespeare's advice that "by indirecttions we find directions out."

Frost insisted that poetry is a series of intuitional leaps, and is never a planned rational process. Writing a poem is like falling in love, a form of lunacy deeply imbedded in our emotional nature, which creates through the special character of language an intimate correspondence between the lover and the object of his love. The Italian words *amante* (*lover*) and *amente* (*lunatic*) apply well to the poet. To reinforce his argument Frost quoted a passage from Shakespeare's *A Midsummer Night's Dream*:

> Lovers and madmen have such seething brains,
> Such shaping fantasies, that apprehend
> More than cool reason ever comprehends.
> The lunatic, the lover, and the poet
> Are of imagination all compact.

One sees more devils than vast hell can hold:
That is the madman. The lover, all as frantic,
Sees Helen's beauty in a brow of Egypt.
The poet's eye, in a fine frenzy rolling,
Doth glance from heaven to earth, from earth to heaven;
And as imagination bodies forth
The forms of things unknown, the poet's pen
Turns them to shapes, and gives to airy nothing
A local habitation and a name.

(act V, scene I, ll. 4–17)

Frost remarked that he agreed with the ancient Greeks, who explained poetry as a divine madness, a gift of the gods to men, through which poets created order in a chaotic universe. Homer and other epic poets invoked the muses for inspiration and guidance, but they never explained their poetry.

If we are to be poets, Frost remarked, there are two qualities we must develop: one is sight, the other is insight. The first pertains to the physical plane; the second to the metaphysical. The first is more important. We always begin with the senses and feelings.

In writing, Frost said, we should have something to say, and we should say it. A finished poem should be at once "sensational and valid." The sensational has a broad scope beyond our senses in our emotions: "It runs the whole gamut from tenderness to blitzkrieg." Frost suddenly shot a question to me: "What is the opposite of valid?" I replied: "Invalid?" Frost shot back, "No! It's wrong as false." I asked: "What do you mean?" Frost replied: "You placed the emphasis on the wrong syllable. It's not invalid, but invalid." He explained that in poor poetry most metaphors are not false but sick. They are "weak, flabby, out-of-focus." In using language metaphorically poets seldom hit the bullseye absolutely. Frost then said: "You can tell where the center of the target is by the number of near misses around the bullseye." Good metaphors have two kinds of appeal: they should be persuasive and appeal to our reason and sense of truth; and they should be charming and appeal to our feelings. "Charming and persuasive," Frost said. That is what is involved in being "sensational and valid." In writing a poem, he added, there is no such thing as a selection or choice of words. There is only one word—the right word. Every word in a poem must be the right word. Each word or phrase in a poem creates an emergency which the next word or phrase solves. I remarked that I agreed with what he had said and that I thought his way of saying it was far better than Ezra Pound's formula: "Make it new but make it true." Frost looked a little startled at my mention of Pound, but said nothing in response.

After we paused to have some ginger ale (I had brought two bottles) Frost remarked by way of reference to a newspaper lying on a table that there had been much criticism of Marshal Henri Pétain for collaborating with the Nazis after the recent fall of France. Pétain had been denounced as a traitor to France and was even charged with being sympathetic with the Nazis. Frost took exception to such criticism. He said Pétain had proven his patriotism and love of France in World War One. At his advanced age Pétain had no personal ambition; he was merely attempting to be a shield between the victorious Germans and the defeated French. It was a sorrowful task; Frost sympathized with Pétain and discounted the criticism against him.

Frost expressed wonder at the swiftness with which the German Blitzkrieg had smashed the British and French armies in northern France. But there had been much heroism on the Allied side, especially in the retreat to Dunkirk and in the evacuation. Frost said: "I can't think of anything more terrible than having to cover the retreat of a beaten army." I asked whether he thought the German victory over the Allies meant the decline and fall of France and Britain. Frost replied that we know about how long a man will live, but we don't know how long a nation or empire will live. He doubted that the war meant the end of Britain. They would fight on. The Germans were now riding high on their victory, but they had many strong enemies. Frost said he didn't know whether to admire the Germans as courageous or to condemn them as foolhardy, for taking on the whole world again. Germany would receive no help from Japan unless she went to war with Russia, which he thought unlikely. Italy was too refined by civilization to fight effectively for the Germans. He remarked that before the United States went to war, or even thought of going to war, we must have a clear-cut issue against Germany. He did not think we yet had such an issue.

I was most eager to hear Frost comment on other poets he had known and steered our talk back to that subject by asking him which American poet looked to him most like a genuine poet. He picked up my word *looked* and treated it literally. He said that "old Edwin Markham," with his long white hair and beard, his self-dramatic, oratorical stance on the stage, and his tremulous elocutionary voice, looked most the way the American public thought a poet should look. "Old Markham" was a funny little man. He wrote poems of social protest that he called "bugle cries" to the world's poor, to rise and revolt. Frost described him as "little boy blue blowing his horn for the proletariat." Frost doubted "Old Markham" had ever read Marx; he was only a muckraking newspaperman and sentimentalist. After he published "The Man With the Hoe," he made a fortune going around the country reciting it and his Lincoln poems. Frost said there were some good blank verses in "The Man With the Hoe," particularly the opening and closing lines. It was a much better poem than most social consciousness verse, which lacked variety and wit. There should be wit in every poem, and variety in the way the sentences are laid down in a stanza. Poems about the virtuous laboring man are labored. The proletarian poets were witless bores.

Frost remarked that "Old Markham" once began a lecture and poetry reading at Bread Loaf, in the late 1920s by saying: "Up to 1900 the world's greatest quatrain was Walter Savage Landor's 'On His Seventy-Fifth Birthday.' But in 1900 I wrote my quatrain Outwitted." He was convinced that his epigrammatic quatrain had eclipsed Landor's. Frost recited Landor's poem:

> I strove with none, for none was worth my strife.
> Nature I loved, and, next to Nature, Art;
> I warmed both hands before the fire of life;
> It sinks, and I am ready to depart.

Chuckling as he spoke, Frost remarked that Landor's quatrain was marvelous as poetry, but the first line was very humorous as fact, because Landor was so short-tempered with everyone that once in a fit of anger he threw his servant out the window and then ran outside to see whether he had ruined his flower bed. Landor loved "Nature," his flowers, and "Art" more than he cared to fight with people. He anticipated our modern pacifists by a century. "Old Markham" thought his poem "Outwitted" beat Landor's quatrain. Frost quoted it:

> He drew a circle that shut me out—
> Heretic, rebel, a thing to flout.
> But Love and I had the wit to win:
> We drew a circle that took him in!

As poetry this quatrain couldn't begin to compare with Landor's poem. Frost argued that any sensitive reader could always tell whether a poem was struck off in a genuine intuition, or whether it was contrived, as "Old Markham's" quatrain was. The first line was genuine enough, Frost said, but the last phrase in the second line, "a thing to flout," was false and labored for the rhyme with "out." The third line too was genuine poetry, but the last part of the final line, "that took him in," had the unfortunate connotation that love deceives.

Frost remarked that a much finer poet than "Old Markham" was Vachel Lindsay. I told him that Lindsay's sister, a Mrs. Wakefield, had come to Middlebury College last spring to read her brother's poems. Frost said Lindsay used to read his poems before large enthusiastic audiences, leading them like a football cheerleader by chanting all the passages up to the refrain lines, then signaling his listeners to join him en masse in a ritual response. This was Lindsay's idea of how a poet should reach his readers in a democracy. It worked pretty well for him. He was an evangelist peddler of poetry. I mentioned that Mrs. Wakefield had tried the same method at Middlebury, but there were too few students in her audience, and they were too self-conscious about shouting the refrain lines in the college chapel. It didn't work for her. Frost said Lindsay had a genuine ear for the tunes of poetry. He remarked that Lindsay had been gulled out of keeping the copyright for his poetry by his publisher, and instead of becoming wealthy he ended up in deep debt, and committed suicide by drinking a can of lye.

Frost had a much harsher opinion of two other midwestern poets,

Edgar Lee Masters and Carl Sandburg. Both poets were committed to writing free verse, which Frost deplored. He dismissed Masters as "filled with animus against his fellow American poets." This was evidenced in his refusal to be part of a group of poets invited by Theodore Roosevelt to visit him in his home at Oyster Bay, Long Island. Masters accepted Roosevelt's invitation on condition that he could come alone. Frost predicted that Masters' poems in *Spoon River Anthology* would not endure.

Frost remarked that Sandburg, like William Butler Yeats, lived a life of affectation. But while Yeats's poses and masks had become a second nature to him and were an unconscious "sincere kind of affectation," Sandburg was artfully and self-consciously folksy. The differences between Yeats and Sandburg could be seen in their poetry. He admired Yeats's poetry very much, but the man was really too much the natural aristocrat to believe the common people were admirable. Yeats thought folk literature was what the courts lost, the kind of overflow or scum inherited by way of the drippings from the king's kitchen. Yeats's appeals to the ordinary people of Ireland were those of a man who knew he was superior to them in most ways, and certainly as a poet. But Sandburg worked hard at creating the appearance of being a common man, and pretended that all common men were really talented, like Lincoln and Walt Whitman. He was more an entertainer than a poet. In his stage appearances he wore a blue working man's shirt, and he would deliberately rumple his white hair and strum his "geetar" while talking sentimental, infantile politics. Frost said his response to Sandburg's "New Deal-Fair Deal propaganda poem," *The People, Yes*, would be "The People, Yes, and the People, No." Frost said he would double the thought and halve the sentiment of Sandburg, whose brand of populist democracy was really popular demagoguery. Frost wanted to see individual freedom under the Constitution, but Sandburg wanted equality of condition under popular will. He attacked Sandburg's free verse, saying, "It's like playing tennis cross-country, without boundary lines or a net." Frost concluded by predicting that Sandburg would be better remembered for his four-volume biography of Lincoln, published the year before, than for his poetry.

I asked Frost what he thought of Archibald MacLeish. He clearly disliked MacLeish's New Deal politics and called him "a true believer." Frost said of New Deal politicians that they think all Americans can be adjusted and readjusted to all their innovations, and they're dead wrong. He would like to see the New Deal replaced with "a new deck." Frost expressed dislike of Roosevelt's "Brain Trust," particularly Harry Hopkins and Guy Tugwell, and said the whole fallacy of a brain trust was that it assumed that politics was primarily a matter of intelligence rather than of moral decency in the use of power. "Archie" MacLeish thought of himself as the cultural leader of Roosevelt's brain trust. But "Archie" strained too hard to play the public role of the intellectual liberal in politics and culture. You could feel the strain clearly in his prose style, filled with repetition and variations of phrases, and self-conscious pauses suggesting he was still searching for the right word or phrase even after he had gone to print. "Archie's" prose style was a pale imitation of Matthew Arnold's essays. The thing that kept him a New Dealer was his belief that love would solve all the world's problems. But misplaced love creates more problems than love or hate can solve. On MacLeish as a poet, Frost remarked that "Archie is too derivative," particularly of Pound and Eliot. He followed the latest literary fashions. The trouble with MacLeish's "America was Promises" was that he made it appear as though America was *only* promises, and nothing more.

Frost expressed great admiration for Edwin Arlington Robinson. He was "the melancholy Jaques of modern poetry," full of tragic grief. He was a patient Platonist. But his good taste and wit saved him from singing the blues like our impatient young reformers. Robinson had the sense of play even about human tragedy and unhappiness. His originality consisted of saying new things in old forms of poetry. This is much harder than trying to say new things by destroying old forms. Poets could no longer express forlorn, aching sadness by saying "She stood in tears amid the alien corn," because Keats had already said it. The poet must find new ways to say this eternal emotion. Robinson found many new ways, and he lodged some good poems where they would endure.

Frost quoted several poems by Robinson, including "The Mill," and "Mr. Flood's Party." I remembered several of his sonnets and "The Dark Hills," and quoted them. During a pause in our quoting I realized it was past midnight, and asked Frost whether he minded if I returned to Bread Loaf since I had early morning chores, and I suggested that I might return for more talk the next night. To my surprise Frost responded favorably. He took his lantern, and we walked together down his side road to route 125, the road to Bread Loaf. He remarked that he liked to make new friends, because he sometimes found it hard to bear the love of old friends whom he had neglected. After we had said good night, as I walked back to campus I reflected that one of the most remarkable things about Frost as a talker was that when we met again after an interval of ten months he had picked up the threads of our earlier talk as though it had been interrupted only the night before. Also, something appeared to have occurred to Frost between the summer of 1939 and the summer of 1940 to make him much less emotionally high strung and tense. He seemed to be far more calm and rationally cool than he had been a year ago.

II

At sunset the next evening I met Frost in front of his barn, and together with Gillie we went to his cabin. I mentioned that I had just bought a copy of "Doc" Cook's *The Concord Saunterer* (1940), an excellent little book, and we drifted into a conversation on Thoreau's *Walden*. Frost had a high opinion of the literary qualities of *Walden* and said that parts of it were like poetry in prose. Thoreau was a very keen observer of nature. Like James Thomson in *The Seasons* he wrote with his senses concentrated upon his subject, not like some writers about "Nature," who seemed to have consulted the *Encyclopedia Britannica*. Thoreau proved to himself and to the world how much of civilization he could live without, while living in it; Robinson Crusoe proved how self-sufficient and independent a man could be apart from civilization. Darwin's *The Voyage of the Beagle*, *Walden* and *Robinson Crusoe* were, Frost said, among the books he most cherished. *Walden* was more than a declaration of independence: it was a story of high adventure and contained much moral wisdom about life.

"Doc" Cook, said Frost, was a truer disciple of Thoreau than he. I asked where he and Cook differed about Thoreau. Frost said he agreed with Aristotle that man is by nature a social animal, and this implied some form of constitutional structure for society. Thoreau was right in protesting abuses by those in political power, but his civil disobedience was anarchical, and directed as much against the very idea of constituted authority as of abuses of power. Philosophically, Thoreau stood for independence from society rather than freedom in society. Thoreau carried out a one-man revolution. He was the apostle of independence, but not as a committed and loyal member of society, not as a citizen. Thoreau thought his relation to society was voluntaristic, rather than a matter of moral necessity. He made a classic case for individual independence against too many claims and demands on us by society and government.

But there is also a case for society against the anarchical claims of individuals who want to live *in* society but behave as though they lived *outside* society. The sweep to collectivism in our time abuses the case for society and leaves little room for individual liberty. Collectivism is a form of organized anarchy; its tyranny recognizes no constitutional restraints on power. Frost said he considered Thoreau's independence "an unchartered freedom." If each of us could live like a monk in a cell in the woods, and be content with a bean patch, Thoreau's social and economic theory would be sufficient. But it isn't enough for any man who isn't a saint, an ascetic, and a bachelor. Frost said he was none of these, and added: "Life among the woodchucks is not for me."

The idea of tyrannical restraints imposed on individuals from without led us to discuss censorship over writers. Frost told an amusing anecdote about how Kipling once sent a short story to a Christian Science magazine in which occurred the sentence: "She tossed off a glass of brandy." The editor knew many of his readers would be shocked by such unbecoming conduct by a member of the fair sex, so he wrote back and asked Kipling to change the sentence so that the word *brandy* would not appear in the story. Kipling was very obliging, and wrote back that he would delete the offensive word. When the manuscript was returned the sentence read: "She tossed off a glass of watermelons." That's the way to handle literary censorship, Frost said.

Frost launched on a related theme. He remarked that all social conflicts and evils in the world may be traced directly to two things which man possesses. The first of these is man's originality; the second is the strength of his conviction that his originality is true and should prevail. The strongest force in the world is our conviction about moral truth. Trouble in society begins when a man, such as Martin Luther, gets a new and original idea which no one has had in quite the same way before. He begins to talk about that idea until someone else gets it too. Then there are two of them. They begin talking about it to other people, and after a while each gets a convert. Then there are four of them. The process is continued until they become a party powerful enough to challenge the ruling authority. Since the ruling authority desires to stay in power the party is told it must get rid of that idea. But the people with the original idea say that since they believe in their idea they will not get rid of it, and if the ruling authority desires to get rid of the idea it must get rid of the people who believe in it. Often those in power are most reluctant to do this, as it would require harsh means, persecution, etc. If the rulers are smart they will incorporate the original idea, and declare the originator of it a saint, rather than excommunicate him as a heretic. That was what the Church did with St. Francis of Assisi. If those in authority cannot absorb the original idea they must destroy it, or they will be destroyed by it when enough people accept the original idea to overthrow their rulers. It is the same within nations and between nations. This is how wars begin. Originality is one of man's greatest virtues, and it keeps the gates of Utopia closed to man.

The right to hold original ideas is necessary for individual liberty. In a great and complex nation such as the United States individual originality often can become eccentricity, and eccentricity can become perverse and lead to madness. But under our system of government, Frost contended, we can absorb all that. The poet's strong nationalism came out in his defence of the many-faceted freedom throughout the United States.

One of the great freedoms he most enjoyed, Frost said, was to use the American language freely in his poetry. For most of the rest of our talk Frost explained his theory of the relationship between phonetics and semantics in poetry. He laid heavy stress upon "the sound of meaning and the meaning in sound." His theory of language was in some ways a subtle refinement of Wordsworth's theory that the natural idiom of common speech provides the basis for poetic diction. Unlike Wordsworth, Frost did not claim that peasants or semiliterate men provided the best source of diction for poetry. But he acknowledged that he had picked up many fine phrases from the motherwit idiom of New Hampshire and Vermont farmers. Among these he cited: "Good fences make good neighbors" (stressing the importance of *good*), in "Mending Wall"; "Sakes/It's only weather," in "The Runaway"; "Tell the truth for once," in "The Witch of Coös"; and "But just the kind that kinsfolk can't abide," in "The Death of the Hired Man." What made these common phrases poetry was the dramatic situation and tone in which they were spoken. Frost remarked that the most naturally dramatic language was gossip and that all literature is good to the extent that it is dramatic. John Synge understood this theory of language in poetry and applied the Irish vernacular and idiom with great skill in *The Playboy of the Western World*. Frost argued that every nation has its own idiom and a poet should not know too many foreign languages, because it dulls his sense of the idiomatic nuances of his own language. While writing a poem a poet is not a linguist but a creator.

Frost recalled that when he was in England, shortly before the First World War, he had pointed out to Walter De la Mare that the rhythm in portions of his poem "The Listeners" was remarkably loose for English prosody. To illustrate what he meant by loose rhythm he quoted a passage from the poem:

> But only a host of phantom listeners
>   That dwelt in the lone house then
> Stood listening in the quiet of the moonlight

> To that voice from the world of men:
> Stood thronging the faint moonbeams on the dark stair,
>   That goes down to the empty hall,
>   Hearkening in an air stirred and shaken
>   By the lonely Traveller's call.

And one later line was a perfect example of loose rhythm: "Fell echoing through the shadowiness of the still house." The number of consecutive unstressed syllables in these lines was most unusual for English, Frost pointed out to De la Mare. But the English poet said he had never noticed anything unusual about these lines. Frost expressed his amazement over De la Mare's insensitivity to the phonetic patterns in his own poem.

I suggested that perhaps sensitivity to the sound of words was buried deep in the unconscious mind. Frost agreed, and said that in his sensitivity to the sound of words, before he understood their dictionary meaning, he "heard" every poem he wrote before putting it on paper. He could understand De la Mare's not being aware of the looseness of his rhythms in "The Listeners" while he was writing the poem, but he felt that afterwards De la Mare should have understood what he had achieved. Perhaps it was like not being aware of an unconscious pun we had made, I suggested. In poetry there were both conscious and unconscious puns. I said that Shakespeare was full of plays on words, conscious puns and deliberate double entendres. Frost agreed and added that Shakespeare's playing with words was a major source of his wit and humor, and made his poetry very rich in meaning. Multiple meanings in sound made for multiple meanings in the content. I asked whether a poet could ever be consciously aware of all the meanings in the sound or the content of his poems. Frost replied that he doubted that was possible. I then asked him whether he was aware of a pun in his poem "Mending Wall"? He looked startled. After a brief silence I quoted the lines with the pun:

> Before I built a wall I'd ask to know
> What I was walling in or walling out,
> And to whom I was like to give offense.

Frost howled with laughter, and shouted: "I'll take it! I'll take it! I'm entitled to every meaning to be found in my poem!" I admired his audacity in rising above the occasion, making valid humor out of what would have embarrassed a more timid man. A bit sheepishly he admitted that although he had said "Mending Wall" many times in public readings, he had been quite unaware of the pun. Perhaps, he added with a mischievous grin, De la Mare wasn't so insensitive after all. He completed his defense by saying: "Something there is that doesn't hear a pun." We laughed together over the whole thing.

In stressing sound as the *vital* element in poetry, Frost said there was danger that the poet could fall into mere jingles if he made his meter too regular, without the grace and variety of rhythm. Tennyson, Swinburne, and Poe were often guilty of that error. I suggested adding Shelley to the list. Frost agreed, but with some qualification. Even in Shelley's "The Cloud" the sound of meaning saves it from becoming a jingle. Frost quoted the last stanza of "The Cloud" in a manner that roughened the too smooth beat of the meter. It wasn't Shelley at his best, Frost admitted. What was Shelley at his best? I asked. Frost quoted the final lines of "Ode to the West Wind":

> Drive my dead thoughts over the universe
> Like withered leaves to quicken a new birth!
> And, by the incantation of this verse,
>
> Scatter, as from an unextinguished hearth
> Ashes and sparks, my words among mankind!
> Be through my lips to unawakened earth
>
> The trumpet of a prophecy! O wind,
> If Winter comes, can Spring be far behind?

In these lines, said Frost, Shelley recognized that his earlier ideas were dead, unacceptable to mankind, and that he had been as Matthew Arnold was to describe him, "a beautiful but ineffectual angel beating in the void his luminous wings in vain." These lines were Shelley's hope or prophecy to himself that he would become a silent legislator to mankind by revitalizing his ideas and his art.

I asked Frost whether he agreed with Shelley's famous claim that poets are the silent legislators of mankind. He said that he did if the word *legislators* was not meant as anything like politicians who pass statutory laws. Poets are responsible for everything that touches the human spirit. Writing is the most powerful weapon for the dissemination of truth. The content of poetry consists of ideas that last. Artists are legislators more in the sense of Biblical prophets than of politicians, more like lawgivers than lawmakers.

We concluded our night together by quoting poems that we liked. Frost was pleased to learn that I knew four odes of Keats and some of his sonnets. Frost recited some English and Scottish ballads, and John Davidson's "A Ballad of Hell." Then with great verve he swung into Masefield's ballad, "Captain Stratton's Fancy" and, like a bard of old, chanted the quatrain that he deeply relished:

> Oh some that's good and godly ones they hold that it's a sin
> To troll the jolly bowl around and let the dollars spin;
> But I'm for toleration and for drinking at the inn,
> Says the old bold mate of Henry Morgan.

The beauty of the third line makes the whole poem live. Masefield disarms every reader by assuming that toleration and drinking at the inn were synonymous.

As we left the cabin Frost stopped at a table on the screened-in porch, scooped up a handful of acorns from a box, and dropped them into his pocket. It had rained for much of the previous night, and the earth along the side of the road was soft and still wet. We walked slowly, and from time to time Frost stopped, dug his heel into the earth, tossed an acorn into the crevice he had made, pressed it down into the soft spot, and covered it with his foot.

When we reached the road to Bread Loaf Frost kept on walking, with Gillie running ahead of us and back occasionally, and I asked Frost whether he was spoofing or serious in claiming that he as the poet was entitled to every "meaning" any reader could get out of his poems. Frost said he really believed he was entitled to every possible meaning. I asked, even if readers get nonsense? Frost said he was not responsible for their nonsense, for their poor reading comprehension. Anything can be abused, including poetry. I asked, suppose two intelligent, sensitive readers, with good taste, get absolutely contradictory but plausible meanings from the same poem— doesn't one cancel out the other? Frost asked how one could be sure they are contradictory. What seems like a contradiction may only be a contrary that can be harmonized in a larger unity. In *Song of Myself*, Whitman says, "I am large, I contain multitudes." The immediate surface meaning in a poem often is enough for one reader, but not for another. It's better to leave a poem alone and read it without straining too hard after any so-called "hidden meaning." Frost cautioned, don't press poetry too far. Like everything in life, metaphors and symbols have a breaking point, and even good readers often don't show good judgment or taste in knowing when the breaking point in figures of speech has been reached. That is why readers can differ so markedly. But the poem is the same statement regardless of what any reader gets from it. And the same reader can get more out of a poem with a second or third reading, or when he has become more experienced with poetry. Does this constitute a contradiction? Or merely growth? Frost also stressed that it is not *what* the poem says that counts but *how* it says it. He quoted himself: "all the fun's in how you say a thing" (p. 44). The mood or tone is everything. The reader has to sense whether a line is coy, or ironical, or questioning, or asserting. The poet doesn't have any obligation to spell things out. Symbols and metaphors don't need to be explained.

And Robert Frost apparently felt he had explained his ideas about the "correspondence" between poet and reader sufficiently for this occasion, for suddenly he shook my hand, turned, and walked back down the road toward the Homer Noble farm. He could drop a conversation with the same sudden abruptness with which he could begin one.

III

The Bread Loaf School session was opened the following day, Friday, June 28, by President Moody, with Dean Harry Owen giving a fine talk on aesthetic theory and the "New Criticism." He paid a special tribute to John Crowe Ransom. On the following Monday evening, July 1, Frost gave his annual poetry reading to the assembled students, faculty, staff, summer resident guests, and visitors, in the Little Theatre.

Before and between reading his poems Frost made comments on the war in Europe and on American politics which were an almost verbatim repetition of what he had said at our two meetings in his cabin. I felt like someone who had attended a preview of a movie, or a dress rehearsal of a play, and was now witnessing its first public performance. He repeated his remark on how terrible it must be to cover the retreat of a beaten army, his comments in defense of Pétain, and his strong conviction that the United States should stay out of the war until we had an important grievance against Germany. But Frost also added some observations to what he had said in the cabin. He was well aware that petitions were being circulated in many American colleges and universities urging the President and Congress to help Britain in every possible way short of going to war. Frost remarked that there were many "Anglophiles" eager to have the United States save Britain but that he was all for Britain saving herself. He did not admire Churchill for making obsequious overtures to the United States for help. There was a stir of protest among some members of his audience. One woman even spoke out loud her strong disagreement with what Frost said. Frost seemed to enjoy her opposition. The poet also expressed concern that President Roosevelt and the "New Deal bureaucrats" would use the war in Europe as an excuse for extending their domestic power over the American people. As long as we were at peace, he remarked, the war in Europe should loosen rather than tighten the controls of government at home. The war was lifting up the American economy, so that there were no longer plausible but fallacious economic arguments for retaining many of the existing regulations over agriculture, business, and industry. Frost was all for expanding freedom from politicians in each of these areas.

Frost read the usual favorites among his poems, "Mending Wall," "Birches," "Stopping by Woods on a Snowy Evening," but he also liked to mix in some of his lesser known and more recent poems. He read "A Drumlin Woodchuck," and then repeated the third stanza, emphasizing the lines

> As one who shrewdly pretends
> That he and the world are friends (p. 282).

These lines, he said, apply to the United States and Japan. Perhaps we have more to fear from Japan than from Germany. Frost also read "Design" and remarked that in this sonnet he had reversed the eighteenth century argument from design, to prove the existence of God, by adding Darwin's theory of natural selection and the survival of the fittest. He read "Departmental," and commented ironically that this poem proved he was not a New England "regional poet," because his ant Jerry was a Florida ant. He read without comments "Provide, Provide," "Not Quite Social," "The Strong are Saying Nothing," and "Neither Out Far nor In Deep."

After Frost's poetry reading he and many people in the audience adjourned to the Bread Loaf Barn for refreshments and informal talk. The woman who had lost her temper and spoken out loud in protest during Frost's poetry reading approached him and berated him vehemently for not supporting Britain. She accused him of being anti-British. Frost was more amused than annoyed. It was ironical to Frost that having fought against Britain in our Revolution, and in the War of 1812, and over boundary disputes with Canada, and over many issues during the nineteenth century, including her anti-Union stand during the Civil War, we had fought on her side in 1917–18, and were now being pressured again to come to her defense. After the woman had lambasted Frost for awhile, he turned to her, and in a loud, mocking voice said: "Why, all those strong nations ought to be ashamed of themselves for picking on Germany." The woman almost collapsed with an apoplexy. Most of those around Frost could see he was spoofing her. Undoubtedly, she left Bread Loaf convinced that Frost was anti-British, when in fact he admired much about the British and simply wanted them to show their best character in the war, without American participation in it. When war came to America with Pearl Harbor he gave up bantering those who semed to him to hold extreme views, out of harmony with the real self-interest of America.

IV

A week after Frost's poetry reading Harry Owen told me he had arranged with Frost for the two of them to have a private lunch with me at Bread Loaf, to celebrate my having received the Elinor Frost Fellowship. On Wednesday, July 10, I was relieved of waiting table for that day, the chef at Bread Loaf, Eddie Doucette, baked

a cake for the occasion, and Frost, Owen, and I enjoyed lunch together in the dining room, sitting at a table along "Fingerbowl Al-
ley" with the paying guests. Owen had bought from the Bread Loaf
Bookstore a copy of the new printing of the *Collected Poems of
Robert Frost* (Halcyon House Edition, 1939), and at the lunch
Frost inscribed the book: "Robert Frost to Peter Stanlis, Bread Loaf,
1940." Next to my name he made an asterisk, and below his inscription he wrote: "For very special reason." As he handed the book
to me Frost said: "People will ask you what was the very special
reason, and then you can tell them about your fellowship." It was
clear that Robert Frost understood the importance of a good public
press. Over the years his prediction proved true.

After my lunch with Frost and Owen, the poet returned to the
campus that evening to attend John Crowe Ransom's poetry reading
from his book *Chills and Fever*. Ransom read his poems without
comments, in a soft, Southern accent, with just a touch of primness
to add an element to his irony. Afterward, Frost commented very
favorably on Ransom's poetry. During the school session Frost visited the campus from time to time, most often to play tennis with
Kay Morrison or another friend. Once he had dinner at the Inn as
the guest of Lee Simonson, the Director of the New York Theatre
Guild, whom Frost admired. Simonson had visited Frost in Ripton
the year before. Later in July Frost attended a talk by Edward
Weeks, editor of *The Atlantic Monthly*, of whom he thought very
well.

On July 27 Frost came to the campus in the morning to hear "The
Vermont Balladeers" sing old ballads of Vermont. These singers
were sponsored by Helen Hartness Flanders, wife of the United
States Senator from Vermont, and they were invited to Bread Loaf
by Donald Davidson, whose passion for old ballads was as strong
as that of Frost. Among the ballad singers was Edward "Grandpa"
Dragon, the head of the numerous Dragon clan in Ripton, famous
throughout central Vermont for his ballad singing, square dancing,
and hard drinking. He was in his eighties and was reputed able to
outsing, outdance, outdrink, and outdo everyone else in everything
in all Vermont. Frost admired him very much. At our lunch together, Harry Owen told Frost and me an anecdote about "Grand-

pa" Dragon which tickled us. Some students at Dartmouth College had invited "Grandpa" Dragon to sing his ballads at a student assembly at Dartmouth. He arrived several hours before he was scheduled to perform, and the students had plied him with liquor, so that he was well-lubricated when he stepped up to the platform. The ballad singing had been advertised as a cultural event, and many dignified matrons and culture vultures were in the audience. "Grandpa" Dragon proceeded to sing some of his bawdiest ballads, to the vast delight of the students and the embarrassed chagrin of the matrons. At Bread Loaf "Grandpa" Dragon was cold sober, and his spontaneous singing charmed everyone. He even made some comments about how the ballads were composed, saying that in the cold Vermont winters, when the mountain folks were snowed in, as they wove baskets they also wove ballads to warm their hearts.

V

On July 29 Sir Wilfred Grenfell spoke at noon to the Bread Loaf School on his work among the poor in Labrador and was very enthusiastically received. That evening Allen Tate, who had come to Bread Loaf to visit John Crowe Ransom, lectured in the Little Theatre on the poetry of John Donne and John Keats and was coolly received. Tate began his lecture by saying that if anyone were to ask where did the Nashville Fugitives come from, no one could answer, but if anyone were to ask whither have they flown, the answer would be "to Bread Loaf." Tate's lecture was centered in a comparison of the techniques of Donne and Keats in introducing and developing images and metaphors in their poetry, in order to convey meaning.

Tate noted that in Donne's lyric, "Go and catch a falling star," the first stanza consisted of a series of seven images, inductively and imperatively ordered, as commands to do impossible things. In the second and third stanzas these imperative impossibilities were applied functionally through two conditional suppositions, to advance the theme. Or as the "New Critics" would put it, the first stanza was the "vehicle" for the "tenor" in the last two stanzas. The "texture" of the detailed images in the first stanza, complicated by the tone of sustained irony, combined to create the "structure" of each stanza and to provide unity and logical coherence throughout the poem. Donne's lyric was unified in structure, logic, tone, imagery, and theme, and therefore it was an excellent poem. Tate then analyzed Donne's "A Valediction Forbidding Mourning" and showed how the same requisite unity was achieved deductively through Donne's famous extended metaphor comparing two lovers to the two arms of a mariner's compass. In contrast to Donne's two poems Tate cited the opening quatrain of Keats's "Ode to a Grecian Urn" and pointed out that each image was made and then broken, without forming a part of any logical induction leading to a later conclusion and without any logical extension of any one image. Only the loosest kind of association existed between the images, and consequently the theme was left very ambiguous. For these reasons and others, Tate concluded, since these characteristics generally prevailed in the poetry of Donne and Keats, Donne was a more unified and better poet than Keats.

Several days after Tate's lecture, I visited Frost at his cabin and summarized at his request the argument, examples, and thesis advanced by Tate. Frost listened with great attention, then remarked that the lecture showed that Tate preferred Donne to Keats, but it didn't prove that Donne was a superior poet to Keats. Donne might be superior in strict logic, but inferior in suggestive connotations in meaning. But logic was only one of several possible principles of arrangement by which to lay out images and metaphors in poetry. The relationship between figures of speech in a poem might be logical, or analogical, or psychological, or grammatical, or associative, or emotional, or tonal—the last being of greatest importance for unity. Tate preferred the inductive and deductive logic of Donne to the psychological, associative, emotional and tonal techniques of Keats, because a logical arrangement lends itself better to the analytical methods of the new critics. But there are many good poems in which sense is conveyed through sound and other non-logical techniques, as well as or better than it could be through strict logic. It is weak reasoning, Frost concluded with an ironical grin, to make reason and logic the supreme criteria for unity in a poem, and weaker still to generalize as Tate had done. Frost added that he thought Tate was a better poet than he was a critic and wished he would write more poetry and less criticism.

I mentioned to Frost that the next day (August 1) Ransom and Theodore Meyer Greene (Princeton University) were lecturing jointly on I. A. Richards's *Principles of Literary Criticism*, to be followed the next night by Philip Wheelwright (Dartmouth College), lecturing on "The Assertion of Truth in Poetry." There would be open discussions after each lecture. I stated that during much of the summer session Ransom had praised Wheelwright highly for illuminating the relationship between linguistic symbols and semantics in poetry. In his "Analysis of Poetry" course Ransom was much concerned with how "meaning" is conveyed in a poem and with the relationship between "belief" and "truth" in poetry.

Frost shook his head sadly. He said he knew all these men and had talked recently with Greene and several times during the summer with Ransom. Both of them, as well as Wheelwright, were paying too much attention to I. A. Richards. The trouble with Richards, Frost said, was that he believed language and psychology were exact sciences and that therefore critical theory could provide a rational and scientific foundation for the practical criticism of poetry and all imaginative literature. Ransom's "New Criticism" was moving dangerously close to that position. It didn't matter that Richards distinguished between how language was used by scientists in its literal sense and how it was used figuratively by poets. Richards's whole object was to make language, however used, as scientific as possible. Frost denied categorically that the methods of appreciating and understanding poetry could be made into an experimental, theoretical or practical exact science. Ever since the seventeenth century the Western world had moved from applying the methods of science to physical nature, or matter, to what has come to be called "social science" and "political science." These terms are misnomers, and create false hopes and delusions, because society and politics cannot be understood with anything like the exactness with which atoms, molecules, and matter in general can be understood. There are still mysteries about what matter is and probably always will be. Richards and others wanted to extend the methods of science beyond the physical and social to include poetry and imaginative literature. Some of these men recognized a qualitative difference between physical nature and human nature, and the extent to which values are human in origin, so they would be shocked by the accusation that they were trying to do to literature what Watson and Pavlov and other sociological behaviorists were trying to do to men in society. Nevertheless, that was what they were attempting to do, and they were doomed to fail. It couldn't work. Frost had become somewhat heated as he talked, and at this point he drew himself upright in his Morris chair, shook his pointed index finger vehemently, and almost shouted: "The twentieth century will be remembered in history for having finally determined the true role of science in human affairs." He concluded by prophesying that men will find that science will fall far short of exact, absolute, predictable knowledge, especially as applied to men.

I asked Frost to explain further why he objected to the term "political science." He said he agreed with Aristotle that politics was a branch of ethics and that ethical principles and values were God-given or man-made, and could not be determined by scientific methods. Politics was concerned with what was "good" for men in their memberships, in society, and not with what was "true" in theory. A political philosophy was best tested by its practical consequences to men in society. Frost objected to speculative theory so far as it reversed the relationship between truth as theory and good in practice, and made men indifferent to the practical consequences of their supposed "truths." Frost put the question to me: "How else can anyone explain Stalin's willingness to 'liquidate' (dread word) millions of Russian farmers in order to establish their collective farms?"

Frost said that from very early life he had rejected any form of radical socialism. He recalled his childhood in California: "In my boyhood I read the radical works of Edward Bellamy and Henry George, but I have never been a radical." He remarked that upon reading George's socialism he rejected it immediately, "because like all socialism it is bad arithmetic, in which two comes before one." Frost said he never believed that politics based upon compulsory social benevolence was superior to politics based upon freedom to pursue legitimate self-interest.

I told Frost I was puzzled, because if science is so important in the twentieth century I wondered why he had not more often used science as a subject for his poetry. Frost replied: "Read my book." Later when I went back to his poetry, I was surprised to discover how many poems dealt with astronomy and botany.

As an example of how scientists revised their claims about knowledge, Frost remarked that scientists used to say the speed of light was absolute but now say light travels faster than they had believed. Geologists are constantly pushing the supposed age of the earth back farther and farther in time. Frost said he had once had a conversation with Niels Bohr, the famous Danish physicist, who had told him what he wanted most to know about atoms passing through a screen. Bohr had said that scientists could predict how many atoms would pass through, but they could not say which ones would pass through. Frost remarked that from this fact we could understand why scientists dealt with statistical averages, and could not say how any individual human being would respond to their experiments. Bohr had confirmed Frost's skepticism about the claims of social scientists that their methods were exact and their results predictable.

VI

Early in August Frost again came to the campus on the invitation of Professor Lucia Mirrielees, to speak to her students, all of whom were high school English teachers, on how to teach writing and literature in high school. He was full of bantering good humor yet deadly serious in the arguments he advanced. He began by claiming to be the greatest expert on American education from having run away from as much of it as he could. He observed the ironical paradox that American public school education was "free and compulsory," that no one was free to stay away from it until he was sixteen years old. He said the greatest failure of American education in teaching fundamentals of knowledge and skill was in our high schools; the greatest failure in teaching students how to think for themselves, instead of going around and repeating what others have said, was in our colleges; the greatest failure to treat the liberal arts humanistically, rather than scientifically, was in our graduate schools. At this point Frost noticed the students all had their notebooks out and were writing furiously. He paused and waited until everyone was looking up, then asked: "Do you know the difference between a student in high school and a student in college? When a high school teacher greets her class 'Good morning,' everyone answers, 'Good morning.' But when a college professor says 'Good morning,' everyone writes it in a notebook." Everyone laughed a bit sheepishly. Some students put their pens away and listened.

Frost admitted that our own best original thoughts often deserved to be recorded, but not someone else's commonplaces on public knowledge delivered in a lecture. He told an anecdote about how his daughter once heard him say that keeping a notebook on a teacher's lectures was a foolish waste of time. When she went to college she was told by her English professor that she had to keep a notebook, and she refused. Her professor became incensed at this insubordination and called her aside one day after class and told her she was setting a bad example for the rest of the class. Frost's daughter said she thought she was setting a good example, but since the teacher thought otherwise she would leave the class. The professor happened to know Frost and feared the poet would be displeased, and being a bit embarrassed over how things stood he called Frost's daughter up and told her she could attend his class without keeping a notebook. Then he hastened to add: "But of course I can't give you an A!" Frost laughed uproariously at his punch line.

Frost's anecdote was a good example of what he meant by a teacher's addiction to foolish required assignments and the binding force of academic machinery. He told of how after he had read his poems at a New England girls' college a student came bubbling up to him and said: "Just think, Mr. Frost, you are required reading in my poetry course!" Frost was not happy to be thus flattered, and replied: "Just think what happened to Longfellow from being required reading!" One of the troubles with institutional education at every level is that teachers feel they must measure a student's performance, and therefore they are primarily testers and graders. Frost admitted that there was probably no way for schools to avoid giving grades, and he would certainly rather give a letter grade to a student than use adjectives on him. But in high school, English teachers could at least avoid assignments of mere busy work in getting factual knowledge and give assignments which truly draw out the intellectual and literary ability of a student. A teacher could ask a student: "Can you recall any simile or metaphor which you made recently which you thought was especially good at the time you made it?" Grade your students on that, he said. Base the final grade for a course on the best original idea, image, metaphor, or analogy the student makes during the course. In high school, students should learn to take wing and soar, instead of which they learn to hate education and poetry by being weighed down with useless heavy requirements. High school is the creative period of a student's life; there will be time enough for him to become critical and scholarly in college. Never ask high school students to be too scientifically exact and thorough; let them disport themselves in playing with ideas and metaphors. Only then will we help young students to grow into writers, and make our literature match our national wealth.

Frost poked hilarious fun at Mortimer Adler's recently published book, *How to Read a Book*, saying that if a student doesn't know how to read he will not know how to read *How to Read a Book*, and if he does know how to read he doesn't need Adler's book. No one acquires a sound taste and critical understanding of literature by a technique or gimmick. Understanding takes place automatically when students experience life and literature together. As we grow older, the more and better we read poetry the more things we can do better with other poems we read. If a student doesn't understand how poetry works, he won't get a poem by having it analyzed for him. But most children naturally love stories and songs and sense the parables in them, from fairy tales and ballads to the most profound fiction and poetry we have. It's all the same thing, saying one thing in terms of another, being playful about the common verities.

So much for education, Frost said. He paused to see if anyone had any questions. A student wondered how it would be possible to enforce class discipline if assignments were not strictly required. Frost replied that of course certain assignments had to be required, as when a class read a play together to act out some scenes. But many assignments could be open invitations for students to perform or write whenever they could. Discipline problems were the result of enforced attendance at school and boredom. Frost told a story of how after he quit Dartmouth College, and took over his mother's school in Methuen, Massachusetts, he had to physically discipline with a cane a group of rowdy students who constantly disrupted his class. The leader of these rowdies was a half-breed Indian named Johnny Howe. The chairman of the Methuen School Board was all for expelling Howe, but Frost insisted he could handle Johnny, and Howe continued in school until after Frost himself quit teaching. Years later Frost was passing through Methuen and visited the former chairman of the school board, long retired. While discussing the past Frost asked: "Whatever became of Johnny Howe?" The former chairman of the school board replied: "Why, Johnny's one of our most esteemed citizens. He's currently chairman of the school board!" After the loud laughter had died, Frost remarked: "Neither in religion nor in education should we shut the gates of salvation on anyone."

On the art of teaching poetry in high school, Frost repeated much that he had said in 1939, but he added some new thoughts. He expressed considerable doubt that poetry could be "taught" through organized education. Perhaps the best a teacher can do is to show by example how much poetry means to him. Show enthusiasm for ideas, metaphors, and the forms of poetry, and hope it rubs off as enthusiasm in the students. Enthusiasm can be crude or very refined, and it is best developed in a sense of play, as on the athletic field. If teachers can make the reading of poetry as much a game as sports, they will teach their students to love poetry, and in time the students will acquire taste and judgment, and will know when metaphor and analogies are fresh and valid and when they are not. Only then will they be educated in poetry.

In teaching writing in high school, Frost wondered, beyond correctness in mechanics what can a teacher hope to do? It is hard enough to pump out mistakes in grammar and logic without also hoping to turn out polished writers. Frost doubted that anyone could "teach" someone how to write a good poem. He threw off an aphorism: "A poem should be at least as good as the prose it might have been." Otherwise stick to prose. Begin with tossing ideas around, and hope it will end in a student's taking fire and throwing off sparks of metaphors. That is a world above having students be parrots or busy work drones. If a person can't think for himself he is better off not saying anything. Then at least he bores or annoys only himself. In teaching how to write good prose, beyond mechanical correctness, teachers can show a student how to back up an abstract statement with a concrete image. For instance, if a student should write, "She clinched the effect," he could add to it, "She stuck its tail down its throat." But above all give the students lots of leisure to write. And if they don't write, or if they fail in writing, what does it matter? Writing, and especially poetry, is the easiest kind of art in which to fail. But mercifully for those who fail—or even for those who would not have failed if they had persisted and had the will and courage to see it through to their maximum talent (and these are the commonest failures in writing)— writing is also the easiest art to slip out of unnoticed. You can leave by the back door and no one will say a word.

VII

The Writers' Conference of 1940 was in many ways a repetition of the patterns established by the various clinics and events in 1939, but with some new staff members, and a totally new body of conferees. Again Frost appeared to be in his true element, far more than at the School of English. He thoroughly enjoyed seeing such old friends as Herschel Brickell, Raymond Everitt, John Gassner, Edith Mirrielees, Fletcher Pratt, and Louis Untermeyer. But this summer "Benny" DeVoto was absent from the staff, and his place in the fiction clinics was taken by John P. Marquand and Wallace Stegner, both of whom had attended the Writers' Conference in 1939 as speakers. They had been so impressive in their comments on fiction that they were invited back for the entire session in 1940. Frost thought that Marquand and Stegner were outstanding fiction writers, although he esteemed Ernest Hemingway as perhaps the best American novelist. Of Hemingway, Frost said: "He's a great one."

One of the most pleasant tasks Harry Owen ever assigned to me at Bread Loaf was to go to Middlebury in the taxi to meet John P. Marquand, to escort him to the campus, and see that he was comfortably settled in Maple Cottage. Owen's attention to such minute details was in part what made him such a fine administrator of Bread Loaf. I had read and admired Marquand's novel, *The Late George P. Apley*, and enjoyed talking a bit about it with the author. The twelve-mile drive from Middlebury to Bread Loaf, spent discussing fiction with Marquand, was one of my most delightful literary experiences during the six years I attended the Writers' Conference.

Marquand was an elegantly cool, sophisticated, dignified, pipe-smoking, quiet-spoken gentleman, with a neat trimmed mustache. He was as impeccably dressed and debonaire as one of his suave fictional socialite Bostonians. Yet he was a friendly and accessible man, and enjoyed talking literary shop. In many ways he was the antithesis of Frost, and differed even more from his young Western colleague, Wallace Stegner, yet all three writers had a profound respect for one another's work, and got along well at Bread Loaf. I enjoyed Marquand's talk so much that on two occasions when Frost did not attend the poetry clinics I sat in on the fiction clinics to hear Marquand.

Edith Mirrielees ran the fiction clinics, and she was a most competent and perceptive critic of fiction, especially strong in technique and form. On one occasion she read a short story by a conferee, and everyone sensed that although it was an interesting story, centered in a common and inherently dramatic human problem, something was subtly and radically wrong with it. Miss Mirrielees prodded the conferees to identify the problem and suggest methods of solving it. A few tried but floundered. Stegner suggested that a change in the point of view, from omniscient author to a participant narrator, would improve it. Everyone agreed on that. Miss Mirrielees suggested that some concrete details in the setting, plot action, and characterizations would improve the story. Everyone agreed with that. Marquand had remained silent throughout the discussion. Finally, Miss Mirrielees turned to him. In a quiet and casual manner he showed how by violating the purely chronological arrangement of the plot, and transposing the episodes so that the reader was plunged into the climactic action at the beginning, through a series of flashbacks gradually leading back to the central conflict, the short story could be redeemed. He noted that an epic structure in miniature was far more dramatic than chronological expository narration. He concluded by urging that much of the description be changed to dialogue. When Marquand had finished there was a sustained moment of complete silence, followed by enthusiastic applause. Everyone knew that his diagnosis and recommendations were absolutely letter right.

Two other newcomers on the staff were Walter Pritchard Eaton (Yale University), in drama, and Barbara Fleury, from Michigan, in children's literature. I had played some hot games of croquet on the West Lawn with Eaton during his visit to the Writers' Conference in 1939, and this summer we resumed our friendly rivalry and played croquet every day through the Conference. Eaton was a tall, thin, wiry man, a salty New England oldtimer, with a keen wit that reminded me of Frost. He and Frost enjoyed talking together.

Barbara Fleury was a very attractive young woman, to whom Frost took an immediate liking because of their many friends in common at the University of Michigan. On one occasion, before the scheduled clinics began, Frost and Miss Fleury stood outside the Little Theatre talking, and Frost introduced me to her, so she could tell me about the extensive creative writing program at Michigan. She and Frost told me about the annual Hopwood Awards in writing at Michigan, the largest money prizes for students in the United States. Miss Fleury had taken writing courses with Professor Roy W. Cowden and others at Ann Arbor, and she had won a major Hopwood Award in fiction and had gone on to success in writing books for children. Frost and Miss Fleury also talked about other people they knew at Michigan, Professors Clarence De Witt Thorpe and Louis I. Bredvold, and Dean Joseph A. Bursley, and Mary Cooley, whom Miss Fleury said ran the Hopwood Room. Frost said that she was one of the original "three graces" who printed the literary magazine the *Whimsies*, when he was at Michigan as poet in residence in the early 1920s. Frost remarked that among large American universities he knew of only two—Michigan and Iowa—which paid much attention to original writing. In addition to its fine writing program the University of Michigan had one of the best departments of English in the nation. It was most unusual to hear Frost speak so warmly about any academic institution. Michigan, as Frost and Barbara Fleury described it, sounded like a school that combined the two things that interested me most—a sound academic program and creative writing. But in the summer of 1940 I had no way of knowing that this conversation, plus others with Frost about Michigan over the next four summers, would send me to Ann Arbor in the fall of 1944.

Early during the Writers' Conference Frost gave a poetry reading, but because I was in Middlebury on an errand for Harry Owen I missed it. I heard afterwards that he spoke on writing poetry as a craft. Frost and Untermeyer again combined to run the poetry clinics. No unusual incidents occurred at the clinics, and the poems submitted by the conferees were better in general than those discussed in 1939. Indeed the whole Conference ran very smoothly, under the humane administration of Ted Morrison, and the clinics, lectures, literary talk, square dances, softball games, tennis matches, and parties at Treman Cottage and the Barn filled the days and nights of everyone at Bread Loaf with pleasant and stimulating activities.

Two memorable speakers were at Bread Loaf that summer, W. H. Auden and Katherine Anne Porter. Auden was a very shy and self-conscious man, most difficult to engage in conversation. But when he stepped up to the podium to give his poetry reading he seemed to catch fire. He brought no book, but quoted his poems from memory in a rapid-fire, nonstop manner, which made it difficult for his audience to absorb what he said. Also, he distracted his listeners by his awkward way of standing at the podium. He lifted one leg almost halfway up the podium, and stood on the other leg and leaned heavily over the podium while he recited a poem. Between poems he would sometimes change legs. About half way through Auden's performance a thunderstorm struck. The Bread Loaf Little Theatre has no partition between the roof and the hall, to absorb sound, and giant hailstones rained an incessant tattoo on the roof, so that no one could hear Auden beyond the first several rows of seats. After a while the podium was moved to the side of the hall, next to the fireplace, and chairs were swung around in a close semicircle. But it was still impossible to hear well, and as the storm continued Auden finally quit reciting his poems. After the storm subsided everyone adjourned to the Barn, where Auden and Carson McCullers huddled together in a corner and talked and sipped their drinks and ignored everyone. Like Auden, McCullers was very shy and introvertive. In her sailor boy's shirt and her hair in bangs she looked like a nineteen-year-old pixie.

Katherine Anne Porter read a brief short story and spoke very sensibly through it on the techniques and art of the short story. She confirmed the theory and practice of writing fiction so richly set forth in the fiction clinics by Miss Mirrielees and Wallace Stegner. During a brief question period following her talk, Eudora Welty engaged her in a pleasant but searching dialogue on several points. When the meeting broke up they converged, and as they drifted off with the rest of the staff to Treman Cottage they continued to talk. The visual image of these two ladies talking about fiction, while oblivious to everyone around them, is almost archetypal.

One of the most entertaining events at the Writers' Conference was Louis Untermeyer's performance as master of revels in a program he organized called "Information Tease," a literary parody of the popular radio show "Information Please." Untermeyer fielded written questions from the conferees, identifications of passages of poetry, obscure facts about author's lives and works, etc., to a panel consisting of Ted Morrison, Fletcher Pratt, and Walter Pritchard Eaton. Every question he read, every answer or nonanswer he received, provoked what appeared to be a spontaneous and outrageous pun. Never was Untermeyer more "the punning pundit of Bread Loaf." Finally, he read a question directed to him: "Which literary man among Bread Loafers was infamous as a punster?" Untermeyer looked blank and professed to be totally baffled by the question. Why was *he* asked to answer it? "Once apun a time, perhaps on opunning night," he might have known the answer, but "upun my word" it was too much for him now. His clowning was clever and lightly amusing, and probably relieved the tension of some nervous conferees. Later, everyone adjourned to the Barn, and Untermeyer conducted a barber-shop sextet of staff and fellows singing summer camp songs. In the choruses of several songs the booming bass voice of John Ciardi lingered on after everyone else's had run out of breath.

On the last day of the Conference I said goodbye to Frost and expressed the hope that I would be back next summer. He suggested that if I should come to Boston before he left for Florida in January I should visit him. He gave me his address and phone number. With that we parted, and several days later I returned to Middlebury, contented with having enjoyed the most stimulating and profitable summer of my life.

VIII

After spending Christmas vacation with my family in Nutley, New Jersey, on December 29, 1940, I went to Hyde Park, Massachusetts, to visit a Middlebury College friend, Robert Burnes. We planned to attend a New Year's eve party in Boston with friends before returning to Middlebury. On New Year's eve, shortly before we were to leave we received word that our host had been rushed to the hospital with pneumonia, so the party was cancelled. I proposed that we telephone Robert Frost to see if he would like us to stop by for a visit. By luck Frost was at home alone and said he would be glad to see us.

We arrived at Frost's apartment around 10 P.M. He lived at 88 Mt. Vernon Street, just off Louisburg Square in Boston. As he greeted us I made a joke in introducing my college friend: "Robert Frost, meet your fellow Scotch poet, Robert Burnes." Bob laughed and admitted to being Scottish but said he was an economics major whose family expected him to go into the family business of selling furniture. We settled down for an evening of good talk.

Frost commented that the idolatry and love the Scottish people have for Robert Burns is incredible. Although the Scots respected James Thomson, and had put up a statue of Allan Ramsay in Edinburgh, and remembered Robert Blair and James Macpherson, among Scottish poets Robert Burns was king. Frost remarked that the Scots quoted Burns everywhere and that celebrations of his birthday in Scotland and in the United States and Canada have been known to last much longer than celebrations of Shakespeare's birthday among the English. I suggested that perhaps the Scots were celebrating Burns's well-known prowess with the ladies. They laughed, and Frost acknowledged that Bobby Burns was certainly filled to overflowing with Romantic sensibility about women. Frost then punned that in the end Burns's "amour was all for Jean Armour." But except for a few really fine poems, such as "The Cotter's Saturday Night" and "To a Mouse," I wondered whether Burns was really as good a poet as many literary critics thought. This heretical remark was politely ignored. Frost said how wonderful it was for Burns's memory that within two hours everyone in the English speaking world would be singing "Auld Lang Syne." That shut me up.

Frost contended that Burns was unique to the Scottish people because in his poetry he so obviously liked everything about his country's past, its language, its songs and stories, its heroes, such as Robert and Bruce Douglas, its people's clannishness and patriotism—everything that made the Scots proud of themselves as a people. Burns's popularity was a sign that the people were returning his love with theirs. Frost recalled that once as a schoolboy in Lawrence, Massachusetts, he had watched his English teacher put on the board some stanzas of William Collins's poem "How Sleep the Brave," which celebrated the heroism of the Scottish soldiers killed in the battle of Culloden Moor. It had made him realize how close poetry could be to the crucial events of life. I remarked on the irony of that battle and poem, that the Highland Scots army of "Bonnie Prince Charlie," Pretender to the throne of Great Britain, was defeated by a combination of Lowland Scots and English. Frost said that religion as well as politics sometimes made strange bedfellows, but if the Stuarts wouldn't be Protestants they couldn't hope to rule in Britain.

Frost recalled that when he and his family had sailed from Boston to Glasgow in 1912, with his first sight of the Hebrides and the shore of Scotland he experienced the special thrill of something like a homecoming. When he had seen battleships at anchor he had made the mistake of referring to "the English navy" in the presence of a Scottish sailor, who corrected him: it was "the British navy." This conscious sense of their nationalism was one of the things that made the Scots among the most energetic and intelligent race the world has ever known. Geography, religion, and nationalism were the chief sources of their strength. I could feel my friend Bob Burnes glowing with pride as Frost spoke.

Frost proceeded to review the contributions which various races had made toward the development of civilization from the dawn of historical time to the present. The yellow race had created a pretty respectable civilization and culture in ancient times, in its laws, customs, and art, but the Chinese and Japanese were hampered by a cumbersome written language, were limited in science and had levelled out several centuries ago. The same was true of the brown races of the Pacific islands, India, and the Near East. India and Egypt had shown their high water marks in creating civilization. In Africa the Negro races had achieved even less in literature and science. Perhaps the tropical climate was a factor in determining where they had levelled off. But what a race the white has been! Its cultural achievements in the arts—witness the Greeks—and in law, government and literature—witness the Romans, British and French —and its intellectual achievements in science—witness Germany, the United States and all Europe—have increased man's hold on the planet beyond what any other races have contributed. Among the most intelligent and energetic of the white race were the Jews and the Scots. Though few in number they had contributed mightily to improve civilization and culture in Europe and America. Bob Burnes remarked that like any impartial and modest Scot he couldn't argue much with that!

We talked and sipped drinks until midnight, then touched glasses and toasted one another with good wishes for a happy new year. While Bob Burnes was in the bathroom Frost asked me in a very quiet voice whether I had heard that his son Carol had committed suicide in October. I told him that Harry Owen had informed me of this tragedy, and I expressed my sympathy. I had seen Carol Frost only once, very briefly during a visit one day to the Homer Noble farm last summer. As I went up to the cabin past the barn I had passed a rather strange and morbid looking man, but had not spoken to him nor he to me. Frost remarked that he had seen his son's tragedy coming on over a long time and had tried to head it off, but that he had failed in this as in so many other things in his family. But he was now determined not to allow this latest failure to get him down. His grandson Prescott had shown him what true courage was, and in this new year he would raise himself up again, as he had done after his wife died. I was deeply moved and very pleased by Frost's words. He was not a man to wear his sorrows on his sleeve. Yet privately he was realistic and courageous in facing the shattering sorrows of his domestic tragedies. I acquired renewed respect and affection for him for that.

Frost inquired about friends and events in Middlebury. I told him that Harry Owen and "Doc" Cook were both well and flourishing, as was President Moody, but that his old friend Vernon Harrington was not at all well. I informed him that a new student literary magazine had been started, called *Directions*, in which I had published an essay on William Blake. Frost said he was interested in student publications, and I promised to send him a copy soon.

We got into a discussion of poetry, and Bob Burnes remarked that he particularly liked Frost's "Stopping by Woods on a Snowy Evening," especially the last stanza. Frost expressed the hope that unlike some readers Burnes did not read the line "But I have promises to keep" to mean unpleasant "promises," duties and practical obligations to others. Frost objected that such an interpretation was too narrow. The "promises" could also be about longstanding ambitions to be fulfilled by the speaker, or other hopes and desires. Frost remarked that there was danger of reading too much into poetry through being too specific while leaving out part of what was there. He acknowledged that William Empson had a valid point about the seven types of ambiguity to be found in poetry, although he did not know why ambiguity should be limited to the magic number seven. Poetry is filled with ambiguities. Some words and phrases are most unfortunate in connotation. As an example, he asked whether we had ever noticed the line in Coleridge's "Kubla Khan," "As if this earth in fast thick pants were breathing." (Even in Coleridge's day "pants" was short for "pantaloons," or men's trousers.) I didn't quite know what to make of Frost's comment, but it appeared to be a preliminary statement to a distinction in dramatic monologues: the contrast was between "rhetorical passages" and "speaking passages," images and metaphors which tended to be descriptive: quick thoughts and direct actions which captured the tone and posture of the speaking voice so completely that in a poem each character could be recognized without the author's identification.

Frost's remarks reminded Bob Burnes and me of a friend of ours at Middlebury, my classmate Douglas H. Mendel, Jr., who performed dramatic monologues of poems and one-act plays in which he alone did all the parts. He had spent the past summer at a large resort hotel in the Catskill Mountains earning money by entertaining vacationers with his monologues. His repertoire included Browning's "My Last Duchess" and "Andrea del Sarto," and Frost's "Mending Wall," "Home Burial," and "The Death of the Hired Man," the last being the most popular monologue. He had also performed these poems in November at a meeting of the Middlebury College Literary Club. Frost was delighted with our account of how Doug Mendel managed to vary the voices of each character without having to identify the speaker. It confirmed his theory that truly dramatic poetry conveys meaning through sounds.

Bob Burnes and I stayed with Frost until around 1:30 A.M. As we were leaving he gave each of us a copy of a little book, *From Snow to Snow* (New York: Henry Holt and Co., 1936), consisting of Frost's selections of his most appropriate poem for each month through the calendar year. He inscribed in mine: "To Peter Stanlis from his friend Robert Frost   Christmas 1940   Boston." He also inscribed Bob Burnes's copy, and gave me another inscribed copy for Doug Mendel. He said he was leaving for Florida in two weeks, so I promised to send him a copy of *Directions* as soon as I returned to Middlebury.

Ten days after I sent Frost our college literary magazine, on January 14, 1941, I received from the poet a letter commenting on it:

Dear Stanlis:
   You sent me a good readable magazine. I like its looks too. My only suggestion is that your quotations shouldn't be altogether from reviews of books. (The quotations are quite an idea.) Your own essay

Dear Stanlis:

You sent me a good readable magazine. I like its looks too. My only suggestion is that your quotations shouldn't be altogether from reviews of books. (The quotations are quite an idea.) Your own essay on Blake smacks a little too much of essay in the sense of effort. It is a hard kind of thing to write at your age. But it is the kind of thing there is the largest lack of and greatest opening for in American letters at this time.

We haven't anyone alive but the soda pop over night critic of the current book of the month. I should think someone could make a modest living and a good position with deliberate criticism of past and present literature blended in the proportion of say two or three to one. You are still too fresh from the classroom. But you make a beginning in the mid of career I wish more of for my country.

Remember me to my friends.

Ever yours
Robert Frost
88 Mt Vernon St Boston Mass
June 11 1941

on Blake smacks a little too much of essay in the sense of effort. It is
a hard kind of thing to write at your age. But it is the kind of thing
there is the largest lack of and greatest opening for in American letters
at this time. We haven't anyone alive but the soda pop overnight
critic of the current book of the month. I should think someone could
make a modest living and a good position with deliberate criticism of
past and present literature blended in the proportion of say two or
three to one. You are still too fresh from the classroom. But you make
a beginning in the kind of career I wish more of for my country.
  Remember me to my friends.

Ever yours
Robert Frost

88 Mt. Vernon St   Boston   Mass
Jan 11 1941

This was to be my last contact with Frost until late in June, just
before the opening of the 1941 Bread Loaf School session.

Robert Frost at Bread Loaf
1941

I

DURING the spring of 1941, to make room for the anticipated
student enrollment, the Bread Loaf Barn had been renovated. Additional classrooms were built downstairs, and a large open dormitory for men was provided upstairs. Dean Harry Owen assigned all
the men students on scholarships to the Barn dormitory. But even before classes began on July 1, it was obvious that the open dormitory
was far too noisy and public for studying and sleeping. I spoke with
Harry Owen, and he arranged for me and another student, Richard
Ellmann, to move to Gilmore Cottage, and we roomed together
there for the summer. Dick Ellmann already had his Ph.D. from Yale
University and was a published poet, and he had come to Bread
Loaf to work with Ted Morrison, hoping to secure a teaching position in the freshman English program at Harvard as the first step
in his academic career. In this he succeeded.

One afternoon very late in June I visited Frost at the Homer Noble farm to arrange for an evening of "good talk." Frost had come up to Ripton much later this summer. He looked in excellent physical shape and had obviously recovered from the emotional shock of his son's death. His farm appeared more flourishing than ever before, with the addition of a horse and a cow and the loud cackling of several hundred chickens. I returned that evening at sunset, and we went up to the cabin. I remarked that since this was my third summer on the Mountain I was fast becoming an "old timer" at Bread Loaf. Frost laughed and responded that he had been coming to Bread Loaf for twenty years and the native Vermonters still regarded him as "summer people." He was accepted at Bread Loaf because the faculty and students were themselves summer people, and besides they all shared the common bond of literature. Frost praised the many good literary and academic traditions blended together among the faculty and students at Bread Loaf. It was good that the Bread Loaf School ran for only six weeks. He wondered whether its virtues would be sustained beyond that length of time. It was that very rare thing—a Brook Farm that worked, without the drudgery and tyranny of a commune. In contrast to the School, the Writers' Conference was more a "Pantisocratic society" rooted in writing, rather than in academics and philosophy. Two weeks was the right length for the Conference.

I remarked that I hoped to have the best of both worlds that summer, since I had signed up for Ted Morrison's "Seminar in Writing," George F. Thomas's "The Platonic Tradition in English Literature," and a course taught jointly by John Crowe Ransom and Theodore Meyer Greene, "The Critical and Philosophical Approaches to Literature." Frost said he hoped I would keep to a poetic approach to poetry and never forget that poetry is a literary art and not a means to advance philosophy or anything else. The themes or content of poetry were often philosophical, but poetry did not consist in *what* was said but *how* it was said. In his myths Plato used the techniques of poetry to illuminate his ideas, but he was too committed to abstract reason, to the world as understood by reason, to be anything but a philosopher. Yet at times, as a mythmaker, Plato was also a poet, and he understood the power of poetry so well that he feared for philosophy, feared that poetry would displace it in the world. Since Plato's whole object was to leap from the physical world to the metaphysical Being of philosophy he was right to use myths, since reason alone was not capable of such a leap.

Frost remarked that we often hear people tell how Plato stands for just one thing, but he stands for many things. Frost told of an encounter he once had about Plato with a college professor friend. The professor insisted that Plato meant only a certain particular thing, and when Frost disagreed, he said: "I know what the trouble is with you. You're a poet, and you know what Plato thought about poets." That was very unfair, Frost remarked, because in reading Plato he was a man before he was a poet. He read Plato as he read anyone else, as himself, not as a member of any one group. Frost insisted that he was himself as a man first, before he was a member of any group, profession, or nation. Plato was most the philosopher in the *Republic*, but he was more poet than philosopher in the *Symposium*, *Ion*, and *Laws*. The professor either didn't know this, or ignored the poet in Plato. Reason was Plato's metaphor, which is why his understanding of Form is so abstract, so far removed from the reality of the senses. I was confident that Frost was not a Platonist, but to confirm my conviction I asked whether he was in any sense a Platonist. Frost replied that he believed in the immanence of the reality of physical presences perceived by the senses more than in a metaphysical transcendence rationally perceived. He had already said this: "Earth's the right place for love: / I don't know where it's likely to go better" (p. 122). As poets we shape the world from our sense of it, what our senses tell us about it. That is our primary reality, the physical, but it does not exclude the metaphysical. Plato made the metaphysical primary, which is why he was more philosopher than poet. Our earth-anchored Platonists are Utopians; they want their heaven on earth. Frost concluded his remarks on Plato by repeating that Plato was many things, that it was hard to get away from Plato, try as we might.

Frost said the real value of the courses I was taking would not be in the body of knowledge I learned, but in the skills I acquired, in the ongoing process of self-development. I indicated a book I had brought with me and told him I was still reading Dryden's poetry, as an outgrowth of my course last summer with Reuben Brower. Frost remarked that Dryden and Pope were our best poets since Horace in using irony and allusion as metaphors of language. The iambic pentameter couplet as a verse form was their metaphor of form. It was ideal for reflective poetry or for brief aphorisms. The couplet as metaphor was the closest thing he retained in salvaging parts of a poem that failed. In his reflective poems he allowed himself to revise lines as couplets. If he could steal a good couplet out of a poem he couldn't write, and include it so naturally in a poem that the joint didn't show, he had no qualms about it. But it was a rare occurrence. It had happened in "Birches," but he wasn't even sure now in which lines.

Frost asked me what of Dryden I had been reading. I had just finished "Religio Laici" and the first part of "The Hind and the Panther." I remarked that they were nonlyrical in tone, rhetorical reflective poems, strong in stating philosophical and religious themes. In each poem I had noted a passage that reminded me of Frost's theme in "The Death of the Hired Man," on the conflict between the claims of justice and mercy, as made by Warren and Mary regarding Silas, their hired man. Frost responded that "the justice-mercy dilemma" had concerned him for a long time, and he was curious about Dryden's views. I had already marked the two passages, and read first the lines from "The Hind and the Panther," in which Dryden described the two unique qualities God compounded into human nature at the time of man's creation, divine qualities which distinguished man from all other animals:

> But when arrived at last to human race,
> The Godhead took a deep consid'ring space;
> And, to distinguish man from all the rest,
> Unlock'd the sacred treasures of his breast;
> And mercy mix'd with reason did impart,
> One to his head, the other to his heart:
> Reason to rule, but mercy to forgive:
> The first is law, the last prerogative.
>   (Part I, ll. 255–62)

While I was hunting for the passage from "Religio Laici" I observed Frost slowly nodding his head in approval of what I had just read.

He noted that Dryden set "reason" rather than "justice" against mercy, and that he left unanswered the crucial question of which of the two should prevail. He said the passage was not as biased in favor of mercy as was Portia's speech in *The Merchant of Venice*.

I remarked that I thought Dryden answered the question in one sense in this passage in "Religio Laici":

> But if there be a pow'r too just and strong
> To wink at crimes, and bear unpunish'd wrong;
> Look humbly upward, see his will disclose
> The forfeit first, and then the fine impose:
> A mulct thy poverty could never pay
> Had not eternal wisdom found the way
> And with celestial wealth supplied the store:
> His justice makes the fine, his mercy quits the score.
> (ll. 99–106)

I shall never forget the sudden startled expression which leaped to Frost's face, and the manner of his response to this passage. He sat bolt upright in his Morris chair and almost shouted: "That's it!" Dryden has reconciled the Old and the New Testament." It answers why men need to look up to God as the final power and arbiter, whose will and wisdom reconciled justice and mercy in judging men. Frost asked to see the two passages and I gave him the book. After he had read them over slowly he noted that in "The Hind and the Panther" Dryden had remained neutral while he mixed "reason" and "mercy" in man, but in "Religio Laici" he had God's will and mercy triumphant over His justice. I asked Frost what that signified. He replied cryptically that it put Dryden closer to St. Augustine than to St. Thomas Aquinas.

Frost argued that there is a natural conflict built into the moral universe between justice and mercy. We see it clearly in how men respond to even the most serious violations of the criminal law. Those who favor capital punishment for murder believe more in justice than in mercy; those who oppose capital punishment believe more in mercy than in justice. Frost remarked that in our age there is danger of destroying justice between men in the name of mercy for all men. This applies to more than the criminal code. In economics mercy is often made to triumph for the poor in the name of distributive justice, which is really injustice to the rich. The redistribution of wealth is becoming more and more the main function of the state. We have "an unholy alliance" between "New Testament Christian sapheads," who take the Sermon on the Mount as having cancelled out the Law of Moses in some of its prohibitions, and sentimental humanitarians, who believe that all the evil in the world is caused by a bad arrangement of social machinery. These religious and secular groups combine to make mercy prevail over justice. Frost said that as the idea applies to God rather than man, they have Milton on their side. In *Paradise Lost* Milton wrote of God: "But mercy first and last shall brightest shine" (Book III, l. 134). Frost said, "Please note, *first and last*."

Frost remarked that he was talking recently to a Unitarian minister, who said his congregation could be divided into two groups—"theists and humanitarians." Frost said that what the minister really meant, though he couldn't bring himself to say it, was "theists and atheists." The first group is in a direct line of descent from Emerson and Channing, idealistic transcendentalists, believers in an "Oversoul," etc. The second group is really secular, recognizes no revelation beyond science and human reason, no Godhead, and believes in the "brotherhood of man." They are "realists rather than idealists," not because they will realize what they want, nor because matter is more real than spirit, but because what they are working with and working for seems tangibly real to their senses. Frost remarked that the "theists" among the Unitarians are really Universalists. They start with God and believe that God is too good to damn any man and that therefore all men will be saved. Salvation is universal. The "humanitarian" Unitarians start with man and believe that men are too good to be damned by any God, if He exists. So they also end up believing in universal salvation, but in a secular rather than a religious sense. I asked Frost what he believed about all this theology. He refused to commit himself to anything. Finally, in a very wary manner, he depersonalized my question and said that none of us deserves salvation, but all men hope to have it. I could see that the subject of salvation was one which agitated Frost's heart, and he was unwilling to put a public label on his private convictions concerning it.

I expressed great wonder how Unitarianism, which preached universal salvation for man, could have derived from Calvinism, which preached "universal depravity" and damnation for all mankind except God's "elect," who were His chosen few. Frost gave the opinion that somewhere between the time of Calvin and that of Emerson the Calvinist doctrine of grace must have been turned inside out, so that either God's "elect" came to include more and more of mankind, or "universal depravity" came to be more and more restricted until even the worst villains and unbelievers were not included.

After a long pause, in which Frost allowed his opinion to register in my mind, he got onto an old familiar subject—Puritanism. Frost expressed his belief that Milton's *Comus* was the greatest Puritan poem ever written. I said that I would have voted for Spenser's *The Faerie Queene*. Frost said there was too much sensuality in Spenser. I perceived that after two years there were still some differences between us regarding Puritanism. According to Frost Milton's greatness as a man and a poet rested on his faith in himself and in his moral courage. His best poems are his shorter, earlier ones, and *Samson Agonistes*, but in *Paradise Lost* Milton proved his courage to the world. Wasn't it a thing to marvel at, Frost remarked, that the two greatest epics in our literature were composed by poets who were blind. What incredible feats of courage Homer and Milton performed. Frost's voice became filled with pathos as he said: "Isn't it a sad world when courage is the supreme virtue in man?" I objected that for a poet talent must be supreme, because without talent all the determination in the world would not get him anywhere. Frost conceded that talent was essential, yet he insisted that the reverse was also true—that talent without courage would not make a poet. Without courage all of our other virtues, including our literary talents, become merely theoretical. Writing a poem is primarily an act of self-faith and courage. And failure in writing is largely the result of a lack of faith and courage. No real agnostic could ever write a true poem, said Frost. Writing the first line of a poem involves a commitment by the poet, and every line thereafter is an act of disciplined will, of courage and faith that he can run the whole course to the finish line and believe the poem into existence. When young writers quit, it is most often a failure of nerve, not of talent.

Frost extended his argument on courage beyond literature to the whole of life. Men should be firm and courageous in their commitments in everything—in love and marriage, in religion, art, politics, and loyalty to their country and their friends. Agnosticism paralyzes the will and makes men cowards. Better a convinced theist or atheist than an agnostic. I remarked that John Henry Newman compared being an agnostic to standing on one leg forever. Frost responded that that was what our political agnostics, the liberals, often did. They couldn't make up their minds and therefore were weak and indecisive as leaders. It was no excuse to say that we didn't know enough yet to take a firm position. It isn't a question of knowing, but of believing and acting. Even the best informed men act from insufficient knowledge; often we can believe our knowledge into existence sufficiently well to take action. Agnosticism is a miserable kind of neutrality about the most crucial questions of life and death.

Our talkathon lasted well beyond midnight, when Frost took his lantern and guided me down his dirt road to the highway. Although we talked about literature, and Frost had occasion further to expound his favorite themes about voice tones in poetry, it appeared to me that since two summers ago a new dimension of moral philosophy and religion had been added to his literary and political interest. This impression was confirmed during the course of the summer of 1941.

II

The Bread Loaf School was opened by Stephen A. Freeman, Acting President of Middlebury College while President Moody was in Washington, D.C., as an adviser to the government. The war in Europe was already reaching the Mountain. Two days after classes began, on July 3, Frost gave his annual poetry reading to the 231 students and faculty. Dean Harry Owen introduced him.

Frost read several of the public's favorites among his poems, and made brief comments on several poems. After reading "The Bear" he remarked that we haven't gone much beyond Plato and Aristotle in our thinking in the liberal arts. "Fire and Ice" elicited a reflection that there was "more passion than petrifaction now in the world." "The Demiurge's Laugh" he described as his "first poem on science." He read "The Generations of Men," and said that although pride in ancestry was a fine thing, the old New England Yankee stock sometimes made too much of the Pilgrims. Recent emigrants to America were also pilgrims in their way. Frost told a story of a Polish boy in a small New England town who outstripped everyone in school. He did so well that the old Yankee families were put out by his superiority. They invented a story that the boy must be illegitimate, that he had a Yankee father. They couldn't accept the idea that the son of Polish emigrants could have more ability than the children of old Yankee families.

The dramatic highlight of Frost's poetry reading followed after he read "Not All There":

> I turned to speak to God
> About the world's despair;
> But to make bad matters worse
> I found God wasn't there.
>
> God turned to speak to me
> (Don't anybody laugh);
> God found I wasn't there—
> At least not over half (p. 309).

Frost addressed his Bread Loaf audience directly and asked whether anyone knew how God got His name. After a long pause the poet said that in the beginning He didn't have a name, and He felt keenly that something was lacking, especially after He had decided to create Earth and man. In creating the earth He took a giant cauldron and built a fire under it. Then He mixed in all the ingredients which were to comprise the earth. And a steam rose from the cauldron, so that He couldn't quite see what He was doing. But He kept on dumping in more ingredients and stirring the cauldron, and more steam rose from it. At last He became curious to see what kind of mixture He had concocted. As the steam cleared off, He looked over the edge of the cauldron into the bubbling mess and gasped, "God!" And that's how He came to be called "God."

The reaction to Frost's anecdote was decidedly mixed. Those who sensed that he was being puckishly whimsical, and treating God in a spirit of play, laughed with good nature. Malicious free thinkers, who thought Frost was denigrating God, laughed in derision. Pious, humorless, religious souls, who felt Frost was being sacrilegious, stirred uneasily in their seats but did not laugh. Frost sensed that his whimsical anecdote had missed fire among many of his listeners. He shifted gears and suddenly became quite serious.

By definition, if not by name, said Frost, God is that by which we explain all things. We can't explain God, because He is a mystery, but we explain things through God. We believe in God as theists; or we stand forever wondering about Him as agnostics; or disbelieve in Him as atheists. Belief, or faith, is the whole basis of knowledge and understanding of God. And men's belief has important practical consequences in their lives. The reason so many people fear death is that they don't understand what God is. God is the One; not any one, but "the ever-ready One." Everything begins and meets in "the ever-ready One." Most people don't think seriously about death until they find themselves in a hospital, or in an old folks home weaving baskets. Frost concluded his remarks by saying that every time he passed a hospital he sensed the smell of death, and his mind wandered up and down the corridors.

After Frost's poetry reading many students went to the Barn and debated his remarks about God and death until well past midnight. I found myself in the small minority who understood Frost as a theist whose faith in God allowed room for a comic treatment of the deity.

III

On the following Sunday afternoon, July 6, the Methodist church in Ripton celebrated its sesquicentennial, and as Bread Loafers were invited I attended. The featured speakers were Bill Meacham, a graduate of Middlebury who had spent many summers in Ripton; Robert Noble, a native of Ripton; and Robert Frost. The poet's grandson, Prescott Frost, around seventeen years old, was in the audience. He had an uncanny physical resemblance to his grandfather. I saw him again at several Friday night square dances in Ripton during July, and each time he made me think that Frost as a teenager must have looked like him.

Frost spoke briefly on how the Hebrew Old Testament provided the basis for the Christian New Testament. His theme was that Christ had fulfilled the Decalogue which Moses had delivered to the Jewish people, providing a new spirit for the letter of the moral law in the Sermon on the Mount. He noted that when Moses came down from the mountain to deliver the Ten Commandments to God's chosen people, even before he could give them the stone tablets he found them violating the first and most important law by worshipping and dancing around the golden calf they had made. In his anger Moses threw down the tablets, and they were broken. This symbolized that the moral laws are always being broken. To this day, he noted, over the entrance of synagogues the Ten Commandments are chiseled in stone, with a crack running across the tablets. The greatest troubles suffered by Jews and Christians occur when they are false to their covenants and reject the revelations of their religion.

Frost's words were well-received by his Ripton audience. His undoubted orthodoxy in religion was clearly evident on this occasion, in contrast to his ambiguous raillery about God three days earlier.

IV

On two other occasions during July I visited Frost at his cabin with student friends; once with Laura Woodard, a student from Vanderbilt University studying at Bread Loaf; and once with George Sullivan, Charley Cotter, and Howard Friedman, friends from Middlebury College. The first talk remained on the social level and produced no serious talk on politics, literature, education, science, or religion—the subjects that really interested Frost. Although the second talk got into some significant matters concerning Emerson, it was dissipated by having too many focal points among Frost's listeners. I concluded after that evening that in the future I would come alone.

Frost expressed his conviction that Emerson was a fine poet and prophet, but not a great philosopher, particularly if we include as poetry some passages of his prose. Indeed, Emerson was really not a philosopher. He was an intuitionalist and a leaper, not a plodding logician. It would be hard to reduce his themes and arguments about things metaphysical to any systematic or coherent form. There are large gaps in his theories and considerable confusion. This didn't bother Emerson much. That was his happy fault. Emerson was a great phrasemaker and symbolist, because he saw the whole of nature; and the facts and particular objects of nature were to him symbols in God's divine plan of the universe. As a poet Emerson fused form and soul in metaphor. At times he was a bit oracular, a priest-poet. There are many good ideas and insights in Emerson's essays, particularly in *Representative Men*, but he is essentially a poet.

Someone asked whether Frost thought Emerson was as good a poet as Emily Dickinson. Frost said both are excellent poets; both are concise and aphoristic, and have a profound sense of form. Dickinson was our best woman poet by far, probably the best ever in Western civilization—better than Sappho, Elizabeth Barrett Browning, or even Christina Rossetti. But, said Frost, toward the end of her life Emily Dickinson was "quite mad." Her garden and home became her universe, and she turned inward more and more. With Emerson it was the other way around. He turned outward from himself and tried to thrust his mind to reach the farthest points of the universe. He knew that all rays return upon themselves and end in the human mind. The more powerful the mind, the more it could penetrate into matter and space. Emerson's expansiveness is concentrated; by contrast, Whitman's is diffused.

Someone also asked what was weakest about Emerson as a philosopher. Frost replied that Emerson's moral theory was monistic. Evil was the absence of good, not a reality in itself. Emerson explained evil by explaining it away. He was too optimistic by far about human nature. He had imbibed the theory of progress in history. Emerson saw only "the good of evil born, but not the evil born of good." Frost asked where in Emerson we could find "the good of evil born," and luckily I identified it as from "Uriel." Frost remarked that the angel Uriel was an orthodox rebel who tried to raise conventional morality to a higher level of understanding than the literalness of the later pharisees, back to the spirit of the prophets. The original pharisees were not pharisaical.

V

On Friday, July 25, at the request of Harry Owen, Frost came to the campus to speak on teaching reading and writing in high school, to Bread Loaf students who taught high school English. He seemed to take his point of departure from a lecture Louis Untermeyer had given at Bread Loaf on July 14, on "How to Hate Poetry." Frost attacked analytical criticism of poetry and said that such critics are to poetry what the scribes and pharisees were to Scripture. He objected to reading assignments which treated poetry as anything other than an art form, as an adjunct of science, history, grammar, or argument. He objected to assignments in source studies or "borrowings." A poem should not be judged by where a poet got his ideas or plot. A poet should be judged by his performance, by what he did with what he borrowed. If students are simply exposed to poetry good poems will dawn in their minds like the dawn of a new day. This happens best not by making a paraphrase of a poem, but by applying the central metaphor to a familiar situation in life. By combining books and life in reading assignments teachers can illuminate two kinds of truth for their students: learning something they knew but had forgotten, which is common in experience; and learning something new, which is rare in experience. Both truths are forms of insight rather than of knowledge. Most students know what they have learned in the order in which they learned it. A teacher should show them how much better it is to get at the premises of ideas in their readings. Frost gestured with his index finger to stress his main points. He said several times: "Never forget the fun of play in reading."

Frost turned from teaching reading to teaching writing. He insisted that a teacher should never assign exercises in writing. Let the students be free in spirit to write what they will, immediately, as well as they can. And never mind mechanics and syntax. If students read with care they will pick up correct usage as they go along; and if they don't, it doesn't matter, because they won't be writers anyway. Teachers who insist on preciseness in mechanics and grammar are big in little things and little in the great virtues in writing—initiative, daring, originality. It is ironical that these mere linguists and mechanists parade their authority and assume to themselves the public image of a teacher of English. They are often majestic in their self-importance. But it's a miserly mistake for a teacher to keep the sleeping spirit in a child sleeping too long. The high school English teacher's job is the same as Prince Charming's, to awake the Sleeping Beauty with a kiss. Prince Charming didn't waste time trying to spoon feed the Sleeping Beauty before he awakened her. From the first writing assignment students should be made aware that their own experiences and ideas are the most vital thing that can engage their minds and hearts in what they have to say. It is important that every student is taught to do his very best every time he writes, to extend himself to his utmost limits, to make his words stand forth as deeds. If necessary, do something shocking and dramatic to get this point across to students. Frost told an anecdote—when he taught English at Pinkerton Academy, in Derry, New Hampshire, he held up a set of papers his students had written and asked: "Is there anything here that anyone wants to keep permanently?" No one said yes, so he shouted to the class: "I am not a perfunctory reader of perfunctory writing," and threw the papers in the waste basket. An undefinable murmer passed through the audience as Frost finished his story.

Frost argued that student aspiration counts for far more than teacher inspiration of students. No one can prod someone else into being a writer. If prodding can create writers why don't the teachers prod each other? He challenged his audience: "Have you ever wondered why so few teachers of English can write well?" Teachers and students would do well to prod themselves. Aspiration is really self-belief. A poet believes and wills himself into existence as a poet. He will know he is a poet before anyone else knows it, but modesty forbids him to announce it to the world. He must wait until the world recognizes it and calls him a poet. A young man who has published a poem or two in a school magazine is hardly qualified to be called a poet, any more than a boy who signs up to become a seminarian should be called a priest. For both poetry and the ministry, many are called but few are chosen.

In teaching we get most from a student not by putting the screws on him but by our example, our presence as a teacher, challenging him to his best efforts, like a coach on the athletic field. We should know in teaching not to teach. There has been much recent nonsense that the student, rather than the teacher, should decide what and how learning should take place. That is to deny that experience has any value in life or in wisdom about life. Youth must go to school to their elders.

Frost emphasized that to write is to think, to have original thoughts by putting together impressions, ideas, and sensations that have never before been combined. To think is to create images, make analogies, and perceive metaphors. When a student succeeds in doing these things he knows it immediately; he does not have to wait a week or a month to know that he has said better what he has never before thought or said as well. He knows intuitively when what he has written is good, just as he knows when he falls in love that the object of his love is good. He knows it the way an archer knows when his arrow strikes the bullseye. He may lack taste and judgment, but these will come in time as he grows. And as a member of society he wants and needs the praise and approval of his teachers and friends.

To illustrate the danger of expecting praise too soon from their teachers, Frost told an anecdote about two green-eyed fishermen. The poet said that young would-be writers often came to him and showed him their work and expected him to tell them they were going to be writers. He generally told them the story of the green-eyed fishermen. It goes like this. Two fishermen lived by a lake, and whenever they wanted some fish they would paddle out to the middle of the lake in their small boat, and one fisherman would say to the other: "Are my eyes green?" "No, not yet," the other would say. Then they would paddle around some more and the first one would say, "Are my eyes green now?" The second fisherman would say, "Yes they're green now." And the first one would dive in and catch some fish. Then one day the two fishermen went out in the

lake to catch fish and the first one asked: "Are my eyes green?"
"No, not yet," the second answered. After they had paddled around
a little more the first one said, "Are my eyes green now?" The other
answered, "No, not yet." Then the first one said, "Oh, come on
now! Say that my eyes are green." Then the second one said, "All
right, then, your eyes are green." Whereupon the first fisherman
dove into the lake and was drowned. Frost remarked that that is
the way it is with so many young would-be writers: they all want
to be told that their eyes are green.

Frost mused that often young would-be poets read a poem to
him and that if he didn't say anything about it they thought he
didn't like it and felt they must say something in the poem's defense.
Often in explaining the poem they said things that were better than
the poem itself. The poet said he often discovered at this point that
the poem was assigned by a teacher, while the remarks about the
poem were "self-assigned," and came from the student. According
to Frost, writing a poem should be self-assigned, so that the poem
unfolds itself as naturally as the opening lines of Keats's *Hyperion*.
But before a young writer can write well with ease he must discipline himself by learning to use his tools. Before a young writer
can experience anything like the intuition in Keats's "wild surmise"
he must have a keen sense of the range of meanings possible in the
sounds and rhythms of the English language, and he must know by
immediate sense recognition the chief verse forms.

Frost spoke at length of meter, rhythm, and the sound of meaning in poetry. He asserted that "there is only one meter in English
poetry, the iambic, more or less loose or strict." A line of English
verse is seldom more than five feet, as it often is in Latin poetry.
We can't be too precise or scientific about meter and rhythm. Robert Bridges had a theory about meter in English poetry which would
have made it as dead to us as Latin is a dead language to most English-
speaking people. Bridges's friend Gerard Manley Hopkins tried to
do the same thing with rhythm—what he called "sprung rhythm"—
that Bridges did with meter. Hopkins's loose rhythm is too contrived, whether viewed as theory or in his own practice as a poet.

In reading a line or passage of poetry out loud, Frost remarked,
there should be no need or reason to consciously stress one word

or phrase more than another, in order to make a point. The stresses should come naturally, from within the word itself, as it were, as if one were speaking common idiomatic English. To illustrate his point Frost quoted a line from "Birches," "It's when I'm weary of considerations," and asked: "Which word is naturally stressed in that line?" If the dramatic effect is to emerge out of the situation of the speaker in the monologue, rather than being put on it from without by the reader, the word "weary" must receive heavy stress. Frost dragged out the middle vowel sounds until they approached being two syllables. By stressing the word "weary" thus, the character speaks in his own true psychological response to his condition. The sound conveys the dramatic meaning, just as in onomatopoeia the sound of a word imitates an action. Frost mentioned *hiss*, *buzz*, *whirr* and *whirl*, *slam*, *suck* and *sizzle*, as examples of words in which the meaning is carried in the sound. Meter alone is too limited and monotonous to convey meaning through sounds. To create "the tune of a poem" the variations in rhythm must cut across the relatively fixed meter. Rhythm provides the range of meanings in a poem. Frost's example for this was to imagine two people arguing in a room, whose voices could be heard rising and falling, even though no distinct words could be made out. A listener would get a very good idea of what was meant by each voice in the argument, even without hearing the words, through the pitch and the rhythm.

It is a common mistake, said Frost, to think of metaphor as only a figure in a verse or stanza. The common verse forms are themselves metaphoric. A blank verse lays down a direct line of image, thought, or sentiment. The couplet contrasts, compares, or makes parallel figures, ideas, and feelings. The quatrain combines two couplets alternatively. The sonnet gives a little drama in several scenes to a lyric sentiment. All of these verse forms have their possibilities and limitations in providing a poet with his means to strip life to form and fix the flux of life for a moment permanently in language. Poetry is not "an escape" from life, as so many people seem to think, but a "pursuit of life," a deeper probing into it, and into ourselves, than ordinary everyday living provides. Comedy and tragedy provide the spirit and style of how we take ourselves in the verse forms we use. Frost said that if we write with obvious outer seriousness, there should always be a subtle core of inner wit or humor; and if we write with outer humor or wit, the inner core should always have a serious theme. To leave out half of life is to make poetry less real rather than more real than life. Only silly, thoughtless people, literal-minded boobs, believe in the slogan "more truth than poetry." They assume that the common verse forms are artificial, not found in life as lived by mundane people, and therefore poetry can't present what is true and real in life. Some writers think this way too. They think they have to dredge the dregs of human depravity to write about what is "real." Their "realism" is "sewer realism," Frost punned. To prove that their potato is "real" they have to give us a peck of dirt with it; Frost said he was content to offer his potato brushed clean. All this concerns the style of content or meaning in the common verse forms. The best way for students to learn these forms is to read much English and American poetry, until they have assimilated the forms and made them second nature. Then when they write they will not think of it as "creative writing," a bad, much abused phrase, Frost said, but as "natural." There were no questions from his listeners, and thus the session ended.

VI

On Sunday evening, August 10, Robert Frost and Louis Untermeyer came to Bread Loaf to hear a program of songs by the famous singer Harriet Eells, a mezzo-soprano of the American Opera Company, from Cleveland, Ohio. During the early forties Miss Eells spent several weeks each summer on the Mountain, preparing her recitals for the coming year in Europe and America. She was a strong, striking woman, with a clear, pleasing, powerful voice, and she completely dominated her accompanist, the well-known Hungarian pianist, Arpad Sandor. After singing some German lieder and folk songs, Miss Eells concluded her program by singing several poems by Frost which had been set to music—"The Pasture," and "Stopping by Woods on a Snowy Evening." I could see that Frost was clearly displeased by these song versions of his poems. He liked Miss Eells, and considered her a fine singer, but after the program he did not congratulate her or speak to her about his poems. On July 23 Madame Elizabeth Schumann had given a recital of German leider at Bread Loaf, and John Crowe Ransom had expressed his dislike of her singing as "too Romantic," because she had tried to charm her audience rather than letting her art speak for itself. But Harriet Eells was a classical singer, so I doubted that it was her singing that had displeased Frost.

Summer school was over on my birthday, August 12, and that night I visited Frost in his cabin for the last time that summer. I immediately asked him what he thought of Miss Eell's rendering of his poems as songs. He said that a poem is already a song, and to add music to it is to change it into something different from itself, to translate it. He insisted that genuine poetry cannot be translated. He remarked that the Italian word to translate, *tradurre*, had the same root as their word to betray, *tradire*. Frost coined an epigram: "To be translated is to be betrayed." Even at its best, said Frost, "a translation is a stewed strawberry." He was glad he didn't know the foreign languages into which his poems had been translated, because it saved him the pain of hearing them mutilated. It was flattering to hear that someone had translated one of his poems, but it was aesthetically painful to hear a translation. More specifically, I asked why can't good poetry be translated into a song without its essence being lost? Frost replied that there's always a conflict between the meter and rhythm of a poem and the meter and rhythm of music. The meter of a poem may be fitted to music, but the rhythm cutting across the meter cannot. That is what is lost in setting a poem to music. The tone and idiom of the spoken language are lost, and something operatic replaces them. Music and poetry are separate art forms, and cannot be combined. The opera is a bastard art form, attempting to be both music and drama, and being neither. No one takes seriously the dramatic plot of an opera. To like opera we must treat it as music. Frost admitted to disliking opera.

With a mischievous twinkle in his eyes Frost said the only kind of poetry that could be improved by translation is free verse. Did he mean Whitman? I asked. He was glad to include Whitman, whose "free verse" was almost as "loose and distended" and sprawling over his page "without compression" and form as most contemporary writing of free verse. Frost remarked that he had once read a long passage of Whitman to some students who said they admired his poetry and asked whether they thought that was good poetry. After they said they thought it was, he told them he had read every other line. "Can you imagine doing that with Pope?" he asked. But the writer he had in mind was Carl Sandburg. Once in the early 1920s, when Sandburg had read his poems at the University of Michigan, Frost said he had thought then that Sandburg accompanied himself on his "geetar" to hide the fact that his free verse had no metrical pattern, only a very loose rhythm. The occasional twangs on the strings supplied the missing meter.

Speaking of the University of Michigan reminded me of the talk we had had with Barbara Fleury last summer, and I asked Frost to tell me about his experience at Michigan. He said he had been the first American poet to be appointed "poet-in-residence" at a university; this had occurred in 1921–22 and was repeated the next year. He was pleased that other colleges and universities have since then had poets- and writers-in-residence; it showed that schools recognize the importance of the arts. I asked him what his duties were at Michigan. Unlike earlier at Amherst, he said, where he was really a teacher and not a poet-in-residence, he had no set courses to teach at Michigan. "I was a poetic radiator," Frost said; "I just sat around and radiated poetry." But, ironically, his freedom from fixed academic duties had been largely negated by the heavy demands of his social life. Such friends as President Marion Burton, Dean Joseph Bursley, and Professors Morris Tilley, Louis Strauss, and Roy Cowden in English, and others, had constantly invited him and his wife out to dinner, afternoon teas, lectures, etc., and he was more a social lion than a poet. Also, the students would frequently invite themselves into his home. He enjoyed talking with them, particularly the staff on the *Whimsies*, but the result was that he neglected to write as much poetry as he wished. His danger was the opposite of that of such poets as Browning and Robinson, who late in life wrote much from habit and fell into the danger of writing commonplace poetry. His danger was that he would dry up.

Did he write anything while in Ann Arbor? I asked. When he returned to Michigan a third time after an interval of another year at Amherst, he lived in a house which he called "chicken Classical," because it had a wing on each side and columns in the middle section. Frost said that this house was later bought by Henry Ford and moved to Greenfield Village, where it is part of that "outdoor museum." He wrote two poems while living in that house, "Spring Pools" and "Acquainted with the Night." He got three lines of "Acquainted with the Night" in an intuitive flash one night while walking alone, when he looked up through some mist or fog at the clock high in the tower of the old Washtenaw County Courthouse:

> And further still at an unearthly height
> One luminary clock against the sky
>
> Proclaimed the time was neither wrong nor right (p. 255).

The whole sonnet had followed from that intuition, just as after he had written "New Hampshire," staying up all night, at dawn the whole of "Stopping by Woods on a Snowy Evening" had come to him in a flash—all except the next to the last line. Later, he had another intuition that all he had to do was repeat the last line to complete the poem. The actual writing of "Stopping by Woods on a Snowy Evening," Frost said, took him only as long as it took to put the words on paper. But in fact he had *lived* the poem for many years before he wrote it. It had simmered quietly for a long time, then suddenly came to a boil.

The University of Michigan had treated him extremely well, Frost remarked. He had nothing but fond memories of it, and among the large universities in the nation he considered it one of the very best. The Hopwood awards in writing were unique, and the writing program made Michigan much less purely academic than most schools. He could have stayed on for the rest of his life, but it would have been his death as a poet. But he finally learned from going to Michigan that his only real permanent home was New England.

From his first year in Ann Arbor Frost recalled one poet in whom I then had a strong interest. He had persuaded the literary students at Michigan to invite a series of poets to the campus, and among them was Amy Lowell. Frost had then known her for over six years, since soon after his return from England early in 1915, when he had visited her in her home in Brookline, Massachusetts, to thank her for having written some favorable criticism about his first two books of poetry. According to Frost, Amy Lowell was "the perpetual show off." She lived in a large sprawling mansion, and when Frost visited her the first time she was talking to some young Spanish poet whom she had befriended. When her servant ushered Frost in, and she became aware that he could see and hear her, she suddenly became very unfriendly to the Spanish poet, and ordered him out. As he was leaving she stuck her fingers up to her nose at him. It was her way of telling Frost that she was the dominant force in any friendship. In private she liked to smoke big black cigars. Whenever she travelled, Frost said, even if it was only for a very short distance, she always took along at least twenty or thirty suitcases. She refused ever to walk any distance and would take a taxi just to cross the street. She liked to boss people around. In Michigan during her lecture, she came out on the stage with a big ball of electric light cord and made Frost and the janitor undo it in front of the audience, while she supervised them and made wisecracks. She put on a vaudeville show whenever she gave a poetry reading.

Despite her liveliness, her outer pleasantness and nastiness, she was a very sick woman during the last years of her life. Frost said Amy Lowell's doctor told him shortly after her death that he had been within quick calling distance of her for a long time, ready to operate on her immediately. About six months before she suddenly died, Frost had invited her to a little party he gave in New York, but she had refused to come. Instead of telling Frost she was too sick to travel, she just said it was too far to go for a party. Frost felt she had snubbed him, so that shortly afterwards when she gave a party to celebrate the publication of her study of Keats and invited Frost, he also refused. Had he known how sick she was, and that illness and not pride or envy had prevented her from attending his party, he would have gone to her celebration. During the last few months of Amy Lowell's life she and Frost were peeved with each other. Frost remarked sadly that he had always been sorry for his part in their alienation.

I asked Frost what he thought of Amy Lowell as an imagist and free verse poet. He remarked that there were two main reasons why many poor poets turned to free verse, apart from its being very easy to write. One group thinks the world picture is too chaotic and dark for any order to be made out of it in the traditional forms of poetry. Therefore, they try to show the world's chaos through free verse. The other group feels that rhymed metrical-cadenced patterns impose too great a burden on them. Amy Lowell belonged to the second group. She was neither a thinker nor a poet, but simply a literary dilettante with a flair for advertising herself.

Frost said he was amused at the inflated literary reputations of some contemporary free verse poets, whose academic admirers praised them by denigrating much better poets who had written in traditional forms. Once during the twenties he was scheduled to give a poetry reading at a socially prestigious Eastern women's college, where he had heard that the professors of English dismissed Longfellow as a sentimental nineteenth-century Eddy Guest. Frost told his audience that before reading from his own poems he would read from the work of a poet he thought they should know. He read several of Longfellow's poems without identifying the author, and each poem was greeted with enthusiasm. When the audience was at a high pitch to know who had written these excellent poems Frost identified him as Longfellow, and a gasp of unbelief went through the coeds. Frost urged the students to read more of Longfellow, and other traditional poets, and to trust their own taste and judgment rather than taking any so-called authority's word about any poet.

There were times during our conversation when I had a unique sense that Robert Frost in the flesh before me, in the flow of his voice, was an imaginary character in a drama of ideas. My role was to ask questions to open the larger drama of life in some future off-stage action. I hoped that action would be in my future teaching and writing.

To move to another subject, I quoted Frost's epigram, "Precaution," "I never dared be radical when young/For fear it would make me conservative when old" (p. 308), and asked him whether that wasn't a conservative statement, in that a radical ran to extremes and was without precaution, and a conservative was the opposite? The real extremes, Frost said, would be "revolutionary and reactionary." As abstractions such terms mean little by meaning too much. But most people are a mixture of both—radical in some things and conservative in others. He remarked that he had known religious radicals who were conservatives in education and politics.

Frost then told an amusing anecdote about a group of students at Amherst who thought they were radical, and asked him if he would introduce a speaker of their choice at their next club meeting. Frost agreed to do this. The students had no money so they asked Frost if he knew of any wealthy alumnus who would pay for a speaker. Frost got a local conservative Amherst graduate to provide the money. The students chose Bertrand Russell as the most radical person they could get. Russell had been lecturing at Harvard, advocating free love and mixed dormitories for men and coeds; he was a militant pacifist and very unorthodox in religion. The day that Russell was to give his talk Frost said he received several telephone calls from the students, who feared he would be afraid to introduce such an avowed radical and therefore would leave town. Frost remarked that he introduced Russell by referring ironically to the introduction of his latest book, in which Russell had said that he was publishing it in a hurry before he changed his mind about his theme. Russell was a very gentle-looking English radical, come to shock the moss-backed conservatives of Amherst, who had come to his lecture in trepidation and fear of what he would say. And there, said Frost, in that paneled room of ardent young radical students, waiting eagerly for the bombs to be thrown, Bertrand Russell delivered one of the most timid and conventional speeches he ever heard.

After we had laughed heartily over Frost's story, we drifted into a discussion of the war in Europe. The poet told a story of something he had witnessed last summer at Bread Loaf. Count Carlo Sforza had told Frost and a group at the School of English of an incident that had happened to him before he was driven out of Italy by the Fascists. The Count had been talking politics to a young Italian Fascist, Emilio Martinetti, who had said to him: "The day is past when discussions between nations will settle disputes. The only solution to arguments between countries is the solid blow in the face." To which Count Sforza had replied: "Do you mean like this?" as he suddenly punched Martinetti full force in the face.

Frost said Count Sforza referred to Fascism as "the philosophy of the clenched fist." His point was that civilized nations and individuals talked their way through problems, and did not resort to war. But, said Frost laughing, by literally beating Martinetti to the punch the Count had proved him right. Of course the Count was right initially, because nations should try to settle their differences by peaceful means. Only an idiot nation would go to war for the sake of war. But when serious differences cannot be settled by diplomacy or negotiation, war is the final means of settling conflicts. In war, said Frost, both sides assume that justice is on their side. Each nation assumes it must win to secure justice over its enemy. War, then, is the final proof of a nation's faith in itself and in its courage to meet the conditions of survival and greatness. The pacifists don't understand this or can't accept it. The conditions of life for survival and greatness include strife and war.

Frost said he was glad President Roosevelt was not a pacifist, as Woodrow Wilson was. However much he criticized Roosevelt's "New Deal," he could not fault him about war. Frost expressed concern that if war came to the United States the nation would not be prepared for it, materially and spiritually. "Archie" MacLeish's theme in "The Irresponsibles" showed a turning of the tide against the cynical defeatism following the First World War. If democracy is the best form of government (and it is) then it must find and elevate the best people in order to survive and triumph—the best poets, politicians, generals, leaders, etc. Frost said he was glad Roosevelt had expressed his courage to fight if it became necessary. Despite their terrible losses in prisoners and land, the Russians had stalled the German armies and were beginning to counterattack. This spoke well for them.

Frost then turned his guns on domestic national politics. The great danger in the world at large—the sweep to collectivism—was present in a mild form in the United States. Collectivism, he said, means "all pigging together," which is what Roosevelt's "New Deal" wanted for Americans. Frost said he didn't believe "truckling to the mob speeds the world's wheels." If Vice-President Henry Wallace's slogan was accurate, if this is "the century of the common man," then our individual freedom will be lost. Wallace, like Sandburg, believed in "The People, Yes," but not in "The People, Yes; and the People, No."

Our founding fathers knew better, said Frost. Being more religious they knew that only God had or should have absolute power. Frost expressed great admiration for George Washington because after the American Revolution, when absolute power was offered to him, he refused it in favor of limited power through divided and balanced parliamentary government. Frost said that next to Washington he most admired Madison, for incorporating the division and balance of power principle into the United States Constitution. Frost expressed concern that Franklin D. Roosevelt had destroyed that principle in 1940 in being elected to a third term. He referred to Roosevelt as "a third termite." But he was not happy about Wendell Willkie either, an international pacifist and "one-worlder."

The greatest branch of our government, Frost contended, was the Supreme Court. He had confidence that it would preserve the American federal-states system long after many other nations disappeared. He didn't always agree with the Supreme Court's decisions, and certainly not with the recent decision upholding the federal statute restricting work for sixteen and eighteen year old youths, and setting hours of labor at a maximum of forty hours per week. He had asked his friend Justice Felix Frankfurter why he had voted to uphold that law. The answer was purely sentimental; it had nothing much to do with law or freedom or labor. Frost said that he asked Frankfurter: "How many hours a week do you work?" Frankfurter had answered: "About seventy or eighty. Oh, but that's different! The poor have nothing else to look forward to." Frost said he had asked Frankfurter how the forty-hours-a-week law would help the ambitious poor who were willing and able to work longer? Wouldn't they just get a second job? Far from helping the self-reliant poor, such a law restricted them from rising from their poverty.

Frost remarked that the state does not create anything: it merely takes through taxes what its citizens create. But then it gives back in a new distribution of wealth. Where before there was only justice or injustice, the state mixes mercy with justice. It can't carry the proportions of mercy and justice too far in favor of mercy without violating the theme of the nursery rhyme about the goose that laid the golden eggs. If it kills the goose, it will not be able to make any more omelets. In our "Robin Hood politics" the state robs the rich to give to the poor. It can't do otherwise, except to leave rich and poor alone. The state can't take from the poor—they have little or nothing to take. It shouldn't give to the rich—they don't need it. The end of every modern government is to create more and more equality of conditions among men. But the great evil is that this is done at the expense of private freedom and justice. The modern socialist state wants a society based on mercy alone. This is impossible. Frost said he favored a society based on justice, but infused with mercy.

I asked Frost why there was always so much corruption in politics. He replied that you don't catch saints going into politics. The saints are contemplatives, not activists. Theirs is the response of character and will to a personal moral dilemma. The best people are morally good without being do-gooders. As Luther said, salvation comes through faith alone. Actions speak softer than prayers to men of faith. Other than saints the best people are good-doers, not do-gooders. That leaves the politicians to do good or do well in society as they see fit. Politics is the seeking out of solutions to social grievances. That involves power and action through statutes and laws. That is why so many lawyers go into politics. In politics, law, power, and money all come together. The premium trait for success is shrewdness, boldness, sociability, prudence, and many lesser virtues that feather off into vices. Manipulating situations leads to swapping favors, patronage, and shyster lawyer tricks: ergo, corruption.

At about two in the morning we took our slow lantern walk down Frost's dirt road to the Bread Loaf highway. It was a particularly pleasant evening. The sky was covered with stars from horizon to horizon, and Frost pointed out and named various constellations. The cool bracing air seemed to put him in an expansive and reflective mood. He expressed his sober confidence that come what may the United States was destined to remain the dominant nation in the world. Our unique constitutional system was still strong, and it would enable us to meet threats from without in war and from within by revolution. Our greatest danger was slow corruption from within through the growth in centralized federal authority. Frost feared the decline of the individual states would also make the American people too reliant on Washington, D.C., with a consequent loss in character and self-reliance. He admired states such as Vermont and New Hampshire, where the old New England Yankee Puritan virtues prevailed. He expected that sooner than we thought —or would wish—the United States would be drawn into the war and that we would prove our mettle as in the past. And, finally, Frost was convinced that American literature would be a match for our power and wealth, as great in the future as in the past. He did not fear for his country.

Frost's words and quiet confidence lifted my spirit. As we shook hands and said good night, I felt closer to him than at any time since we had known each other over the past three summers. As Bread Loafers we had in common our love of poetry. But Frost's love of the United States, his nationalism without jingoism, enlarged and intensified our common identity as Americans. It was more personal than social, like the family feeling that is bred in the bones. Yet Bread Loaf was America at its literary and intellectual best. It was our magic mountain. Its humanized landscape, peopled with the most intelligent, stimulating, and pleasant academicians and professional writers I could wish for, made me aware, that night, through Frost that Bread Loaf was the closest thing to the lost Eden that I would ever know.

VII

The annual gathering of the clan of would-be writers and highland chiefs of the staff at the Writers' Conference of 1941 again found Frost frequently on the Bread Loaf campus. He read his poems, talked to young writers on the West Lawn or in the Barn, played tennis with Kay Morrison, Louis Untermeyer and Dick Ellmann, autographed books, and regularly took part in the poetry clinics with Untermeyer, who did all the leg work with student manuscripts.

During the School of English session there had been a healthy mixture of academic and literary lectures: Padraic and Mary Colum, Edward Weeks, Louis Untermeyer, Professors Irwin Edman (Columbia) and Marjorie Nicholson (Smith), the novelist Julian Green, the poet May Sarton, and the critic Edmund Wilson. Frost had attended only those by his friends. Although he did not attend the special lectures of Elizabeth Drew, a new Bread Loaf faculty member from Cambridge, England, he was well aware through me and several other friends that in her popular course in modern British and American poetry she ranked as the four greatest modern poets Yeats, Eliot, Pound, and Auden, with Frost nowhere in sight. This neat and frail lady with her impeccable clipped English accent was widely accounted one of the leading authorities on modern poetry. She considered "Two Tramps in Mud Time" as Frost's most representative poem. She found it thin and conventional in its fixed stanzas, without anthropological myths, archetypal symbols, or esoteric allusions of the kind found in Yeats, Eliot and Pound, and without the proletarian social consciousness of Auden. Frost's diction was to her indistinguishable from that of a New England farmer's casual talk. She dismissed Frost as a nineteenth century relic in the John Greenleaf Whittier tradition of verse. Several years later Miss Drew changed her mind about Frost as a poet, but in 1941 she was the one important anti-Frost dissenter at Bread Loaf.

Apart from Miss Drew, the speakers at the School made easy the transition to the Writers' Conference staff, which included besides Ted Morrison and Frost, such veterans as Walter Pritchard Eaton, John Gassner, John P. Marquand, Fletcher Pratt, and Louis Untermeyer. From the previous summer's staff Edith Mirrielees and Wallace Stegner were absent, but I was delighted to see Barbara Fleury back, and Bernard De Vote also returned after a year away. Frost was very friendly with Marquand and Barbara Fleury, but his relationship with De Voto was clearly cool and strained. Whenever Frost joined a group which included De Voto, his old friend would appear ill at ease and soon would move away by himself. Everyone was aware of their enmity and felt uncomfortable. De Voto stayed at Treman Cottage and spent all his spare time there, rather than around the campus and tennis courts, as in previous years. His closest friend was the petite Fletcher Pratt, wispy in his new beard, about whom there was always a squirrel-like aura. Everyone liked the paradoxical Pratt.

Early in the Conference Frost read his poems in the Little Theatre. He prefaced and interspersed his reading with comments on the war in Europe, and on American politics, very similar to those he had made to me earlier in his cabin. In reading "Mending Wall" he noted that he had gotten the central metaphor of the poem from the idea that human biological life is cellular. The cells of the body constantly break down and are built up again, so that everyone is a wholly new and renewed person every seven years or so. Frost observed ironically that some readers were known to have found political implications in "Mending Wall." He had no objections to that. He noted that good walls are necessary to keep things properly in and properly out. Good walls define good geography, which is necessary for a sound national life. Frost also read "The Bearer of Evil Tidings" and quipped that it contained his version of the Immaculate Conception, oriental style.

But the highlight of Frost's poetry reading was "The Lesson for Today," particularly because the poem was not yet published. It appeared the following year in *A Witness Tree*. After his reading many were convinced that "The Lesson for Today" was an important poem for understanding Frost as a thinker. Like "New Hampshire" it was a reflective poem, in the Horatian tradition, less ironical than "New Hampshire," but more concise and polished in its aphorisms. Frost's contention that it is dangerous to have more knowledge than can be safely assimilated and utilized was well summarized:

> They've tried to grasp with too much social fact
> Too large a situation (p. 351).

Other outstanding touchstones included some magnificent individual lines:

> The groundwork of all faith is human woe.
> Art and religion love the somber chord.
> Earth's a hard place in which to save the soul. . . .
> We're either nothing or a God's regret.
> One age is like another for the soul.

The final line, "I had a lover's quarrel with the world," was conceded by everyone as a permanent touchstone in the canon of Frost's best lines. Someone prophesied that some day the line would be chiselled in stone on Frost's grave. Indeed, I heard only two listeners voice any dissent about "The Lesson for Today," Cedric Whitman and Theodore Roethke, both Fellows at the Conference, who preferred Frost's lyrics to his philosophical and didactic poems.

After one poetry clinic, a woman who assumed that Frost's poems were autobiographical—not fictional art but personal history—began to discuss one of Frost's lyrics in those terms. He put her in her place with one concise rhetorical question: "When I use the word 'I' in a poem, surely you don't believe I mean ME?"

At the poetry clinics Louis Untermeyer, as usual, could hardly speak a sentence without making a pun. Some of his puns, like his allusion to Shakespeare's "The Merchant of *Venus*," duly elaborated, were quite ribald, like limericks. Frost felt that Untermeyer was rather overdoing his puns and became a bit annoyed with him. To Frost Bread Loaf was neither Bohemian, nor Marxist, nor a place for precious aesthetes, and although he relished good wit and humor as much as anyone, he believed that Untermeyer's clowning sometimes interfered with the serious purpose of the poetry clinics. In light of this fact Frost particularly relished an incident in which I triumphed over Untermeyer. One day while waiting table I was asked to go upstairs with a dinner tray for a sick member of the Conference. As I came back into the dining hall, Louis Untermeyer came past me through the door in company with a lovely Writers' Conferee. He reached into his pocket, pulled out a penny, tossed it nonchalantly on the tray, and said, "Have a tip." When the penny stopped spinning, and I saw the value of the coin, I responded: "Looie, what kind of an animal throws a cent?" Before Untermeyer could come back with a pun or quip, and with the loud laughter of his young partner ringing deliciously in my ears, I slipped past him into the dining hall. Frost remarked on hearing this story that it was good enough to keep "Looie" subdued for a whole morning session.

One of the highlights of the Conference was the guest lecture by William Carlos Williams. His subject was writing poetry "in the American grain," by which he meant to use, or "put over," or "catch," the American vernacular, in the tradition of Whitman. Slang was an excellent source for the diction of poetry, Williams argued. He said that the early Imagistes were really objectivists, content merely to name their subject. But this was not enough for poetry. The present imagists, such as he, aimed to "catch" the idiom of common speech in ways that were diametrically opposed to T. S. Eliot, with his classical allusions. Williams said: "Eliot is a good poet, but he uses the wrong words." Today's imagists don't just *tell* it; they *show* it. A thing that is shown well needs no comment to explain it. Suppose, for example, a cat is lying on a rug and a man comes into the room and deliberately steps on the cat. We don't have to say the man is cruel.

Among his final points Williams said that the sonnet is not a form of poetry, but a word, an obsolete outmoded word. He agreed with what E. E. Cummings was doing with words, splitting them up by syllables, or combining them in new ways, but he favored extending this technique beyond words to include conventional verse forms.

Afterwards I asked Frost what he thought of Williams's argument. Frost replied that some of it was obvious and much of it was dubious. But there was nothing more in the current imagist poetry than there was in their original work back in 1912. Frost was politely unimpressed by Williams.

Wyman Parker, the librarian at Middlebury College, came from Rutherford, New Jersey, Williams's home town, and they had known each other for many years. Parker introduced me to Williams the day after his lecture, and told him I was from Nutley, just across the Passaic River from him. After we had talked about poetry for an hour, Williams invited me to visit him in Rutherford on my trip home after the Writers' Conference, and I accepted. Out of this grew an invitation for Williams to speak at the Middlebury College Literary Club, and a long talk about Ezra Pound, whom Williams knew very well. These were significant epilogues to the Writers' Conference for me and for my third summer at Bread Loaf. But that is another story, just as my five later summers at Bread Loaf, in 1942–44, and 1961–62, are another story.

Since Frost visited Bread Loaf frequently over a period of forty-two years, from 1921 through the summer of 1962, and was after

1938 often there from May or June through September, any balanced understanding of his character and temperament must take
into account his life at Bread Loaf—the kinds of activities he engaged in, what he said, whom he knew, how he impressed people,
what he liked and disliked. These three pre-war summers of our
Bread Loaf talks form but a small part of the total record of the
man. It may take years to complete the record. Yet even from the
existing incomplete evidence, certain tentative conclusions can be
made. There is no question that Frost was one of the greatest con-
versationalists in all English and American literature, comparable
to Dr. Samuel Johnson and Coleridge. His intellectual brilliance is
beyond dispute. I learned more from Frost about the nature and
function of poetry in my Bread Loaf talks with him than I did from
all the professors I ever had, from the B.A. through the Ph.D. What
I learned was of immense practical value to me, both as a student
and subsequently over decades as a college and university teacher of
literature. From Frost's talk I received a conception of poetry and
the power of words from which I never recovered. Undoubtedly,
Frost's philosophical convictions about religion, politics, education, and science are open to dispute, even when they are clearly
ascertained. Yet he presented his principles so brilliantly, and with
such wisdom, that even where we may differ from him his position
commands intellectual respect.

   In addition to his intellectual virtues Frost possessed the social
virtues to a very high degree. As a raconteur he had few equals,
and his stories almost always carried an important theme. They
were generally comic, humorous or satirical, and his spirit of fun
and play in telling a good story was often joyous and full of infec-
tious laughter. To hear Frost tell a story was a shared aesthetic experience, and his listeners often ended up laughing as hard as Frost
at his punch line; it was never a didactic lesson inflicted by a superior creature on dullards. At such times no one could ask for a
more companionable and likeable man than Frost. His skill in putting a visitor at ease included not merely a deep sense of prudence
and social tact, but a warm and empathetic feeling toward another
person's interests and concerns. It is doubtful that when Frost was
candid or caustic in his negative criticism of ideas, events, institu-

tions, or persons, insecurity, envy, or hatred, as has been often asserted without proof, but a philosophical difference between himself and the ideas, institutions, or persons he criticized. For example, throughout his life Frost was thoroughly consistent in his theory of poetry, and this included what he favored and opposed, so that his harsh criticism of the theory and practice of free verse had nothing personal in it, but was directed against free verse regardless of who defended or practiced it. The same may be said regarding his philosophical positions in religion, politics, and education. Behind all of his negative criticism was a positive set of principles he wished to defend. It is no more valid to condemn Frost *as a man* because of his strong criticism of ideas and people he opposed than it would be to castigate Jonathan Swift *as a person* because in his satires he bullwhipped the pride, vices, follies, errors, and bad taste of mankind.

It is a very grave and crude error to separate Frost's or any man's moral nature and psychological or emotional temperament from his intellectual and social virtues. Every Middlebury and Bread Loaf friend of Frost I knew—Vernon Harrington, President Moody, Deans Harry Owen and "Doc" Cook—men who altogether knew him over a period of forty-two years, thought Frost was not only a brilliant man and talented poet but also that he was socially attractive, morally sound, and healthy in his overall harmonious whole. All of these men also agreed that Frost was an extremely intense and emotional man, that his psyche was most complex. Yet this did not prevent them from getting along wonderfully well with Frost. Their relationship with him was not merely professional but personal; there was mutual affection between them. My eight years on the Mountain confirmed to the hilt their view of Frost.

It should be clear that almost everything in my experience of Frost at Bread Loaf contradicts the view of his psychological nature and emotional temperament presented in Lawrance Thompson's three-volume biography. This is neither the time nor the place to examine in any systematic way the portrait of Frost as a man in Thompson's work. But a few basic facts may be noted. Thompson's biography barely mentions Frost at Bread Loaf. A summary sketch of Frost's visits between 1921–36 appears in volume two. In the third volume there is only a brief reference to Frost at the Writers'

Conference in 1937; the account of Frost's bad behavior at the Conference in 1938; and a few sentences on a momentary encounter with Bernard De Voto in 1947. And that is all. Twenty-three summers of Frost's life at Bread Loaf are totally omitted by Thompson. Never once does he even mention—much less describe or discuss—Frost's important and intimate relations with the Bread Loaf School between 1938 and 1962, while far less important periods or events receive extensive treatment. At the very least these vital omissions make Thompson's biography terribly lopsided and out of focus.

Much ado is made by Thompson and others of the crisis summer of 1938 in Frost's life, after his wife died, when the poet's so-called "demon" broke loose, when he called himself "a bad man," and was called that by De Voto. The lack of balance and proportion in making this period the basis for understanding Frost as a man is evident in the enormous stress laid on Frost's behavior during this time. Thompson and those who accept him at face value present Frost as a pathologically warped and disturbed man, insecure, childish, petulent, gloomy, filled with despair and nasty guilt feelings of remorse about his family, at times morose and suicidal, and always filled with malicious envy and hatred of contemporary rival poets; in short, a thoroughly disagreeable man, hounded and consumed by his raging "demon." It is significant that in Thompson's index under "Robert Frost," the subject headings are heavily weighted with negative emotional and psychological terms, such as "Badness," "Confusion," "Cowardice," "Death," "Enemies," "Fears," "Hate," "Insanity," "Jealousy," "Sadness," "Self-centeredness," "Suicide," and "Wildness." All of these subjects are in themselves legitimate inquiries in a biography, but very rarely does Thompson provide any opposed or different but positive headings. There is nothing on Frost's "Goodness," "Charity," "Bravery," "Love of Life," "Friends," "Hopes," "Loves," "Sanity," "Benevolence," "Gladness," or "Sociability." Thompson's Freudianism carefully filtered out these traits in Frost as illusory disguises, attempts to conceal the reality of Frost's negative emotions. As a result, the real imbalance in Thompson's biography, stemming from his own Freudian theories, is in his interpretation of the inner nature of Frost, especially his emotional nature. It is ironical that Thompson, who thought of himself as an objective, scientifically rational man and scholar, above the common superstitions of religion, should have created a demonology about Frost.

There is no doubt that Frost had a great ego and much literary vanity, and that the negative emotional traits found in all men, so emphasized by Thompson, existed in Frost in an intense form, larger than ordinary life. But these traits are no more nor any less "real" than their positive opposites, which also existed larger than life in Frost. The specific origins of fears, hatreds, jealousy, etc., are not easily uncovered by the speculative probings of amateur psychoanalysis, which has often been known to attribute to a single simple cause emotional problems which are complex and many-faceted. Undoubtedly, Frost's incredibly difficult personal emotional dilemma derived in general from his early and total commitment to his life of poetry, with all that it entailed in economic sacrifice and emotional suffering in failing to meet his necessary responsibilities to his family. Frost could have avoided this dilemma by never marrying. But he believed in and loved family life as much as poetry, and he paid the terrible price of trying to have both. The personal tragedies which afflicted his family, which had nothing to do with his commitment to poetry, intensified his emotional problems.

My experience of Frost at Bread Loaf, in these three pre-war years, and later, provides some of the positive elements missing from Thompson's biography. Frost's dictum that only those who approached poetry in the true spirit of poetry, and accepted it on its own terms, can understand it and be saved by it, applies as well to individual human beings, and to Frost himself. Thompson approached Frost too much through Sigmund Freud (whom Frost once dubbed "Sigmund Fraud"). I have presented Frost descriptively as a conversationalist, and in the main have allowed him to speak for himself, on his own terms.

A view from the front of The Gully, a former (1929–1938) home of Robert Frost, now the summer home of artist Kenneth Noland, South Shaftsbury, Vermont

In Aladdin's Lamp Light

LESLEY FROST

A question being asked periodically is somehow demanding an answer: did Robert Frost believe in God, in an Almighty? How religious was he? I have always considered it a quite superfluous question, when all one has to do is count the number of times God's name appears in the collected poems. I did just that the other day and even surprised myself. Then I looked for members of the jury to back me up, and came upon several strong affirmations. For instance, there are two fine studies of the poem "Directive": one, " 'Directive' and the Spiritual Journey" by Robert K. Greenleaf; another, "A Reading of Robert Frost's 'Directive' " by John Robert Doyle. There are sermons of Rabbi Victor Reichert, and many other men of the church; essays in academic journals and dissertations; and now the forthcoming book *Robert Frost: Contours of Belief* by Dorothy Judd Hall. Often too the subject has been raised in an interview with Frost himself, such as one given to Seldon Rodman (*Tongues of Fallen Angels*) during the Bread Loaf days. The two are discussing a certain poem, "The Bear," and Rodman asks whether it isn't meant to be "a sly criticism of preachers," to which Frost replies, "Could *be*. I despise religiosity. But I have no religious doubts. Not about God's existence, anyway." Then, as further documentary evidence, there was always a Bible within easy reach, including a Latin one (Paris 1865) with his mother's inscription (Belle Moodie), which is now mine.

As for my own approach to the matter, it was and is something answered in the affirmative long before my time. My father was early steeped in the religious thinking of a mother to whom he was strongly attached: a gallant, intelligent woman of Scotch descent, with poetic leanings of her own. Isabel (Belle) Moodie Frost was a devout Swedenborgian, as her church in San Francisco can testify. After her husband's death she returned East and founded a private grade school for the education of the two children, Robert

313

and Jeanie. Robert lived at home through high school in Lawrence (Massachusetts), where a classmate was Elinor White—a case in point for "love at sight"—"Meeting and Passing," "The Telephone." After high school he spent a few months at Dartmouth, but he soon returned home to assist his mother in her school. Three years later he added Elinor to the teaching staff by marrying her.

(Elinor inspired him. He once told me, "Every love poem I ever wrote was to one person—your mother." The early "A Prayer in Spring" was written to her; so was "The Silken Tent," which I can remember typing out, along with my brother Carol, the winter before my mother died.)

The direct influence of Isabel Moodie Frost on her son should not be underestimated. The reason he could claim he read his first book through at the age of fourteen (one of his slight exaggerations) was that he had been read-aloud-to during his boyhood from the books of *her* choice; the poems of Robert Burns (that were to give me my name—Lesley); Scott's *Tales of a Grandfather*; the teachings of Swedenborg; MacDonald's *At the Back of the North Wind*; Prescott's *Conquest of Mexico* and *Conquest of Peru*; anything and everything relating to Scottish history. My father's first poem to appear in print, in the Lawrence High School *Bulletin*, was of Cortez driven from Mexico City.

True, now that my attention is being called to it, I find it interesting to mark a certain development of religious position from, shall we say, "A Prayer in Spring" to "A Steeple on the House" and "Directive." In 1962 or thereabouts he remarked to me, "I have always lived according to my emotions, perhaps too much so, but I wouldn't have had it otherwise." Comes the next question: what did he mean by emotions? I suspect, for him, they were the "passionate preferences such as love at sight" ("Accidentally on Purpose"). Love, then, was the original source, the instinctual way, through nature, of being in touch with Divinity. Perhaps love *was* Divinity.

For me, I can only say that the question of my father's belief in God, however asked, was answered unconsciously during those faraway evenings of being read-aloud-to (an inherited custom) on the Derry farm—now open to the public as The Derry Farm—in front of the wood fire in the Franklin stove, in the light of an Aladdin lamp. (And speaking of wishes didn't my father say that a wish wished hard enough would bring it to pass, would be a way of projecting the future?) There were passages from the Old and New Testaments, the Psalms, *Pilgrim's Progress*, Maeterlinck's *Blue Bird*, Gayley's *Classic Myths*, the *Odyssey*, the *Aeneid*, *Marco Polo*, "The Ancient Mariner," "Horatius at the Bridge," Tennyson's Arthurian legends, Shakespeare—poetry and more poetry (with a lot of memorizing)—in which the heroic and the divine rubbed shoulders with the not so heroic and the not so divine, for my father insisted that one age is much like another, for better or worse, in how it adjusts to Good and Evil. There has to be bad for there to be good.

Yes, such poems as "The Trial by Existence" and "Two Tramps in Mud Time" charted the life course of Robert Frost. "I Could Give All to Time," "Directive," and many others, saw him across the finish line. And since he hasn't returned, nor has anyone, we may assume ("Away!") that he approved of what he found.

The world he left behind he vividly set forth in two lines ("From Iron—Tools and Weapons"):

> Nature within her inmost self divides
> To trouble men with having to take sides.

In other words, we *elect* to choose between love and hate, war and peace, right and wrong, God and the Devil.

An Old Testament Christian

DOROTHY JUDD HALL

PREFACE

I number among the students, teachers and writers who are starting to be called a "second generation of Frost scholars." I know Robert Frost primarily in his poetry—and in his letters and essays. During his last years, however, I had the good fortune of meeting him in person. And since that time I have become a close friend of his daughter Lesley, whom I met in Florida through an unexpected coincidence of events (too complicated to detail here) and a bit of my own ingenuity. She arranged for me to visit her father at his winter home next to hers in South Miami. It was February 4, 1960; I was on a short escape from the northeast snows. When Lesley reached me by telephone at my motel on the Beach she said to be at her home at four in the afternoon. (Padraic Colum was "coming at five.") I drove through the downtown business traffic and tried to believe my luck. But as I pulled into the driveway of her Florida-style pink stucco house, I began to know it was real.

Lesley led me down behind her home to a secluded pine thicket, to her father's white frame cottage. It was not much bigger than a freight-train caboose. In fact, Lesley told me, he had shipped the cottage on a flatcar from New England. Another tiny house (for guests) stood nearby. I remember that I had to sit on Frost's "good ear" side, on an old leather sofa. He talked about the fruit trees around his cottage, and how he enjoyed tending them. On the whole, though, he asked me more about *my* interests than he spoke about himself. He was an avid collector of news about people. After about a half hour he shuffled over to a worn wooden desk to sign for me "A-Wishing Well," his Christmas card poem that winter; and I saw that I should leave.

I had lived in Texas and Indiana for some time, but now, back East again, I determined to make up for lost years and track down the poet on his lecture circuit. My master's thesis at Purdue on Frost's "Lyric Voice" made me want all the more to hear the living

316

man. I recall with pleasure his skillful handling of large crowds in New York City—at the Poetry Society of America annual banquet; at Hunter College; at the Y. M. H. A. uptown on Lexington Avenue. But my fondest memories are of the summers I spent at Bread Loaf School of English, high in the Green Mountains of Vermont, where Frost came over some evenings from his nearby log cabin in Ripton. There, it seemed, sunsets mingled with poetry in an aura almost mystical. He read a lot: from British and American poets he particularly liked, and from his own works. Besides his *Complete Poems* he brought along his cherished *Oxford Book of Verse*.

His tastes were catholic, ranging from Shakespeare to Emily Dickinson. He was drawn to her instinct for just the right word: "Parting is all we *know* of heaven,/And all we *need* of hell." Mad Kit (Christopher) Smart was also a favorite; Frost thundered forth heroically the rhythms of "A Song to David." And he resurrected with affection poets that had come to be pretty much ignored, like Coventry Patmore. He admired Shakespeare most, I think, especially the sonnet (cxvi) with the image of the star "Whose worth's unknown, although his height be taken." (Was that line an inspiration for Frost's "Take Something Like a Star"?)

"Saying" his own poems—from his early to, as he called it, his "Post Late" period—he interspersed the reading with many witty asides. You couldn't tell which remarks were supposed to give hints to his meanings (he often denied that *any* were) and which were calculated to throw dust in our eyes, a phrase he used to Lawrance Thompson (*SL*, p. 529).

Coming to Frost, as I did, mainly through the poetry is, I discovered, a valid way to know him. At Bread Loaf once he threatened that he wouldn't write his own biography—"because I'd lie!" Then his voice dropped and he added, "Don't trust me, trust the poems." I have tried to heed the admonition. And yet the sparkling asides in his talks did, I think, give insights to the poetry. In my writing I have sought to blend these fleeting glimpses with my thoughts about his lines of verse, lines that he meant "for keeps."

Lesley Frost, in her own way (which mixes New England directness with warm affection), has helped me to build a more intimate knowledge of her father than his words alone, even with the "asides," could give. Her reminiscences from her childhood with him, her memories of both her father and her mother, her interpretations of Robert Frost as poet, man and parent, have given a perspective that (though inevitably subjective) has a psychological and emotional sureness unreachable by the detached analysis most of us champion.

While I met Frost personally—in Florida—rather late in his life, I had been in pursuit of his *words* since early in mine. I encountered him first in my high school anthology, where the usual photograph (apparently from his Ann Arbor teaching stint) displayed him with proper dignity in a modest business suit. My earliest impression of him was the (then) conventional grandfather image—simple farmer turned sage and bard. The poems I read confirmed me in a sense that he had escaped the disillusionment, the cynicism that infected much twentieth-century literature.

My picture of him altered sharply when he came to Barnard College, where—in the early fifties—I was an undergraduate. Here he stood, down from the solid granite rock of Vermont, shattering my naive assumptions—hedging on religious issues, playing the nonbeliever. That spring day my quest began in earnest. I was after his deeper meanings. My search took me into the ambiguities of his wisdom—and afield into Emerson, William James, Henri Bergson. Also into the Bible, as I discovered how Frost was steeped in it.

I have come to know Frost as a complex thinker, a complex man—in fact, a highly controversial figure. For decades various critics have tried to label him an agnostic. At times he seemed to wonder if life makes "much sense"—a doubt he offered to reporters shortly before his death (*Interviews*, p. 295). Taken by itself, such a comment suggests that Frost thought life had no ultimate meaning. But a comprehensive look at his lifelong self-revelations in poetry and prose—however guarded they were—reveals to us a deeply religious man.

A more recent problem in Frost criticism involves an *ad hominem* approach to his poetry. Seeing something insidious in Frost's private life, in his character, a few readers have challenged his reputation as a poet. The question is not new in the annals of criticism: Can a bad man be a good poet? In my view, to call Frost, in effect, *bad* is a misguided oversimplification—one that not only lacks compassion but ignores his great complexity. He may have been partly responsible for tragedies in his life. His letters at times delineate a man tormented with guilt. Yet in the letters many other sides of his nature surface as well. And his poetry shows a far-reaching grasp of the problem of good and evil on a universal scale. Frost once asked his friend Rabbi Victor Reichert (the rabbi tells me), "If you can love your neighbor as you love yourself, doesn't that also mean you can hate your neighbor as you hate yourself?" In this remark, and in the poem "Fire and Ice," we discover a man who understood the devastating force of hate in the world. That depth of understanding surely contributed to his greatness as poet.

A few years before he died, Lawrance Thompson wrote me his opinion that Robert Frost's religious belief "provides more problems than any other part of his art—and it happens to be inseparable from his art." Some critics—Yvor Winters, Joseph Warren Beach, George W. Nitchie among them—hold that Frost was an agnostic; put more subtly, "a spiritual drifter." I object to the charge of agnosticism, but here I am concerned with two important influences on Frost's religious thinking: the Bible and the philosophy of Henri Bergson.

Frost's acquaintance with scripture began when he was a child in San Francisco, listening to his Swedenborgian mother read aloud to him. He came, Thompson told me, to be "actually soaked in The Bible." When he was thirty-seven he discovered Bergson's *Creative Evolution* (the English translation, 1911), and his fascination with the French philosopher was immediate. While his initial enthusiasm eventually waned, his thinking—we find in later poems—received an indelible, if indistinct, mark. "Kitty Hawk," "The Grindstone," and "West-Running Brook," for example, are colored by Bergson. They show too the pressure that Frost's reading of Bergson had exerted upon his much earlier and more sustained familiarity with the Bible. He had turned to Bergson, as (in his Harvard days) he had to William James, to buttress what he called his "freethinker" tendencies (Thompson, I, 119). In these two philosophers he noticed a skepticism about orthodox religious structure combined with a need for private faith. Bergson furnished also a way of giving spiritual meaning to the prevalent theories of material evolutionists.

Frost's poetry accommodates Bergson to the Bible, the mainspring of his faith. But defining Frost's religious belief is not an easy task. His fondness for calling himself, ambiguously, "an Old Testament Christian"[1] tends more to confuse than to clarify. Where did he intend the emphasis in the phrase to lie—in the Old Testament or the New? I am convinced he saw in the Bible a continuum of revelation, but his self-definition does not allow one to convert him into a *New* Testament Christian.

He did give clues to the meaning of "Old Testament Christian"— in and out of his poetry. The question of his intent clearly hinges on his view of Christ's role in the total Biblical story. Some might argue that he ignored Christ altogether. He certainly did not. In a deathbed letter (12 January 1963) to his friends Roy and Alma Elliott he was still pondering the relation of Christ to mankind: "Why will the quidnuncs always be hoping for a salvation man will never have from anyone but God? I was just saying today how Christ posed Himself the whole problem and died for it. How can we be just in a world that needs mercy and merciful in a world that needs justice" (*SL*, p. 596).

The way Frost understood Christ is tied directly to his reflections on the meaning of religious salvation and mercy, reflections which at times occupied him intensely. A notebook (unpublished, housed in Boston University Mugar Library) which he kept during the decade of the forties reveals the darker undercurrents of thought that surface as banter in the two masques (1945, 1947). Personal sorrows (the recent deaths of his daughter Marjorie, his wife, and— tragically, by suicide—his son Carol) were no doubt related to his spiritual questioning. Under the guise of humor in the masques he explores troubling religious paradoxes: rational man's vexing "submission to unreason" (*A Masque of Reason*, p. 481), the enigma of "mercy-crossed" justice, and the "irresistible impossibility" of the ideal in Christ's Sermon on the Mount (*A Masque of Mercy*, pp. 510, 512).

A Masque of Mercy draws themes from *both* Testaments of the Bible; *A Masque of Reason* draws only from the Old. But it is significant that both works give their starring roles to *Old* Testament characters, Job and Jonah. We can believe that the "Old Testament Christian" saw strong continuity in the Biblical texts and used his masques to press his point. In fact, he cited with approval Rabbi Victor Reichert's opinion that Judaism and Christianity both "study the same book." The rabbi, Frost contended, "knows the New Testament as well as he knows the Old, and he maintains that all the material in the New can be found in the Old."[2]

In what sense then was Frost a "Christian"? The "Old Testament" modifier is the key. Although the Elliott letter and, two decades earlier, *A Masque of Mercy* show him considering Christ in connection with mercy and salvation, nowhere in his writings does Frost refer to Christ as divine. His attitude toward Christ's divinity remains a puzzle. He seems to have regarded Christ's birth as a unique event in a series of Biblical revelations. The letter suggests that he ranked Christ among all God's *suffering servants*. It sees Christ dying for "the whole problem" (the paradox of justice and mercy), not—by his crucifixion—resolving or alleviating it. And *A Masque of Mercy* extends, to all religious faiths, the cross which man must bear. The "crucifix" in the play has been painted on a cellar wall by "a religious Aztec Indian" (p. 516). It represents—we may conclude from the theme of the play—the eternal crossing of justice by mercy.

I do not think—to go one step further—that Frost took seriously the felix culpa concept: that Adam's fall anticipated mankind's redemption through Christ. While the Eden myth figures prominently in Frost's poetry—from "After Apple-Picking" in his first volume to "Kitty Hawk" in his last—it does not involve the idea of the "fortunate fall." It remains throughout Frost an Old Testament metaphor. His twentieth-century Job in *A Masque of Reason* carries Adam's burden still, his plight unchanged by the message of New Testament gospel. Even "God's own descent/Into flesh . . ." ("Kitty Hawk," p. 435) does not refer in particular to "the coming of the second Adam (the Christ)," as one critic thinks.[3] The image (I will show) is more inclusive. Admittedly, in a 1941 letter to Louis Untermeyer, Frost reports having "good talk" on the "two-word phrase *felix culpa*" with some "intelligent priests in San Antonio." But he protests being "safe from all [the church's] moonshine however significant I can make it seem to myself." Then he gives the Latin expression his typically Emersonian twist: "Felix culpa—that is only the good of evil born in Emerson" (Untermeyer, p. 327).

In the letter Frost may "smile at the easy way the church has of saying deeply," but he was—especially in the forties—deeply concerned with spiritual salvation. His most soul-searching treatment of the subject occurs in "Directive" (1946). Here, Christian overtones (references to "the Grail" and "Saint Mark," p. 379) may lead us to suspect Frost of conversion from the Old Testament to the New. But he explicitly denied that the road to salvation, in the poem, is narrowly Christian. He told Hyde Cox that the narrator-guide "is not offering any general salvation—nor Christian salvation in particular." The journey back to childlike innocence, to a state of *wholeness*, may, he implied, lead down the path mapped out by Christ. He emphasized, though, that "the key word in the whole poem is source—whatever source it is." "The source might even be a conventional religion . . . but religion is most of all valuable when something original has been contributed to it."[4]

Frost's comments on "Directive" neither acknowledge nor deny a personal belief in Christ as saviour. What *is* significant is Frost's concept of salvation as actively pursued, not passively received; granted to one at a time, not wholesale to all comers. The route the traveler in the poem must follow—to become "whole again beyond confusion" (p. 379)—is solitary.

> And if you're lost enough to find yourself
> By now, pull in your ladder road behind you
> And put a sign up CLOSED to all but me (p. 378).

As for any solace Frost might have sought in salvation through Christ, we have—to my knowledge—only one clear statement. His notebook from the forties takes a dim view of the idea: "Christ sacrificed himself rather to show us that we must sacrifice ourselves on the altar of his impossible ideals than to suffer vicariously to save us from sacrifice. No atonement/quite vicarious."

The notebook further confirms Frost's view of the two Testaments as sequential; it interprets Jonah as a forerunner of Christ in the divine drama of *crossed justice*. "God seems first to have become self conscious in his mercy," Frost observes, "in the book of Jonah." The entry illuminates his casting an Old Testament figure in his "New Testament" masque. Like *A Masque of Mercy*, the notebook focuses on the difficulty of living up to the Sermon on the Mount: "God breaks us on his Sermon, then gives us Heaven if we own up broken." Grimly in the notebook, more playfully in the masque, Frost recognizes the moral weight that Christ's Sermon places upon the *individual*. Frost's spiritual tough-mindedness resisted "mass mercy," as Paul calls it (*A Masque of Mercy*, p. 509), and any *general* kind of salvation—Christian or other. He was unsympathetic toward all neat theological formulae, and he had reservations even about Emerson's facile "good of evil born." Emerson, Frost pointed out, "couldn't bring himself to say the evil of good born" (*SL*, p. 584).[5]

Frost shunned religious doctrine and shied away from church ritual. "I don't go to church," he once quipped, "but I look in the window."[6] In 1946 he ventured further; he went inside his friend Rabbi Reichert's temple in Cincinnati and delivered a "sermon."[7] Apparently, he wouldn't let "a foolish consistency" (to quote Emerson correctly) keep him out of church altogether. On the whole, though, he probably shared Keeper's sentiment: "I'd rather be lost in the woods/Than found in church" (*A Masque of Mercy*, p. 513). Keeper very likely speaks for Frost also when he explains that his "approach to Christ" is "more through Palestine" than "through Rome" (p. 513). In a 1947 letter to Roy Elliott (*SL*, pp. 525–526) Frost makes essentially the same point: "My approach to the New Testament is rather through Jerewsalem than through Rome and Canterbury." We may infer from these remarks that Frost was less attracted by (New Testament) theology than he was drawn to dark Biblical mysteries. His sermon, for instance, dwells on "the fear of God" and the inadequacy of "human wisdom." His masques delve into the meaning of human sorrow and the acceptability, to God, of human sacrifice.

Following in Emerson's footsteps, Frost was an unorthodox believer. (He named Emerson and William James as the thinkers who had influenced him most.)[8] Both Emerson and Frost were symbolists. That is, they considered the physical universe to be a "constant symbol" (Frost's phrase, *SP*, p. 23) of spiritual reality. But Emerson's universe is virtually "transparent," as he claims in *Nature*: "The visible world and the relation of its parts, is the dial plate of the invisible." In Frost's universe the earthly and the extraterrestrial are interchangeable; it is hard to tell fallen star from building stone ("A Star in a Stoneboat"). Spiritual insights are brief and partial, experienced as "A Passing Glimpse" (p. 248) or "an intimation, a shot of ray" ("One More Brevity," p. 421). Ultimate truth is wreathed in "mist," veiled by "smoke" ("A Cabin in the Clearing," p. 414).

Frost and Emerson are the intellectual heirs of American Puritanism and the typological tradition. They open the book of nature in the way the Puritans turned to scripture, as a compendium of spiritual "types" or symbols. Frost has the firmer hold on the real world. With Emerson, "facts"—as Hawthorne once confided in his diary (*American Notebooks*, entry for 15 August 1842)—"seem to melt away and become unsubstantial in his grasp." Frost, by contrast, believed that "a poet must lean hard on facts, so hard, sometimes, that they hurt."[9] He chided Emerson for being "too Platonic about evil" (*SP*, p. 118). Frost's universe is more opaque than Emerson's; his vision, his way of perceiving, is darker.

Frost's essential vision is, however, difficult to pinpoint. If it is not tragic, or "terrifying"—as Lionel Trilling labelled it in his controversial talk at the poet's eighty-fifth birthday celebration[10]—neither is it Dantesque. For Frost's universe, like that of Henri Bergson, is continually being *made*; God has not thought it through in advance. And the earth therefore is not a stage setting for a preconceived divine comedy, climaxing in the coming of Christ. Frost viewed life on earth as a spiritual trial ("The Trial by Existence") where the conditions of judgment are undisclosed (*A Masque of Reason*);

where the quality of mercy often seems capricious (*A Masque of Mercy*).

Frost's God has a sense of humor, it is true. He has His "great big [joke]" on man ("[Forgive, O Lord . . .]," p. 428), and He enjoys playing divine "hide-and-seek" ("Revelation," p. 19). But He remains the inscrutable "Secret . . . in the middle" of Frost's universe ("The Secret Sits," p. 362). He is like the mysterious Old Testament Jehovah of whirlwind and burning bush—a God of conundrums. By way of New Testament analogy, He speaks through parable, "so the wrong ones . . . can't get saved, as Saint Mark says they mustn't" (p. 379). The line, from "Directive," is based on the theory (advanced in Saint Mark's Gospel) that Christ's parables were intended to make it harder, not—as generally thought—easier to understand Him. (Frost was delighted with this idea when Hyde Cox pointed it out to him.)[11] Though Frost's God is in hiding, he does have unmistakably "human" traits—qualities discernible in his handiwork. Stated conversely—and more accurately, as Frost looked at creation—man has *divine* characteristics: chiefly, a sense of humor, a free will, and the courage to use his freedom.

In "Kitty Hawk," the central poem of *In the Clearing*, Frost considers man decidedly God's creature. The poem sums up Frost's thinking about the role of mankind on earth. Its significance in Frost's last book is hinted at in his earlier intention—at the time of a 1959 interview (*Saturday Review*, 21 March)—to title his upcoming volume "The Great Misgiving," a phrase that occurs in the poem. (An earlier version of "Kitty Hawk" had already been published in *The Atlantic Monthly*, November 1957. There the phrase appears as "the soul's misgiving.") His subsequent decision to call the volume—which came out in 1962—*In the Clearing* (echoing "A Cabin in the Clearing," included there) was very likely prompted by his recognition of poetry as "a clarification of life" (*SP*, p. 18). The title rounds out a lifelong metaphor that can be traced back to *North of Boston* (1914)—in the image of "wait[ing] to watch the water clear" ("The Pasture," p. 1).

Most careful readers agree that "Kitty Hawk" is a crucial statement of Frost's belief. They disagree, however, over its meaning. It has been interpreted—as *A Masque of Mercy* was some decades ago [12]—as a profession of Christianity (the New Testament variety). At the other extreme, it has been read as a secular credo. Wade Van Dore told me, when I visited him on the gulf coast of Florida recently, that he sees in the poem Frost's "turning to science as man's salvation." (Van Dore, poet and naturalist—and a friend of Frost since 1922—had already said, "I'm not as much interested in Frost's religion as you are.") I teased him a bit, asking if he thought Frost had ever been *against* science. Our conversation got side-tracked when the telephone rang. The point I was about to make, though, was that I think "Kitty Hawk" does celebrate science—and man's ingenuity—and, behind it all, a *divine experiment*. The poem is a tribute to scientific enterprise, epitomized in the flight of the Wright brothers' biplane, which propelled man into the Space Age. But the lines that Frost chose from "Kitty Hawk" for his frontispiece to *In the Clearing* take *experimentation* beyond the laboratory and the workshop. Before the Wrights went up, God had to come down. The frontispiece begins:

> But God's own descent
> Into flesh was meant
> As a demonstration
> That the supreme merit
> Lay in risking spirit
> In substantiation (p. 435).

Not long ago, Father Arthur MacGillivray (Boston College) showed me a copy of the *Complete Poems* that Frost gave him in May 1958. "Kitty Hawk" was not, of course, printed in the volume, but Frost penned, inside the cover, the six lines quoted above. Although the poem had already been called "Kitty Hawk" when it appeared in 1957, Frost added over his inscription, as a heading, "The Risk." Obviously the lines were important to him in 1958, and still in the 1962 frontispiece. And his writing them out for a Jesuit priest raises the question of their religious appropriateness. Clearly they deal with the idea of incarnation. But what kind of incarnation?

A clue to this question may be found in the heading, "The Risk." I do not think incarnation here is exclusively Christian, although certainly I would include that interpretation. The phrase "Risking spirit/In substantiation" (p. 435) should be read in the light of some lines from the next stanza in "Kitty Hawk," lines which describe the risk as an ongoing process:

> Spirit enters flesh
> And for all it's worth
> Charges into earth
> In birth after birth
> Ever fresh and fresh (pp. 435–436).

"Kitty Hawk" interprets God's risk of spirit *vicariously* (in the way Frost's notebook views Christ's crucifixion)—as a "demonstration" (p. 435) of the highest form of behavior available to man. Man is enjoined to repeat God's performance. The poem implies also that God repeats His own performance, "In birth after birth" (p. 436). The two kinds of repetition blend Biblical and Bergsonian elements. God's first entrusting His spirit to the material universe— the initial act of creation—is depicted in the Book of Genesis. *Creative Evolution* paints with a broader brush. There the élan vital— life force—continually reenacts the drama of creation in a universe that is perpetually evolving through the free-wheeling intercourse of spirit and matter.

"Kitty Hawk" expands the Bergsonian drama by introducing the element of risk, on a theological plane. Actually, the theme of risk recurs in Frost in various guises. (It has a philosophical parallel in William James's taking the plunge of faith, with insufficient knowledge; and Frost found James's *The Will to Believe* congenial to his own thinking.) Risk has personal resonances in Frost's father's propensity for gambling—the origin, perhaps, of the poker-game metaphor of "In Divés' Dive," with its philosophical overtones. The idea surfaces also in "Two Tramps in Mud Time," where "work," at its best—when it unites "love and need"—is called "play for mortal stakes" (p. 277). To gamble is to put up a bold front, even to the verge of recklessness—especially when the stakes are life itself. The stars we once thought fixed in crystal spheres can suddenly arc crazily, testing our nerve ("Bravado"):

> Have I not walked without an upward look
> Of caution under stars that very well
> Might not have missed me when they shot and fell?
> It was a risk I had to take—and took (p. 383).

In religion, too, taking a risk demands courage, the daring to be-lieve in the unseen—even the intellectual audacity to question tra-ditional belief. Reginald Cook reports that Frost called Emerson "profoundly subvertive," "a great disturber of the peace." Frost admired Emerson's wit, his "sense of freedom" and his bold play at "the dangerous edge of things."[13]

For Frost, risktaking was a moral imperative, following a prece-dent set forth by God. "Someone asked me," he observed—in con-nection with "Kitty Hawk," during his 1959 interview—"if I thought God *could* take a chance. I said it looked to me as if he had —right from the start."

Both Frost and Bergson insist upon the preeminence of freedom in the creative process and, consequently, upon the universal inter-action of order and chance. But Bergson seems more optimistic about the progressive realization of cosmic design, through man's increasing intellectual development. In Frost, the spectre of the Biblical Fall darkens human prospects. It casts its long shadow east of Eden, where man plays life's game of chance while God, un-daunted, bets on him to win. Frost's notebook from the forties ap-plies the gambling metaphor to Christ's Sermon on the Mount: "God too is out to win. . . . (In one view The Sermon makes the game like the one at Monte Carlo all in favor of the house.)" As we learn in *A Masque of Reason*, Frost recognized that even a God-rigged contest is not a sure thing. In the masque, God concedes to Job:

> Virtue may fail and wickedness succeed.
> 'Twas a great demonstration we put on (p. 475).

Job's scene was indeed "splendid" and he was "flattered proud/To have been in on anything with [God]" (p. 481). He was only one actor, though, in the human drama; through the ages, Satan hangs around the casino, waiting for *his* opportunities to change man's luck.

Frost, with his Biblical emphasis, identifies a disturbing paradox in life which Bergson tends to ignore: risk of spiritual loss is inherent in man's freedom—is inseparable from material progress. The risk is reciprocal between God and man. *God must risk creating man free to fall,* in order that He may be *free* to save man. Concurrently, *man must risk acting freely* with no assurance of God's salvation. The dual risk makes earth a trial ground for man's individual soul, and, ultimately, for the testing of God's spirit in material form.

The Eden myth in Frost's poetry symbolizes the "chance" God took in Genesis—an Old Testament risk that is perpetuated in the New. Adam's plucking the fruit of the tree of knowledge gave him a foretaste of mankind's spiritual penetration—after God's example, according to "Kitty Hawk"—into matter. The word *substantiation* in that poem goes for pay-dirt. It has the force of an affirmation, a confirmation, of the spirit, with all the attendant danger. In the 1959 interview Frost speaks of the "fear that we won't be able to substantiate the spirit." With "science plunging deeper into matter . . . into the smallness of particles and . . . into the hugeness of space," we are all left with a "great misgiving"—"that the spirit shall be lost." Yet, in a universe where freedom is a guiding principle, risk of failure is inevitable.

"Kitty Hawk" projects the Biblical metaphor of the Fall into the Space Age—an age when, with aid of telescope and microscope, human knowledge reaches ever further into galactic and molecular space. Scientific (from the Latin *scire, to know*) investigation is viewed in the continuum of risk initiated by Adam's yielding to temptation. The poem (p. 435) argues that

> All the science zest
> To materialize
> By on-penetration
> Into earth and skies
> (Don't forget the latter
> Is but further matter)

contains both promise and peril.

Frost has sometimes been accused of being against science. "The Egg and the Machine," for example, removed from the corpus of his poetry, might lead to this assumption. It was not science itself, but man's use of it, that Frost was wary of. "It's knowing what to do with things that counts" ("At Woodward's Gardens," p. 294). Not technology only, in Frost's opinion, but all knowledge—mis-used—can lead man morally astray. Human probing into the ma-terial universe follows, symbolically, "God's own descent/Into flesh" (p. 435), and it incurs a similar risk in the sustaining of spirit.

The Book of Genesis provides Frost with an appropriate meta-phor to develop the relationship of spirit to matter. "The spirit of God moved upon the face of the waters" when "the earth was without form, and void." Like the Old Testament writers, Frost believed that an informing spirit is needed to give structure to chaos. "The only materialist," he said in 1931 at Amherst, "is the man who gets lost in his material without a gathering metaphor to throw it into shape and order. He is the lost soul" (*SP*, p. 41). Long before writing "Kitty Hawk," Frost probably had seen a similarity be-tween God's role and man's as bringers of order. And, as his "the lost soul" suggests, he evidently connected order—in poetry and elsewhere—with man's salvation.

Frost's letter to Roy Elliott (c. 21 February 1938) jests about "us[ing] poetry for the salvation of souls" (*SL*, p. 460). His tone only partly conceals his firm conviction that "The Figure a Poem [or a life] Makes" (*SP*, p. 17) constitutes its meaning—saves it. Thus God's initial "descent" in "Kitty Hawk" (p. 435) demon-strates vicariously not only the risk required of man but also the opportunity open to him for salvation. In life and art, "a gathering metaphor" brings *wholeness*, leads to a *healing* of shattered psyche and broken spirit.

"The Holiness of Wholeness," title of the next-to-last section of "Kitty Hawk," plays upon etymology to indicate the integral bond-ing of body and spirit. ("Whole," "heal," and "holy" derive from a common Old English root, *hal*.) The section places human salva-tion under a divine "covenant" which provides man the chance to save himself through metaphor—specifically, through synecdoche, through a *part-for-the-whole* grasp of reality. God permits man, in the face of cosmic vastness, to discover meaning; grants him a way, in "our [chaotic] dump of learning," of "Getting thought ex-pressed" (pp. 441–442).

> But the comfort is
> In the covenant
> We may get control,
> If not of the whole,
> Of at least some part
> Where not too immense,
> So by craft or art
> We can give the part
> Wholeness in a sense (p. 441).

Like the Biblical Yahweh, God here has a compact with man. Man has been *loosed* into material space, but he need not become *lost* in it.

In "Kitty Hawk" man is given a special place in the hierarchy of creation. Focusing on the Wright brothers' flight, the poem affirms the upward thrust of all human effort: "Keep on elevating. . . . Let's keep starring man/In the royal role" (p. 441). The differentiation between the human and lower species has, of course, a Biblical parallel: God's giving man (in Genesis) "dominion over the fish of the sea, and over the fowl of the air . . . and over all the earth." The distinction also has Bergsonian resonances. *Creative Evolution* separates man *in kind* "from the rest of the animal world." Man's "consciousness breaks the [evolutionary] chain" and sets him free; he is therefore "the 'term' and the 'end' of evolution." "Every human work," Bergson stresses, "in which there is invention . . . brings something new into the world." In "Kitty Hawk" too, man's intellect shapes his universe—"by craft or art" (p. 441) launching planes and poems. His plastic imagination releases "one mighty charge/On our human part/Of the soul's ethereal/Into the material" (p. 436).

"Kitty Hawk" shares with *Creative Evolution* a vision of matter invigorated by spirit; an insistence upon man's total freedom; faith in the power of the human mind to collaborate in cosmic order. But just as Bergson tends to play down the element of spiritual risk, he likewise bypasses the problem of evil, of human sin, that, Biblically —and in "Kitty Hawk"—is a condition of God's creating Adam, a being (in Milton's phrase) "Sufficient to have stood, though free to fall." In other Frost poems—for example, "The Grindstone"—the Eden myth adds a rather sombre dimension to man's hope of accomplishment. "Kitty Hawk" is more sanguine about the human condition, despite man's "great misgiving" in the pursuit of knowledge. At the end of the poem, Frost does seem—as Wade Van Dore thinks—to turn to science; a prayer of "thanks" is offered to the "God of the machine . . . Some still think is Satan" (pp. 442–443). Frost, however, had long been a (qualified) "friend" of science, as he affirms in "The Constant Symbol," where he offers a "soft impeachment" to remind science that it, like poetry and philosophy, "is simply made of metaphor" (*SP*, p. 24). The closing lines of "Kitty Hawk" signal no conversion in their author. They merely reaffirm what he had long believed: that the engines of technology are ignited by a divine spark in man's mind.

While Bergson tends to gloss over the way evil functions in the world, and to depersonalize "God"—as Frost does not—there is a great deal in *Creative Evolution* that evidently appealed to Frost's thinking. The cooperation of man in a divine experiment that combines accident and design seemed to meet some psychological need. Frost liked to watch unpredictability operate in conjunction with order. "I like a coincidence," he wrote in a 1912 letter, "almost as well as an incongruity" (*SL*, pp. 45–46). In his life and his poetry, he enjoyed discovering form in unforeseen ways.

The letter, in the winter of 1912, was addressed to Susan Hayes Ward, literary editor of the *Independent* and one of few people around the turn of the century to respond to Frost's talent. (The magazine published "My Butterfly" in 1894; "The Trial by Existence" in 1906.) The letter describes a doppelgänger that Frost experienced in the New Hampshire woods. Approaching the spot where two snow-covered paths ("neither . . . much travelled") converged, "I felt as if I was going to meet my own image in a slanting mirror. Or say I felt . . . as if we [the real traveler and his double] were two images about to float together with the uncrossing of someone's eyes." Oddly, the year 1912 was to find Frost at a crossroad in his career. A few months later, his flip of a coin sent him—a little known poet—to England, rather than to Vancouver, British Columbia. We know in retrospect that the apparent gamble led to the publication of his first two volumes abroad. A superficially inconsequential act—like some decision at a fork in a road—"made all the difference" ("The Road Not Taken," p. 105).

As artist too, Frost liked to be surprised by form. A poem "has an outcome that though unforeseen was predestined from the first image of the original mood." The ending "must be more felt than seen ahead like prophecy" (*SP*, pp. 18–19). He let design evolve gradually, as "Pertinax" tells us:

> Let chaos storm!
> Let cloud shapes swarm!
> I wait for form (p. 308).

The principle of *waiting* applied to individual poems and to his poetry as a whole. He looked "backward over the accumulation of years," he told Whit Burnett in 1942, "to see how many poems I could find towards some one meaning it might seem absurd to have had in advance, . . . to learn if there had been any divinity shaping my ends and I had been building better than I knew" (*SL*, p. 501).

Did Frost really expect to find the hand of God outlining the "figure" his poems made? Perhaps he did. For he was not the "refined modern agnostic" that Joseph Warren Beach once called him.[14] Frost was not altogether lacking in "superstition" at the highest level: "the first step in the descent of the spirit into the material-human at the risk of the spirit" (*SP*, p. 118). He might, furthermore, have turned to Bergson for a rationale. *Creative Evolution* may have led Frost to consider man *as poet* (by derivation, as *maker*) to be a vehicle through whom cosmic order is realized.

Yet Frost did not claim that his poetry embodied any grand design. He merely wondered—in the Burnett letter—whether "any fragment of a figure [could] be discerned among the apparently random lesser designs of the several poems" (*SL*, p. 501). With Bergson too, order evolves hit-or-miss. The élan vital is a "centre from which worlds shoot out like rockets in a fire-works display . . . a continuity of shooting out. . . . God thus defined, has nothing of the already made; He is unceasing life, action, freedom."

The randomness in Bergson's scheme survives in Frost's accommodation of *accident* to the more traditional concept of an infallible divine plan. In Frost (as in Bergson) form tends toward comprehensiveness. But it is incomplete; it is organic, changing, growing out of a series of coincidences. Order is continually approached through an apparently haphazard fulfillment of divine "purpose" ("Accidentally on Purpose," p. 425):

> Grant me intention, purpose, and design—
> That's near enough for me to the Divine.

The lines do not mean that the way man tries to arrange events in patterns—or shapes poetic images—furnishes a workable substitute for an outmoded belief in myth. They mean, quite literally, "near enough": the evidence of "design," however minimal, in an unfinished universe is as close as man can come to knowing God.

"Design," Lawrance Thompson wrote me (22 September 1970), "is a sacred word to [Frost], and he's being tricky in his poem entitled 'Design.' " (I had questioned its if-y conclusion.) I have come to agree that Frost did look upon design as something sacred. I think now that the final line of the poem, while deliberately ambiguous, *underscores* (not undermines) the premise inherent in its title. "If design govern in a thing so small," so small as that particular sonnet, what might be the *larger* implications of form-making? "Assorted characters of death and blight" may weave only "design of darkness to appall" (p. 302). But when we observe *any* configuration in natural events, we observe the presence of purpose in the universe. Similarly, in *A Masque of Reason*, Job concludes that even a form that evil can take—"devilish ingenuity of torture"—bears the imprint of God: "there is nothing You are not behind" (p. 482).

Frost's penchant for contraries probably accounts in large measure for the way he was drawn to the cosmic tensions in Bergson's philosophy. The juxtaposition of accident and order, the interpenetration of spirit and matter satisfied the dual leanings of a poet who was part mystic (on his Swedenborgian side of the family), part empiricist. The conclusions of materialist thinkers were insufficient. Frost looked to *Creative Evolution* to help explain an impulse that *resists* the downward flow of matter into—as in "West-Running Brook"—"the abyss's void." In that poem, "there is something" which defies the "death/That spends to nothingness"; there is a "backward motion toward the source,/Against the stream." And Frost hints that the (spiritual) countercurrent is "sacred" (pp. 259–260). (Bergson would have noted a *design* in the contrary currents of the brook, but he probably would avoid the religious ring of "sacred.")

The reverential tone throughout Frost's poetry is solidly grounded in his reading of the Bible, and it appears that his interest in Bergson is primarily on a philosophical plane. We can guess from "West-Running Brook" that he had already found an emphasis on tensions in Heraclitus's idea of the perpetual strife which resolves itself into harmony. Yet *Creative Evolution*, beyond all its polarities, appealed to Frost in another way: by helping to confirm his belief in the value of form-making as a human endeavor. To compose a poem is to join in spirit, he liked to think, with a greater creative power in the universe—call it (we may) the élan vital, or (he would prefer) God. All acts of ordering "stroke faith the right way," he put it in an open letter to *The Amherst Student* in 1935 (*SP*, p. 106). Sometimes he hid his belief in form behind a pun. "There's nothing so composing as composition," I heard him say toward the end of his life. Or he might bury his conviction under a homely image, like Silas—in "The Death of the Hired Man"—building his load of hay in careful bundles. He might inject a casual aside: "Nothing not built with hands of course is sacred" ("New Hampshire," p. 171). But the Amherst letter reveals, a bit more, his seriousness about the art of composition—about making "a basket, a letter, a garden, a room, an idea, a picture, a poem. For these we haven't to get a team together before we can play" (*SP*, p. 107). Frost sees all kinds of *composing* as aspects of the existence of "good in the world." He points to "the suggestions of form in the rolling clouds of nature" and asserts that such discovered structure "admits of," indeed "calls for," our imitation (*SP*, p. 106). The universe itself evokes man's talent for design.

In Frost, man's relationship to the creative process is organic and reciprocal. Although man's *vision* of design is partial, he is an *agent* in its operation. He embodies both its vital and its degenerative tendencies. He is indissolubly wed to his world. "West-Running Brook" talks about this union, about mankind's interaction with natural forces; and about human marriage, human discourse.

Cast as a dialogue between husband and wife, the poem demonstrates the principle of contrariety in its framework and its central image. "The black stream, catching on a sunken rock,/Flung backward on itself in one white wave" (p. 258) is an emblem of opposing material and spiritual currents in the universe. The lovers' quarrel over the interpretation of the phenomenon illustrates conflicting modes of apprehension. Ultimately, they arrive at a position which goes beyond reconciliation. They come by different routes to a place where contradiction itself is a source of enrichment. Their apparently divergent faculties of intellection (the male factor) and intuition (the female factor) bring them to deeper understanding. Such an interdependence between the two faculties had been described by Henri Bergson, who saw the "two procedures" working in "opposite direction[s]." "The philosopher" rejects intuition (he wrote) "once he has received from it the impetus," then proceeds self-reliantly along the paths of logic toward a conclusion—until, needing a firmer "foothold," he brings himself "into touch with intuition again."

Initially in the poem, the wife indulges what seems a private fantasy. Humanizing the countercurrents, she guesses "It must be the brook/Can trust itself to go by contraries"—the way lovers do in marriage (p. 258). She imagines that the stream is "waving to us with a wave/To let us know it hears me" (p. 258). Her matter-of-fact mate gently rebukes her. He counters her fancy with a mild disparagement about "lady-land" (p. 258) and threatens to drop the subject: "It is your brook! I have no more to say" (p. 259).

For all his level-headedness, though, the man already has shown his own inclination for mythmaking:

> "That wave's been standing off this jut of shore
> Ever since rivers, I was going to say,
> Were made in heaven . . ." (p. 258).

Less sentimental than his wife, he too apparently enjoys pressing physical fact for moral significance. His tendency to symbolize moves toward intellectual abstraction; hers is homespun and intuitive.

Coaxed after a moment to break his silence, he brims with analogies. He reads in the crosscurrents of the brook a metaphor of both waste and resistance to waste in the universal scheme. He picks up from her initial idea about "contraries" (a case in point for Bergson's theory that intuition sets logic in motion), and muses at length on the downward drift of things, and the reverse impulse in life to "Get back to the beginning of beginnings" (p. 259).

His long, eloquent speech spans centuries of thought, drawing upon the Bible and biology (the origin of life in water); upon Heraclitus and Bergson (existence as perpetual flux); upon the materialism of Lucretius (the impending dissolution of nature). He talks in sad Lucretian tones of the disintegration of matter. The stream becomes all life flowing toward oblivion—"even substance lapsing unsubstantial" (p. 259).

Then suddenly he rallies; he checks the downward sweep. He sees in the very "cataract of death . . . some strange resistance"— "Not just a swerving, but a throwing back" (p. 259).

At a public reading in 1949, Lawrance Thompson relates, Frost paused after "Not just a swerving" and said parenthetically to the audience, "as in Lucretius." Here the poem turns from the influence of that ancient Roman to the dominance of Bergson, to his view of the universe as a composite of "physical" and "psychical existence" —mutually dependent, dynamic opposites. One force, he thought, is the inverse of the other. If materiality tends toward physical decline, then, he speculates, must not psychic energy *retard* (though not stop) the downward flow of matter? The stream in "West-Running Brook" behaves in Bergsonian fashion:

> And the white water rode the black forever,
> Not gaining but not losing . . . (p. 258).

The wave that catches on the rock cannot reverse the mainstream, but it can impede its deathward course.

The husband in the poem interprets the resistant action as a symbol of man's spiritual essence, as something linking him to his origins —to "that in water we were from" (p. 259). (Is the reference to

338 An Old Testament Christian

primordial slime? Or to the spirit of God that, in Genesis, moved upon the face of the deep?) The resistance operates throughout nature; it reaches its height in mankind. The husband calls the "backward motion"

> The tribute of the current to the source.
> It is from this in nature we are from.
> It is most us (p. 260).

"West-Running Brook" and *Creative Evolution* alike wrestle with the concept of immortality, but the tones are vastly different. Bergson thinks metaphorically of "the whole of humanity, in space and in time," as "one immense army galloping . . . [to] clear the most formidable obstacles, perhaps even death." The husband's eloquence in "West-Running Brook," by contrast, is understated and quietly evocative. The militant clamor, the (implied) human pride with which Bergson storms the gates of immortality is far different from the piety that binds "current" back to "source" in Frost's poem. (The word *religion* means *a binding back*.) The brook's "wave" (p. 258) of resistance is not a collective siege, but—characteristic of Frost—an *individual* "tribute"—"As if regret were in it and were sacred" (p. 259).

At the conclusion of her husband's philosophical excursion, the woman deferentially concedes, "Today will be the day/You said so." He replies, also conciliatory, "No, today will be the day/You said the brook was called West-Running Brook." (She had suggested the name at the start.) The closing line, the wife's, resolves the dramatic tension: "Today will be the day of what we both said" (p. 260). The integrity of what each has contributed is to be preserved, commemorated. In Bergsonian terms, "the philosopher"—the husband—has regained his foothold of intuition.

The wife's final comment is not mere verbal politeness, for their underlying agreement is substantial. Her romantic notion, earlier, of their "both be[ing] married to the brook" (p. 258) is corroborated in her husband's vision of an all-embracing stream of life that "flows beside us . . . between us, over us, and *with* us" (p. 259). There is subdued irony in the way he has spent his efforts in discursive logic merely to confirm the point she had made with a simple image. She had interpreted natural sign language (the brook's "waving" to them) instinctively. His elaborate speculation, finally, puts him in a position compatible with her seeming foolishness.

Creative Evolution treats intellection and intuition in the abstract. "West-Running Brook" clothes the abstractions in flesh, joining the human pair to a grand design that "Can trust itself to go by contraries" (p. 258).

Robert Frost confronted life on its own often illogical terms, seeing, thinking, speaking, writing "by contraries." He found in Bergson, especially, a rationale for his vocation of poet, a maker of form. Yet despite his dedication to form—"form true to any chance bit of true life," he told Sidney Cox in 1929 (*SL*, p. 361)—he was peculiarly skeptical of "finished art." "I thank the Lord for crudity which is rawness, which is raw material, . . . the part of life not yet worked up into form, or at least not worked all the way up." (*SL*, p. 465). We taste the Bergsonian flavor here; a perpetually evolving creation is forever incomplete. If life itself is unfinished—that is, imperfect—how much perfection ought we to expect of art? At Bread Loaf in 1962 I heard Frost call Shakespeare's genius "slapdash." Years earlier (1921) he wrote Louis Untermeyer: "the only great art is inesthetic" (Untermeyer, p. 136).

Polished form, to an artist, is an abstract ideal. In practice, he must accept some unhoned roughness. The limitations of perfection in art, in life, are examined in "The Grindstone," which asks metaphorically: when is a "blade" ground fine enough? Mythic in scope, the poem brings into partial alignment Bergsonian theory and the Biblical story of the Fall. It places man the maker in the shadow of Adam's transgression and weighs, in sacrifice and suffering, the cost of human endeavor.

The poem is as obstinate in yielding meaning as the cantankerous grindstone is in granting satisfaction to the man who cranks it. As lines and grindstone grind laboriously along, though, sparks fly off at odd angles: ideas about time and so-called progress, about creativity, about discord and destruction, about striving, toil, and woe.

The basic metaphor draws upon a grindstone theory of the universe which Frost attributed to Sir William Herschel; the grindstone is intended as an analogue for the turning world.[15] Getting off to a deliberately "cumbersome" start, the poem backs into its sub-

ject by way of participial phrase and circumlocution. Irregular
rhythm intensifies the roughness of motion:

> Having a wheel and four legs of its own
> Has never availed the cumbersome grindstone
> To get it anywhere that I can see (p. 188).

Not all wheel-spinning, the lines suggest, can be considered progress.

> I wondered what machine of ages gone
> This represented an improvement on.
> For all I knew it may have sharpened spears
> And arrowheads itself (p. 189).

The stubborn grindstone, "worn" by usage to "an oblate/Spheroid
[like the planet earth] that kicked and struggled in its gait" (p.
190), had been rendered less effective through the passage of time
than its ancient predecessor which "sharpened" primitive weapons.
If scientific advance is measured by sophisticated modern warfare,
then the presumption of progress is indeed questionable.

The grindstone world continues to rotate on its axis, but how far
has mankind come from prehistoric times? The effort of cranking
takes its toll in suffering:

> I gave it the preliminary spin,
> And poured on water (tears it might have been). . . .

Man's burden of sorrow is symbolized in the machine's location:
"It stands beside the same old apple tree" (p. 189). The shade from
the tree—like the darkness cast from the Garden of Eden—falls
upon the grindstone as it turns season after season.

> The shadow of the apple tree is thin
> Upon it now; its feet are fast in snow (p. 189).

In the late world of winter the grindstone is still "standing in the
yard/Under a ruinous live apple tree" (p. 189). The conjunction
of thought in "ruinous live" is curious. Though full of rot, the tree
survives—a living emblem of decay and mortality. The blight in-
fecting the tree spreads ruin to things under its apparently protec-
tive, potentially pernicious "shadow."

Stylistically intricate, the poem is also ponderous in overall structure. Frost abandons his more familiar dramatic beginning (the

initial "I" that launches directly into action). The opening stanza—twenty-five lines—does little but set the scene for the drama of the second. Moreover that action is distanced, introduced as a glimpse of a summer long ago. Some vague sense of Adam's Fall seems to jar memory, as if by associative guilt; the man tries to deny any significance (for him) of the grindstone. It "Has nothing any more to do with me,"

> Except that I remember how of old
> One summer day, all day I drove it hard,
> And someone mounted on it rode it hard,
> And he and I between us ground a blade (p. 189).

His denial is refuted by a haunting reminiscence that crowds in upon his consciousness and spills forth, in stanza two, remote and dreamlike—a kind of ancestral reverie from some primeval time. The nameless "someone" emerges as a mysterious "Father-Time" figure who peers "funny-eyed" (p. 190) over "spectacles that glowed" (p. 189). Embodiment of human mortality, he is a natural antagonist to the man driving the wheel. It is a dubious cooperative venture, for the design of the grindstone requires that the two men work at odds. The harder the one presses the blade against the wheel, the more slowly it turns, and the more arduous becomes the other's cranking. The turning grindstone, like the earth in its rotation, is a measure of our wearing out. The time a man *spends* on a task *expends* his energy, bringing him closer to death. (Recall the opposition of life and time in "West-Running Brook": "Our life runs down in sending up the clock," p. 259.) Life, whatever its rewards, eventually grinds us down; suffering and sacrifice are inherent. Time, not man, has the last word.

> I wondered who it was the man thought ground—
> The one who held the wheel back or the one
> Who gave his life to keep it going round?
> I wondered if he really thought it fair
> For him to have the say when we were done.
> Such were the bitter thoughts to which I turned (p. 190).

There is further irony in this drama of grinding: not only must the two men, in performing a job both want to complete, work against each other, but their objective is of doubtful merit. They are sharpening the blade of Time's "scythe," symbolic instrument of human destruction. A moral cloud hangs over their endeavor; the end-product can be used for either good or evil. (Time's being "armed" indicates *his* malicious intent.) A scythe, like any other blade, is either a tool or a weapon depending on the vantage point. It may help a man to maintain a farm, but it may also be turned against him; and to the living grass, of course, the scythe is a weapon. (In "The Objection to Being Stepped On," a humorous reversal of swords-into-ploughshares, "an unemployed hoe" delivers a sharp crack to the head, p. 450.)

Good and evil throughout "The Grindstone" are inextricably intertwined. So also are harmony and discord, creativity and destruction. Two antagonists "pass the afternoon . . . grinding discord out of a grindstone" (p. 190) to make a blade perfect. Looked at one way, the "gritty tune" (p. 190) of their grinding tends toward a creative, harmonious goal. The finer the blade becomes, the less raucous will be the "tune." But from another perspective their aim is destructive, for to grind a finer blade is to produce a sharper, more lethal weapon.

Such a network of moral ambiguities leaves finally unreconciled Bergsonian theory and Biblical myth. If creative evolution leads toward higher levels of cosmic order, the story of the Fall lends a darker coloration to mankind's lot. In the last stanza, the moral center of the poem, the philosophic emphasis is distinctly Biblical rather than Bergsonian. Here it develops that the two men labor in vain, since they strive for an unfeasible ideal. Without knowing, the grinders may be "only wasting precious blade" (p. 190); error in human judgment always stands between man and the abstract goal of *fineness*. Not only is perfection beyond man's grasp, but to strive to attain it is, in religious terms, to usurp divinity—like Adam, to pluck the forbidden fruit, to be (warns Genesis sternly) "as gods."

> Wasn't there danger of a turn too much?
> Mightn't we make it worse instead of better?
> I was for leaving something to the whetter.
> What if it wasn't all it should be? I'd
> Be satisfied if he'd be satisfied (p. 191).

"Disinterestedly" (p. 191), the figure of Time grinds on; the other, sensing the imperfection of their attempt, all but cries out in fear. He knows that only a hand-held whetstone, not the coarser grindstone, can hone to a finer polish, and he is "satisfied" to leave their present edge well enough alone.

Is "the whetter" some ultimate judge of mortal effort—maybe God? We can only guess. "Unfinished business," a phrase Frost dwelt upon in a talk he gave in his last summer at Bread Loaf, comes to my mind when I read the end of "The Grindstone." So too does the final line of "Good-by and Keep Cold" where, in winter, an apple orchard "sinks lower under the sod":

> But something has to be left to God (p. 228).

I think of another Eden-myth poem, "After Apple-Picking," and the feeling of drowsy contentment although work remains to be done. And of "Unharvested"—also an "apple fall" poem (p. 304)— where nature compensates for human negligence. Finally, I think of "The Wood-Pile" and the woodcutter's abandoned "cord of maple" that "warm[s] the frozen swamp as best it could/With the slow smokeless burning of decay" (pp. 101–102). Like "The Grindstone," these poems recognize human frailty and imply trust that somehow man's deficiencies may be offset—that, though imperfect, he may (as Paul requires in *A Masque of Mercy*) have given "the best [he has] to offer" (p. 520).

Though it is an ars poetica poem, the central issue in "The Grindstone" is moral. Beyond the expectation of death that Time's scythe represents, looms the veiled prospect of judgment upon the grinder's deeds. Here, as elsewhere in Frost's poetry—and in his life itself— earth is a trial ground.

Robert Frost's life came full circle. Those who knew him well saw his early prophecy borne out ("Into My Own," p. 5): "They would not find me changed from him they knew—" In his last illness he wrote his daughter Lesley from a Boston hospital (12 January 1963): "I am too emotional for my state. Life has been a long trial yet I mean to see more of it" (*SL*, p. 596). We might be led to take his use of "trial" lightly, in its reduced colloquial meaning.

But Lesley was aware of the religious implications in his remark. For the idea of life as a mortal trial, a test of the soul, had been with him since his youth.

Young Rob was just eleven when his father died, and the family, left with little money, returned from San Francisco to his father's people in New England. In the spring of 1892, at eighteen, he had a mystical experience, a flash of second sight. As he walked alone on his way to high school, he saw that private sorrow is part of a metaphysical design. He suddenly felt that in some prior plane of existence our souls must heroically choose to be tested by the ordeal of life on earth. For the test to be valid, the soul must surrender any memory of having chosen to be tested.

> But the pure fate to which you go
>   Admits no memory of choice,
> Or the woe were not earthly woe
>   To which you give the assenting voice (p. 21).

That visionary moment on the road to school inspired these lines, but it was not until 1906—on the Derry Farm in New Hampshire—that they were born, in the poem, "The Trial by Existence." Elizabeth Shepley Sergeant's biography of Frost, which takes the poem's title for its own, tells us that he never read the poem in public. Perhaps he feared that listeners would regard it as mere fantasy. We may suspect from his thorough knowledge of the classics (he slept with copies of Horace and Catullus by his bed) that the poem derives in part from the myth of Er in the tenth book of Plato's *Republic*. It carries nonetheless a feeling of conviction that is largely subdued in his poetry. Here, though he gives his lines the cloak of myth, he speaks unequivocably about the destiny of the soul.

In various guises throughout Frost, a picture of earth as trial ground emerges. It is revealed by the glass of wit in *A Masque of Reason* where God apologizes to Job in modern times "For the apparently unmeaning sorrow/You were afflicted with in those old days."

> But it was of the essence of the trial
> You shouldn't understand it at the time.
> It had to seem unmeaning to have meaning (p. 475).

Job's wife picks up the "trial ground" theme:

> Job says there's no such thing as Earth's becoming
> An easier place for man to save his soul in.
> Except as a hard place to save his soul in,
> . . . .
> It would be meaningless. It might as well
> Be Heaven at once and have it over with (p. 484).

Like "Kitty Hawk," *A Masque of Reason* emphasizes the experimental nature of creation. God needs man's collaboration to prove His risk of spirit worthwhile. God wryly admits to Job,

> You would have supposed
> One who in the beginning *was* the Word
> Would be in a position to command it.
> I have to wait for words like anyone (p. 475).

He thanks Job for "releasing [Him]/From moral bondage to the human race./The only free will there at first was man's" (p. 475).

> I had to prosper good and punish evil.
> You changed all that. You set me free to reign (p. 476).

Man is given the starring performance in God's creative action, but the Devil has a role too. His is the "originality," God says, of "invent[ing] Hell" (p. 480). "As for the earth," He continues (speaking still of the Devil), "we groped that out together"—much as, "together," God and Job "Found out the discipline man needed most/Was to learn his submission to unreason." God speculates,

> Society can never think things out:
> It has to see them acted out by actors,
> Devoted actors at a sacrifice—
> The ablest actors I can lay my hands on (p. 481).

The drama metaphor is accurate, so long as we remember that the script is Bergsonian—not written beforehand. Life is no scenario rolled up on a reel for future display. Men retain free choice and "God must await events,/As well as words" (p. 478). Frost's earth is a stage where a continual *happening* takes place—where the spirit of love itself is tried out, *essayed* ("Too Anxious for Rivers," p. 380):

> Time was we were molten, time was we were vapor.
> What set us on fire and what set us revolving,
> Lucretius the Epicurean might tell us
> 'Twas something we knew all about to begin with
> And needn't have fared into space like his master
> To find 'twas the effort, the essay of love.

"The Trial by Existence" is a somewhat neglected, but seminal, poem. Its premise, man's "obscuration upon earth" (p. 20), anticipates by several decades Job's plight in *A Masque of Reason*. It underlies also one of Frost's most terrifying poems, "The Draft Horse," an excursion in the dead of night. Grim companion to "Stopping by Woods . . ." (1923), it was written—according to Frost—about 1920, though not published until 1962 (*In the Clearing*). It is an acquiescence to the symbolic darkness enshrouding man. In this respect it resembles "Acceptance," but there nightfall induces a feeling of security. In "The Draft Horse" "a pitch-dark limitless grove" (p. 443) is a setting for nightmarish irrational cruelty. For the couple who drive "In too frail a buggy . . . Behind too heavy a horse," darkness is absolute. Even their "lantern . . . wouldn't burn" (p. 443). The grove becomes a chamber of horror.

> And a man came out of the trees
> And took our horse by the head
> And reaching back to his ribs
> Deliberately stabbed him dead.
>
> The ponderous beast went down
> With a crack of a broken shaft.
> And the night drew through the trees
> In one long invidious draft (p. 444).

The night wind is filled with hate; the killing is brutal and apparently unprovoked. Yet it is interpreted as "deliberate." It is "assumed" by this "most unquestioning pair/That ever accepted fate" to have some undisclosed purpose. The end of the poem finds them not bitter, just resigned:

> We assumed that the man himself
> Or someone he had to obey
> Wanted us to get down
> And walk the rest of the way (p. 444).

The couple are cast in the Job mode. Or they are latter-day Adam and Eve prototypes,[16] accepting their human ordeal without demanding reasons. They take for granted what Job (*A Masque of Reason*) waited thousands of years to learn, that "unreason" (p. 481) is a condition of life. Still, in some obscure way, they sense that they are being tested. Trusting in an unrevealed design, they invent a rationale for their baffling situation. The unspecified "someone" behind the scene is like a diabolical stage director artfully manipulating the characters ("ablest actors," p. 481, God calls all Joblike figures) to express his own will. But who can say whether he is diabolical or divine? Recall the "heroic" souls in "The Trial by Existence," accepting their "earthly woe,"

> In the pain that has but one close,
> Bearing it crushed and mystified (p. 21).

During Frost's own "long trial," his poetry bore witness to a questing, patient, religious spirit. Once, talking with his friend Elizabeth Sergeant, he gestured toward his thick green volume of the *Complete Poems* on the arm of his beloved Morris chair: "There I rest my case." If there is any verdict beyond time and human judgment, may his case stand up well.

His self-styled "Old Testament Christian" label sticks. Nevertheless, Bishop Henry Wise Hobson, at the Memorial Service for Frost (Amherst, 17 February 1963), brought him into somewhat more modern times. "Robert Frost had the spirit of a true Protestant in that he thought all valid belief had to be suffered for and 'hard won.' . . . He had a reverent admiration—almost an awe—for Jesus of the Gospels from whom he seemed at times to shield his eyes. He felt some dogmatists and theologians had robbed us of the Gospel Jesus, and was bitter and angry about it. At times he spoke of himself as an 'Old Testament Christian,' which may have been his protest against the harm he felt had been done to the Christ of the New Testament." Once (the Bishop said) Frost remarked, "What an enemy of dead and stultifying tradition Jesus was . . ." and so, certainly, the poet himself remained.

Drawn alike to a priest, a rabbi, or an Anglican bishop, Robert Frost was, always, his own person. In the late fifties the Jesuit priest,

Father Arthur MacGillivray, took Frost out to dinner at a Cambridge restaurant. When they got back to Frost's home on Brewster Street, Frost said he wanted to go upstairs "to change my shoes." (He was, in fact, surreptitiously getting a copy of his *Complete Poems* to sign.) On the way up, he turned. "Father Arthur, why do you think we're such good friends?" Father Arthur, who told me about the evening recently, was perplexed and amused. "I don't know, Robert." "Maybe," Frost pursued, "it's because you don't try to convert me." He was, to the end, "Only more sure of all I thought was true" (p. 5).

Notes to "An Old Testament Christian" by Dorothy Judd Hall

1. Victor E. Reichert, "The Faith of Robert Frost," *Frost: Centennial Essays* (Jackson: University Press of Mississippi, [1974]) says "Frost loved the Scriptures and liked to call himself an Old Testament Christian. He was soaked in the King James version and might have agreed with John Livingston Lowes that it is the noblest monument of English prose" (p. 421).

2. Daniel Smythe, *Robert Frost Speaks* (New York: Twayne Publishers, 1964), p. 136.

3. Alfred R. Ferguson, "Frost and the Paradox of the Fortunate Fall," *Frost: Centennial Essays* (Jackson: University Press of Mississippi, [1974]), p. 427.

4. Theodore Morrison, "The Agitated Heart," *The Atlantic Monthly*, 220 (July 1967), 79.

5. Frost voices his objection to Emerson in a letter to Lawrance Thompson, 11 July 1959, where he places Emerson in "the great tradition of Monists," calling him "an Abominable Snowman of the top-lofty peaks." See also Peter J. Stanlis, "Robert Frost's Masques and the Classic American Tradition," *Frost: Centennial Essays* (Jackson: University Press of Mississippi, [1974]), p. 454. Stanlis discusses "Frost's ethical dualism" and quotes the passage from Emerson's "Uriel" that Frost had in mind in the Thompson letter.

6. Reginald L. Cook, *The Dimensions of Robert Frost* (New York: Rinehart & Company, Inc., 1958), p. 149.

7. Lawrance Thompson and R. H. Winnick, *Robert Frost: The Later Years, 1938–1963* (New York: Holt, Rinehart and Winston, 1976), p. 140. The notes (pp. 406–407) refer the reader to the complete text of Frost's talk in *Sermon by Robert Frost* (1947) which was issued in a privately printed, limited edition, published by Spiral Press, at the instance of Victor E. Reichert.

8. Hyatt Howe Waggoner, "The Humanistic Idealism of Robert Frost," *American Literature*, 13 (November 1941), 209.

9. Sidney Hayes Cox, "The Sincerity of Robert Frost," *The New Republic*, 12 (August 25, 1917), 109.

10. "A Speech on Robert Frost: A Cultural Episode," *Twentieth Century Views: Robert Frost*, ed. James M. Cox (Englewood Cliffs: Prentice-Hall, Inc., 1962), p. 156.

11. Morrison, p. 78.

12. William G. O'Donnell, "Parable in Poetry," *Virginia Quarterly Review*, 25 (Spring 1949), 278. O'Donnell interprets Jonah's death as "the death of the Old

Covenant and the natural man. Jonah dies as St. Paul died on the road to Damascus."

13. "Emerson and Frost: A Parallel of Seers," *The New England Quarterly*, 31 (June 1958), 215–216.

14. *The Concept of Nature in Nineteenth-Century English Poetry* (New York: The Macmillan Company, 1936), p. 551. "Robert Frost is a refined modern agnostic in religion and philosophy, a clear-headed and fastidious realist. He has retained the aura of New England transcendentalism without a trace of its philosophy."

15. John F. Lynen, *The Pastoral Art of Robert Frost* (New Haven: Yale University Press, 1960), p. 91. Lynen explains that, although Frost attributed a grindstone theory of the universe to Herschel, the comparison actually originated with Simon Newcomb in discussing Herschel's theory of the shape of the universe.

16. Robert Pack also makes the comparison in "Robert Frost's 'Enigmatical Reserve,'" *Robert Frost: Lectures on the Centennial of his Birth* (Washington: Library of Congress, 1975), p. 51.

A Note on the Notebook

Mr. Jeffrey Jarvis of Boston University, Special Collections, referred me to Mr. Paul C. Richards, donor of the Frost collection to Boston University in 1975. Mr. Richards, who lives in Templeton, Massachusetts, dates the Frost notebook approximately 1950, since it contains a handwritten version of "A Cabin in the Clearing," Frost's Christmas card poem for 1951. However, Mr. Richards agrees with me that some entries were probably made prior to 1950. Loose pages are inserted into the notebook—when, or by whom, Mr. Richards has no idea. The material quoted in my essay is from pages *bound* into the notebook, not from inserted pages. Mr. Richards says he purchased the notebook at a Parke Burnet Gallery auction in 1975 from the estate of William Stockhauser, who had collected a good deal of Frostiana. Mr. Richards could not recall whether he ever knew how Mr. Stockhauser acquired the notebook and concluded only that sometimes Frost just gave things away. In any case, the notebook has no previous auction record.

The Two Frosts
and the Poetics of Confession

RICHARD FOSTER

Is biographers and a number of those otherwise close to the facts and patterns of his life, from friends and colleagues to family, have let the world know that Robert Frost was not only a troubled and difficult man, but a divided man as well. To put the matter simply, the "real" Frost—a flawed man of extraordinary sensitivity, deep fears, and destructive impulses—was screened and protected from wide detection by the remarkable intactness of another Robert Frost, the important public personage. Both Frosts live expressively in the poetry. But with a few exceptions, such as the late Randall Jarrell, most commentators on the poems have tended to read them under the influence chiefly of the public Frost. This essay is an examination of the poetry in terms of "the two Frosts," how they express themselves in it, how they develop, what their relationship to each other is as the years and the volumes accumulate, and of how, finally, "confession," oblique or direct, becomes the rhetorical medium in which the two come together as one.

I

The two Frosts appear early, and purely literarily, in the form of a "false" versus "true" poet—the derivative young poet writing by the book versus the emerging unique voice and vision of the authentic Frost. "My November Guest" (1912), an obviously quite early verse essay on Melancholy in which the poet preens and postures literarily over certain stockly "poetic" thoughts and feelings, exemplifies the young Frost's capacity for fabricating a piece of versified false feeling. Of course, Frost soon got over this weakness of youth and found his own mature voice, a voice, in fact, in which he cast some strong confessional poems ("The Wind and the Rain," 1942, for example), on the theme of how experience and aging cruelly mock the callow emotional posturings of youth with the facts of real pain, real grief.

But even after this maturing had taken place, Frost showed a tendency to another kind of stylistic falseness, possibly one related to what Jarrell calls the "irresponsible conceit" of his worst work as opposed to the "responsibility and seriousness" of his best[1]—his tendency increasingly, as he grew older, to handle serious matters with a relentless whimsy, as if mature emotion required a show of pointedly al fresco lightness in talking about it.

A poem called "One More Brevity" (1953) provides an example. In it Frost tells how a stray Dalmatian dog darts in to stay the night with him when he opens his door a last time before going to bed. The dog is in trouble, clearly, and the two seem to understand each other. "You're right, there's nothing to discuss," the poet says to his visitor:

> Don't try to tell me what's on your mind,
> The sorrow of having been left behind,
> Or the sorrow of having run away.
> All that can wait for the light of day.

But in the morning, the poet's tender understanding is repaid by the dog's blind urgency to be gone:

> I opened the door and he was gone.
> I was to taste in little the grief
> That comes of dogs' lives being so brief.

Had the poem ended here it would have conveyed the stilling force and poignancy of a Thomas Hardy poem. But Frost "copes" with the feeling in seventeen additional lines of literary fancy in which he imagines the stray as an earthly incarnation of the heavenly star Sirius who had come down to remind the poet of "having depended on him so long, / And yet done nothing about it in song" (pp. 419–21). One is vexed with such a poem for its coyness and seeming vanity. And yet one is moved, as the poet clearly was, by the ironies of the mute and accidental encounter it describes, which makes annoyance at the poet's self-consciously clever playing with his subject all the sharper. The problem is that there are two incompatible Frosts in the poem: a real man delicately and wonderingly

examining his true feelings, and a self-consciously professional literary personage keeping a shrewdly appraising eye on his performance of the role that he seems to believe his public expects him to
play.

II

"New Hampshire" (1923), the title poem of Frost's fourth volume,
was perhaps the first poem that signaled unmistakably the impulse
of a second Robert Frost to get born: Robert Frost the public man,
the folksy, shrewd, but affirming New England guru, the authentic
poet who was nevertheless down to earth and common-sensical, who
could charm the WASP masses by saying, in public appearances,
"gonna" and "it don't" while clearly knowing better, who scoffed
at "big government" and "socialistic" schemes for reform, all the
while extolling the self-reliant virtues of the small farmer toughing
out his survival on the hostile soil of Vermont and New Hampshire.
In "New Hampshire" this second Robert Frost went so far as to
boldly contradict his own original mentor, Ralph Waldo Emerson,
who wrote in his great "Ode" to his abolitionist friend William
Ellery Channing (1846) that "the God who made New Hampshire
/Taunted the lofty land/With little men." New Hampshire's people, Frost retorted, are not at all inferior in stature to the mountain
land they inhabit:

> The only fault I find with old New Hampshire
> Is that her mountains aren't quite high enough.
> I was not always so; I've come to be so.
> How, to my sorrow, how have I attained
> A height from which to look down critical
> On mountains? (pp. 168–69).

There is no true irony in this "ironic" question. None, at least,
of any kind that would not serve to puff out further the apparently
well-expanded chest of the speaker, whose voice in these lines and
the answering lines that follow suggests that he is already in possession of final certainty about most philosophical matters. It is, at
best, a voice of swaggeringly self-congratulatory irony. And such
a speaker, this other Frost, might have done well indeed to wonder,

one feels, and to worry, about how he had attained a height superior to all he once understood from the point of view of ordinary folk who had no voice but the kind that Frost—the original Frost—could lend them.

The "other" Frost was a glibly complacent optimist easily made impatient by fears, doubts, and the human fact of failure. It was this Frost who wrote "On a Tree Fallen Across a Road" (1921), a poem which starts as a true-seeming country poem (one kind of poem written by the "real" Robert Frost) but which quickly turns into a jingoistic hymn of praise to the dawning age of space technology:

> We will not be put off the final goal
> We have it hidden in us to attain,
> Not though we have to seize earth by the pole
>
> And, tired of aimless circling in one place,
> Steer straight off after something into space (p. 238).

Frost's poem "Riders" (1929) has the same sort of message:

> The surest thing there is is we are riders,
> And though none too successful at it, guiders,
> Through everything presented, land and tide
> And now the very air, of what we ride (p. 267).

And so on. And there are many more Frost poems, too many, in the same vein.

III

If this occasional shallow cleverness and provincial smugness were all there were to the "other" Frost, one who cared for Frost's best poems could just forgive him these lapses and glory in that best. But alas there is worse. Frost in his maturity had a capacity for being cruel and inhumane as well as cute and glib. And as he indulged that capacity in life, so did he in a number of poems—"A Lone Striker" (1933), "The White-Tailed Hornet" (1936), "Build Soil" (1936), his attack on Franklin Roosevelt in "To a Thinker" (1936), and others—many of them written as verse tracts against movements for remedial collectivism in the decade of the great depression.

354 The Two Frosts and the Poetics of Confession

The reactionary prejudices of "A Roadside Stand" (1936) are partially redeemed by the poem's expression of genuine compassion for the trials of country folk suffering hard times, a compassion not in evidence in his display of brittle cleverness in "Departmental" (also 1936), an outrageously rhymed satire on the bureaucratic state which was for years a favorite Frost showoff piece on the reading circuit. Certain other Frost poems are unmistakably disagreeable. One of the best known of them is Frost's ceremonial poem for John F. Kennedy's presidential inauguration. Subtitled "Gift Outright of 'The Gift Outright'" (1961), it prophesies "a next Augustan age" for a truculent imperial America "eager to be tried,"

> Firm in our free beliefs without dismay,
> In any game the nations want to play.
> A golden age of poetry and power
> Of which this noonday's the beginning hour (p. 424).

From the early twenties onward, such assertively "bad" Frost poems increased in number, encroaching noticeably more, with each succeeding volume, on the rich territory of Frost's "good" poems. Although *New Hampshire* (1923) announced and initiated the trend, it was still a remarkably strong Frost collection. But *West-Running Brook* (1928) and *A Further Range* (1936) showed a progressive dilution until in *A Witness Tree* (1942) there was a mix of approximately equal parts of fine and awful, such true and beautiful Frost classics as "Once by the Pacific," "Tree at my Window," and "Acquainted with the Night" strangely neighboring with such glib and easy pieces of hackwork as "A Peck of Gold," "A Soldier," and "Riders."

IV

There is an almost conscious nakedness of uncertainty in *A Witness Tree* as a whole, an uncertainty (or is it perhaps really a paradoxicalness?) which is adumbrated in its two opening poems, "Beech" and "Sycamore." "Beech" presents a harsh emblem of the limitations imposed by natural circumstances on human life and dreams:

Where my imaginary line
Bends square in the woods, an iron spine
And pile of real rocks have been founded.
And off this corner in the wild,
Where these are driven in and piled,
One tree, by being deeply wounded,
Has been impressed as Witness Tree
And made commit to memory
My proof of being not unbounded.
Thus truth's established and borne out,
Though circumstanced with dark and doubt—
Though by a world of doubt surrounded (p. 331).

But "Sycamore," an adaptation from *The New England Primer*, hints at miraculous possibilities:

Zaccheus he
Did climb the tree
Our Lord to see (p. 331).

Two of Frost's finest small poems follow: "The Silken Tent" (1939), a beautiful oblique love sonnet which presupposes an untainted idealism in the speaker, and "All Revelation" (1938), a wittily composed justification of total philosophical skepticism. The next four poems, all of them among Frost's best on a small scale—"Happiness Makes Up in Height for What It Lacks in Length" (1938), "Come in" (1941), "I Could Give All to Time" (1941), and "Carpe Diem" (1938)—explore further into reality's contradictions.

Then comes the cryptic and strangely powerful "The Wind and the Rain" (1942), which seems to erase all dallying with thoughtful alternatives in an explosion of inexplicit but powerful grief. Part I of the poem is a bitter meditation on how cruelly Fate rewards the naive emotional melodramatics of youth, implicitly recalling and renouncing such an exercise as "My November Guest": "I sang of death—but had I known / The many deaths one must have died / Before he came to meet his own!" (p. 336). Part II is a brokenly intense statement of the poet's final understanding of the meaning of real grief: It ends,

I have been one no dwelling could contain
When there was rain;
But I must forth at dusk, my time of day,
To see to the unburdening of skies.
Rain was the tears adopted by my eyes
That have none left to stay (p. 337).

"The Wind and the Rain" is a "confessional" poem. In it the poet confesses a failing: a blindness, a callowness, a selfishness of feeling, which he believes marks him as a defective human being. And the poem seems to be written somehow to make up for that fault, to compensate for that failing.

Lawrance Thompson has shown how many and how deep were Frost's personal faults, how arrogant and selfish and vain he could be, and how cruel, especially to those closest and dearest to him. And as Thompson also shows, Frost's periodic fits of extreme guilt over these failings all too frequently took the form of further exhibitions of unattractive egotism. But what is significant for Frost's art is that these deep-seated feelings of personal guilt, amply justified and rich in their variations, bore true and often beautiful fruit indeed in the poems he wrote about those feelings.

V

It is hard to say just when Frost began to write "confessional" poems about his personal faults and failings, but at least one can say that such poems began appearing early. Frost's second book, *North of Boston*, was his most objective and dramatic volume of poems, the volume in which he came closest to achieving the depersonalization of the Joyce-Eliot type of modern artist who is supposed to disappear into or behind the densely real objectivity of the world he creates in his art. The last poem in the volume is called "Good Hours," and rings confessionally of some deeply personal regret.

"Good Hours" is a delicately Frostian emblem poem in which the poet seems indirectly to meditate upon the human dangers of becoming a purely detached observer of life. Though the speaker of the poem has "No one at all with whom to talk" during his "winter evening walk," he savors his detached perspective on "the cottages

... / Up to their shining eyes in snow," with their muted sounds of music coming from within, and their glancing images "through curtain laces / Of youthful forms and youthful faces." Something like a confession of human error and ignorance, possibly of arrogance, comes in the terse third stanza:

> I had such company outward bound.
> I went till there were no cottages found.
> I turned and repented, but coming back
> I saw no window but that was black.

The poem ends with a rueful verse about how the sound of the poet's steps creak on the snow of the empty village street,

> Like profanation, by your leave,
> At ten o'clock of a winter eve (p. 102).

"Good Hours" nicely complements "The Vantage Point" (1913), that little sermon on the virtues and pleasures of detachment which enriched *A Boy's Will*, Frost's somewhat too "poetic" first collection of poems, with a bracing and welcome touch of rather elegant acerbity. "Good Hours" is also a harbinger of the hauntingly Eliotic "Acquainted with the Night" (1928), where another late night walk is associated with a much darker awareness of personal guilt, a nearly desperate desire for forgiveness, and a much more terrible sense of aloneness:

> I have passed by the watchman on his beat
> And dropped my eyes unwilling to explain.
>
> I have stood still and stopped the sound of feet
> When far away an interrupted cry
> Came over houses from another street,
>
> But not to call me back or say good-by ... (p. 255).

Frost was a reticent poet. And although there are not many of his poems which give more definite tints to the rather generalized picture of confessed human failure contained in those already cited, there are a few. One of these few, and one of the best of them, is "The Thatch," a poem not published until 1928 (in *West-Running Brook*), but apparently reflecting Frost's marital problems (Thompson, I, 464–65) as his friendship with the English poet Edward

Thomas, a similarly troubled man, brought him to understand those problems in 1914 during Frost's sojourn in England with his family:

> Well, we should see which one would win,
> We should see which one would be first to yield.

Outside, it is a dark and winter world. And as the poet angrily swings along, he flushes birds from their unsuspected winter housing in the thatch of his cottage "out of hole after hole, / Into the darkness." His self-righteous anger is suddenly muted by "a grief":

> To think their case was beyond relief—
> They could not go flying about in search
> Of their nest again, nor find a perch.
> They must brood where they fell in mulch and mire,
> Trusting feathers and inward fire
> Till daylight made it safe for a flyer.

Self-righteousness and self-pity begin, at this touch of reality, to transform themselves into something like guilt and compassion as the poet's "greater grief" starts to melt and he finds himself grieving for the frightened, dispossessed birds "without nest or roost." The poem concludes with five lines which starkly and chillingly place its account of petty human furies in perspective with the relentless laws of time and nature:

> They tell me the cottage where we dwelt,
> Its wind-torn thatch goes now unmended;
> Its life of hundreds of years has ended
> By letting the rain I knew outdoors
> In onto the upper chamber floors (pp. 252-53).

A major part of the "other Frost," it must be recognized, is the Frost that finds himself compelled to confess to the kind of pettinesses and failings as are portrayed in such poems as "The Thatch." "Egotism" was the hard core of Robert Frost's human imperfection, as Frost himself told his friend Louis Untermeyer more than a few times,[2] and Frost's confessions of fault in his letters to the friends he was sure of, like Untermeyer, could turn very quickly and easily into more "egotism." But in his poetry, where reality was given the distancing of art, Frost was often able to be sharply honest about himself, able to confront the worst of himself and tell the truth of what he saw.

VI

Frost could play to perfection, as Randall Jarrell wittily wrote, "the Grey Eminence of Robert Taft, or the Peter Pan of the National Association of Manufacturers" (p. 37), both in person and in his poems. But he also continued to write and publish, as if in despite of this carefully sustained public self, remarkably true and piercing poems about the realities of life as it is lived by most ordinary people. In "The Investment" (1928), for example, Frost was close to marveling at the ability of the poor, deprived, and unlucky to take joy in life. It isn't quite a "confessional" poem, but it supports the effect of such poems in Frost's work because it vigorously gives the lie to the easy cant of the "other" Frost:

> Over back where they speak of life as staying
> ("You couldn't call it living, for it ain't"),
> There was an old, old house renewed with paint,
> And in it a piano loudly playing.
>
> Out in the plowed ground in the cold a digger,
> Among unearthed potatoes standing still,
> Was counting winter dinners, one a hill,
> With half an ear to the piano's vigor.
>
> All that piano and new paint back there,
> Was it some money suddenly come into?
> Or some extravagance young love had been to?
> Or old love on an impulse not to care—
>
> Not to sink under being man and wife,
> But get some color and music out of life? (pp. 263–64).

The "digger" referred to in the poem seems to be identical with its speaker. And it is the speaker, known to us from the context of the rest of Frost, upon whom the light of the poem's revelation falls. It is pretty clear that the speaker, or the poet, all other appearances to the contrary, "understands."

In 1943 Frost remarked that he should have been an "archeologist" because of his "love of desolation." "The evidence," he said to a young questioner, "is written large in my books all down the years" (SL, p. 514). Such evidence is easily provided by "The Need of Being Versed in Country Things" (1920), "The Census-Taker"

(1921), "Directive" (1946), and another dozen or more great Frost poems in the elegiac mode—tender, grieving poems about the "archeology" of human mortality. Bernard De Voto, a colleague of Frost's at the Bread Loaf School of English, accused Frost in 1938 of being a "bad man" even though a "good poet." Frost called his correspondent's attention to his powerful and clearly professional, if somewhat cryptic, poem titled "To Earthward." "To Earthward" is a poem about maturing, about the shock of loss and grief which must be experienced if one is to grow up:

> I had the swirl and ache
> From sprays of honeysuckle
> That when they're gathered shake
> Dew on the knuckle.
>
> I craved strong sweets, but those
> Seemed strong when I was young;
> The petal of the rose
> It was that stung.
>
> Now no joy but lacks salt,
> That is not dashed with pain
> And weariness and fault . . . (p. 227).

"One of the great changes my nature has undergone," Frost wrote passionately and indignantly to DeVoto, "is of record in To Earthward and indeed elsewhere for the discerning. . . . I began life wanting perfection and determined to get it. I got so I ceased to expect it and could do without it. Now I find I actually crave the flaws of human handiwork. . . . I'm telling you something in a self-conscious moment that may throw light on every page of my writing for what it is worth, I mean I am a bad bad man" (SL, p. 482).

This petulant little storm of confession to all charges was meant, of course, to capsize DeVoto in a tidal wave of guilt feelings for having been critical in the first place. But there is also in Frost's squeal of defensiveness at having been "found out" an oblique, unspoken confession to defects of weakness and vanity, a confession to being less good than he seemed to ask others to be, and than perhaps he himself really wanted to be.

During his last illness, Frost received words of praise from his daughter, Lesley Frost Ballantine, for his "bravery." The aged poet wrote back to his daughter, perhaps with the final honesty of the knowledge of years of fault behind his words, that he would "rather be taken for brave than anything else" (*SL*, p. 594).

Many times in earlier years Frost had written poems of great power around muted, indirect, or seemingly unwitting confessions that the "other" Frost—the Frost created by his clever, optimistic, conservative, "Emersonian" poems which the majority of his readers seemed to like best—was at worst a self-serving fraud, at best a frightened posturer. The *real* Frost was a man not of certainties, but of deep and intense fears—fears of night, of isolation, of exposure, of death. As "The Thatch" indicates, this real Frost had capacities for cruelty, selfishness, and inhumanity that could earn him the profound feelings of guilt and rejection that permeate such a poem as "Acquainted with the Night."

VII

When Frost heard of the death in action during World War I of his English friend Edward Thomas, he wrote an elegy ("To E.T.") which is full of his sense of guilt at having failed Thomas humanly during the years that they were neighbors in England:

> I slumbered with your poems on my breast,
> Spread open as I dropped them half-read through
> Like dove wings on a figure on a tomb,
> To see if in a dream they brought of you
>
> I might not have the chance I missed in life
> Through some delay, and call you to your face
> First soldier, and then poet, and then both,
> Who died a soldier-poet of your race.
>
> I meant, you meant, that nothing should remain
> Unsaid between us, brother . . . (p. 222).

Another poem apparently about the Frost-Thomas friendship and its aftermath of regrets is "Iris by Night" (1936), a memory-poem recalling an early evening walk taken by the two friends through a world of twilight mist which was suddenly transformed by an encircling, moon-created rainbow:

> And we stood in it softly circled round
> From all division time or foe can bring
> In a relation of elected friends.

Thomas was long dead, of course, when Frost wrote these words, and his ecstatic description of the seeming miracle, which concludes the poem, contains this poignant revelation:

> And then we were vouchsafed the miracle
> That never yet to other two befell
> And I alone of us have lived to tell (p. 315).

"Iris by Night," a very beautiful poem, first appeared in *A Further Range* (1936), a volume published almost at the midpoint of Robert Frost's career. Like its successor, *A Witness Tree*, it is a divided book, a mélange of junk and gems. But unlike *A Witness Tree* it does not show the telling internal signs that the poet, in putting it together, had begun to be conscious of the division in himself, and in his art, between the good and the bad. The book begins with "A Lone Striker" (1933), a decently done verse essay in cliché anti-industrialism, and ends with a rather dense and abstract, and also rather engaging poem called "A Missive Missile" (1934), which develops the theme that time and history can make two yearning sensibilities inaccessible to each other across the years. The poem ends with these memorable lines:

> Two souls may be too widely met.
> That sad-with-distance river beach
> With mortal longing may beseech;
> It cannot speak as far as this (p. 328).

A Further Range contains several Frost classics, including "Two Tramps in Mud Time" (1934), "Desert Places" (1934), "Neither Out Far nor In Deep" (1934, "Design" (1922), and "Provide, Provide" (1934), all of them exemplary of the best Frost, the truest Frost, the Frost least afflicted by the unattractive characteristics of the "other" Frost, the Frost represented in the same volume by such poems as "Departmental" (1936), "Build Soil" (1936), and "To a Thinker" (1936).

VIII

A Further Range is thus an incoherent book of poems, but it is in-coherent in an interesting way, with the confessional note breaking out again and again, telling eloquently of the fears, self-doubts, and personal guilts that the poet finds it hard to face up to. "Desert Places," for example, can't be mistaken for anything other than the confessional poem that it is. But "The Figure in the Doorway" (1936), a poem of similar mood from the same period, is less direct in declaring its theme. It simply tells what the poet saw as he rode in a train through an unfamiliar mountain landscape:

> The grade surmounted, we were riding high
> Through level mountains nothing to the eye
> But scrub oak, scrub oak and the lack of earth
> That kept the oaks from getting any girth.

This is not a New England landscape; but like New England's it is a harsh landscape, indicating little hospitality to humankind. Sud-denly a cabin appears in the midst of this grim wilderness, its owner, a great gaunt giant, filling the doorway: "The miles and miles he lived from anywhere / Were evidently something he could bear," the poet thinks as he gazes on this man from the dining car of the passing train. Then Frost begins a strange, oblique apologia in which he catalogues what he imagines to be sufficient consolations in the life of this native of a foreign soil: lots of wood for heating and light, a hen and a pig, a well, a "ten-by-twenty garden patch," and for "entertainment," the passing of the train in which the poet is riding:

> He could look at us in our diner eating,
> And if so moved uncurl a hand in greeting (p. 292).

It is on this note that the poem ends, the note—how to define it?—of the poet's dread of the hostility of the object of his poem, and perhaps of a knowingly deserved guilt vis-à-vis that object. The last lines hint at Frost's yearning to be accepted, to be forgiven even, as he passes at a distance in his privileged dining car. He wishes, it seems, that the clenched fist of the peasant giant would "uncurl" understandingly to the outlander "in greeting." But of course it doesn't.

This way of reading "The Figure in the Doorway" seems to be encouraged by "On the Heart's Beginning to Cloud the Mind" (1934), the poem immediately preceding it in *A Further Range.* "On the Heart's Beginning . . ." published in the middle of the desperate and troubled 1930s, the period when Frost's great popularity encouraged him in some of his grossest poetic exhibitions of triviality, vanity, and inhumanity, is again a train poem with the poet looking out on passing lives made foreign to him by geography, distance, and social position:

> Something I saw or thought I saw
> In the desert at midnight in Utah,
> Looking out of my lower berth
> At moonlit sky and moonlit earth.

What he sees is a dark enough vision: only a scattering of stars in the heavens, and on earth "a single light afar,"

> A flickering, human pathetic light,
> That was maintained against the night,
> It seemed to me, by the people there,
> With a Godforsaken brute despair.
> It would flutter and fall in half an hour
> Like the last petal off a flower.

But just here the poet catches himself: "But my heart was beginning to cloud my mind." He knows "a tale of a better kind," he says to himself and his reader; and as in "The Figure in the Doorway," he proceeds to distract himself and his reader from unhappy thoughts by spinning a consoling tale about what the custodians of the light are probably "really" like: they are very probably a young and harmoniously married couple with lots of character and courage, and their light is the affirmative symbol of their shared strengths:

> They can keep it burning as long as they please;
> They can put it out whenever they please.

The prevailing darkness does not mean that the couple is alone, furthermore, but just that their neighbors have gone to bed and put out their own lights. The flickering of the light does not suggest the fraility of the lives of the people tending it, but only the intervention of ordinary cedar trees on the desert between the house and the passing train in which the poet is riding. And the trees are nothing to fear, for they "Have no purpose, have no leader, / Have never made the first move to assemble. . . ." Marriage has strengthened rather than worn down this couple, and "they fear not life." The poet made his original error, he says, due to his "heart's beginning to cloud his mind" as he made his wakeful nighttime "surface flight" across an unknown landscape.

Thus does the poet, troubled by fears and self-doubts and a perhaps unhappy marriage of many years, moralize to himself. But the poem does not end here. After a space indicating a pause there are four more lines:

> This I saw when waking late,
> Going by at a railroad rate,
> Looking through wreaths of engine smoke
> Far into the lives of other folk (pp. 290–92).

The tone of these last lines is wistful, yearning, perhaps a little sad, as if the mind-chastened heart is not quite satisfied. Not surprising, if the heart is that of the poet who wrote such hauntingly tender poems about mortal lives and dreams as "After Apple-Picking" (1914), "An Old Man's Winter Night" (1916), "In the Home Stretch" (1916), "On the Need of Being Versed in Country Things" (1920), "The Census-Taker" (1921), "Paul's Wife" (1921), "Iris by Night" (1936), "Directive" (1946), and so many others.[3]

IX

"Wild Grapes" (1920), a worthy sister-poem to "Birches" (1915), tells about a young girl who is suddenly transformed into an adult when, trying to gather wild grapes growing in the crown of a birch tree bent to earth for her by her brother, she is swept dangerously heavenward as her brother releases the tree. The brother, who is older, makes the moments of her hanging frightened up there in the air ("It wasn't," she recalls, "my not weighing anything / So much as my not knowing anything") an occasion for learning. He engages her in a colloquy of mixed cruelties and tendernesses; and all the time he cares. What she learns from the occasion is expressed in the closing lines of the poem, which are spoken from the vantage point of adulthood:

> I had not taken the first step in knowledge;
> I had not learned to let go with the hands,
> As still I have not learned to with the heart,
> And have no wish to with the heart—nor need,
> That I can see. *The mind—is not the heart.*
> *I may yet live, as I know others live,*
> *To wish in vain to let go with the mind—*
> *Of cares, at night, to sleep; but nothing tells me*
> *That I need learn to let go with the heart* (my italics, p. 199).

The "true" Frost speaks from the viewpoint of the matured woman in "Wild Grapes." He knows what her brother knows. And as the older brother is loved by his younger sister, the "true" Frost is loved, as Lionel Trilling said on the occasion of Frost's eighty-fifth and "Sophoclean" birthday in 1959, not because he charms with easy cheer, but because he has "made plain" to his lasting readers "the terrible things of human life."[4]

Even so, the "other" Frost has his contribution to make. His existence makes the "true" Frost more complex, more real, perhaps ultimately more fully human. Admitting the fact of slighter and richer, worse and better, poems by Robert Frost, and taking stock of what characteristics make for both kinds, the best reader of Frost, and I venture to judge the best rewarded, takes Frost's work as a whole. "Robert Frost" is all there in the poems, virtues beside vices, pettiness mixed with greatness, for a good reader to know as perhaps no one ever knew Frost in life. And this kind of knowledge, the poignant and immediate knowledge of the ebb and flow of a human being's moral and emotional experience through a lifetime, is the rare and invaluable bequest to us of Robert Frost's poetic art.

Notes to "The Two Frosts and the Poetics of Confession" by RICHARD FOSTER

1. "The Other Frost," *Poetry and the Age* (New York: Vintage, 1953), p. 29. Cited later in text with page number only.

2. See, for example, Frost's letter to Untermeyer dated 7 July 1921, and the mea culpa poem ("To prayer, to prayer I go . . .") accompanying it (p. 130), and his similar letter quoting the same poem, 15 January 1942, *Selected Letters of Robert Frost*, pp. 27 and 497–98.

3. Radcliffe Squires writes that "On the Heart's Beginning to Cloud the Mind" is a "curiously self-defeating poem" because it "prepares the mind for being clouded by the heart—not at all for the mind's clarifying everything" (*The Major Themes of Robert Frost* [University of Michigan Press, 1963], p. 44). This commentator's puzzlement is produced by his failure to see Frost as a divided man who in this poem, as in a few others, is looking at his own dividedness with a remarkable objectivity and wholeness of self-understanding. "On the Heart's Beginning . . ." is, in other words, an oblique or dramatized "confessional" poem.

4. "A Speech on Robert Frost: A Cultural Episode," *Partisan Review*, 26 (Summer 1959), p. 452.

William James, Robert Frost, and "The Black Cottage"

LEWIS H. MILLER, JR.

WHERE Robert Frost may have acquired his persistent passion for the "speaking voice" in writing cannot be rigidly determined; but in William James, specifically in *Pragmatism*, Frost could have found a useful precedent. James's propensity, in *Pragmatism* and elsewhere, to play down his own urbanity and sophistication by employing a simple, colloquial, and chatty manner of speaking must certainly have been congenial, if not tonic, to Frost's imagination. Even without the biographical evidence which underscores Frost's enduring respect for William James the teacher, psychologist, and philosopher, one is struck by affinities of temperament, tone, and thought pervasive in the work of the two men.[1] Just as James strove to be a philosopher of and for the people, Frost strove in his poetry, prose, and public performances to project the image of a wise, earthy farmer highly distrustful of the intellectual establishment. Both writers offered unusually modest claims for the importance and novelty of their achievements, and both exhibited a deep, conservative strain beneath an active engagement with a changing world; while James significantly extended his title, *Pragmatism*, to include *A New Name for Some Old Ways of Thinking*, Frost extolled the virtues of "the old-fashioned way to be new" (*SP*, p. 60).

Behind the amiable poses of these crackerbarrel philosophers lies a view of the universe and of the human predicament which is uncompromising in its recognition of man's loneliness and vagrancy in a world that remains, and always will remain, discontinuous and piecemeal. Where James emphasized the "tangle" of concrete experience and looked steadily at what he called the "rich thicket of reality," Frost used similar metaphors—the "pathless wood" ("Birches") or "alien entanglements" (*SP*, p. 25)—to account for the pressures of contingent reality. Despite their apparent optimism, both writers assumed that truth is multivalent and shifting and that to rest comfortably in a universe fixed, final, and closed is to hibernate. Thus we find James's insistent asseveration that the world is malleable and plastic and that man engenders truths upon it; thus we find Frost's refusal to accept with any finality the comfort and control implicit in his fictions. In *Pragmatism* especially—with its numerous references to rooming houses, corridors, and hotels—James offers a view of man in isolation, always searching, but never completely at home.[2] Turning away from abstractions, fixed principles, or closed systems, the pragmatist welcomes "open air and possibilities of nature"; he seeks his momentary stay inside the flux. In short, the pragmatist's search for some sort of a home within a homeless world is marked by the same spirit of risk and openendedness which characterizes so many of Frost's strategies to make himself at home in an alien world.

Nowhere in the Frost canon is the pragmatistic method so explicitly and consecutively realized as it is in "The Black Cottage," a grossly underrated poem whose "figure"—as I shall argue—can be most successfully perceived in the light of those lectures delivered by William James in 1906 and published in 1907 under the title *Pragmatism: A New Name for Some Old Ways of Thinking.* This is not to posit a straight line between James and Frost (Frost usually invoked a dotted or crooked line when he addressed the vexed issue of literary influence) or to suggest that Frost's dramatic narrative is merely a poeticized version of James's *Pragmatism.* My intention is to provide a meaningful and appropriate context for a frequently misunderstood poem by demonstrating Frost's uncanny ability in "The Black Cottage" to dramatize and epitomize the philosophic temperament of one of America's most original thinkers. For "The Black Cottage" provides, I believe, one of those rare instances in American letters where philosophy and poetry mingle strenuously to form one seamless, artistic whole.

I

Striving to be a truly "popular philosopher," James deliberately invoked the homey, colloquial phrases and rhythms most familiar to the nonspecialized audiences to whom his lectures were addressed.

And in his effort to bring philosophy out of the classroom, James became, like Frost, a confirmed practitioner of writing with his ear on the speaking voice. Such a practice served James especially well in *Pragmatism*; for by assuming a voice of remarkable leisure, expanse, geniality and openness, James could exhibit and reinforce the thoroughly democratic basis of the philosophic attitude he fostered: "You want a system that will combine both things, the scientific loyalty to facts and willingness to take account of them, the spirit of adaptation and accommodation, in short, but also the old confidence in human values and the resultant spontaneity, whether of the religious or of the romantic type. . . .

"The pragmatistic philosophy of which I hope to begin talking in my next lecture preserves as cordial a relation with facts [as does Herbert Spencer] and, unlike Spencer's philosophy, it neither begins nor ends by turning positive religious constructions out of doors—it treats them cordially as well.

"I hope I may lead you to find it just the mediating way of thinking that you require."[3] One of James's prime achievements as a philosopher was his ready ability to link his philosophical "systems" with what he called "this actual world of finite human lives"; in *Pragmatism*, he achieved this linkage through a convincingly flexible, accommodating, and cordial manner of addressing his listening and reading public. Similarly, the minister of Frost's "The Black Cottage" (pp. 55 ff.) reaches *his* audience—through a voice which in its absence of dogmatism, in its cordial, accommodating, and inclusive gestures (e.g. "Pretty . . . Come in"; "Why not sit down . . ."; "Dear me, why abandon a belief. . . ?") quite tangibly bodies forth the "mediating way of thinking" proposed by William James.

The minister's rambling and discursive voice-ways have, however, troubled readers who seem to expect a more commanding presence than the one offered by the main speaker in a narrative which purports to deal seriously with major issues of the American experience: the Civil War, slavery, the Constitution, religious freedom. Casually assuming the role of guide to an abandoned little cottage, the minister approaches these large issues almost incidentally —as if they were subsidiary to his fascination with the black cottage itself, and with the old lady who had lived a lifetime in it. The min-

ister reveals, in roundabout fashion, that the old lady was a parish-
ioner of his and that she managed to cope with loneliness and suffering in a most self-reliant and resilient manner. She had met Garrison
and Whittier, the minister tells us, but for her, the Civil War meant
more than freeing the slaves or preserving the Union. The minister
reflects on the old lady's "innocence" as well as on her experience,
her "art of hearing and not hearing the latter wisdom of the world";
and he refers to the lasting effect she had upon him in persuading
him to "keep hands off" the traditional version of the Apostles'
Creed. Throughout, the minister punctuates his expression with
parentheses, dashes, self-interruptions and asides—as in the following account of the old lady's devotion beneath a rough crayon portrait of her soldier-husband:

> She always, when she talked about the war,
> Sooner or later came and leaned, half knelt,
> Against the lounge beside it, though I doubt
> If such unlifelike lines kept power to stir
> Anything in her after all the years.
> He fell at Gettysburg or Fredericksburg,
> I ought to know—it makes a difference which:
> Fredericksburg wasn't Gettysburg, of course.
> But what I'm getting to . . . (ll. 26–34).

These oft-cited lines are typical of the freewheeling, unassertive
discourse which pervades "The Black Cottage" and which has
prompted readers to dismiss the narrative as "ordinary" or to detect
"deep uncertainties" within a narrator who seems basically naive
and uninformed: "The minister seems hardly to understand that kind
of devotion. . . . His interest in the past is so dim that he does not dis-
tinguish Gettysburg from Fredericksburg."[4] Yet viewed within a
pragmatistic context, the minister's "uncertainties" reflect the informal, plastic, and mediating approach to experience so persistently
extolled and practiced by William James. Despite the nature of his
calling, the minister exhibits—through shifting, repetitive, self-
qualifying patterns of speech—a bold skepticism which refuses to
rest comfortably among fixed principles or dogmatic certainties.
The minister's expression of doubt about the crayon portrait's intrinsic "power to stir" anything in the old lady is an indication

neither of ignorance nor of callousness. It is a recognition of the subjective condition of the old lady's beliefs and devotions, of the deep private sources of grief, memory, and desire which alone could animate the "unlifelike lines" done sadly from an old daguerreotype. As for his "interest in the past," the minister, true to the pragmatic spirit, is more concerned with what James called the "tangled, muddy, painful and perplexed" world of concrete personal experience than he is with the more public world of historical record. Thus the minister will not quibble over alternatives (Fredericksburg or Gettysburg) which, in relation to his perception of the old lady's innermost feelings, mean practically the same thing. James's concluding statements about the "trivial" dispute concerning man, tree, and the scurrying squirrel are pertinent here: "The pragmatic method . . . is to try to interpret each notion by tracing its respective practical consequences. What difference would it practically make to anyone if this notion rather than that notion were true? If no practical difference whatever can be traced, then the alternatives mean practically the same thing, and all dispute is idle" (*Pragmatism*, p. 42). Whether the husband fell at Gettysburg or Fredericksburg may make a "practical difference" to someone, somewhere, as the minister admits; but the question is unrelated to the minister in his role as sympathetic spokesman for the old lady and her quest after meaning in the face of a husband's sacrifice in the Civil War. In the tradition of James, the minister realizes, and makes us realize as we share in his process of thought, that "a truth must always be preferred to falsehood when both relate to the situations; but when neither does, the truth is as little of a duty as falsehood."[5]

II

Frost's distillation of James's pragmatism is more faceted and comprehensive than I have indicated thus far. Frost obviously took to heart James's well known elaborations concerning toughness and tenderness of mind. Like James, Frost respected both the empiricist's and the rationalist's points of view, and he recognized that most men harbor what James called a "hankering for the good things on both sides" of these philosophic positions. Indeed, Frost is usually at his best whenever he succeeds in dramatizing this two-pronged "hankering" by fashioning a speaker whose tough and tender habits of mind emerge naturally from one integrated personality. In "The Black Cottage," the minister's summary treatment of the "unlifelike lines" under which the old lady "half knelt" reveals only one side of a temperament which, for all its tough-minded skepticism and uncertainty, also displays—as I shall show—a strong attraction to abstract and eternal principles, to a tender-minded conception of experience in which basic desires for permanence, simplicity, and order are satisfied. James's detailed descriptions of the tender-minded temperament are especially pertinent to a consideration of "The Black Cottage": "There are outlines and outlines. . . . An outline in itself is meagre, truly, but it does not necessarily suggest a meagre thing. It is the essential meagreness of *what is suggested* by the usual rationalistic philosophies that moves empiricists to their gesture of rejection. . . . Your typical ultra-abstractionist fairly shudders at concreteness: other things equal, he positively prefers the pale and spectral. If the two universes were offered, he would always choose the skinny outline rather than the rich thicket of reality. It is so much purer, clearer, nobler. . . . But from the human point of view, no one can pretend that it doesn't suffer from the faults of remoteness and abstractness. It is eminently a product of what I have ventured to call the rationalistic temper. It disdains empiricism's needs. It substitutes a pallid outline for the real world's richness" (*Pragmatism*, pp. 36–37, 55, 57).

James can be (and has been) accused of oversimplifying and overstating the rationalist position; but there is no arguing with his underlying assumption that all of us, whenever we are weary of considerations and life is too much like a pathless wood, are prone to "choose the skinny outline rather than turn to the rich thicket of reality." Trenchantly aware of this psychological fact, Frost explores it dramatically in "The Black Cottage" through the tough-tender mind of his minister who, in his shifting perspective on the black cottage itself, translates into rich symbolic action the mediating way of thinking prescribed by William James.

The "little cottage" is set back syntactically from the reader just as it is "set well back" from the road:

> We chanced in passing by that afternoon
> To catch it in a sort of special picture
> Among tar-banded ancient cherry trees,
> Set well back from the road in rank lodged grass,
> The little cottage we were speaking of,
> A front with just a door between two windows,
> Fresh painted by the shower a velvet black (ll. 1–7).

Framed as a "sort of special picture" among the "cherry trees" and "rank lodged grass," the cottage assumes the qualities of a still life, a primitive painting or a child's drawing the stark simplicity of whose two-dimensional outlines contrasts sharply with the depth and variety of its surroundings. As readers, we are led momentarily to choose the skinny outline rather than the rich thicket. Holding the cottage "at arm's length," the minister, in his distancing, appreciative gesture, prolongs the aesthetic perspective defined by the opening lines of the poem and further endows the cottage with qualities of fixity, stability, and quaintness:

> We paused, the minister and I, to look.
> He made as if to hold it at arm's length
> Or put the leaves aside that framed it in.
> "Pretty," he said. "Come in . . ." (ll. 8–11).

It is important to note here that the minister's invitation to "Come in" invites his companion only up to a windowsill of the framed cottage in the clearing[6] and that his initial remarks about the cottage's interior are directed towards its imperviousness to change: "We pressed our faces to the pane. 'You see,' he said,/'Everything's as she left it when she died'" (ll. 14–15). Set off from the flux by the geometry and protection of a windowpane, the cottage's drawing room answers to the minister's tender-minded hankering after a sacred space where he might pause to take stock of himself and of the relentless pressures of an ongoing world: "It always seems to me a sort of mark/To measure how far fifty years have brought us" (ll. 45–46). Like James's rationalist, the minister is again drawn to the simplicity of outlines: by focusing specifically on the "unlifelike lines" of a portrait "done sadly from an old daguerreotype" (l. 24), he places himself strategically at several removes from the lives that "had gone out of" the cottage. Yet the black cottage offers more than a correlative for what James called a "classic sanctuary in which the rationalist fancy may take refuge from the intolerably confused and gothic character which mere facts present" (*Pragmatism*, p. 27). Leading his companion (and the reader) up to a "weathered window-sill" (l. 13), the minister moves from a safe, "arm's length" mode of viewing to a close engagement with the confused and gothic character which mere facts present: "The warping boards pull out their own old nails/With none to tread and put them in their place" (ll. 49–50). This is to say that the minister's perception of the black cottage, and of experience in general, persistently mediates between a tender-minded monism with its commitment to pure, simple, and noble "lines," and a tough-minded pluralism characterized by a rich intimacy with the tangled and muddy facts of a contingent reality.

III

Throughout his career as psychologist, theologian, and moral philosopher, James expressed a deep-seated distrust of abstractions or fixed systems of thought; he spoke in behalf of "truths" rather than of "Truth," and he kept his eyes steadily on the sheer multitudinousness of concrete facts and concrete personal experiences. In *Pragmatism*, however, he "unstiffened" some of his own predilections by arguing for a mediate position which could accommodate abstract ideas along with concrete realities, which could provide a middle ground where rationalist and empiricist temperaments might meet and mingle. Rather than reject the rationalist's "pallid outline," James urged that any concept—no matter how abstract—can and should be viewed as a "truth" when that concept leads its proponent into "satisfactory relations" with concrete aspects of experience. Insisting on the redirecting function of abstract ideas or principles, James argued that metaphysical and theological propositions become true (are "verified" or "validated") insofar as they prove helpful or instrumental in dealing with life's practical struggles. "What," he asked again and again, "is the truth's cash value in experiential terms?" And for one who believed emphatically that temperament plays a controlling role in determining belief, James

could logically extend his "cash-value" nexus to include basic feelings and desires, what he called "instinctive human reactions of satisfaction or dislike." James's instrumental view of truth has been attacked and abused by analytic philosophers, defended half-heartedly
by James's apologists, but has nowhere been so compellingly restated
and applied as in Frost's "The Black Cottage." Meditating on the old
lady's means of coping with the loss of her husband in the Civil War,
the minister speaks like the true pragmatist he is:

> Her giving somehow touched the principle
> That all men are created free and equal.
> And to hear her quaint phrases—so removed
> From the world's view today of all those things.
> That's a hard mystery of Jefferson's.
> What did he mean? Of course the easy way
> Is to decide it simply isn't true.
> It may not be. I heard a fellow say so (ll. 60–67).

The minister's mock credulity, here, gently chides but does not
reject James's conviction that "apart from abstract propositions of
comparison . . . we find no proposition ever regarded by anyone as
evidently certain that has not either been called a falsehood, or at
least had its truth sincerely questioned by someone else."[7] Indeed,
the minister's wry disclaimer alerts us to the remarkable extent to
which he has assimilated James's assumptions about truth. Not-
withstanding Jefferson's eloquent pronouncements in the Declaration of Independence, the minister does *not* "hold these truths to be
self-evident," but insists on viewing "truth" in terms of its cash
value, its potency in helping specific individuals come to terms with
life's practical struggles. Insofar as Jefferson's principle that all men
are created free and equal has had its traceable, salutary effects upon
the old lady (and upon the minister himself), then that principle is
"true." The pragmatist's propensity to locate truth within a dynamic interaction of abstract ideas with concrete human experience
is nicely captured by the minister's use of the verb *touch*. Like the
"unlifelike lines" of the old crayon portrait, Jefferson's principle—
so the minister perceives—has been animated or "touched" by the
old lady's personal experience, her outright "giving" which has, in
turn, been rendered meaningful by that "hard mystery of Jefferson's."

The same pragmatic habit of mind which informs the minister's response to Jefferson's ideals also informs the minister's treatment of the Apostles' Creed. Recounting his temptation to change the Creed "a very little," the minister explains that his decision not to drop the words "descended into Hades" was based less on intellectual or metaphysical consideration than on his own and the old lady's instinctive human reactions of satisfaction and dislike:

> Such a phrase couldn't have meant much to her.
> But suppose she had missed it from the Creed,
> As a child misses the unsaid Good-night
> And falls asleep with heartache—how should *I* feel? (ll. 100–103)

In his expression of concern for the old lady's feelings and for the feelings which her heartache might have engendered in him, the minister not only reveals a pragmatist's respect for the temperamental grounding of beliefs, but he offers a dramatic confirmation of James's conclusion that "feeling is the deeper source of religion," that "philosophies and theological formulas are secondary products."[8] And as the minister reflects upon his decision to resist change, he proceeds to expound a view of history which, in its stark conservatism, goes to the heart of James's belief in the absolutely controlling part played by the "older truths":

> I'm just as glad she made me keep hands off,
> For, dear me, why abandon a belief
> Merely because it ceases to be true.
> Cling to it long enough, and not a doubt
> It will turn true again, for so it goes.
> Most of the change we think we see in life
> Is due to truths being in and out of favor (ll. 104–110).

This rather flat, sermonizing portion of the minister's narrative is remarkable for its demonstration of Frost's acute responsiveness to an aspect of James's thought which too often passes unnoticed. Like Ralph Waldo Emerson, James has been criticized for a lack of historical consciousness and an attendant disregard of objective conditions for belief. It is important to note here that while Frost's minister is often a spokesman for some of James's most radical notions about the plasticity of truth, the minister also exhibits—as in lines 104–110—James's latent distrust of novelty and his commitment to "truths" which Common Sense has validated over the centuries. The minister's talk of "truths being in and out of favor" neatly summarizes a basic assumption in James's *Pragmatism*; namely, that there exists a large storehouse of tried and tested principles readily available for practical application (and hence for verification) as they are removed from "cold storage" to become once again instruments for action.[9]

IV

At this point in "The Black Cottage," Frost's pragmatist seems to ignore James's vigorous call to action; carried away by the comfort and security implicit in his own rhetoric, the minister once again exhibits a tender-minded inclination to shun the rich thicket of reality:

> As I sit here, and oftentimes, I wish
> I could be monarch of a desert land
> I could devote and dedicate forever
> To the truths we keep coming back and back to.
> So desert it would have to be, so walled
> By mountain ranges half in summer snow,
> No one would covet it or think it worth
> The pains of conquering to force change on.
> Scattered oases where men dwelt, but mostly
> Sand dunes held loosely in tamarisk
> Blown over and over themselves in idleness.
> Sand grains should sugar in the natal dew
> The babe born to the desert, the sandstorm
> Retard mid-waste my cowering caravans— ... (ll. 111–124).

Situating himself protectively within the guarded precincts of his utopian vision, the minister provides a correlative for the idyllic state of mind which James attributes to the rationalist with his "exclusive interest in the remote, the noble, the simple, and the abstract in the way of conception" (*Pragmatism*, p. 61). Caught up in the lyricism of this passage, the reader momentarily shares the minister's entry into a timeless, stable world sustained by "the truths we keep coming back and back to." But such a pristine vision is hard to hold for long, especially when projected by a pragmatist seated on a

doorstep whose "warping boards pull out their own old nails . . ."
(l. 49). The tough-minded questions which James put to the claims
of "tendermindedness" seem to me particularly appropriate here not
only because they provide a useful grid against which to evaluate
the minister's reverie, but because they anticipate so well the cloying
details which fill that dream world: "May not the notion of a world
already saved *in toto* anyhow, be too saccharine to stand? May not
religious optimism be too idyllic? . . . is the last word sweet?" (*Pragmatism*, p. 190). Both Frost and James craved the bitter with the
sweet; and Frost, in a variety of contexts, staunchly seconded
James's formulation of the pragmatist's close involvement with raw
experience: "He turns away from abstraction and insufficiency, . . .
from fixed principles, closed systems, and pretended absolutes and
origins. He turns towards concreteness and adequacy, towards
facts, towards action and towards power. . . . [Pragmatism] means
the open air and possibilities of nature, as against dogma, artificiality,
and the pretence of finality in truth" (*Pragmatism*, p. 45).

It should not surprise us to find that Frost's minister follows
James's injunction and breaks off his meditation by turning away
from a closed system and towards concreteness, adequacy, facts,
action and power:

> "There are bees in this wall." He struck the clapboards,
> Fierce heads looked out; small bodies pivoted.
> We rose to go. Sunset blazed on the windows (ll. 125–127).

These six, crisp assertions contrast markedly with the loose, mean-
dering rhythms to which we have become accustomed; for Frost
would have us feel along our pulses the insistent, often disruptive
claims of the real world's richness. Yet Frost is concerned with more
than bringing his readers up sharply against the pressures of contingent reality. Working within a pragmatic tradition, Frost sought
to reconcile a scientific loyalty to facts with what James called an
"old confidence in human values"; and in the final lines of "The
Black Cottage," he achieves such a reconciliation.

Although the minister, in his deliberate thrust toward the bee-
infested cottage, cuts himself off from the protected and static
world of his reverie, that ideal world of truths we keep coming back

and back to is not left irrevocably behind. Much as "lives" have "gone out" of the black cottage, the fierce, yet graceful and delicate, bees have not; and the sheer inevitability of their presence (the minister knows they are there before he strikes the clapboards) bespeaks a continuity and order in the real world similar to that projected by the minister in his vision of sand dunes blown over and over. Redolent of sweetness (honey), and ablaze with light, the abandoned little cottage looms larger than life in answering to the minister's longing for stasis and simplicity. Whether sitting on its doorsteps or catching it in a special picture among tar-banded ancient cherry trees, the minister *is* "monarch" of a sanctuary which he "devotes and dedicates to the truths we keep coming back and back to." This is to say that the minister's utopian dream is actualized in the tangled, muddy, and perplexed world of facts. No meagre outline, the black cottage bristles with vitality as it emerges from Frost's tough-tender handling to become a symbol for the only kind of "truth" suitable to the pragmatic temperament: "For pluralistic pragmatism, truth grows up inside of all the finite experiences. They lean on each other, but the whole of them, if such a whole there be, leans on nothing. All 'homes' are in finite experience; finite experience as such is homeless. Nothing outside of the flux secures the issue of it. It can hope salvation only from its own intrinsic promises and potencies" (*Pragmatism*, p. 169). Immanent in the flux, yet transcending it, Frost's black cottage provides the home that James was looking for.

Notes to "William James, Robert Frost, and 'The Black Cottage' " by LEWIS H. MILLER, JR.

1. Lawrance Thompson, in *Robert Frost: The Early Years, 1874–1915* (New York: Holt, Rinehart and Winston, 1966) discusses Frost's avid reading of James's *Pragmatism* and Frost's pedagogical use of James's *Principles of Psychology*. For a more theoretical and general account of Frost's literary indebtedness to James, see Frank Lentricchia, "Robert Frost and Modern Literary Theory," in *Frost: Centennial Essays*, ed. Jac L. Tharpe, (Jackson: University Press of Mississippi, [1974]), 315–332.

2. I am here indebted to Beverly Lawn's interesting discussion, "From Temple to Streets: The Style of *Pragmatism*," *New England Quarterly*, 45 (December 1972), 526–540.

3. William James, *Pragmatism*, ed. R. B. Perry, (New York: World Publishing Co., Meridian, 1955) pp. 26, 37; other references are in the text.

4. Margaret V. Allen, " 'The Black Cottage:' Robert Frost and the Jeffersonian

Ideal of Equality," in *Frost: Centennial Essays*, p. 224. Also, see William H. Pritchard, *"North of Boston*: Frost's Poetry of Dialogue," in *In Defense of Reading*, ed. R. A. Brower and R. Poirier (New York: E. P. Dutton, 1962), 49ff.

5. *Pragmatism*, p. 151; in his homey way, James elaborates: "If you ask me what o'clock it is and I tell you that I live at 95 Irving Street, my answer may indeed be true, but you don't see why it is my duty to give it. A false address would be as much to the purpose."

6. Readers of "The Black Cottage" tend to assume incorrectly that the minister physically enters the cottage; see Allen and Pritchard.

7. "The Will To Believe," in *The Will To Believe and Other Essays in Popular Philosophy* (New York: Dover, 1956), p. 15.

8. *The Varieties of Religious Experience* (New York: Longmans, Green, and Co., 1916), p. 431.

9. My discussion of James's conservatism draws from *Pragmatism*, pp. 50–51, 134–135, 150.

"The Death of the Hired Man": Modernism and Transcendence

WARREN FRENCH

For Don and Paco,
who brought me to the "Frost Country."

Literary critics are generally quarrelsome; but one thing all seem agreed upon is that we have recently reached the end of that period now being called Modernist. (I suspect this name will not last. As it becomes increasingly inappropriate historically, a new label will arise, as Art Deco already has for the related modernistic decorative arts. I think that T. S. Eliot will finally win the honor of providing the tag for "The Age of the Waste Land.")

Although there is little agreement about anything concerning this period (or most others), I thought it might be profitable to explore with a recent seminar in twentieth-century American literature a theory of Modernism to see to what extent the celebrated writers of the period illustrated it. To determine who was celebrated, we built the project around anthologies designed for undergraduate college courses.

The experiment proved quite fruitful. We proved to *my* satisfaction at least that most of the writers winning spots in the anthologies were, despite vast differences, alike in sharing that sensibility that I had designated Modernist. All, that is, except Robert Frost.

I have observed earlier in my essay "Frost Country" (*Centennial Essays II*) that we rarely think of Frost as an artist ahead of his time; yet the proceedings of the seminar confirmed my opinion that indeed he was. Despite his extraordinary popularity, Modernist critics I think never felt quite comfortable with him. I think the reason was not that he had not caught up with them, but rather that they had not caught up with him. "The demiurge's laugh" is Frost's own.

I

Before I can pursue this argument, however, I must summarize my own perhaps idiosyncratic concept of Modernism as I have set it forth in an earlier paper.[1] The term was given vogue through a lecture that Harvard's distinguished comparativist, Harry Levin, delivered in 1959 to Stanley Burnshaw's seminar in modern literature at New York University. Subsequently the lecture was published in Burnshaw's *Varieties of Literary Experience* (1962), and the rapid and wide adoption of the term that Levin used to ask "What Was Modernism?" indicates that he provided a useful label for something that needed naming.

Levin's essay, however, goes only a little way toward answering the question it poses. Concerned primarily with an international style of art and life, Levin equated Modernism particularly with the expatriate writers of the 1920s and provided less an essay in definition than a nostalgic reminiscence. More important actually than Levin's essay is another in Burnshaw's collection, Lionel Trilling's "On the Modern Element in Modern Literature," in which after observing that Thomas Mann had "once said that all his work could be understood as an effort to free himself from the middle class," Trilling proposes that this effort describes "the chief intention of all modern literature." "I venture to say," he concludes, "that the idea of losing oneself up to the point of self-destruction, of surrendering oneself to experience without regard to self-interest or conventional morality, of escaping wholly from the societal bonds, is an 'element' somewhere in the mind of every modern person who dares to think of what Arnold in his unaffected Victorian way called 'the fulness of spiritual perfection.' " (Trilling borrowed his title from an essay that Matthew Arnold had delivered at a nineteenth-century turning point in British literary history.)

When Jacques Barzun, Trilling's colleague at Columbia University, published *Classic, Romantic and Modern* in 1961, he considered "Modernism" a sufficient neologism to require quotation marks; but he contributed little to the definition of the phenomenon, because he was interested only in denouncing what he called "its intellectual vices, its perverse critical deficiencies," which led him to describe it as "an artificial survival of the last phase of romanticism."

As befits the founder/editor of a *Journal of Modern Literature*, Maurice Beebe tried to isolate the defining characteristics of Modernism in "*Ulysses* and the Age of Modernism," presented at a James Joyce colloquium in 1972. He quoted a key paragraph from this essay in his contribution to the July, 1974 issue of his journal, which was devoted to the theme "From Modernism to Post-Modernism." Beebe turned Levin's earlier question into a declaration, "What Modernism Was," and finally settled on four characteristics which he thought clearly differentiated Modernist literature from that of the nineteenth-century and that of the 1970s:

> First, Modernist literature is distinguished by its formalism. It insists on the importance of structure and design—the esthetic autonomy and independent whatness of the work of art—almost to that degree summarized by the famous dictum that "a poem should not mean but be." Secondly, Modernism is characterized by an attitude of detachment and non-commitment which I put under the general heading of "irony" in the sense of that term as used by the New Critics. Third, Modernist literature makes use of myth not in the way myth was used earlier, as a discipline for belief or a subject for interpretation, but as an arbitrary means of ordering art. And, finally, I would date the Age of Modernism from the time of the Impressionists because I think there is a clear line of development from Impressionism to reflexivism. Modernist art turns back upon itself and is largely concerned with its own creation and composition. The Impressionists' insistence that the viewer is more important than the subject viewed leads ultimately to the solipsistic worlds-within-worlds of Modernist art and literature (Vol. 3, p. 1073).

Beebe seems to me, however, to come closer to capturing the essence of the Modernist sensibility when he abandons this elaborate categorical approach and observes that he finds Philip Stevick's essay "Sentimentality and Classic Fiction" correct in pointing out that "one could almost define modernism by its irony, its implicit admiration for verbal precision and understatement." Certainly *irony* was the quality most prized in literature by the "New Critics," who composed the most prominent school of academic tastemakers during the Modernist years.

II

Irony, however, has been used in so many ways that it has become almost as vague a term as A. O. Lovejoy found *Nature* in " 'Nature' as Aesthetic Norm." One must specifiy just what kind of *irony* one has in mind if one speaks of this quality as definining Modernism. (I am here, however, speaking only for myself. I have no idea what Beebe or Stevick would think of my theorizing.) I argue that this kind of irony is most exactly specified by a definition from Kierkegaard's *Concluding Unscientific Postscript* that Marston LaFrance used to focus the argument in his *A Reading of Stephen Crane* (1971): "Irony is a synthesis of ethical passion which infinitely accentuates inwardly the person of the individual in relation to the ethical requirement—and of culture, which infinitely abstracts from the personal ego, as one finitude among all other finitudes and particularities." LaFrance takes Kierkegaard's statement to mean that the individual endowed with this type of "ironic vision" has "a perception or awareness of a double realm of values where a different sort of mind perceives only a single realm" (pp. 3–4). LaFrance finds Hamlin Garland representative of the writers who perceive only a "single realm" of values, but William Dean Howells is a more conspicuous exemplar to place in contrast with the writers of the succeeding age.

The relationship between *irony*, as Kierkegaard defines it, and the alienation that has been widely characteristic of Modernist art and lifestyles is apparent. As I understand the definition, the "passion" that leads to imaginative creation arises from the tension between the individual's ethical judgment of his environment in the light of his private vision and an increasingly technological culture that seeks to suppress as intolerably deviant the expression of a private vision and to exploit the individual not in his full complexity as a human being but as a two-dimensional "thing" like the characters in Elmer Rice's play *The Adding Machine* or the workers in Fritz Lang's film *Metropolis*. Since artists' judgments of this culture have been almost unexceptionably negative and hostile, the tension has resulted in the presentation of our world as waste land from the Bowery in Stephen Crane's *Maggie* to the dying universe

of T. S. Eliot's landmark poem to the ravished landscapes of Kurt
Vonnegut, Jr.'s *Breakfast of Champions*. The self-conscious individual's reaction to an increasingly dehumanizing culture has ac-
celerated his retreat into his private vision and has resulted in his
denunciations of the Establishments' efforts to turn him into a statis-
tic becoming increasingly despairing, like Samuel Beckett's plays or
Thomas Pynchon's novels, or annoyingly preachy like Faulkner's
A Fable or John Steinbeck's *Burning Bright*.

   This kind of ironic vision did not, of course, suddenly spring into
being with the withering away of the pre-Modernist, genteel, Victorian period. Writers like Melville had possessed it, but Melville's
contemporaries deplored and ignored those works like *The Confidence Man* that have been elevated to preeminent rank during the
Modernist years after long being out of print. What distinguishes
the Modernist period from others is the special, exalted value it
placed upon this particular sensibility. What might have proved
in an earlier age of "faith" a serious—even fatal—liability, cutting the
possessor off from the censorious guardians of taste, became during
the first two-thirds of the present century a characteristic so highly
prized that those lacking it fell into critical disrepute (though it remains dangerous to the individual in persisting nineteenth-century
cultures like Russia's official one.)

   I argue that the first writer of the Modernist period in American
literature is Stephen Crane, who appears at the very time that the
protocols of pre-Modernism are being codified in William Dean
Howells's *Criticism and Fiction*. (The sacred scriptures appear—as
often others have—not at the height of an expanding movement, but
during the decadence of a once powerful force now driven to last-
ditch efforts to maintain the status quo.) Howells's effort peaks in
a famous statement: "The manners of the novel have been improv-
ing with those of its readers. . . . Generally people now call a spade
an agricultural implement; they have not grown decent without
having also grown a little squeamish, but they have grown compara-
tively decent; *there is no doubt about that*. They require of a novelist whom they respect unquestionable proof of his seriousness, if he
proposes to deal with certain phases of life; they require a sort of
scientific decorum" (italics mine).[2]

As the term "scientific decorum" in the above passage suggests, the central tenet of "pre-Modernism" as embodied in America's "Genteel Tradition" was that the best interests of the individual are identical with the best interests of society and that utopia will be reached when—as with the aid of one of the nineteenth-century's favorite family toys, the stereopticon—differing views are resolved into one. (The 1890s witnessed one of the great outpourings of utopian tracts, most of them depicting the triumph of tendencies that were already beginning to lose their hold on rebellious young artists.)[3] These pre-Modernist rallying cries found their apogee and ultimate degradation, ironically, at the very height of the Modernist period in the 1920s in the doctrines of Dr. Emile Coué, who made a fortune by advocating that millions of mindless wastelanders hypnotize themselves by repeating over and over, "Every day in every way I am getting better and better." Of course, such pre-Modernism is still very much with us in many popular forms of writing and especially in our politics; but I am concerned here with creative, imaginative forces, not those who perpetuate stereotypes.

At first the as yet unstereotyped Modernists felt great exhilaration about the superiority of their "double vision" to the simplistic single vision of those who accepted the "infinite abstraction" of their institutional exploiters. The Modernist age begins in American letters when Stephen Crane's Henry Fleming in *The Red Badge of Courage* says, in "a half-apologetic manner" to his conscience, that "he could not but know that a defeat for the army this time might mean many favorable things for him." Although Fleming subsequently has misgivings about his ability to substitute his private fantasy for what has actually happened in the face of doubting questions, the novel is not—as it has often been misconstrued—an initiation story (which involves someone's winning a place in an established group), but the narrative of the slow, unsteady, but ultimately self-confident development of an individual consciousness that enables Henry as he reviews "the battle pictures he had seen," to feel "quite competent to return home and make the hearts of people glow with stories of war. He could see himself in a room of warm tints telling tales to listeners."

Fleming's discovery of this competence leads to the conclusion that some critics have argued does not fit the book, when the young Henry smiles, "for he saw that the world was a world for him, though many discovered it to be made of oaths and walking sticks." The world is "a world for him," because Crane has depicted him as developing consciously the double vision that makes him the master rather than the slave of circumstances. Fleming is elated at his ability to manipulate circumstances to his own advantage, and the tale of his quest ends entirely fittingly with "over the river a golden ray of sun [coming] through the hosts of leaden rain clouds."

Such elation is to prove shortlived. Henry Fleming was not to prove the model for the Modernist hero—or, as many insist, anti-hero—because the Establishments exerted more power than even the most perceptive manipulators could overcome. Increasingly those endowed with the Kierkegaardian "ironic vision" had to take refuge in disillusioned flight. The prototype of the Modernist sensibility is James Joyce's Stephen Dedalus, who at the end of *A Portrait of the Artist as a Young Man* vows, "I will not serve that in which I no longer believe, whether it call itself my home, my fatherland, or my church; and I will try to express myself in some mode of life and art as freely as I can and as wholly as I can, using for my defense the only arms I allow myself to use—silence, exile, and cunning."

Artists sadly or angrily recognized it was unlikely that an individual could defeat society and yet preserve the integrity of his own sensibility, "the following of a grail," as Nick Carraway describes the title character's behavior in F. Scott Fitzgerald's *The Great Gatsby.*

Certainly a most vivid and memorable embodiment of the "ironic vision" in American fiction is Carraway's paradoxical opening comment, "When I came back from the East last autumn I felt that I wanted the world to be in uniform and at a sort of moral attention forever.... Only Gatsby ... was exempt from my reaction—Gatsby, who represented everything for which I have an unaffected scorn." Because he is able to perceive that Gatsby embodies the extreme opposites of complete innocence and complete corruption rather than merely looking at this remarkable figure and the world in terms of some "uniform" set of values, Nick possesses the principal characteristic valued during the Modernist era. It is interesting in the light

of the development of the following argument, however, to observe that Nick distrusts utter commitment to his private vision and
chooses to return to a life that he wishes to embody the "single realm
of values" of pre-Modernist culture. Hence he does compromise his
own sensibility when he shakes Tom Buchanan's hand; but he places
self-preservation above following Gatsby's tragic example. As early
as the 1920s Fitzgerald has produced a *Götterdämmerung* of Modernist art.

This is not the place to outline the history of the rise and decay
of the Modernist sensibility, though something of the last days can
be suggested by contrasting the transformation of *The Great Gatsby* into J. D. Salinger's 1959 story, "Seymour: An Introduction,"
in which Gatsby's ingenuous sacrifice to his vision becomes Seymour Glass's self-conscious self-sacrifice. "The true artist-seer . . .
is mainly dazzled to death by his own scruples, the blinding shapes
and colors of his own sacred human conscience," Seymour's brother
Buddy tells us when he explains the suicide; and Buddy himself
does not, like Fitzgerald's Nick Carraway, try to go home again,
but takes to the woods (like his creator J. D. Salinger) to devote
himself in utter alienation from the world to the celebration of
his private saint.

And I do not intend to try to enter either into the controversy
about the ending of the Modernist period, which Maurice Beebe
dates as early as 1945, while Monroe Spears proposes 1957. I will
only say that I think the Kierkegaardian "ironic vision" continued
to inspire significant artistic creations until the early 1970s when
Thomas Pynchon's *Gravity's Rainbow*, John Barth's *Lost in the
Funhouse*, and Kurt Vonnegut, Jr.'s *Breakfast of Champions* appeared. These works are, however, I think, the end of the road, for
in them the protagonists' retreats into their private visions have
become so complete that the "double realm of values" characteristic
of the Modernist sensibility has become once again a "single realm,"
although one exactly opposed to that of the pre-Modernist sensibility. The protagonists have become so isolated and alienated from
their cultures that they "see" only what is going on in their own
heads. While this phenomenon occurs in all of these novels and in
other works like plays by Samuel Beckett and Tennessee Williams,

the end of the Modernist road can be most summarily illustrated by an exchange of words from *Breakfast of Champions*: the novelist/ protagonist (the difference between them has disappeared) is sitting in a darkened cocktail lounge with his sunglasses on. "Can you see anything in the dark, with your sunglasses on?" a waitress asks; and he replies, "The big show is inside my head." When "the big show" is entirely in one's head, the "double vision" of the Modernist has become once more a single vision, but one exactly the opposite of Howells's or Dickens's, which perceived an ideal state of affairs in the total identification of the best interests of the individual and the culture. (This ideal was theoretically to be realized, of course, in the Marxist state; and Marxist art is still pre-Modernist.)

The last significant Modernist artists have developed the exact opposite of this optimistic, nineteenth-century vision; totally alienated from their "abstracting" culture, they entirely ignore the external world, so that any passionate synthesis of conflicting external and internal visions has become impossible. Undoubtedly alienated writers will continue to follow Modernist models for many years, but any genuinely "new" literature is going to have to move in some new direction. Vonnegut's gesture of "liberating" his fictional creations at the end of *Breakfast of Champions*, which has puzzled many critics and has been denounced as an affectation by others, is the only appropriate one that he could have made at that point. If we need to single out a precise end for the Modernist age, this is it.

III

Where do we go from here? Before speculating about possible new directions, I wish at last to contemplate Robert Frost against this background I have sketched in.

Maurice Beebe's extended definition of Modernism scarcely fits the bulk of Frost's poetry, which is rarely formalistic or greatly concerned with its own composition—as the work of T. S. Eliot and Wallace Stevens was. Frost occasionally uses mythological references and is at times noncommittal; but myth is introduced— as in his late masques—for its own sake and does not provide an ordering framework for his narratives as for some of Eliot's. The stances of his speakers are usually unequivocal—"I advocate a semi-revolution" (p. 363), "[New Hampshire's] one of the two best states in the Union" (p. 164). Most of his poems—especially those most often repeated both by himself in public performances and by anthologists—are firmly rooted in a strong personal reaction to the occasionally heart-warming, but more usually bleak and bitter, experiences of life in "Frost Country."

Nor in dealing with these experiences was Frost often "ironic" in the sense that Fitzgerald is in *The Great Gatsby* or T. S. Eliot in "The Love Song of J. Alfred Prufrock" (". . . human voices wake us and we drown"). While occasionally—as in "The Lovely Shall Be Choosers"—Frost suggests the existence of "a double realm of values," in which "culture" (if indeed that can be said to be *the* "Voice" behind the "Voices") "infinitely abstracts from the personal ego" overwhelming the inward accentuation of the personal requirement, even in this poem the individual's "joys" seem superficial satisfactions rather than externalized embodiments of deep-seated ethical commitments. Usually, although we may sympathize with the plight of Frost's characters, he presents them as having gotten if not (to avoid moralizing as Frost himself did) what they deserved, at least the inevitable consequences of their own approach to life and pattern of behavior. (I gather this is what Maurice Beebe calls the "contingency" that he finds characteristic of post-Modernism). Frost presents not the customarily fragmented and increasingly internalized vision of the Modernist, but most characteristically the unified vision described at the end of "Two Tramps in Mud Time":

> Only where love and need are one,
> And the work is play for mortal stakes,
> Is the deed ever really done
> For Heaven and the future's sakes (p. 277).

But perhaps—as I suspect many people think because of Frost's concentration upon country life and his seeming resurrection of Whittier's "independent yeoman"—Frost's poems are pre-Modernist, a defiant call for a return to the single value system of the "good old days," the kind of thing that Nick Carraway expects of the world after his return to the Midwest.

Yet if Frost's vision of the world seems remote from Eliot's, Faulkner's, O'Neill's, it is even more remote from Hamlin Garland's and Howells's, from Longfellow's and that of other standard bearers of the "genteel tradition," for the people in Frost Country have little regard for "scientific decorum" and are definitely not "getting better and better."

As the quotation from "Two Tramps in Mud Time" indicates, the speaker harbors a concept of work as play that would be anathema to the "earnestness" of the arbiters of nineteenth-century refinement, and the emphasis is placed upon the future and not a retreat to the past. Frost is looking, I maintain, beyond the wasteland.

I do not believe, moreover, that a dynamic art could move backward from Modernism (or any other contemporary contagion), as I do think that John Steinbeck attempted to do in such late works as *The Pearl* and *The Winter of Our Discontent*. Despite the frantic exertions of cultists, the clocks of culture have never been turned back successfully. The question is not, as T. S. Eliot phrases it in "Gerontion," "After such knowledge, what forgiveness?" but what reconciliation, what—to use a currently touchy word—amnesty? Once we have perceived the world as wasteland, we cannot abandon this perception, this knowledge without shutting ourselves off sentimentally from our milieu as totally as the extreme Modernists have shut themselves off distraughtly. If literature is to continue to grow and to help man to grow, it must begin to cope with the problem of accepting the culture without approving it or succumbing to it, of devising strategies by which the individual can retain his integrity without losing consciousness of his environment—as Frost's characters rarely do.

These characters do, however, share some important attributes of the Modernist sensibility. They prize highly their own integrity, and they find their greatest satisfaction in isolation. Yet, except in the rare cases of such pitiable figures as the speaker in "A Servant to Servants," they are not withdrawn from the external world into their own heads and alienated from their environment; they simply value solitude. They are stubbornly determined, however, to find a place of dignity *within society*. They live within "a world they never made," yet they *transcend* it.

Often they have not been understood because of a confusion about the distinction between *escapism* and *transcendence*. Transcendence is not a physical or hallucinatory flight; it is a conscious ethical triumph. The escapist retreats—like Joyce's Stephen Dedalus or Salinger's Buddy Glass—from institutions that threaten him, and he ceases to regard the world about him. Who *transcends* his environment keeps his eyes open and holds his ground; but he marches, like Thoreau, to "a different drummer" from those around him who lead "lives of quiet desperation." As Wallace Stevens somewhat more disconsolately puts the matter in his poem "A Glass of Water" —"Even among the dogs and the dung / One continues to contend with one's ideas." Stevens, however, provides no post-Modernist model, because his personae transcend their environments by retiring into art or other abstract patternings, not—like Frost's characters—by dealing directly with the harsh physical realities of an inescapable environment. Once overly popularized, but now too much neglected, an analysis in David Riesman's *The Lonely Crowd* is useful in explaining the distinctions involved here. The "autonomous," Riesman argues, are "those who on the whole are *capable* of conforming to the behavioral norms of their society—a capacity the anomic usually lack—but who are free to *choose* whether to conform or not," while the anomic is "a characterological nonconformist, who is frequently neurotic." Frost's characters are generally what Riesman calls *autonomous* rather than *anomic*, as many of the characters in the outstanding productions of the "Modernist decadence" have become.

IV

There is even less agreement about the likely nature of a possibly burgeoning "post-Modernism" than about Modernism itself. While some literary journals are already dedicated to post-Modernist studies, some wonder if works appropriate for consideration will ever appear. As Maurice Beebe observes in his essay, "What Modernism Was," it is "difficult to point to successful works of literature" that illustrate a post-Modernist sensibility. Beebe lists as the characteristics of this sensibility, "preferences for content over form, emotional commitment over irony, 'contingency' over 'mythology' and the group over its members." I agree with the first three of these selections; and I think that Frost remarkably foreshadows them, especially in "The Death of the Hired Man." I disagree with Beebe's fourth point if he means to suggest a pre-Modernist assertion of the ethical priority of the group over the individual. I would agree, however, that there must be a recrudescence in the individual's perception and recognition of the group, making possible what David Riesman calls *autonomy* to replace the *anomie* of the Modernist sensibility. Curiously, the successful work that recently best illustrates these characteristics is not one in a traditional form, but Stanley Kubrick's film, *2001: A Space Odyssey*. Perhaps we are going to have to look primarily to new media for evidences of a new sensibility.

My principal argument, however, is that long before Kubrick took to the screen—at the very height of Modernist dominance—Robert Frost produced works displaying post-Modernist characteristics, an achievement that may lead at last to Frost's being recognized as the same kind of precursor of post-Modernism that Poe can now be seen to have been of Modernism.

I think the very characteristic that has bothered traditionalist critics like Yvor Winters and accounts for my own friendly quarrel with George Nitchie's *Human Values in the Poetry of Robert Frost* is that these astute critics have sensed Frost's differences from his contemporaries, but expected him to turn back to the past and embrace some religiophilosophical system that would reunify the vision of man and society. They are disturbed that Frost is a "spiritual drifter" who supports no "system"; but I think the very thing the post-Modernist artist may have to contend with is that as Thoreau—grandfather of post-Modernism—argued in "Slavery in Massachusetts," no "system" works except as an "expedient." If we believe in "infinitely abstracting" systems, we will eventually be absorbed into them and our individuality will be destroyed—in the very manner that Frost satirizes in the poem "Departmental." We must find a sophisticated way of holding ourselves above "systems" without fancying that we can escape their influences by ignoring them and alienating ourselves from our supporting environment. Frost himself made this point forcefully in these often quoted but rarely fully comprehended lines from "Birches":

> I'd like to get away from earth awhile
> And then come back to it and begin over.
> May no fate willfully misunderstand me
> And half grant what I wish and snatch me away
> Not to return. Earth's the right place for love (p. 122).

Frost's relationship to the pre-Modernist and Modernist sensibilities and to the possibilities of post-Modernism is most clearly dramatized, however, in the struggles between the characters in "The Death of the Hired Man." This poem may be read simply as a poignant revelation of failure, the epitaph for a loser; yet we are told a good deal more than we would need to know to appreciate Silas's situation. Some of the most magic words, like the final description of Mary's watching the sky, have nothing directly to do with the business at hand. Since Frost is not a man to waste words, more is going on than the title event—life is moving on even at this moment of stasis. Although the narrative can be contorted into an "ironic" social fable, such a reading necessitates a sentimental overvaluation of "the hired man" that is at odds with the steady toughness of Frost's stance. Silas can be said to have been badly used, but we get no indication that he ever did amount to much.

There are actually five characters involved in the episode, though we see and hear only two. They conjure up the others, including the title figure. The five offer intriguing contrasts if we look at them in a framework of pre-Modernist, Modernist and post-Modernist sensibilities, though this remains but *one* way of looking at them. Certainly I do not mean to suggest that Frost had any such scheme in mind. To urge that he told his stories to illustrate philosophical doctrines would exactly reverse my own point about him; mine is an after-the-fact classification of material that he presents with experiential immediacy. What makes a great writer great is that he seizes upon situations that have greater potential significance than he apprehends at the moment.

The hired man's unnamed brother, "A somebody—director in the bank," comes through in even this brief reference as the perfectly self-abstracted exemplar of the pre-Modernist sensibility. The statement that the shiftless Silas is "just the kind that kinsfolk can't abide" reveals more about the relatively uncomplicated kinsfolk than about the complex and elusive Silas. The brother is the only character not given a name; he is simply a type, and Frost is not interested in him. Mary, the wife, will see that he provides help if it is needed; his systematic behavior is entirely predictable. Frost slyly insinuates that he isn't even really "a somebody," he's just a "something." So much for the genteel tradition as far as this poem is concerned and virtually as far as Frost is concerned! It was dutiful, but passionless. As George Santayana observes in "Genteel American Poetry," his subject is "without sensuous beauty, splendor, passion, or volume," like "the life it expressed." Though the banker "may be better than appearances," he can be counted on for nothing but emergency aid on conventional terms. I find in the poem no hint of regret that Silas has strayed from his birthright (all quotations from p. 39).

The young college professor, Harold Wilson—dignified at least with a name—is almost a parody of the Modernist sensibility as Maurice Beebe has categorized it: "He studied Latin like the violin / Because he liked it" (p. 37). Silas makes this point disparagingly; but we can look through this shadowy figure and see some of the giants of Modernism—from the precursor French Symbolists to A. E. Housman, Ezra Pound, James Joyce, Amy Lowell, Ernest Hemingway, Edmund Wilson, especially T. S. Eliot, putting up with the message of the church for the sake of its ritual. Frost understands Wilson; but the character remains a decadent refugee that we meet only at second hand.

Perceived in its relationship to these two distant figures, Silas's real tragedy manifests itself. Like many amiable but limited people during a transitional period, he has been fatally confused by his incapacity either to escape the past entirely or to reject the present wholly. As the husband Warren presents Silas, the hired man is really much like Harold Wilson, a consummate but limited formal craftsman whose "one accomplishment" is "to build a load of hay":

> 'I know, that's Silas' one accomplishment.
> He bundles every forkful in its place,

And tags and numbers it for future reference,
So he can find and easily dislodge it
In the unloading. Silas does that well' (p. 37).

But Silas cannot recognize his kinship to young Wilson, cannot like James Joyce's Stephen Dedalus, entirely "fly the nets" of family and culture to find self-fulfilment in his craft, because he cannot entirely escape the "do-gooder" philosophy that Thoreau damned in *Walden*, but that someone like Silas's brother would still embrace. Thus his ability to realize himself, to become his own man, is defeated by a detritus of irrelevant moralism of the kind that dominated his culture during his childhood. Silas wants to teach Wilson to stack hay, because "He thinks if he could teach him that, he'd be / Some good perhaps to someone in the world" (p. 37). Silas shares enough of the pride of the family that rejects him to be "coaxed off" at crucial moments by the shallow promise of a little pocket money. Silas is a "hired man" in other than the usual signification of the term. It is clear from the beginning, in fact, that he is never really Warren and Mary's "hired man," since they cannot afford to pay him regularly. Rather he is a "hired man" in the sense that he can be bought, his integrity can be compromised; he is at the mercy of conflicting drives and debilitated philosophies that he cannot comprehend. Like the unenlightened neighbor in "Mending Wall," "He will not go behind his father's saying." He has no sense of "ownership" in his culture. Rather he has been reduced to a thing, a skill for sale. Like the migrants in John Steinbeck's *The Grapes of Wrath*, there is really no place in the world for him between brief seasons of exploitation.

This sorry perception of Silas brings us to the central confrontation in the poem—the conflicting views of "home" voiced by Warren and Mary. The husband observes that "Home is the place where, when you have to go there, / They have to take you in." The wife counters, "I should have called it / Something you somehow haven't to deserve" (p. 38).

Different as these two concepts are, neither reflects either a pre-Modernist or Modernist sensibility. "Home" in genteel culture is the "woman's sphere," the ultimate center, *the* place where one belongs. If the best interests of the individual and society are indistinguishable, the home is the mediator where values are taught and exemplified. To be driven from home is the greatest disaster one can experience; to be accepted, the greatest triumph. It is the place where the decorous artist presides in the otherwise unused parlor and never visits the bedroom except to comfort the dying.

The growing oppressiveness of this self-suffocating concept of home was probably the principal force in leading to the Modernist revolt. Home became the place to be renounced, to be fled, to be wistfully castigated in works from *Dubliners* through *Winesburg, Ohio* and *The Great Gatsby* (in Gatsby's case) to *The Glass Menagerie* and *Breakfast of Champions*. One feels that Harold Wilson in the Frost poem has rejected his home and home ways just as surely as Silas's banker brother cherished and sought to entrench his. Wilson might have grown up into the affected Harvard professor that J. P. Marquand exhibits at length in *Wickford Point*.

Warren and Mary, however, offer propositions that would antagonize and enrage both the banker and the scholar. *Home* becomes in the husband's sentence like Thoreau's concept of government—an expedient, a legalism, a useful servant but an unworthy master. There is nothing in this vision of genteel pride or Modernist rejection. There is only the cheerlessness we find in other Frost poems like "A Servant to Servants" and "The Hill Wife."

Mary's opposing view, however, dissolves all the tensions of both genteel repression and Modernist alienation. Without rejecting the view that the home may be an expedient, she dismisses the quibblings of legalism and the traumas of pride. If her husband's matter-of-fact attitude undercuts all the tensions and hostilities and aspirations of the other characters and reduces man to an existential burden, the wife transcends all these petty barriers and reasserts man's inherent spiritual participation in something like Emerson's oversoul.

Mary—bearing the name of the figure who at the beginning of our era brought "The Light" to the world—is a creature of light. At three moments we see her spotlighted against the surrounding darkness. In the opening line we see her sitting "musing on the lamp-flame at the table," involved not in the terror of the surrounding darkness that might beset many in her situation but rather in the contemplation of the light's flickering challenge to this dark.

Just before the crucial confrontation over the view of *home*, we learn

> Part of a moon was falling down the west,
> Dragging the whole sky with it to the hills.
> Its light poured softly in her lap. She saw it
> And spread her apron to it (p. 38).

Light is no longer just energy, but a physical thing. With the disappearing moon, the whole reality of the environment seems to be disappearing. Without light, the sky will be gone. Darkness is an absence like Emerson's evil. Mary provides a receptacle for the falling light, as though she might actually shelter and preserve it there when it was gone from the sky.

Finally, while her husband goes into the house to find the hired man dead, Mary sits outside to "see if that small sailing cloud / Will hit or miss the moon." The narrator reports:

> It hit the moon.
> Then there were three there, making *a dim row*,
> The moon, the little silver cloud, and she.
> (p. 40; italics mine)

The row is "dim"; Mary, like the moon, is not a vivid force. Yet the description clearly dissociates her from the dark earth and makes her the point of projection into the sky from which the light comes as well as the end of this line from the heavens. Her associations lie beyond the earth. All four male characters in the poem are earthbound: Silas's brother is tied to concepts of family and community influence, Wilson is solipsistically infatuated with the creations of the human mind, Silas understands only the physical act of haying, Warren is a covenanter (like his probably Puritan forebears). He appears out of the darkness at the beginning of the poem and disappears into it at the end to make the final discovery. Only Mary is constantly before us and constantly associated with the light—the flickering lamp, the changing and disappearing moon, the transient silver cloud, the unstable glorious forces in the sky that illuminate our lives, the forces that are ever changing and transmuting themselves rather than petrifying themselves into systems.

I think it is toward the contrasting visions of these two characters that the post-Modernist artist must move. We must transcend the petty barriers that separate people without destroying people's integrity in the process. There is a choice. Warren dramatizes the alternative of law—*not*, notice especially, of any kind of *perfectible* system, but of the law as expedient that man must, however reluctantly, accept in an environment in which he can no longer afford the illusions of superiority and perfectibility. His vision is most likely to lead, however—as it already has—to an increasing preoccupation with "non-fiction" narratives, presented as factual, however outrageously the facts may be manipulated, because of a seemingly increasing literal-mindedness that reveals an inability to grasp even how fiction works. But Mary dramatizes the alternative of light, of utter openness, of lack of niggling discriminations, of an all-embracing love. It is her *vision* that I think is most likely to provide the impetus for a significant new fiction—a fiction whose viewpoint is perhaps too coyly intimated by this passage from a recent work by Tom Robbins, a still sputtering novelist who may bear watching as post-Modernist:

> Ritual, usually, is an action or ceremony employed to create a unity of mind among a congregation or community. The Clock People see the keeping of the clockworks as the *last* of the *communal* rituals. With the destruction of the clockworks, that is, at the end of time, all rituals will be personal and idiosyncratic, serving not to unify a community/cult in a common cause but to link each single individual with the universe in whatever manner suits him or her best. . . . paradoxically, the replacement of societal with individual rituals will bring about an ultimate unity vastly more universal than the plexus of communal rites that presently divides peoples into unwieldy, agitating, and competing groups (*Even Cowgirls Get the Blues*, p. 191).

Of course, Robbins's idea of universality through individuality is Walt Whitman's "Song of Myself" revisited—"I teach straying from me, yet who can stray from me?" But Whitman, like Thoreau, looks across the wasteland to the post-Modern; and he was never especially trusted by the Modernist critics.

True also that Frost gives the last word "Dead" to the darkness and the husband in "The Death of the Hired Man." Yet before we are snatched back to earth, we have gotten away a while and moved up into the dim light of the sky with the wife. While death is the inevitable end of all men, we need not spend our lives in the narrow confusions of the "hired man"—nor the self-indulgences of banker and professor. Recognizing along with the husband in the poem the inescapableness of our journey through the dark, we must muster all the toughminded skepticism we can and still strive with the wife to become a part of the light, to make earth a place for love. And we may do this without ever leaving our stoop, by traveling—like Thoreau—"much in Concord." Flourishing though he did during the Modernist period, Robert Frost transcended it and has yet, I maintain, to find his true artistic "contemporaries." May they come out into the light!

Notes to " 'The Death of the Hired Man': Modernism and Transcendence" by WARREN FRENCH

1. "John Steinbeck and Modernism," *Steinbeck's Prophetic Vision of America: Proceedings of the Bicentennial Steinbeck Seminar*, ed. Tetsumaro Hayashi and Kenneth D. Swan (Muncie, Indiana: The John Steinbeck Society of America, 1976), pp. 34–55.

2. Although the term *pre-Modernism* is not introduced, one of the central concerns of this sensibility—its concept of woman as "a redemptive figure"—is outlined and the decay of its influence suggested in Paul John Eakin's *The New England Girl: Cultural Ideals in Hawthorne, Stowe, Howells and James* (Athens: University of Georgia Press, 1976), especially in the chapter on "The Howells Heroine" (pp. 83–130).

3. The unequalled outpouring of utopian tracts during the twelve-year period when the enlightened gentility were making a last-ditch stand against the collapse of old values is examined in Kenneth Roemer's *The Obsolete Necessity: America in Utopian Writing, 1888–1900* (Kent, Ohio: Kent State University Press, 1976).

Bibliographical Note

The following list is intended to identify major items cited by abbreviation in the text. Notes mention other secondary materials, and the preface refers to two recent bibliographies of Frost.

Anderson, Margaret B. *Robert Frost and John Bartlett: The Record of a Friendship*. New York: Holt, Rinehart and Winston, 1963.

Cox, Hyde and Edward Connery Lathem, editors. *Selected Prose of Robert Frost*. New York: Macmillan, Collier Books, 1968. Abbreviated as *SP*.

Lathem, Edward Connery, editor. *Interviews with Robert Frost*. New York: Holt, Rinehart and Winston, 1966. Abbreviated as *Interviews*.

Thompson, Lawrance. *Robert Frost: The Early Years, 1874–1915*. New York: Holt, Rinehart and Winston, 1966.

————. *Robert Frost: The Years of Triumph, 1915–1938*. New York: Holt, Rinehart and Winston, 1970.

———— and R. H. Winnick. *Robert Frost: The Later Years, 1938–1963*. New York: Holt, Rinehart and Winston, 1976. Abbreviated as Thompson, with roman numeral and page number.

Thompson, Lawrance, editor. *Selected Letters of Robert Frost*. New York: Holt, Rinehart and Winston, 1964. Abbreviated as *SL*.

Untermeyer, Louis, editor. *The Letters of Robert Frost to Louis Untermeyer*. New York: Holt, Rinehart and Winston, 1963. Abbreviated as Untermeyer.

Contributors

Lesley Frost Ballantine is the daughter of Robert Frost.

N. Arthur Bleau is Superintendent of Parks and Recreation at Goshen, Indiana.

Reginald L. Cook is Dana Professor Emeritus of American Literature at Middlebury College, Middlebury, Vermont.

Charles H. Foster was professor of English (1958–1974) at the University of Minnesota and now lives in Luray, Virginia.

Richard Foster (deceased) was professor of English at the University of Hawaii, Honolulu, Hawaii.

Warren French is Director, Center for American Studies at Indiana University-Purdue University at Indianapolis, Indiana.

Dorothy Judd Hall is lecturer and free-lance writer and formerly instructor at Boston University and Emerson College, Boston, Massachusetts.

Luella Nash LeVee, a disabled former newspaperwoman and publicist, now attempting to launch a new career writing for and about the handicapped, resides at Ft. Mitchell, Kentucky.

T. H. Littlefield is associate professor of English at State University of New York at Albany, New York.

Lewis H. Miller, Jr. is professor of English at Indiana University, Bloomington, Indiana.

Victor E. Reichert is Associate Professor Emeritus of Biblical Literature at the University of Cincinnati.

Peter J. Stanlis is Distinguished Professor of Humanities at Rockford College, Rockford, Illinois.

Dorothy Tyler is a writer and editor residing in Troy, New York.

Index